Putin's Russia

Putin's Russia

Past Imperfect, Future Uncertain

SECOND EDITION

Edited by
Dale R. Herspring

ROWMAN & LITTLEFIELD PUBLISHERS, INC.
Lanham • Boulder • New York • Toronto • Oxford

ROWMAN & LITTLEFIELD PUBLISHERS, INC.

Published in the United States of America
by Rowman & Littlefield Publishers, Inc.
A wholly owned subsidiary of The Rowman & Littlefield Publishing Group, Inc.
4501 Forbes Boulevard, Suite 200, Lanham, MD 20706
www.rowmanlittlefield.com

P.O. Box 317, Oxford OX2 9RU, UK

British Library Cataloguing in Publication Information Available

Library of Congress Cataloging-in-Publication Data

Putin's Russia : past imperfect, future uncertain / edited by Dale R. Herspring.—2nd
ed.
    p. cm.
    Includes bibliographical references and index.
    ISBN 0-7425-3004-3 (cloth : alk. paper)—ISBN 0-7425-3005-1 (pbk. : alk. paper)
       1. Russia (Federation)—Politics and government—1991– 2. Putin, Vladimir
Vladimirovich, 1952– I. Herspring, Dale R. (Dale Roy)
    DK510.763.P88 2005
    947.086—dc22   2004008435

Printed in the United States of America

♾ ™ The paper used in this publication meets the minimum requirements of
American National Standard for Information Sciences—Permanence of Paper for
Printed Library Materials, ANSI/NISO Z39.48-1992.

To the long-suffering Russian people
in the hope of a new, and better, future.

I would like to suggest that at this point the country does not need a leader of strategic proportions, but an effective manager.

—P. Vayl

Contents

Foreword   xi
Ambassador James F. Collins

Preface to the Second Edition   xvii

1   Introduction   1
Dale R. Herspring

Part I: Politics

2   Putin and Democratization   13
Timothy J. Colton and Michael McFaul

3   Putin, the Duma, and Political Parties   31
Thomas F. Remington

Part II: State and Society

4   Putin and the Media   55
Masha Lipman and Michael McFaul

5   Putin and Culture   75
Boris Lanin

6   Putin, Demography, Health, and the Environment   89
David E. Powell

Part III: The Economy

7   Putin and the Economy   121
James R. Millar

8   Putin and Agriculture   141
Stephen K. Wegren

9 Putin and the Oligarchs   161
  Peter Rutland

Part IV: Military and Security

10 Putin and Military Reform   185
  Dale R. Herspring

11 Putin and Russia's Wars in Chechnya   205
  Jacob W. Kipp

Part V: Regional and Foreign Policy

12 Putin and the Regions   237
  Nikolai Petrov and Darrell Slider

13 Putin and Russian Foreign Policy   259
  Dale R. Herspring and Peter Rutland

14 Conclusion   293
  Dale R. Herspring

Suggested Reading   301

Index   305

About the Contributors   313

Foreword

Ambassador James F. Collins

One unexpected outcome of the terrorist attacks on New York and Washington was Russia's return to centrality in America's foreign policy and security calculus. President Putin's embrace of the U.S.-led antiterrorist coalition and the outpouring of sympathy from Russia's people captured the imagination of Americans and rekindled interest in this complex, rich, but elusive country whose fate has been inextricably tied to our own over the past two-and-a-half centuries. This volume provides an excellent introduction to the multihued tapestry of today's Russia and to the personality, vision, and politics of its president. The authors discuss the individuals, issues, and circumstances central to Russia today, and they help us understand the environment that is defining Russia's transition from its Soviet imperial past. The book is especially valuable for its portrayal, when taken as a whole, of the ambiguities and inconsistencies that characterize a Russia still deeply in search of itself as a society, its place in the international system, and its future direction.

For most readers, Russia's direction and future is directly linked to the personality and vision of Vladimir Putin, its enigmatic, often controversial young president. When Boris Yeltsin sprang his own Y2K surprise on the eve of the new millennium by announcing early retirement and selecting Putin to succeed him, this last confounding stroke by Russia's master of the political surprise was greeted by most of his compatriots with a mixture of hope that the aimless drift of the late Yeltsin era had ended, and deep uncertainty about the man to whom their country had been entrusted. The uncertainty was understandable. Emerging from Russia's faceless bureaucracy, Putin at that time was all but unknown. He had neither known political affiliation nor political experience anyone could point to. In St. Petersburg he had worked in the shadow of the city's reformist mayor, Anatoly Sobchak, and his earlier activities as an intelligence officer had for obvious reasons been hidden from public view. Nor had his short tenure in office at the national level—as Kremlin staffer, director of the Federal Security Service (FSB), and national security adviser—given Russia's political class familiarity with his views. Indeed, it was only in his few months as prime minister that this unexpected president-to-be had come before the public, and that tenure, dominated by the renewal of warfare in Chechnya, raised as many questions as it resolved. So it was scarcely surprising that on the mind of nearly every Russian, foreign official, journalist, and political figure on New Year's Day 2000 was the question, "Who is Vladimir Putin and what does he represent?"

Nevertheless, Putin was not unfamiliar to everyone. As ambassador I had come to know the new acting president in different capacities. I had encountered him occasionally as a Kremlin insider working in the presidential administration. I had met with him more often during his service as FSB director, national security adviser, and prime minister. In those encounters Putin came across to me as an intelligent, exceptionally well-informed interlocutor. He addressed issues pragmatically and logically, without emotion. He was precise in presenting his positions and views. He impressed me as a man who internalized issues and spoke to them from a base of solid understanding and mastery of detail. Putin also had a personable side, although he was often difficult to read as an individual. With visitors he was a gracious host, employing a sense of humor effectively to put guests at ease at the outset of meetings devoted even to the most difficult issues. And in conversation he was a careful listener who responded to his partners' points and made clear where he agreed or disagreed, or deliberately chose to leave an issue open. But with all this, Putin revealed little of himself or his personal thinking, and he remained a political mystery to the nation he would lead.

Four years of the Putin presidency have now changed that. The contours of the Putin vision have emerged more clearly as he and his team addressed Russia's pressing economic and social issues and defined their nation's international role. Nevertheless, even as President Putin prepares for a second term, many of the critical issues of his first term remain unresolved and many of the uncertainties about the direction in which he will take his country are yet to be defined.

The chapters that follow discuss how the new administration has shaped the Putin presidency to date by confronting the critical issues of Russia's revival and recovery. They offer a good beginning for those who seek to understand not just who Mr. Putin is and how he seeks to define and direct his nation, but also to comprehend the environment within which this Russian president must make the critical decisions for his country.

As the authors of the subsequent chapters discuss, Putin first developed as a presidential candidate many of the ideas that would later define his presidency. Certain political themes served to differentiate him from his predecessor while establishing his credentials to deal in new ways with Russia's pressing problems. Thus, he emphasized restoring the strength and authority of the Russian state and promoted his image as a decisive, active, and engaged leader. Sensing the emotional appeal of patriotic themes, he stressed from the very first moment that as president he would insure that Russia set its own domestic and international course and define its own interests. And, taking account of the fatigue from political stalemate between the pro- and anti-Yeltsin camps, he conveyed readiness to make room for all who shared his goal of restoring Russia to greatness, specifically including those who felt alienated by Yeltsin's determined struggle with the communists. This was, it seemed at the time, very much the leader of a new generation who understood and accepted the dynamics of Russia's post-communist and post–Cold War international circumstances, the necessity to find accommodation with the forces at work in Russia's fledgling and imperfect market democracy, and the need to create and maintain the support of a centrist majority if he were to become an effective political leader of the Russia of the twenty-first century.

That Russia, it is important to recall, was already far removed from its Soviet past. A decade of the Yeltsin revolution had dismantled the Soviet empire, uprooted the communist political structure, and planted the roots of a market-based economic system. Russia also had taken giant steps to end the Soviet era's self-imposed isolation and to normalize relations with its neighbors and the broader international community. Nevertheless, Yeltsin, as he observed poignantly in his farewell to the Russian people, had failed to achieve a recovery from economic collapse. Moreover, after several years of weakened and increasingly ineffective leadership by an ailing president, Russia's fragile political system had become dysfunctional. Reform efforts had stalled; immature democratic institutions provided weak and unresponsive governance; and Russia's citizens suffered from lawlessness, corruption, and arbitrary bureaucratic rapacity that seemed to drag the country down with each passing crisis of leadership.

It was this Russia that Yeltsin entrusted to his successor, and these issues that Putin began to address as he took up his duties at the stroke of midnight, January 1, 2000. He began to set in motion a program of radical change no less ambitious than that begun by his predecessor a decade earlier. That program, developed by a close group of young advisors whom Putin assembled around him in his earliest days, and implemented subsequently by a newly formed Putin-structured coalition, has not only defined the Putin presidency but has already been instrumental in setting Russia on a new course. At home, the components of this program have already done much to jump-start a second phase in the modernization of Russia's society, political system, and economy. It has also included actions in the name of managed democracy that have raised questions about the degree of commitment the Putin administration has to democratic principles and the development of the rule of law. Several chapters of this book examine key elements of this program as they document some of the Putin team's greatest achievements as well as its shortcomings. Among these are market reforms that have carried Russia farther than was possible in much of the previous decade and have fostered a remarkable economic recovery, the passage of a major legislative package that is transforming fundamental elements of Russia's socioeconomic and legal culture, and an ambitious program to redefine the relationships between central and regional authority in a way that will answer the eternal challenge of governing Russia's vast territory effectively. At the same time the authors raise many of the persistent questions that Putin's agenda has posed for the future health of Russian democracy and economic recovery. The implications for human rights and democracy of the debilitating and dehumanizing war in Chechnya remain a scar on the Putin record for which neither he nor any in his team have answers; and the handling of press and media issues in ways that suggest discomfort with truly pluralistic freedom of expression leave serious questions about the Putin leadership's capacity to subject government to open public scrutiny. Finally, the highly controversial Yukos affair involving the incarceration of one of Russia's leading industrial magnates renewed the controversy surrounding the government's respect for property rights and the status of privatization transactions during the Yeltsin years, leaving major question marks around the economic policies President Putin would pursue in a second term.

The final chapters of this volume are devoted to issues that in recent years have been at the heart of Russians' efforts to define themselves and their place in the post–Cold War world. Much attention has been paid to President Putin's moves in response to the attacks on New York and Washington on September 11. But, as the chapters on Russia's defense and foreign policy suggest, Putin's realism and sense for realpolitik have guided his vision for Russia's future place as a great power from his earliest days in office. Central in this regard, Putin has been almost brutally frank with his own people about Russian weaknesses—military, economic, and diplomatic—and the limits thus imposed on his nation's options and choices for national defense and international leadership. The authors of these chapters rightly point to Putin's repeated return to the need to restore and modernize Russia's economic, military, and political structures to revive its international fortunes. And they note that Putin has consistently urged his people to take a realistic view of their international circumstances. He has thus crafted pragmatic responses to actions by the West that have reshaped the structures of European security and transformed the strategic framework of relations with the United States, preserving his options and avoiding confrontations that Russia would not win.

For many, the declaration of his intent to take Russia into the coalition against terrorism came as a surprise, one not without serious controversy internally. But Putin's conviction that his country's destiny lay with Europe and the West was evident almost from the outset of his presidency and appeared to represent a core element of his vision for Russia's future. In his first meetings with Western leaders, including Secretary of State Madeleine Albright for example, Putin set forth certain principles he maintained would guide his approach to Russia's international position. Most significantly, I recall, he categorically insisted almost from the first moment that in his worldview Russia was a part of the West and would develop only in that context. He made clear, of course, that Russia would actively pursue normal and productive relations with all its neighbors. But, his early comments were a not-very-subtle rejection of competing strategies that emphasized a multipolar world in which Russia stood as a counterweight to American dominance or a Eurasian school of thinking that sought to set Russia apart from its European roots. That he later would seize on the opportunity afforded by September 11 to push his country dramatically westward was fully in keeping with these early inclinations. And even as the Iraq conflict strained elements in Russia's relations with the United States, the orientation of Russia's policy remained wedded to the idea of its place as a part of the greater European and Euro-Atlantic civilization.

Readers of this volume may well ask themselves at the end many of the same questions they had at the outset. They will look in vain for a unidimensional answer to the question, "Who is Putin?" Nor are there uniform or consistent answers to critical questions about the future of Russia's fragile democracy and developing market economy. Rather, what emerges is a complex and uneven tapestry whose design and weaving are far from complete. For Americans, with an abiding and deep interest in how Russia will evolve, it is perhaps of greatest significance that President Putin remains steadfast in his conviction that Russia's future lies with the Euro-Atlantic world. The challenge will be to recognize the opportunity that conviction represents and to approach the accomplishments and failures of this Russian president with patient realism about the difficult and complex transition through which he must guide his nation.

Preface to the Second Edition

No sooner had we published the first edition of *Putin's Russia* than it became apparent that a number of critical changes were taking place in Russia. Students often approached me asking about some comment in one of the chapters, and I often had to respond, "Yes, but the situation has changed." Some of the information was outdated. For this reason, we decided to do an updated book to provide students, specialists, and the general reader with a better understanding of what has happened in Russia since January 2000.

Putin has been in power for four years, and all signs indicate that he will be in office for at least another four years. During his first term, he laid the foundation for his second. And he has made significant changes in his nation. To begin with, Putin increased the role of the Russian state significantly. Moscow has far more power than it did four years ago in controlling the country. The country is much more centralized, and the amount of freedom enjoyed by the average Russian at the beginning of Putin's time in office has decreased. The economy and agriculture are stronger now than they were when he came to office, and there are signs that in spite of serious problems, he is serious about reforming the military. Putin has taken on some of the oligarchs, and he has tightened controls on the media and on culture. He has control of the Duma and the Federation Council, and political parties remain in their infancy. Nevertheless, it is important to keep in mind that, as opposed as many Westerners may be with regard to Putin's actions to strengthen central control over the country, he has not implemented the kind of repressive measurements of the communist period.

On the foreign policy front, Putin has shown himself to be an expert diplomat in spite of the many upheavals the world has witnessed since he came to power. Russia is taken far more seriously now than it was four years ago. One suspects that although Russia will never be the superpower it was twenty years ago, in the foreseeable future it is an international force to be reckoned with.

All of these changes color how we see and understand critical developments in one of the world's most important countries. Because there is more to Russia than the material covered in the first edition, I turned to three experts on Russia, asking them to help us fill in some of the blank spots. Steve Wegren provided a stimulating essay on the role of agriculture, clearly one of the critical components of Putin's hope to create greater stability by raising the standard of living. Boris Lanin filled in another major gap with his essay on Putin and his relationship to Russian culture, an area often overlooked by volumes such as this one. One of the most interesting, thought-provoking, and upsetting essays was written by David Powell on demographics, health, and environmental problems. I suspect that very few readers realize how serious these problems are. Unfortunately, Virginie Coulloudon was not able to update her very useful chapter on the Russian legal system and felt that, in light of the changes that have taken place in the last four years, it should not be included in this volume. Readers who are interested in an introduction to the approach Putin began taking toward the legal system will profit by reading her essay in the previous edition.

Convincing contributors to update their contributions—not to mention getting scholars to agree to provide new chapters for a revised and expanded volume—is seldom easy. At least generally it is not easy. However, in this case I was very lucky because all of the contributors faithfully updated their contributions and the new articles came in on time. I am deeply grateful for all of the help—and patience—they showed me, especially as I harassed them. These authors represent some of the "best and brightest" among American and Russian specialists on Putin's Russia.

On a personal note, I would like to once again thank Dr. Jon Wefald, president of Kansas State University, for his continued support. I would also like to express my appreciation to Dr. Charles Reagan, associate to the president, for his valuable advice and counsel over the years. Matt Hammon, of Rowman & Littlefield, did an excellent job of helping me with the many problems that arose in putting this book together. I do not think I could have put everything together were it not for his assistance. Finally, and most important, I want to thank my wife, who not only put up with me while I worked on the second edition of this book, but showed incredible patience because I was writing another one at the same time. To say that she was often an academic widow would be an understatement.

Chapter One

Introduction

Dale R. Herspring

When Vladimir Putin became interim president of Russia on January 1, 2000, he was confronted with a staggering array of daunting problems. As he put it, "Russia is in the midst of one of the most difficult periods in its history. For the first time in the past 200–300 years, it is facing a real threat of sliding into the second, and possibly even third echelon of world states."[1] The country's economy was in shambles, its political system was in chaos, and its social and moral structure was in an advanced state of decay. To make matters worse, Putin was virtually unknown, both in Russia and abroad. A former KGB officer, he had returned to his native Leningrad from a KGB assignment in East Germany only ten years previously to become an assistant to Anatoly Sobchak, his former professor, at Leningrad State University. And now the obscure Putin was the country's president!

Putin's reign has been short in the context of Russian history, but these few years have been critical in Russia's development and allow us to begin to make some tentative judgments about his and his regime's performance to date. With this in mind, we will focus on two key questions in this book. First, to what degree has he and his regime been successful (or unsuccessful) in dealing with Russia's problems? Second, and perhaps even more important, where does he seem to be leading the country? What are his goals for Russia, or does he even know where he is taking this beleaguered nation? Before we attempt to shed light on these questions, however, let us take a closer look at this man, an individual who is attempting to rebuild Russia internally, while at the same time regain the international prestige it lost under Yeltsin.

PUTIN, THE MAN

The published facts about Putin's career are sketchy, but the following discussion will at least permit the reader to understand the major events that influenced his life.[2]

Putin was born in 1952 in what was then Leningrad (now again St. Petersburg). While in school, he trained in judo and in 1974 became the Leningrad city champion. In his autobiography he credits judo as the turning point in his life. "If I hadn't gotten involved in sports, I'm not sure how my life would have turned out. It was sports that dragged me off the streets."[3] His lifelong dream was to become a member of the KGB. Indeed, he recalls going to the local KGB office while still in high school and telling a somewhat startled officer, "I want to get a job with you."[4] He was advised instead to attend the university and study law.

After graduating from Leningrad State University in 1975 with a degree in law, Putin applied again to the KGB, this time successfully. He was sent to Moscow for initial training and was then assigned to foreign intelligence in Leningrad, where he spent the majority of his time spying on foreigners and Russians who had contacts with them. He studied German and was eventually posted to Dresden in the German Democratic Republic, where he and his wife spent five years and their two daughters were born. This was also where he perfected his German. Putin was no "natural" in the world of espionage, but he learned the craft quickly and effectively, according to one German agent he controlled.[5]

In 1989, Putin returned to Russia and became head of the Foreign Section (Inotdel) at Leningrad State University. In that capacity he served as an assistant for international affairs to his former law professor, Anatoly Sobchak, who was the university's rector. A year later, Sobchak, becoming a major force in Leningrad politics, asked Putin to move to city hall as his advisor on international affairs. In 1991, Sobchak became Leningrad's mayor and appointed Putin chairman of the city's foreign relations committee. It was not long before Sobchak gave him responsibility for a number of reform programs, including foreign investments, where Putin impressed those who dealt with him as a man who could get things done.[6] Indeed, it was during his time in St. Petersburg that he made his reputation as an outstanding administrator.[7]

In 1996 Sobchak failed in his bid for re-election amid charges of corruption, and it appeared that Putin's post-KGB career was at an end. Having heard of Putin's reputation as a "doer," however, Anatoly Chubais, a well-connected advisor to Yeltsin, got him a job working with Pavel Borodin, who was head of a staff closely associated with Yeltsin. Yeltsin took notice of Putin, and in the tumultuous administrative upheavals of the Russian executive in 1998, he was appointed first deputy head of the presidential administration in charge of relations with the regions, and later that year head of the Federal Security Service (the successor to the KGB), a move he claimed made him unhappy because of the secretive life it would entail. "It put you in a constant state of tension. All the papers are secret. This isn't allowed, that isn't allowed."[8] Shortly thereafter, he was put in control of the body that coordinated all of Russia's security and intelligence ministries. Not bad for a former KGB lieutenant colonel.

On August 9, 1999, the ailing Yeltsin surprised the world by appointing Putin as his prime minister and designated successor. On December 31, Yeltsin again astonished everyone by resigning his post and making Putin Russia's acting president. Yeltsin knew his time was limited and wanted to ensure his protégé had the best possible chance to win the forthcoming presidential elections. On March 26, 2000, Putin stood for election and won over 52 percent of the vote in the first round—enough to avoid a runoff. He became Russia's only second elected president.

PUTIN'S APPROACH TO POLITICS

Perhaps because of his KGB background, Putin gives the impression that he believes that even the most difficult problem can be resolved, provided the decisionmaker will follow through and take personal responsibility for the outcome. In short, his past experience made him into a dedicated problem solver. Anatoly Sobchak called him a "determined, even stubborn young man."[9] Once he made up his mind—whether it was to be a judo champion, a KGB officer, or a presidential aide—his bosses could rely on him to see a problem through. Graham Humes, who dealt with Putin while Humes was director general of CARESBAC, an international humanitarian organization in St. Petersburg, talks of the important role Putin played in the city. He overcame one bureaucratic obstacle after another to ensure that humanitarian aid from abroad was delivered in a timely and fair manner.[10] Putin faced a different challenge during his tenure in charge of regional affairs in dealing with the country's regional governors while working for Yeltsin. The latter, who had given the governors considerable autonomy in return for their support, was concerned about their tendency to side with former Russian Prime Minister Yevgeny Primakov and the mayor of Moscow, Yuri Luzhkov, in the battle for political power. Yeltsin asked Putin to break up this budding alliance, which Putin took on. In a short time, the governors had become more neutral when it came to power struggles in Moscow.[11]

In contrast to his predecessors, Putin claims to be nonideological. As he put it in his millennium speech shortly after he took over from Yeltsin, "I am against the restoration of an official state ideology in Russia in any form."[12] Putin appears less interested in an ideological system, than in using any strategy that will work to attack a problem. The ultimate pragmatist, he has been known to try the solutions of left as well as right.

Putin also gives the impression that he tries to be highly rational in his approach to dealing with issues. As a former KGB colleague put it, "He's always in control of his emotions, keeping his cards close to his chest. He must have a weakness, but I don't know what it is."[13] In the policymaking arena, he seems both thoughtful and methodical. To quote two Russian writers, "We have to say this for Putin: he is not in a hurry to make a choice with regards to the reforms and the methods of their implementation. He is taking his time, waiting for his team to be formed to the end."[14]

Putin's style is also administrative, in that he expects the bureaucracy to implement his mandates, and his decisions tend to be of the gradual, incremental type that one would expect from someone who spent his life in an organization like the KGB. As Bortsov put it in comparing Putin with Aleksandr Kerensky (the ill-fated head of the short-lived noncommunist government in the immediate aftermath of the czar's fall in 1917), "Aleksandr Fedorovich Kerensky was an irresponsible romantic, but Vladimir Putin is pragmatic, and it is for that reason in his policies from the beginning he has taken the tactical approach of 'the possible.' Putin is a statesman—Kerensky was not, Putin is for stability, Kerensky was for a revolution, Putin is a man of action, Kerensky was an outstanding orator."[15] In this sense, Putin also stands in contrast to Yeltsin, who was a revolutionary in the sense that he destroyed the old system, especially the control of the Communist Party, and attempted to introduce a new one. In short, Putin is a leader who appears to believe in structured, stable decisionmaking.

Despite his early reputation as a "laid back" KGB agent,[16] during his civilian period he quickly developed a more active image. Putin delegates, but he is also deeply involved in dealing with the problem of the moment. Bortsov put it best when he commented on the difference between Boris Yeltsin and Vladimir Putin: "The principal difference was that the text was written for Boris Nikolaevich, while Vladimir Vladimirovich writes the theses."[17] This hands-on approach is also evident in Putin's dealings with the various departments and agencies in the Russian government. Take Chechnya, for example. As he noted in his autobiography, his initial response to the conflict was centralization and improved coordination. "I met with the top officials of the Ministry of Defense, the General Staff and the Interior Ministry. We met almost every day—sometimes twice a day, morning and evening. And with a lot of fine-tuning, the ministries were consolidated. The first thing I had to do was overcome the disarray among the ministries."[18] In the same vein, Putin believes in personal responsibility—a trait that has again been evident in Chechnya, where Moscow's military operations have been anything but successful.[19]

Pragmatic solutions to immediate tasks, however, depend on the definition of the problem. And Putin's worldview appears to play a role. He spent his career in the state apparatus, within an agency tasked with being the sword and shield of the regime. He comes to problem solving with a bias toward governmental actions and a notion of society as subservient to the interests of the state. He belongs to a long tradition of Russian statesmen who have sought change through autocratic action from above to mold society.[20]

If Putin's character contains an "ism," it would be a statism that, like nationalism, embraces a deep-seated desire to restore Russia to the greatness of its Soviet years, especially through the exercise of state power. His words are instructive: "Patriotism is a source of courage, staunchness and strength of our people. If we lose patriotism and national pride and dignity, which are connected with it, we will lose ourselves as a nation capable of great achievements."[21] Revealingly, Putin's personal hero is Peter the Great, the leader most associated with opening Russia to the West.[22] Indeed, if Putin has a bias in the foreign policy realm, it is toward the West in general, and the United States and Germany in particular. German was one of his best subjects in school and he served there long enough to become quite comfortable in the language—fluent enough to address the Bundestag in German when he visited in 2001. Indeed, his affinity for Germany was strong enough that one of his biographers called him the "German in the Kremlin."[23] Those who worked with him, however, considered him primarily a Europeanist,[24] and his actions in the aftermath of the attack on the Pentagon and the World Trade Towers show that he also favors strong ties with the United States.

Despite Putin's desire to restore Russia to its great-power status, there is no evidence that he is allied with the jingoistic right. He is clearly what Bortsov called a "healthy conservative."[25] Putin's major concern is to rebuild Russia so that it plays the kind of role in the world it did twenty or thirty years ago, and he is not bashful about saying so.

This brings us to the question, how well does the short biographical sketch match up against Putin's first years in office? To what degree did he act in accordance with the personality characteristics described earlier? To try and shed some light on Putin, the man, we asked Ambassador James Collins, newly returned from four years as U.S. ambassador in Moscow, to comment on Putin and his regime. Ambassador Collins observed Putin's rise at close range, and met with him on numerous occasions. Ambassador Collins not only sat in on many private meetings with Putin, including many of the U.S.–Russian summits, he also met and talked with almost all of the individuals mentioned in this book. His perspective on the issues covered in this book is unique.

RUSSIA IN CONTEXT

As a number of analyses of the Yeltsin period have shown, Yeltsin's primary concern was to maintain his own power. Toward that end, he did nothing to create the kind of political infrastructure that would establish a functioning democracy in the Western sense of the term. As Lilia Shevtsova put it, "His worst mistake both for Russia and himself, has been his failure to establish strong political institutions and stable rules of the game. He has displayed little respect for the law. More often than not, he has obeyed only his sense of political expedience, apparently placing the highest priority on his own political ambitions."[26] Indeed, for a while one of the best sports for Moscow watchers was to bet on (a) how long Yeltsin's current prime minister would last, and (b) who would replace him as Yeltsin proceeded to play musical chairs with his top officials. The minute anyone appeared to grow too powerful or became a political liability, Yeltsin removed him. Yeltsin believed that Russia could only survive if it had a strong president.

One could argue that in the aftermath of his 1993 war with the Duma, Yeltsin had no choice but to create a constitution that enshrined the idea of a super-presidency. With recalcitrant legislators, communists, and hundreds if not thousands of other opponents, he had no alternative. However, as Shevtsova noted, "Many people, even in Russia, at first hoped that the 'super-presidency' that Yeltsin established was only temporary. But this structure, designed to overcome deadlocks and to serve as a major reform force, has now become the main source of political disarray."[27]

A temporary super-presidency might have worked if Yeltsin had been a different leader. However, his ill health, his alcoholism, his acceptance of cronyism and corruption, and his fear of competitors undermined his effectiveness. Furthermore, as time wore on, instead of developing political institutions such as the Duma, he fought one battle after another with it until he generally ignored it in favor of presidential decrees. His actions were often contradictory and his leadership weak at best.

This meant that when Putin came to power Russia had a constitution that put almost all power in the hands of the country's president. In the meantime, nothing had been done to create a "rule of law," a system that would not only enable justice to be dispensed in a fair and impartial manner, but would allow the millions of daily interactions between individuals and firms and the government to be regulated. Similarly, political parties—with the exception of the Communist Party—were nonexistent. By Soviet standards, the press was free, as was the media in general. However, as a result of Yeltsin's need of their support during his 1996 election campaign, the majority of the country was owned by the oligarchs, a small group of powerful and wealthy individuals. In the meantime, many of the country's eighty-nine regions paid little attention to Moscow. They passed whatever local laws they preferred, even if they ran counter to the Russian constitution. The country's economy was in shambles after the August 1998 crash of the ruble. Finally, the military was mired in what appeared to be an unwinnable war in Chechnya, and the Kremlin's standing on the world stage was at an all-time low.

Putin and his followers have attempted to deal with these problems. It would be wrong, however, to look upon Putin either as Russia's savior or as its Satan. I personally am agnostic. I believe it is too early to say where Putin is taking Russia. As citizens of a Western democracy, we may disagree with many of his and his colleagues' actions. Yet the most important issue, at least in my opinion, is how effective has he been in creating a politically stable and economically viable polity. Here, the jury is out; and indeed the reader will find disagreement among this book's contributors on this question.

Some will argue that he has done very little; that his actions are half-measures at best, while others will maintain that he has taken some (admittedly small and preliminary) steps toward moving the country in the direction of political and economic stability. Some will also note that this "progress" has come at a cost. They will maintain that democracy (as that term is understood in the West) has been weakened, while others will suggest that the creation of viable economic and political institutions may have to take priority at this stage, considering Russia's disastrous state.

One of the key prerequisites of any democracy is the existence of attitudes that support it—the presence of beliefs in support of concepts such as compromise, secret ballots, respect for the law, a belief that power comes from the people (i.e., the presence of an active as opposed to a passive citizenry), the existence of groups of individuals who are not controlled by a single party or state, etc.

Timothy Colton and Michael McFaul struggle with this vitally important issue by looking at grassroots attitudes in Russia, especially toward democracy and political practices. Contrary to popular wisdom, they conclude that despite Russia's illiberal tendencies, most citizens support democratic values and ideas. Just as important, however, is the problem of institutionalizing democracy. Toward this end, Thomas Remington focuses on the oft-overlooked Duma, Russia's parliament, and the issue of creating viable political parties. Yeltsin fought with parliament, while Putin is trying to work with it, even if not as democratically as many in the West would prefer. The key point is that unless democratization is institutionalized in the form of genuinely functional political parties, many argue that the outlook for democracy in Russia is mixed at best.

When it comes to the question of democracy, there are no more important issues than press freedom and corruption. In the first instance, Masha Lipman, herself a journalist, and Michael McFaul take a critical look at how the relatively free media that existed under Yeltsin has fared under Putin. The trends are disturbing—at least if one supports the kind of free press we have in the West.

Indeed, almost all observers are united on one point: unless Russia is able to create a stable, healthy economy, there is little chance that it will evolve in the direction of the kind of democratic polity that most Russians seek. Indeed, Putin has focused repeatedly on this problem, and noted just how critical it is in his millennium speech when he observed, "It will take us approximately fifteen years and an annual growth of our Gross Domestic Product by 8 percent a year to reach the per capita GDP level of present-day Portugal or Spain, which are not among the world's industrialized leaders."[28] Toward this end, James Millar takes a careful and critical look at the evolution of the Russian economy under Yeltsin and then Putin in an effort to shed light on the prospects for success in this area. Furthermore, it is clear to anyone who has followed events in Russia that if there is one group that has had the most profound impact on the country's economic and political structure, it is the oligarchs. Peter Rutland considers their role and his chapter on the oligarchs looks at how Putin has approached these highly influential individuals.

Too often books such as this one tend to ignore security and military questions. It reminds me of a book published in the 1930s that I read long ago that said it would not discuss the military "because it is an occupation that we hope will not be used again." However, in the case of Russia, it is impossible to overlook the issue of security. It plays a vital role in Russia's future whether we like it or not. Thus, Dale Herspring considers whether Putin has been successful in reforming that beleaguered institution. At the same time, no analysis of the military would be complete without an in-depth discussion of the never-ending wars in Chechnya, which Jake Kipp provides. As a historian, Jake Kipp knows only too well the key role that historical animosities play in this part of the world.

Chechnya is far from Putin's only regional worry. Nikolai Petrov and Darrell Slider explore Putin's efforts to reassert Moscow's authority, first over the rest of the country, and second in the world at large. One of the strategies Yeltsin used to gain the support of local politicians was to give them as much autonomy as they could seize. While that may have helped Yeltsin in his battle with the communists, it left Putin with a highly decentralized political system—one in which the Kremlin exerted only limited authority over its far-flung territory, as Nikolai Petrov and Darrell Slider note. Putin appears to have regained some of the control that Yeltsin lost, but at a cost to local autonomy.

Dale Herspring and Peter Rutland consider Moscow's attempt to influence the world beyond the near abroad, the realm of foreign policy, where Russia has fallen from the cosmic heights of a superpower to what some observers have referred to dismissively as "a third world country with nuclear weapons." Putin both wants to see Russia reestablish its position in the world for nationalistic reasons and because he understands that Russia's economic recovery is to a large degree dependent in particular on its ties with the United States and Western Europe.

This leaves us with our first question noted earlier: Where is Putin taking

Russia? Dale Herspring explores this issue in his conclusion. What can we (and the Russian people) expect from Putin in the future? Political prognoses are an inexact science at best, and none of us would claim to know the future. Yet the more we understand the present and the past, the better are our chances to prepare for what may come.

NOTES

1. Vladimir Putin, "Russia at the Turn of the Millennium," *Pravitel'stvo Rossiyskoy Federatsii*, January 17, 2000, at www.government.gov.ru/english/statVP_engl_1.html.

2. Much of the following biographical information is taken from Herspring and Kipp, "Searching for the Elusive Mr. Putin," *Problems of Post Communism* (September/October 2001).

3. Vladimir Putin, *First Person* (New York: Public Affairs, 2000), 19.

4. Putin, *First Person*, 23.

5. Mark Franchetti, "Spy Tells How Putin Blew It as KGB Rookie," *New York Times*, March 11, 2001.

6. See Graham Hume's discussion of Putin's role and effectiveness at this time. "Vladimir Vladimirovich Putin in 1994: A Personal Reflection," E-Notes, Foreign Policy Research Institute, January 14, 2001.

7. Yuri Bortsov, *Vladimir Putin* (Moscow: Feniks, 2001), 132.

8. Putin, *First Person*, 131.

9. Ann-Marie O'Neill, Julian Varoli, John Garelik, and Glen Mikelbank, "Vladimir Putin, Russia's Martial-Arts-Loving President in Waiting Remains an Enigma," *People's Weekly*, February 28, 2000.

10. Hume, "Vladimir Vladimorovich Putin in 1994."

11. Masha Gessen, "Putin Himself First," *New Republic*, January 17, 2000, 23.

12. Putin, "Russia at the Turn of the Millennium," 5.

13. Franchetti, "Spy Tells How Putin Blew It as a KGB Rookie."

14. "Putin in 2001: A Burden of Choice," *Ponedelnik*, no. 6 (February 2001) in *Johnson's List*, February 13, 2001.

15. Bortsov, *Vladimir Putin*, 215.

16. Rahr, Alexander, *Wladimir Putin, der "Deutsche" im kreml* (Munich: Universitas, 2000), 64.

17. Bortsov, *Vladimir Putin*, 175.

18. Putin, *First Person*, 140–41.

19. Bortsov, *Vladimir Putin*, 199.

20. Ariel Cohen, "From Yeltsin to Putin," *Policy Review*, no. 100 (April/May 2000): 35–49.

21. Putin, "Russia at the Turn of the Millennium," 6.

22. See Bortsov, *Vladimir Putin*, 111.

23. Rahr, *Wladimir Putin*.

24. Bortsov, *Vladimir Putin*, 122.

25. Bortsov, *Vladimir Putin*, 277.

26. Lilia Shevtsova, *Yeltsin's Russia, Myths and Reality* (Washington, D.C.: Carnegie Endowment for International Peace, 1993).

27. Shevtsova, *Yeltsin's Russia, Myths and Reality*, 3.

28. Putin, "Russia at the Turn of the Millennium," 5.

Part One

POLITICS

Chapter Two

Putin and Democratization

Timothy J. Colton and Michael McFaul

Is Russia a democracy? Is democracy in Russia developing, eroding, or not changing—for either better or worse? The answers to these questions have tremendous implications for social scientists and policymakers. If Russia is a democracy, then theories that explain democratic transitions may provide a meaningful framework for understanding regime change in Russia. If Russia is not a democracy, then other metaphorical lenses may be more appropriate. If Russia is a democracy, then its entrance into Western multilateral institutions may be justified and Western aid for democracy assistance is no longer needed. If Russia is not a democracy, or if Russian democracy is eroding, then the exact opposite policy recommendations may be more appropriate—delayed membership in Western unions and more assistance that is democratic. If Russia is stuck in the middle—caught in the twilight zone between dictatorship and democracy—then this too has implications for theory development and policymaking.

The answers offered in this chapter to these difficult and politically charged questions are unlikely to please anyone. They are based upon a mixed and contradictory assessment. Although some might disagree, it is clear that some form of democracy emerged in Russia after the collapse of Soviet communism in 1991.[1] While not displaying the thick structures and norms typical of a mature "liberal democracy," the Russian regime that put down roots under Boris Yeltsin in the 1990s has many of the features of an "electoral democracy."[2] Especially after the enactment of Yeltsin's super-presidential constitution in 1993, mass-based interest groups were consigned to the fringes, pluralist interest intermediation became feeble, individual liberties began to be abridged by arbitrary practices, and institutions that could have helped to redress the imbalance—parliament, the party system, the judiciary—lost strength and independence. Nonetheless, the Russian state and Russian society displayed features of democratic development.[3] Elections took place under a set of rules recognized by all. The results of these elections were not entirely certain beforehand, and no authority intervened after Election Day to reverse the outcome of the voting. The playing field for competitors in elections was never equal and has steadily become less so. Nonetheless, the rulers of Russia were selected in competitive elections. The regime that emerged in the 1990s was qualitatively different from the communist and tsarist dictatorships.

Since Vladimir Putin became president at the beginning of 2000, democratic institutions have eroded. When Yeltsin appointed Putin prime minister in the fall of 1999, the regime's uncertain and unconsolidated nature lowered the barriers for institutional change. Putin soon put his imprint not only on policy but on institutions. He has not amended or radically violated the 1993 constitution, and he has not upended the institutional configuration of Yeltsin's regime. Nor does he seem to have any coherent plan for doing so. He has, however, initiated or tolerated a series of discrete changes that have diminished the democratic legacy of the reform years. Yeltsin, in recruiting Putin from the closed world of the security agencies and announcing him as the "steel core" of a revitalized government, undoubtedly expected a course correction toward discipline and order. He now thinks that Putin has gone too far in certain respects. However, Yeltsin's feelings are irrelevant. What is important and worrisome is the cumulative impact of the changes.

Putin's innovations coincide with a spate of revisionist thinking about democratization in the contemporary world. Some say that autocracies are being replaced, as often as not, by hybrid regimes entwining democratic with authoritarian principles. Others go further, asserting that Russia and a series of other countries are best thought of as "competitive-authoritarian" systems, in which the authoritarian element has the upper hand.[4] Much ink has been spilled in recent years on the failure of the promising "third wave" of global democratization, which extended from the 1970s into the 1990s, and was capped by the fall of the Soviet dictatorship and its satellites in Eastern Europe. Although there have been democratic success stories in the former Soviet Union, there have been terrible failures and disappointments as well.[5]

It is premature to pigeonhole Russia into any of these autocratic categories. The phrase "managed democracy" will do as a marker for the current condition of its polity. If it is too early to sign the death certificate for democracy, it is too late to ignore tokens of a backing away from the liberal and democratic ideals in which name the Soviet regime was overthrown. Having begun on Yeltsin's watch, the retreat has gathered momentum under Putin. Russia's present rulers are modernizers in the economic and socioeconomic sphere and pro-Western realists in foreign policy. In the political domain, they take the electoral mechanism and the trappings of democracy for granted. They accept that they must periodically renew their popular mandate and that when they do, society must be afforded alternatives to the status quo. They are also reconciled to a limited diversity of opinions and interests within the state machinery. Without setting out to extinguish it, they aim to contain this diversity within boundaries they alone fix. For those at the rudder, democracy is neither good nor evil. It is an existential product of larger forces that, like gravity, cannot be stopped, yet, with the appropriate engineering, can be harnessed to one's own purpose. Institutional change under Putin has reflected this odd blend of preserving formal democratic practices and at the same time weakening the actual democratic content of these political rules and norms.

THE NEW BALANCE OF POWER IN THE DUMA

Putin took office bent on resuming the economic reforms that had been stymied by governmental disorganization and legislative resistance in Yeltsin's second term. Although he selected a face from the Yeltsin era, Mikhail Kasianov, to head his first cabinet, Putin inserted a team of market liberals into the next tier, most of them known to him from his St. Petersburg days. Key players were the new first deputy prime minister and minister of finance, Aleksei Kudrin (a fellow vice mayor with Putin under Anatolii Sobchak), the minister for economic development and trade, German Gref, and the president's personal adviser on economic affairs, the iconoclastic Andrei Illarionov. The team came in with an ambitious program encompassing tax reform, land privatization, deregulation, changes in labor and welfare policy, and incentives for foreign investors.

The 1999–2000 electoral cycle put in place a Duma and a president with the same basic political orientation, enabling rapid progress on this reform agenda. The Unity bloc, partnering with the People's Deputy faction (consisting of pro-Kremlin deputies from the districts) and Regions of Russia (which parted from Fatherland–All Russia [OVR] after the Duma election), materialized as the pivotal force in the Duma.[6] These political partners made a deal with the Communist Party of the Russian Federation (KPRF) to divide the chairs of major committees, cutting out OVR, the Union of Right Forces (SPS), Yabloko, and the Liberal Democrats (LDPR).[7] The pact gave the KPRF's Gennadii Seleznev a second term as speaker. Seleznev's subsequent departure from the communist hierarchy made it apparent that he now had a binding commitment to Putin and the Kremlin. Unity's alliance with the KPRF was purely tactical and unwound in the course of 2000 and 2001. Unity increasingly counted on rightist deputies to help it pursue its legislative agenda, leaving the jilted KPRF leader, Gennadii Ziuganov, to huff at Putin as a "liberal dictator."[8]

For the first time since 1993, the balance of power in the Russian parliament is decisively anti-communist. The Duma has not indulged in squabbling with the president by debating impeachment and censure resolutions. Pushed to act on the economy by Putin and his government, the Duma has enacted new sections of the Russian tax code, which had been in legislative limbo for years, putting in place a flat income tax of 13 percent and a lower profits tax.[9] It has gone along with a new labor code, considered very friendly to business interests, and a land code that allows for the ownership and sale of farms and urban land. Putin and the executive branch have also managed to work with the Duma to pass balanced and feasible budgets, a feat rarely accomplished in the Yeltsin years, when parliament and president were so bitterly estranged.[10] Putin has not yet sent the Duma draft legislation on some of the most painful structural changes, such as those touching on pensions and social assistance. Nevertheless, much has been accomplished since the polarization of executive and legislature was eased as a consequence of the 1999–2000 elections.[11]

The new relationship between the Duma and the president is not "antidemocratic." Every president around the world wants to work with a pliant parliament. Executives in liberal democracies most certainly spend considerable political and material resources to achieve a pro-presidential majority in their legislatures. The anti-democratic flavor of current executive-legislative relations in Russia comes from the way in which the new pro-presidential majority was achieved, that is, through an election in which the playing field was not level for all participants. Unlike any previous parliamentary election in Russia, the Kremlin intervened actively in the 1999 contest to assist Unity and destroy Fatherland–All Russia. The Kremlin relied on its allies in the country's two largest television networks, ORT and RTR, to unleash a negative assault against Fatherland–All Russia. Although other factors contributed to Unity's strong finish and Fatherland–All Russia's disappointing showing in the 1999 parliamentary vote, the playing field for the two parties was not equal.[12]

WEAKENING THE FEDERATION COUNCIL

Putin has assembled super-majorities in the Duma—majorities capable of overriding vetoes of bills handed down by the Federation Council, the upper house of parliament. As a result, he has been able to transform the organization of the upper house and therefore the federal system. To everyone's surprise, Putin made reform of the Federation Council one of his top political goals in his first months in office.

The Russian constitution states that after an interim period during which members would be directly elected (1993–1995), each region of the federation was to send two deputies to the Federation Council: one representing the province's legislative assembly, and one representing its chief executive. The constitution did not specify how these representatives were to be selected. By the end of the two years, the regional governments had won agreement on a law mandating that all provincial leaders were to be popularly elected—until then, Yeltsin had appointed many governors—and that governors and legislative heads would henceforth sit *ex officio* in the Federation Council. This formulation gave the governors and their legislative colleagues increased local legitimacy and greater autonomy from Yeltsin and Moscow. By granting the governors and republic presidents a direct voice in the national parliament, it also created a constitutional anomaly in that these figures would be concurrently executives and legislators. The Federation Council functioned mostly as a lobby for regional interests.

Two weeks after he was sworn into office, Putin proposed a new recipe for the upper house that replaced the regional leaders with persons designated by them under an intricate formula.[13] The members of the Federation Council resisted tenaciously, knowing they would lose their apartments and offices in Moscow, their parliamentary immunity, and much of their clout with the federal government. After a heated battle, in which the Duma said it would override a Federation Council veto and the Kremlin allegedly threatened governors with criminal investigations if they did not support Putin's plan, the law was adopted in July 2000. As a sop, many governors and retired governors were appointed to a new presidential advisory body, the State Council.

The reform has emaciated a significant institutional counterweight to the president. Council members, being unelected, do not have the same authority as their predecessors. Many, in fact, are Muscovites with patronage ties to Putin—they obtained their seats with his administration's backing and have put the Kremlin's interests ahead of their constituents.[14] The new setup also makes it more difficult for regional leaders to take collective action vis-à-vis the central government. As the Duma deputy Vladimir Lysenko stated in 2001, "The president had managed to get rid of one of the strongest and most authoritative state bodies in the country. Under the old structure, the Federation Council provided somewhat of a check and balance on the other branches of power, especially the executive, which is fast evolving into an authoritarian regime."[15]

Putin's reforms of the Federation Council did not formally transgress the democratic rules of the game outlined in Russia's constitution. Moreover, the prior method of constituting the upper house was far from perfect, since it blurred the lines between executive and legislative authority. Putin's correction to this odd formation, however, was not the democratizing measure that many had proposed for years—that is, direct election of senators. Instead, his reform decreased the role of the citizenry in selecting its governmental representatives and thus weakened another check on the Kremlin's power.

MOSCOW VERSUS THE REGIONS

Putin's clipping of the governors' wings was extended to their home turf by a decree enacted on May 13, 2000. The decree established seven super-regions ("federal districts"), accountable to Moscow, and super-imposed them on the eighty-nine units of the federation. Each super-region was to be headed by a plenipotentiary appointed by the president and sitting on his Security Council. Five of the seven envoys named in 2000 were from the Federal Security Service (FSB), the army, or the police.[16] Their writ extends to every federal agency in the regions other than the military forces, and thus they have access to officials in the politically most sensitive and influential agencies, such as the treasury, the tax inspectorate, the procuracy, the FSB, and the regular police. Their mission is to oversee the activities of the bureaucracy and report to the president's office on any regional noncompliance with the constitution or the law.

Three other changes accompanied the super-regions. First, a law passed in July 2000 authorizes the president to suspend elected governors accused of wrongdoing by the procurator-general's office. Inasmuch as criminal proceedings can drag on indefinitely (especially if it suits the president), the law is tantamount to a presidential right to fire governors. Putin has used the power only once, and indirectly at that (when he orchestrated the ouster of Governor Evgenii Nazdratenko of Primorskii Krai in 2001),[17] but the mere threat of it has had a chilling effect on gubernatorial initiative. Putin can also dismiss any regional legislature that passes laws contravening federal laws or the constitution. Second, Putin's government has stopped signing the bilateral agreements with the provinces that were one of Yeltsin's favorite instruments for winning their acquiescence. As of 2003, the division of labor among the national and subnational governments is to be governed by an omnibus law that in principle is to be applied uniformly across Russia. Third, Moscow has pushed through a more centralized allotment of tax receipts. As of 1999, roughly 45 percent of the revenues collected in the regions were supposed to be transferred to the central government, but the amount that reached it was often smaller. Under a law signed by Putin in 2000, about 55 percent is to go to Moscow and 45 percent to the regions, and the balance is to be reviewed regularly. Regions like Bashkortostan, which for years paid almost no federal taxes by virtue of bilateral agreement, are once again contributing to the federal budget.

PARTY FRACTURES, ELECTION MACHINATIONS

Russia's party system does not perform the role that party systems play in working democracies. Most of the country's parties lack a distinct identity or a stable following. They have little effect on the elections that count, the ones in which the president and the regional administrative heads are chosen. Russian electoral law assigns political parties a pivotal role in parliamentary elections, but nonpartisans and weak party organizations continue to play a critical role. Finally, there is little internal cohesion within the parties that remain.

Fatherland–All Russia

The Fatherland–All Russia bloc (OVR), the founding of which initiated the electoral struggle, spoke for current and recent officeholders who sought control of the national government on the assumption that Yeltsin and his entourage were a spent force. Unity, the response to OVR's challenge, was initially created by some pro-Kremlin governors and businessmen like Boris Berezovskii who were concerned about the problems they would face if OVR and former prime minister Evgenii Primakov came to power.

Both founding groups miscalculated. OVR made the biggest blunder when it fumbled the Duma election and then concluded that it could not field a credible candidate for president. All Russia and the Regions of Russia caucus defected in January 2000 and mended fences with the Kremlin. In due course, the entire coalition followed abjectly into Putin's camp.

Unity

The original masterminds of Unity miscalculated in a different way. Unity achieved electoral success and incorporation into the power structure, but its architect, Berezovskii, did not survive as a political insider. Anticipating Putin's gratitude, Berezovskii got the back of his hand, because Putin feared that the "Family" group around Berezovskii and his business ventures had too much influence. He first ostracized Berezovskii and then pushed him into exile in London in 2001. Unity thrived without Berezovskii, upgrading its legal status from electoral bloc to civic movement and then, in 2002, into a political party named Unified Russia. OVR agreed to a phased-in merger with Unified Russia to be complete in time for the 2003 parliamentary election. Whereas Yeltsin discarded two consecutive parties of power, Russia's Choice and Our Home Is Russia, Putin favors strengthening Unity/Unified Russia as an organization and endorsed and assisted it in the 2003 parliamentary elections.

Communists

A smoldering disagreement in the Communist Party of the Russian Federation (KPRF), the main opposition party, between the leader, Ziuganov, and the parliamentary speaker, Seleznev, burst into flame in 2002. Seleznev resigned from the party but, with Kremlin support, kept the speaker's job. He has formed his own political organization, Russia (*Rossiia*), and vows to battle the KPRF for leftist votes in the next elections. Many members are disgruntled with Ziuganov's inflexibility, and thus the KPRF may very well nominate a younger, less hidebound individual, such as Sergei Glazev, as its presidential standard bearer in 2004. Despite these internal battles, the KPRF is poised to benefit from its loyal and stable electorate. Compared to all of Russia's other parties, the KPRF has the most promising short-term future.

Union of Right Forces

On the right, the SPS has made the transition from a coalition of parties and movements to a political party. The head of its 1999 slate, Sergei Kirienko, withdrew from partisan activity when he became Putin's plenipotentiary in the Volga super-region. This left Boris Nemtsov as parliamentary chair, with Anatolii Chubais, Yeltsin's privatization tsar, lurking in the wings. Having cooperated with the government and seen it institute a liberal economic policy, SPS worried that it would not have an attractive platform to sell to the electorate in 2003—and its failure to clear the 5 percent barrier for representation in the Duma bore this out. Several veterans of the Russian democratic movement, most prominently human rights advocate Sergei Kovalev, have quit the party in disgust at its pro-war stance on Chechnya.[18] With Unity creeping to the right and the Kremlin ever more hostile to its leaders, SPS witnessed large inroads into its slightly right-of-center electoral base in the 2003 parliamentary elections.

Yabloko

SPS's liberal rival, Yabloko, suffered a number of defections after March 2000, including the manager of its 1999 campaign, Viacheslav Igrunov, who left to form his own boutique political movement.[19] Grigorii Yavlinskii remains at the helm and has firmed his relationship with Mikhail Khodorkovskii, the CEO of Yukos and the richest man in Russia. Sporadic negotiations with SPS about a common slate in 2003 or other forms of collaboration have been in vain.[20] After years of standoffishness toward the government, Yavlinskii has edged closer to Putin, perhaps aware of how much the president's blessings could help him in the next election. Putin's attitude toward the liberals was apparently influenced by their conduct during the crisis sparked by the seizure of hundreds of hostages in a Moscow theater by Chechen fighters in October 2002. He accused Nemtsov of exploiting the disaster for political gain and praised Yavlinskii for not doing so. His reaction fueled suspicion that Putin may back Yabloko as his liberal ally instead of SPS.[21]

Long-Term Effects

Whatever comes of these partisan intrigues and squabbles, there are two other changes under way that must be watched for their long-term effects. The first stems from the interest of the Russian leadership in revamping the rules for party formation and State Duma elections. Addressing Unity's convention in February 2000, Putin spoke in favor of a "workable" party system made up of "two, three, or four parties."[22] Streamlining was the main aim of a new law on parties passed in 2001, which stiffened the requirements for registration and stipulated that electoral blocs would now have to include one political party. In 1999, Unity called for an end to proportional representation and for all deputies to be elected in districts. Its motivations were not altruistic. Unity's poor showing in the districts in 1999 notwithstanding, its founders calculated that a party of power would do better in a district-based system, especially if it could polarize the district races and then prevail in the runoff. Unity and its Duma allies have so far failed to institute such a change, but in 2002, they raised the threshold for the party list from 5 to 7 percent, effective in 2007 (they originally proposed 12.5 percent), which will decrease the number of parties that get into parliament. Putin's brain trust hopes eventually to push all parties other than Unified Russia and the KPRF to the sidelines.[23] If the communists and Unified Russia were to cooperate in getting rid of proportional representation altogether, Russia's proto-multiparty system might easily become a hegemonic party system dominated by Unified Russia.[24]

The second and more alarming trend is toward arbitrary interference by the central authorities in regional elections, usually with the connivance of local politicos, electoral commissions, and courts. The tone was set in November 2000, when Kremlin officials pressured a judge to remove the incumbent, Aleksandr Rutskoi, from the gubernatorial ballot in Kursk on the eve of the election. Rutskoi, a supporter of Unity in 1999 and Russia's vice president from 1991 to 1993, had, among other things, offended Putin during the controversy about the sinking of the submarine *Kursk* several months before.[25] In April 2002, the scenario was repeated with the front-runner for president of Ingushetiia, a republic bordering Chechnya.[26] The same year, Moscow intervened on behalf of clients in gubernatorial elections in Krasnoiarsk and Nizhnii Novgorod, and there were charges of fraud in the vote counting.[27] Such practices, whether or not they spread to the national level, compromise Russia's functioning even as an electoral democracy. As Andreas Shedler has observed, the process of assessing electoral democracies is like multiplying by zero, as opposed to adding: "Partial compliance to democratic norms does not add up to partial democracy. Gross violation of any one condition invalidates the fulfillment of all the others. If the chain of democratic choice is broken anywhere, elections become not less democratic but undemocratic."[28]

The lack of strong opposition parties and the central state's ability to intervene in local elections underscore the weakness of the checks on the Kremlin's power. Rather than consolidating, these potential balancers of presidential power have weakened with time.

CHECHNYA AND CIVIL LIBERTIES

Putin's rise to power dovetailed with a cruel war in Chechnya, the second Russia had fought there since 1994. In the 1999–2000 electoral cycle, voters saw Unity and then Putin as the political players who could best handle this tormenting issue. The initial use of force against the Chechen fighters making raids on nearby Dagestan in 1999 was justified. Russia also had a sovereign right to deal with the lawlessness that enveloped Chechnya after the Khasavyurt Accord ended the first war in 1996, a plague whose barbarous manifestations included a wave of kidnappings and the execution of hostages. The Russian government's response—full-scale reoccupation, bombardment by heavy weaponry, oppressive patrols and "filtration camps" for segregating and interrogating suspects—has not brought about the promised result. Putin has pledged military reform, as did Yeltsin before him, and appointed a civilian, Sergei Ivanov of the FSB, as defense minister in 2000, but this objective has taken a back seat to prosecuting the war with archaic military forces consisting of sullen conscripts led by a Soviet-era officer corps.[29]

Wars are always brutal, and Chechnya is no exception, but the violence of the guerrillas and the terrorists linked to them does not exonerate Russia's routinely inhumane actions. Human Rights Watch has documented atrocities that include summary shootings, the torching of villages, the rape of Chechen women, and the mistreatment of prisoners of war.[30] Experts reckon that the fighting has displaced 400,000 refugees.[31] Moscow has no strategy for either withdrawal or a negotiated settlement. The March 2003 referendum on Chechnya's status, in which more than 90 percent of its citizens supposedly endorsed all three of Moscow's questions, was a farce, emphasizing yet again the lack of a serious plan to end the bloodshed. To stanch the flow of information about human rights violations, Russia has expelled the observer mission of the Organization for Security and Cooperation in Europe from the republic.

President Putin has loosened the leash on the FSB, which he headed in 1998–1999 and which is now directed by his associate Nikolai Patrushev. The agency has stepped up its harassment of targeted human rights activists and environmentalists, Western non-governmental organizations, and religious groups affiliated with outside organizations.[32] New guidelines on foreign contacts for academics have been issued, and contacts with scientists in so-called closed nuclear cities are restricted. Several academics and environmentalists have been prosecuted for espionage, although the most conspicuous cases ended with acquittals or pardons.[33] At the end of 2002, the FSB became more aggressive about limiting contacts between Russian citizens and foreigners. The Ministry of the Interior must now review most visa invitations to non-Russians. In addition to evicting the OSCE from Chechnya, the Russian government canceled its agreement with the U.S. Peace Corps and refused reentry to Irene Stevenson, the long-time director of the AFL-CIO's Solidarity Center in Moscow.

MUZZLING THE INDEPENDENT MEDIA

Putin has also tightened the state's grip on the mass media, assigning priority to national television.[34] The commercial network NTV supported OVR in the Duma campaign and, though less warmly, Yavlinskii in the presidential campaign, and provided the most candid coverage of the two Chechen wars. Putin moved to settle scores in the spring of 2000. His Kremlin administration leaned on prosecutors to investigate alleged past misdeeds of Vladimir Gusinskii, president of the Media-MOST company, which owned NTV. Gazprom, the natural gas conglomerate with strong ties to the Kremlin, then called in a large loan to NTV. In the space of several months, Gazprom's media holding company took control of the network, Gusinskii fled abroad, the staff of the weekly newsmagazine *Itogi* was fired, and most Media-MOST ancillaries were shut down. Gazprom purged NTV a second time in January 2003, removing Boris Jordan, the Russian-American director it had appointed in 2000, due to NTV's critical coverage of the government's handling of the hostage crisis in a theater in downtown Moscow in the fall of 2002. Evgenii Kiselev and many of NTV's best journalists and producers migrated to TV-6, a much smaller station owned by Berezovskii, only to have the government close it. The former NTV employees got back on the air on a channel called TVS in 2002, but it has only a small fraction of the national audience. One of the original TVS board members, Evgenii Primakov, "called on editorial staff to exercise 'internal censorship' in order to keep the network 'responsible.'"[35] By the time Berezovskii relinquished TV-6, he had already ceded his large minority stake and editorial control in ORT, and Sergei Dorenko, the sarcastic newscaster who was his and the Kremlin's battering ram against OVR in 1999, had been sent packing. Governmental agencies have severely restricted access to Chechnya by Russian and foreign correspondents, and have arrested and intimidated several print journalists whose war stories they found inconvenient.[36]

The struggle about the media involves business and personality issues as well as questions of free speech. The losers to date are not blameless. Gusinskii's financial practices were questionable, and NTV did not offer equal access to all comers during the 1999–2000 elections. Nevertheless, the pluralism that comes from multiple owners and multiple biases is preferable to the monotone that would result from a total state monopoly of the news. In nationwide television broadcasting, Russia is closer to such a monopoly today than at any time since the establishment of NTV in 1993. In its Global Survey of Media Independence for 2003, Freedom House listed Russia as "not free" for the first time since the collapse of the Soviet Union. As the 2003–2004 round of elections approaches, even moderate opponents of Putin have many fewer outlets for delivering their message than in 1999–2000.[37]

PUTIN'S AGENDA AND THE FUTURE OF RUSSIAN DEMOCRACY

Putin and his statecraft cannot be appraised on one level or by one criterion. Enough is not yet known to make it possible to sort through the ellipses and contradictions in the thinking of the public man. The private man is hidden behind many veils.

Some of what is here called managed democracy is a pragmatic response to the trying circumstances Russia found itself in at the end of the 1990s. Boris Yeltsin, capable of flashes of imagination and boldness, was bored with the minutiae of government and preferred changing officials to rethinking policies. To buy support and stability in tumultuous times, he repeatedly made concessions to groups like the provincial governors and the new business elite, barely considering the costs. Putin inherited these arrangements, found many of them lacking, and set out to enforce or negotiate better terms. The particulars often reflect common sense more than ideology, and might very well have been implemented no matter who succeeded Yeltsin. Although the means have sometimes been suspect, there is nothing objectionable in Putin's ending the polarization of executive and legislature, removing the anomaly of governors sitting in the upper house of parliament, squeezing more tax revenues from the provinces, tinkering with the electoral system, putting one or two of the most arrogant oligarchs in their place, and retaliating against the Chechen incursion into Dagestan. In economic policy, Putin has listened to liberal advice and converted it into legislation more consistently and effectively than Yeltsin did. His reforms, along with the 1998 devaluation and the rise in world oil prices, have helped sustain an economic recovery now in its fifth year, a welcome respite after so long in the doldrums.

Prolonged economic growth should be conducive to democracy, for it will grow a middle class that will demand freedoms and accountable governance.[38] This could end up being Putin's most benign legacy to Russia. Nor should one ignore the institutional and political projects he supports that may ultimately strengthen democratic governance. To his credit, for example,

Putin favors legal reforms that will pare the power of prosecutors, introduce jury trials nationwide, and lessen the incarceration rate. In 2002, he vetoed restrictive amendments to the law on the mass media passed by parliament after the Moscow hostage crisis. On occasion at least, Putin says the right things about democracy and human rights. In November 2001, he attended a Civic Forum sponsored by his administration with the purpose of bridging the chasm between state officials and grassroots activists. The sight of a former KGB agent, Putin, sitting at the same table as a former Soviet dissident and Helsinki Watch leader, Ludmila Alekseeva, was a stirring one, although some fretted that it was all a ploy to co-opt activists.[39] A year later, Putin met with a similar group on International Human Rights Day and proclaimed that his heart was with them:

> Protecting civil rights and freedoms is a highly relevant issue for Russia. You know that next year will see the tenth anniversary of our constitution. It declares the basic human rights and freedoms to be the highest value and it enshrines them as self-implementing standards. I must say that this is of course a great achievement.[40]

Unfortunately, Putin's actions are all too frequently at variance with his words. He has worked assiduously to weaken the ramshackle checks and balances built up during Yeltsin's tenure and to impose the tidy logic of the rationalizer and controller but not, as a rule, the logic of the democrat. Yeltsin loved adding pawns to the political chessboard. Putin is happier subtracting them, as he has with Fatherland–All Russia, the oligarchs who got too close to the throne (Berezovskii and Gusinskii), the governors who rashly meddled in Moscow politics, the parties he wants to limit to "two, three, or four," and the elected government of Chechnya. When the chips are down, Putin has shown himself to be, if not actively antagonistic to democratic values, indifferent to their application. In his pursuit of a strong state that can solve Russia's problems, he tends to forget what he said in his open letter to the electorate in February 2000—that a strong state, capable of promoting popular freedom and welfare, must itself be "bound by the laws." A presidential administration that schemes to have candidates whisked off the ballot hours before a gubernatorial election is not one bound by the law. Neither is a government that invokes phony legal excuses to seize control of an NTV or a TV-6 or that lets ill-trained troops run amok in the North Caucasus.

It is not the trees that one should dwell on here but the forest. Democracy as practiced by Putin is partly about practical problem solving, but it is also about eliminating external checks on the power of the state and the leader without scrapping the constitutional framework bequeathed by Yeltsin. Russia's political institutions were never more than partly democratic and were not properly consolidated during the Yeltsin period. This makes it all the more deplorable that Putin has diverted the country further away from democratic development. After the critical set of elections in 1999–2000 and the first several years in office of the talented leader who triumphed in them, the future of Russian democracy is, in fact, more uncertain than before. Theorists and policymakers must come to grips with the regime trajectory in Russia today. The country is not following the democratic-transition script. Contrary to what some in the Bush administration believe, Russia is very unlikely to graduate to liberal democratic status by 2008.

The impact on the regime of Putin's rise to power suggests that the current political system has not consolidated. Russia's nascent democracy is on a negative trajectory, but the unconsolidated state of the regime gives some cause for hope. The regime has not become a total dictatorship.[41] Whether Putin even wants to create such a regime is an open question. Whether he could is also uncertain. Although weak throughout the 1990s and weaker today than just two years ago, democratic rules and procedures are still embedded in the regime, and democratic norms permeate society.[42] Above all else, every major political actor in Russia today believes that elections are the only legitimate way to choose national leaders. No serious leader or political force in Russia today has articulated an alternative model to democracy. For the near future, Putin and his advisers seem likely to manage a version of democracy that limits real political competition and blocks the strengthening of alternative sources of political power. During new crises or after unforeseen events, "managed democracy" can become unmanageable, and pseudo-democratic institutions may suddenly gain real democratic content. The experience of Slobodan Milosevic in the former Yugoslavia and Leonid Kuchma in Ukraine demonstrates how formal democratic rules can suddenly and surprisingly undermine the best plans for "managing" democracy.

In Russia, though, the most likely outcome for the near future is neither more democracy nor more autocracy—neither liberal democracy nor dictatorship—but a stable regime somewhere in between. Putin has eroded democratic institutions and practices but has not destroyed them, nor has he articulated a plan for their further erosion. Russian society seems content with the current quasi-democratic, quasi-autocratic order. Russians value democracy but are too exhausted, from decades of turmoil, to fight for better democracy. Stability is the greater priority. Managed democracy could be around in Russia for a long time.

NOTES

This chapter was published in *Problems of Post-Communism* 50, no. 4 (July/August 2003), copyright © M. E. Sharpe, Inc., and appears here by permission.

    1. For more skeptical assessments, see Vladimir Brovkin, "The Emperor's New

Clothes: Continuities of Soviet Political Culture in Contemporary Russia," *Problems of Post-Communism* 43, no. 2 (March/April 1996): 21–28; Peter Reddaway and Dmitri Glinski, *Market Bolshevism: The Tragedy of Russia's Reforms,* (Washington, DC: U.S. Institute of Peace Press, 1999); Stephen Cohen, "Russian Studies Without Russia," *Post-Soviet Affairs* 15, no. 1 (1999): 37–55; Lilia Shevstova, *Yeltsin's Russia: Myths and Realities* (Washington, DC: Carnegie Endowment for International Peace, 1999).

2. On the differences between electoral and liberal democracies, see Larry Diamond, *Developing Democracy: Toward Consolidation* (Baltimore: Johns Hopkins University Press, 1999).

3. For elaboration of the authors' views on this subject, see Timothy J. Colton, *Transitional Citizens: Voters and What Influences Them in the New Russia* (Cambridge: Harvard University Press, 2000); Michael McFaul, *Russia's Unfinished Revolution: Political Change from Gorbachev to Putin* (Ithaca: Cornell University Press, 2001).

4. See Larry Diamond, "Thinking About Hybrid Regimes," *Journal of Democracy* 13, no. 3 (July 2002): 21–35; Steven Levitsky and Lucan Way, "The Rise of Competitive Authoritarianism," *Journal of Democracy* 13, no. 3 (July 2002): 51–65; Larry Diamond and Marc F. Plattner, eds., *Democracy after Communism* (Baltimore: Johns Hopkins University Press, 2002).

5. Michael McFaul, "The Fourth Wave of Democracy and Dictatorship: Noncooperative Transitions in the Postcommunist World," *World Politics* 54, no. 2 (January 2002): 212–44.

6. See Thomas F. Remington, chapter 3 in this volume.

7. The pact scrapped a rule of thumb that assigned committee chairs in proportion to the size of the respective fractions. OVR and the two liberal groups, SPS and Yabloko, boycotted Duma sessions for several weeks, to no end.

8. Quoted by Susan Glasser in the *Washington Post* (June 8, 2002): A14.

9. For details on the package, see Erika Weinthal and Pauline Jones Luong, "Resource Wealth and Institutional Change: The Political Economy of Tax Reform in Russia," Yale University, December 2002.

10. See Alexander Sokolowski, "Bankrupt Government: The Politics of Budgetary Irresponsibility in Yeltsin's Russia" (Ph.D. dissertation, Princeton University, 2002).

11. Political polarization generally results in bad economic policy. Polarization between institutions produces especially bad policy, as the 1998 financial crisis in Russia starkly demonstrated. On the first issue, see Timothy Frye, "The Perils of Polarization: Economic Performance in the Postcommunist World," *World Politics* 54, no. 3 (April 2002): 308–37. On the second issue, see Sokolowski, "Bankrupt Government"; Vladimir Mau, *Ekonomicheskaia reforma: skvoz prizmu konstitutsii i politiki* (Economic Reform: Through the Prism of Constitutionalism and Politics) (Moscow: Ad Marginem, 1999).

12. For details, see Timothy J. Colton and Michael McFaul, *Popular Choice and Managed Democracy: The Russian Elections of 1999 and 2000* (Washington, DC: Brookings Institution Press, 2003).

13. One representative is selected by the speaker of the regional assembly and confirmed by the assembly as a whole. The governor selects the second representative,

but the assembly can veto the nominee with a two-thirds majority. Representatives serve at the pleasure of those who select them.

14. Aleksei Makarkin, "Sovet Federatsii: novyi sostav, novye problemy" (Federation Council: New Structure, New Problems), in *Politika v regionakh: gubernatory i gruppy vliianiia* (Politics in the Regions: Governors and Groups of Influence), ed. Rostislav Turovskii (Moscow: Tsentr politicheskikh tekhnologii, 2002), pp. 53–75.

15. Vladimir Lysenko, "The Federation Council Fails to Become a House of Lords," in *Russia on Russia: Administrative and State Reform in Russia*, ed. Yuri Senokosov and John Lloyd (Moscow: Moscow School of Political Studies, June 2002), p. 20.

16. Many of the "federal inspectors" reporting to them from the administrative regions also have backgrounds in the FSB/KGB and the uniformed police. Natalia Zybarevich, Nikolai Petrov, and Aleksei Titkov, "Federalnye okruga—2000" (Federal Districts—2000), in *Regiony Rossii v 1999 g* (Russian Regions in 1999), ed. Nikolai Petrov (Moscow: Moscow Carnegie Center, 2001), p. 190.

17. Nazdratenko, who supported the Unity bloc in 1999, was removed mainly because his government was incapable of dealing with power outages in the region. He was allowed to resign and given the comfortable Moscow post of head of the national fisheries agency.

18. Viktor Pokhmelkin and Sergei Yushenkov also quit SPS, ostensibly for the same reason. They joined forces with Berezovskii in 2002 to form a new movement, Liberal Russia. They severed ties with him in 2003 and have demonstrated little appeal for voters.

19. Other defectors included the well-known Duma deputies Nikolai Travkin and Elena Mizulina.

20. In January 2003, SPS offered to support Yavlinskii as presidential candidate and to sever its ties to Anatolii Chubais, whom Yavlinskii abhors, but Yavlinskii rejected the proposition.

21. There were reports after the hostage crisis that Yavlinskii was considering taking a senior position in Putin's government. See Boris Sapozhnikov at www.gazeta.ru (December 23, 2002).

22. *RFE/RL Newsline* (February 28, 2000).

23. See the perceptive report by Olga Tropkina in *Nezavisimaia gazeta* (October 8, 2002).

24. Pointing in a more positive direction is the 2002 federal law mandating proportional representation for 50 percent of the seats in local and regional legislatures. The law creates incentives for party building at the subnational level, where it has gone at a snail's pace for the past decade. See the statement by Aleksandr Veshniakov of the Central Electoral Commission (www.cikrf.ru/_1_en/doc_2_1/).

25. The incident was widely reported at the time. See, for example, *Novosti Rossii* (November 9, 2000), available at www.newsru.com/russia/. Rutskoi confirmed the main elements of the story, but did not blame Putin personally, in an interview with Colton in Moscow on June 5, 2001.

26. *Novosti Rossii* (April 29, 2002).

27. See Anatolii Kostukov in *Nezavisimaia gazeta* (October 1, 2002).

28. Andreas Shedler, "The Menu of Manipulation," *Journal of Democracy* 13, no. 2 (April 2002): 41.

29. Some Russian observers speak of the "militarization" of civil government, as opposed to what Putin promised. See Olga Kryshtanovskaia, "Rezhim Putina: liberalnaia militokratiia?" (Putin's Regime: Liberal Military Rule?), unpublished manuscript, December 2002; "KGB vo vlasti," (KGB—There Is the Power), *Kommersant-Vlas,* (December 23, 2002), available at www.compromat.ru/main/fsb/kgbvovlasti1/.

30. See, for instance, articles in the OSCE publication *Russia/Chechnya*: "Now Happiness Remains: Civilian Killings, Pillage, and Rape in Alkhan-Yurt," 12, no. 5 (April 2000): 1–33; "February 5: A Day of Slaughter in Novye Aldi," 12, no. 9 (June 2000): 1–43; "The 'Dirty War' in Chechnya: Forced Disappearances, Torture, and Summary Executions," 13, no. 1 (March 2001): 1–42; "Burying the Evidence: The Botched Investigation into a Mass Grave in Chechnya," 13, no. 3 (May 2001): 1–26. John Dunlop's *Chechnya Weekly,* published by the Jamestown Foundation, also provides full coverage of the war, including human rights violations. There is extensive discussion of the first and second wars in Matthew Evangelista, *The Chechen Wars: Will Russia Go the Way of the Soviet Union?* (Washington, DC: Brookings Institution Press, 2003).

31. This figure is cited in Sarah Mendelson, "Russia, Chechnya, and International Norms: The Power and Paucity of Human Rights?" working paper, National Council for Eurasian and East European Research, Washington, DC, 2001, p. 11.

32. Details may be found in the special issues on civil society in Russia in *Demokratizatsiya* 10, nos. 2–3 (spring and summer 2002).

33. Those involve Aleksandr Nikitin and Grigorii Pasko, who were accused of leaking classified information about the Russian navy's mismanagement of nuclear waste. Both were arrested when Yeltsin was still president.

34. For details, see Masha Lipman and Michael McFaul, chapter 4 in this volume.

35. *RFE/RL Russian Political Weekly* (April 2, 2002).

36. Criminal prosecutions by the national and regional authorities have also been widely utilized. According to Oleg Panfilov, the director of the Center for Journalism in Extreme Situations, the number of criminal cases against journalists under Putin already exceeds the total under Yeltsin. Quoted in *RFE/RL Russian Political Weekly* (January 11, 2003).

37. The parties are thus devising new information strategies. These include expensive means for distributing programming to regional and cable stations.

38. See the argument in Adam Przeworski, Michael Alvarez, José Antonio Cheibub, and Fernando Limongi, *Democracy and Development: Political Institutions and Well-Being in the World, 1950–1990* (New York: Cambridge University Press, 2000).

39. Alexander Nikitin and Jane Buchanan, "The Kremlin's Civic Forum: Cooperation or Cooptation for Civil Society in Russia?" *Demokratizatsiya* 10, no. 2 (spring 2002): 147–65.

40. Remarks translated and circulated by Federal News Service (December 10, 2002).

41. On the differences between "politically close authoritarian," or full-blown dictatorship, and "competitive authoritarian," see Diamond, "Thinking About Hybrid Regimes"; Levitsky and Way, "Rise of Competitive Authoritarianism."

42. Timothy J. Colton and Michael McFaul, "Are Russians Undemocratic?" *Post-Soviet Affairs* 18, no. 2 (April/June 2002): 91–121.

Chapter Three

Putin, the Duma, and Political Parties

Thomas F. Remington

The contrast between the Yeltsin and Putin presidencies is nowhere more visible than in president-parliament relations. Whereas President Yeltsin never commanded a majority of votes in the Duma, Putin's legislative record is filled with accomplishments. On some controversial issues where Yeltsin was blocked by a hostile parliament—land reform, political parties, ratification of START—the president and government have won majorities. To get his legislation through, Yeltsin bullied the deputies with threats of decrees and dissolution and wooed them with material inducements. On a number of issues, unable to win passage of his preferred legislation, Yeltsin simply allowed legislation he supported to die, allowing the legal vacuum to be filled by regional acts or government regulations, or issuing a decree (*ukaz*). Putin, however, has enjoyed consistent support in both the State Duma and the Federation Council and has established an accumulating record of successes in enacting an ambitious legislative agenda. Moreover, he has tackled issues on which Yeltsin never tried to develop legislation, such as breaking up the natural monopolies and reforming the system of state bureaucracy.

Putin has also altered the institutional setting for politics in the parliamentary and larger electoral arenas. The heavy-handed actions by the police and procuracy against selected business figures and accused spies have chilled open political opposition to the president, while significant changes in legislation on federal relations, political parties, and regional elections have strengthened the power of pro-Kremlin "parties of power" vis-à-vis potential partisan and regional opposition. Less dramatic but of some significance is the development of a new form of institutional relations between president and parliament, under which the executive branch relies on a standing majority in the Duma to pass its legislative agenda. While this arrangement demonstrates the Putin-era Kremlin's domination over the Duma, it may also set a

31

precedent for the emergence of a less asymmetric relation between legislative and executive branches in the future.

Although the 1993 constitution gives the president major political prerogatives, he must obtain the consent of parliament if he seeks to pass legislation. In all cases, the Duma must approve draft legislation before it can be signed into law. There are certain categories of legislation that the Federation Council must consider, and it can consider any bill if it takes it up within two weeks of passage by the Duma. The Federation Council's vetoes of legislation, however, can be overridden by the Duma. The two chambers can also override a presidential veto by a concurrent two-thirds vote. Therefore, if the president wants to enact a law, he must obtain the consent of a majority of members of the Duma. The president can enact measures by edict if a law is not already in force, but even then, experience has shown that a law is more stable and therefore more authoritative than a decree, which can be more easily reversed. Putin has preferred to operate by the normal legislative process, in contrast to President Yeltsin, who often relied on presidential decrees (*ukazy*) to enact important policy changes, particularly in 1992–94. Under Putin, the number and importance of presidential decrees has continued to decline.

Thanks to a reliable base of support in the Federal Assembly, Putin's administration and the government have enacted a comprehensive body of legislation, much of it aimed at stimulating economic growth. More than did President Yeltsin, President Putin has used his annual messages to parliament to lay out his legislative priorities. To an impressive degree, he has then followed up these signals by submitting legislation to parliament. By tracking the flow of legislative proposals from the president's message as they are developed into specific bills, introduced to the Duma, and subjected to the legislative process in the two chambers, we can examine the nature and degree of Putin's control of the policy process.

As in the United States, the president's annual message to the legislature is an occasion for the staff responsible for policy development in the executive branch to insert references to issues on which legislative action is a high priority. Under President Yeltsin, the president's advisors often used the preparation of the message as a way to attract Yeltsin's attention to issues they considered important. Lacking significant support from the president, the government, or particular agencies, many of the general points that the president emphasized died as soon as the speech was over.[1] Under Putin, the annual message to parliament has served to signal the president's direct commitment to developing policy in a number of areas. In most cases, when the president called for legislation on a particular issue, presidential and government staff responded by drafting packages of legislation that were submitted to and shepherded through the Duma and Federation Council. To be sure, the legislative process has often been subject to many more delays than Putin desired. In some cases, the president still has not won passage of desired legislation, or the legislation that passed ended up taking forms that he opposed. In most cases, presidential and government staff in charge of policy development have had to negotiate with their friends in parliament to win support for Putin's program.

Putin's far more focused approach to policy development was evident from the start. In his first message to parliament in July 2000, Putin listed several far-reaching and fundamental policy reforms that he wanted to enact into law. These included a flat income tax rate, lower taxes on profits, a lower social tax, firm protections on property rights, less intrusive regulation of business, banking reform, property rights in land, labor relations, reform of the customs regime, and a new law on political parties. The following year, in his April 3, 2001, message, he called for new legislation on federal relations, criminal and civil procedure, administrative reform, reducing the regulatory burden on business, further tax cuts, reform of the pension system, a system of mandatory federal health insurance, a new labor code, and intellectual property rights protection. His 2002 message was still more ambitious. Here he called for legislation demarcating the jurisdictions of the federal government and federal territorial subjects, reform of local government, a series of judicial reforms (including delineation of the jurisdictions of general and arbitration courts, reform of the criminal code, new codes of civil and arbitration court procedure, a law on arbitration tribunals [*treteiskie sudy*], amendments to the law on the procuracy, and penal reform), reform of the structure of the state bureaucracy and the rules governing state employment, reform of banking, reform of bankruptcy law, and legislation harmonizing Russian trade law with WTO standards. Moreover, he called for breaking up the large natural monopolies (the gas industry, electric power, and railroads), and for reform of the housing and utilities sector. This was the most ambitious program of his first term. In 2003 he made very little mention of new legislative priorities, calling only for the acceleration of the development of reforms of the state administration, and development of a new law on citizenship.

Putin won some significant early victories in enactment of his legislative agenda. In July 2000 his bills reforming the manner of formation of the Federation Council and giving the president the right, under certain circumstances, to remove sitting governors passed. The first several bills of his package of tax reform passed by the end of the spring 2000 term. His bill radically reforming the rules under which political parties could compete was introduced in January 2001 and passed by July 2001. Other proposals, however, were significantly delayed. The first legislative steps toward legalizing a market for property in land were only taken in early 2001, and the land code itself did not pass until September 2001. Even then, it passed after the most controversial element—concerning the regulation of sales of agricultural land—had been removed. Legislation on the sale of agricultural land did not pass until June 2002. The new labor code required lengthy negotiations between the government, the trade unions, and the employers' associations, and only passed in December 2001. A new customs code did not pass until April 2003.

Serious reform of federal relations, which Putin called for in 2001 and 2002, has taken a particularly long time to move from policy development to the introduction of legislation. The task of developing new legislation demarcating jurisdictions and reforming the basis for local government was assigned to a commission headed by Dmitri Kozak, deputy head of the presidential administration, in 2001. Not until January 2003 did the Kozak commission submit legislation to parliament, and only in September 2003 did the Duma pass the controversial bills. Judicial reform, in contrast, moved more quickly. The president called for reform of the criminal and civil procedure codes in 2001 and emphasized judicial reform still more explicitly and comprehensively in the 2002 message. Dmitri Kozak headed another commission drafting legislation in the area of judicial reform and submitted a package of four bills to the Duma in May 2001, and more bills later. The package passed relatively quickly in the year between fall 2001 and fall 2002. Reform of the state bureaucracy and the state employment was a theme emphasized in Putin's 2002 message, but legislation has moved at a glacial pace: a bill regulating the terms of state employment was submitted to the Duma in November 2002 and passed in April 2003, but as of late 2003 there still has been no major overhaul of the organizational structure of the state bureaucracy, or even an initial draft proposal. Still, parliament has generally passed Putin's proposals. In the spring 2001 term alone, the Duma enacted the Land Code (in second reading; the third reading occurred as soon as the Duma reconvened in September); the first bill in a package of pension reform bills (first reading); a new Labor Code (first reading); comprehensive tax reform, including a low flat income tax rate, a unified tax for all social assistance funds, a lower excise tax, a lower profits tax, a lower rate on transactions in hard currency, a new sales tax, and a lower tax on production-sharing agreements (all in second reading); the first bill in a package of judicial reform legislation (first reading); Part 3 of the Civil Code, liberalizing inheritance rights (first reading); a set of reforms lowering the regulatory burden for business, including laws on the registration of businesses, licensing of businesses, regulation of stock companies, money laundering, and three laws on banking reform (all passed through third reading); and a law on the regulation of political parties (through third reading). The spring 2002 term was similarly productive from the standpoint of the government. The Duma passed legislation on standards and on bankruptcy, elimination of the last remaining turnover tax, reduced taxes on small businesses, a new code of procedure for arbitration courts, and a law on sales of agricultural land. All of this legislation would have been difficult if not impossible to pass in the Yeltsin-era Duma. Putin's success reflected both the changed balance of political forces in the parliament and the Kremlin's skillful management of its relations with parliament in building majorities for its policy program.

This chapter reviews Putin's strategy for dealing with parliament. It addresses his relations with both chambers and the means by which he has built up his base of support in each. It examines the process by which legislation is developed and enacted by parliament, surveying relations between the presidential administration and the government, and the executive branch and the factions in parliament, in deciding on the legislative agenda. It concludes by exploring the implications of Putin's strategy for passing his legislative agenda for the development of Russia's constitutional framework in the future. The argument of the chapter is that Putin has skillfully managed relations with parliament and the parties represented in it by creating a regularized but asymmetric environment for bargaining. In this arrangement, parties favoring Putin and his policies are granted minor policy concessions in return for reliable support of Putin's agenda in parliament. Like his predecessors Gorbachev and Yeltsin, Putin has traded off representational rights in certain arenas that do not threaten his power in return for their support of his control over policy in major issues. While in the future the institutionalization of a pro-presidential majority coalition in parliament may create a precedent leading to a more parliamentary form of rule, for the present it ensures Putin's domination of the policy environment.

BUILDING THE KREMLIN'S MAJORITY

From the very beginning, Putin demonstrated his mastery of parliamentary tactics in dealing with the third Duma, which convened in January 2000. His adroit manipulation of interfactional negotiation resulted in a temporary alliance between the Unity faction and the communists, which was joined by a group of single-member district independents called People's Deputy. Controlling a bare minimum majority in the Duma, they succeeded in electing communist Gennadii Seleznev to the speakership and in allocating the committee chairmanships among themselves. Factions excluded from the arrangement—the Fatherland / All-Russia coalition (OVR), Yabloko, and the liberal SPS—walked out in protest and refused to return to the Duma for three weeks. But the communists' triumph was ephemeral. Quickly it became apparent that they had very little power within the Duma. Their committee chairmanships did not include any of the committees with jurisdiction over the main policy issues that were politically important to them or to Putin: they did not control the defense, security, foreign relations, budget, legislation, property, or banking committees. Nor could they determine the majority, as they had done in the two previous Dumas. In 1994–95 and 1996–99, the communists were the dominant faction by virtue of the interaction of two crucial advantages: their size and their cohesiveness. In the first two Dumas it became extremely difficult to form a majority that did not include the communists. As the pivotal faction, they could usually dictate the terms on which they would join a majority coalition. Now, in the third Duma, they were marginalized, despite holding the speakership and ten committee chairmanships. Their role as the pivotal faction was taken over by Unity. Unity had nearly as many members as the communists (eighty-nine initially for the communists, eighty-one for Unity), and a level of voting discipline that rivaled the communists, but they also had one additional crucial advantage: direct access to the Kremlin. Unity became the Kremlin's majority-maker in the Duma, and the Duma's major intermediary with the Kremlin. Given the asymmetry in constitutional powers between president and parliament, it became clear that Unity's strength and cohesiveness gave the Kremlin the ability to form majorities around nearly any bill it wanted to pass.[2]

Putin's handling of the upper chamber of the parliament has been equally effective. The law that he succeeded in getting passed in both chambers in the summer of 2000 that overhauled the method by which the members of the Federation Council are chosen has had the result of giving him a secure base of support in that chamber as well.[3] Under the new procedure, the Federation Council comprises members chosen by the chief executives and the legislatures of the eighty-nine territorial subjects of the federation. Previously, the chamber's members were the chief executives and chief legislative officials of the regions, who held their seats ex officio. The new members generally lack independent resources and tend to reflect the influence of the presidential administration. In 2001 around one hundred of them joined a caucus called "Federation," which firmly supported President Putin and his policies and has delivered resounding majorities for Putin-backed legislation, even against the preferences of their principals in the regions. Then, in January 2002, the Kremlin engineered a major change in the governance of the chamber. It successfully backed the candidacy of Sergei Mironov, considered a Putin loyalist, to be chair of the chamber, and it persuaded the members of the chamber to banish all political caucuses, including Federation. Henceforth the Kremlin conveyed its guidance on each piece of legislation directly to the leadership of the chamber and its committees. This mechanism has been remarkably successful in guaranteeing overwhelming majorities for almost every piece of legislation that the Kremlin supports.[4]

THE "COALITION OF THE FOUR"

Table 3.1 indicates the breakdown of members of the Duma factions as of July 2003 by electoral mandate type. (Note that the figures do not reflect all changes in Duma membership and faction membership as of that time, so

Table 3.1. Duma Faction Membership by Electoral Mandate Type, July 2003

Faction	N/%[a]	SMD??	Party List	Total
Independent	N	11	8	19
	%	58.0	42.0	100.0
Russia's Regions	N	40	7	47
	%	85.0	15.0	100.0
CPRF	N	36	47	83
	%	43.0	57.0	100.0
People's Deputy	N	53	1	54
	%	98.0	2.0	100.0
Unity	N	19	63	82
	%	23.0	77.0	100.0
Yabloko	N	2	13	15
	%	13.0	87.0	100.0
SPS	N	4	27	31
	%	13.0	87.0	100.0
OVR	N	22	32	54
	%	41.0	59.0	100.0
APG	N	23	20	43
	%	53.5	46.5	100.0
LDPR	N	—	13	13
	%	0	100.0	100.0
Total	N	210	231	441
	As % of total	48.0	52.0	100.0

[a] N = Number; % = percentage of faction

they should be taken as approximations.) The table shows that factions vary in the electoral backgrounds of their members: the communists are relatively balanced between party list and single-member district (SMD) deputies, whereas factions such as LDPR, Yabloko, and even Unity are highly dependent on their list contingents for their membership. Groups such as People's Deputy and Russia's Regions are entirely made up of SMD deputies, except for a few deputies elected on other parties' lists who have changed factional affiliation since their election.[5] The agrarians would also be an all-SMD group, but the communists seconded some of their members to them to bring the group up to the strength required for registration.

The differing electoral composition of different factions directly affects the ability of the pro-Kremlin forces to command a voting majority in the Duma. The coalition supporting Putin and the government consists of Unity and three allied factions: People's Deputy, Russia's Regions, and OVR. In spring 2001, this coalition formed an organizational structure for coordinating positions on major legislation, although they faced continuing difficulty in imposing voting discipline. Unity and OVR are factions formed on the basis of deputies elected on the Unity and OVR party lists, plus deputies who won single-member district races and chose to affiliate with those factions. People's Deputy and Russia's Regions are, technically speaking, not factions but groups; groups are formations that are not based on successful list parties, but rather comprise deputies elected in single-member districts who did not have other party affiliations. Groups that can claim at least thirty-five members can register for the same rights and status as party factions, so both groups and factions will sometimes be referred to here (as they often are in the Duma) as factions when speaking of Duma political formations generally. But an important distinction between groups and factions in practice is that groups, precisely because they are formed out of single-member district members, usually without a party affiliation, and for the purpose of providing such members with political teammates, tend to be much less cohesive in voting than party factions. Therefore Unity, which boasts a high level of voting discipline even in comparison with other party factions, has a difficult time holding its coalition partners in line on divisive votes. If the coalition of the four vote cohesively, they can command a majority of votes; when they are joined (as they usually are) by Zhirinovsky's small LDPR faction, the majority is more secure, and when SPS supports the item, the coalition can afford to lose some defectors. This insurance is needed because the coalition cannot count on disciplined voting within People's Deputy and Russia's Regions, especially on matters where their members feel strong pressures from their constituencies.

Unity faces a different problem with OVR. OVR was originally led in the Duma by Yevgeny Primakov. Under Primakov, OVR tended to adhere to an independent line in Duma voting. When Primakov stepped down as leader in September 2001, the faction agreed formally to join the Unity coalition in the Duma, and its external party organization led by Luzhkov agreed to merge with Unity. Even then, OVR deputies indicated that they would maintain a distinct political line and would decide whether to side with Unity on a vote-by-vote basis. Therefore Unity has had some difficulty in forming and maintaining its majority coalition. Deputies cannot be blackmailed into voting discipline by the threat that defection from the party program will lead to the collapse of the government: there simply is no parliamentary responsibility for maintaining a government in power in Russia as there is in a true parliamentary system. Given the dependence of pro-government deputies in the Duma on the presidential administration for material benefits and electoral assistance, the possibility that they might bring about the dissolution of either the government or the Duma through a vote of no confidence is too remote to give faction leaders any leverage to use against straying members. Moreover, the government can look for a majority by building agreements with other factions, bypassing its ostensible Duma allies. Still, leaders of the pro-government forces have some leverage. Faction leaders can and do threaten members who defect on key votes with exclusion from the faction, although this is a weak sanction; it may mean, however, that the errant deputy will lose the Kremlin's administrative assistance at the next election. The pro-government factions have enough bargaining resources that when the government needs their support on particular pieces of legislation, they can bargain for concessions. Consequently, there is a reciprocal interest on the part of the executive and the pro-executive factions in building a more institutionalized relationship. The government's objective is to consolidate its influence so that the bargains are less costly and support more reliable; Unity and People's Deputy both aspire to expand their influence (and access to the Kremlin) by regularizing the coalition arrangement so that they can count on the votes of all four factions in the coalition and minimize its dependence on other factions for votes.

The prospect of parliamentary elections strongly affects the alliances and policy positions of Duma factions. Unity formed the electoral party "Unified Russia," and in fall 2003 both Unity and OVR changed the official name of their Duma factions to "Unity–Unified Russia" and "Fatherland–Unified Russia," respectively, to emphasize their electoral alliance. The People's Deputy faction is a particularly good example of the effect of prospective Duma elections on the political strategy of Duma factions. In the Duma the People's Deputy group has competed with Unity to be the Kremlin's favorite partner, looking to win benefits by positioning itself as a more viable electoral force than Unity in future parliamentary elections. In the fall of 2001, as the People's Deputy Duma group was cementing its parliamentary alliance with Unity, Gennadii Raikov, leader of People's Deputy, decided to form a separate political party called "People's Party." In 2003, Raikov decided to challenge Unified Russia by running its own separate party list in the 2003 elections as a rival "party of power" with a center-left political profile, rather than sharing a single list with Unified Russia. By contrast, Russia's Region has chosen not to organize itself into an electoral party. Evidently its members prefer to obtain what policy and election benefits they can from joining the pro-government coalition. However, they have so little voting discipline that they bring rather limited bargaining leverage to the table.

The first hints that the Duma was moving toward a more majoritarian pattern of governance was the tactical alliance created by Unity, the communists, and People's Deputy in January 2000. Following the Kremlin's strategic direction, they found that they commanded the minimum necessary number of votes in the Duma and could divide up the lion's share of the office benefits that came with majority status. These three factions were the three largest in the Duma; by uniting, they represented the smallest number of factions as well as the smallest number of deputies that could have controlled a majority. Their alliance represented a sharp departure from the traditions of proportional representation that had previously governed the distribution of committee chairmanships, and of course a still greater departure from the parity principle used to form the Council of the Duma. Other factions protested the violation of these practices. The coalition of Unity, CPRF, and People's Deputy was short-lived, however. It was evidently intended to keep Primakov from winning the speakership and to co-opt the communists by giving them numerous but largely nominal leadership offices. It left Unity free to forge other tactical alliances, depending on the issue. This Unity proceeded to do, always closely adhering to the Kremlin's legislative goals and strategies.

In the 2000–2003 period, Unity was on the winning side of nearly all major votes, but its alliance partners varied. Sometimes Unity allied with the factions of the left (the communists, the agrarians, and some of OVR), and on other issues its partners were SPS and Yabloko. Unity was the pivotal member of nearly every winning coalition. It delivered the president and government a string of victories, but at a price. The government had to make concessions on a number of policy fronts in order to win passage of its highest-priority legislation, such as the modifications to the annual budget, and tax reform. On land reform, for example, the government simply dropped the provisions which would have legalized the buying and selling of agricultural land as a condition for winning passage of this landmark law. (As table 3.2 shows, it passed in second reading with 253 votes, 27 more than the bare minimum required.) The new bill dealing specifically with agricultural land then passed in 2002. The convergence of interests of the government and the key pro-government factions in the Duma led to their efforts to create a more durable alliance structure that would lower the bargaining costs of building a majority.

The coalition began in April 2001 when Luzhkov, as head of Fatherland (one part of the electoral coalition of Fatherland and All-Russia, whose joint list produced the Duma faction OVR), joined with Minister of Emergency Situations Sergei Shoigu, as head of the Unity movement, in announcing that they were forming a united party. They held a meeting with President Putin the same day, reporting that the president supported the idea. Several days later, their Duma factions joined with People's Deputy and Russia's Regions in forming a "coordination council" that would harmonize the positions of the factions in passing legislation. The head of the Unity faction, Vladimir Pekhtin, observed that their goal was to "unify the efforts of deputies of the center and thus to facilitate the accelerated passage through the Duma of decisions necessary for ensuring stable economic growth."[6] The head of the Russia's Regions faction, Oleg Morozov, went further in describing the goal of the new council. Eventually, he said, they intended to form a government of the parliamentary majority.[7] Together, the coalition of the four commanded 234 members at the time of its formation—enough to pass ordinary legislation if all members voted cohesively, although not enough to pass constitutional laws, which require 300 votes.

Since its formation, the coordinating council has been active, although it is far from exercising the disciplined voting power that a majority coalition in a parliamentary democracy would normally exhibit. The fall 2001 term began with sparring over the 2002 budget between the Duma and the government. The coalition of the four demonstrated its potential by preempting the usual committee deliberations and negotiating separately with the government over the shape of an acceptable compromise. After a series of meetings between the finance ministry and the four factions, the government and the coordinating council announced that they had reached a compromise that would enable the four pro-government factions to support the budget in first reading. The government, with a show of reluctance, agreed to raise its estimate of revenues for 2002 by another 123 billion rubles, thus allowing the four factions to direct additional spending into electorally profitable directions: pensions; defense; regional aid; industrial investment; and highway construction.[8] Four days later the budget passed the vote in first reading with 262 affirmative votes. Unity, People's Deputy, OVR and Russia's Regions voted by overwhelming margins in favor of the bill. Clearly, the deal with the government satisfied the coalition members; their support in turn made it more advantageous for other factions to join them than to oppose the bill. Thereafter, the "zero reading" procedure by which the government met with the leaders of its four allied factions in the Duma before formally submitting the annual budget bill to parliament, in order to accommodate some of the majority coalition's interests, has been followed each year. The procedure for handling the budget is efficient in that it allows the government to concentrate its bargaining leverage on the smallest number of factions that can deliver it a majority.

Analysis of a number of important votes this year indicates that voting cohesion among the four is high but not 100 percent. Unity can usually count on a majority of People's Deputy members to join it on close votes but not Russia's Regions or OVR. Table 3.2 lists the breakdown by faction of support for thirty major votes in 2001. All are votes where fewer than 65 percent of the Duma voted on the winning side, and all are items of high salience for the government and Duma. They concern issues such as tax policy, land reform, imports of nuclear wastes, regulation of political parties, electoral reform, federal relations, labor relations, and the budget. Unity was on the winning side in twenty-four of the cases (80 percent), but more striking is the high level of voting discipline: in nearly all cases, at least 90 percent of its members voted on the same side. OVR was relatively cohesive as well; 80 percent of the time its members could call upon at least three-quarters of

Table 3.2. Voting on Key Votes by Faction (percent voting "Yes" in each faction)

Vote No.	Date	Subject	Total "Yes"	CPRF	APG	LDPR	Rus Reg	Nar Dep	Yabloko	Unity	OVR	SPS	Indep
V34970	22-Feb-2001	Profits tax, 2nd reading	233	0.000	0.000	1.000	0.578	0.831	0.944	0.952	0.205	0.737	0.467
V34990	22-Feb-2001	Tax on securities, 2nd reading	226	0.012	0.000	1.000	0.422	0.542	0.778	0.940	0.659	0.763	0.400
V37580	22-Mar-2001	State regulation of foreign trade, 2nd reading	213	0.977	0.977	0.417	0.778	0.169	0.389	0.000	0.523	0.053	0.267
V38000	4-Apr-2001	Single tax-agreemt commiss report	253	0.965	0.953	0.083	0.711	0.831	0.000	0.024	0.795	0.000	0.533
V39910	18-Apr-2001	Use of atomic energy, 2nd reading	244	0.465	0.512	0.917	0.467	0.695	0.000	0.843	0.591	0.000	0.467
V40020	18-Apr-2001	Environmental protection, Art. 50, 2nd reading	230	0.384	0.419	0.917	0.467	0.644	0.000	0.831	0.591	0.000	0.533
V40080	18-Apr-2001	Special ecological programs, 2nd reading	267	0.488	0.558	1.000	0.378	0.763	0.000	0.916	0.818	0.026	0.533
V41860	26-Apr-2001	Tax Code part 2, Chap 23, 2nd reading	269	0.000	0.000	1.000	0.733	0.712	1.000	0.916	0.977	0.921	0.600
V42850	23-May-2001	Production-sharing agreements, 2nd reading	275	0.128	0.140	0.833	0.756	0.644	1.000	0.952	0.818	0.921	0.467
V44260	24-May-2001	Political parties, 2nd reading	261	0.035	0.116	0.917	0.800	0.949	0.889	0.964	0.977	0.079	0.467
V44570	6-Jun-2001	Principles of org of power in subjects, 2nd reading	250	0.884	0.791	0.000	0.689	0.220	1.000	0.024	0.795	0.895	0.467
V44710	6-Jun-2001	Law on militsiia, 2nd reading	235	0.012	0.163	1.000	0.756	0.949	0.722	0.976	0.477	0.105	0.400
V45610	13-Jun-2001	Basic guarantees of elec rights, 2nd reading	289	0.895	0.953	0.583	0.711	0.610	0.889	0.060	0.932	0.711	0.467
V46700	14-Jun-2001	Social development of rural settlements, 2nd reading	236	0.953	1.000	0.000	0.689	0.610	0.000	0.000	0.818	0.000	0.533

V47170	15-Jun-2001	Take up Land Code on floor	254	0.000	0.000	1.000	0.378	0.797	0.944	1.000	0.864	1.000	0.133
V47250	15-Jun-2001	Give floor to Gref for Land Code debate	251	0.000	0.000	0.917	0.356	0.746	0.944	1.000	0.818	0.818	0.467
V47310	15-Jun-2001	Land Code, 1st reading	236	0.000	0.000	1.000	0.333	0.542	0.944	0.988	0.818	0.818	0.267
V48630	21-Jun-2001	Political parties, 3rd reading (2nd try)	238	0.000	0.000	1.000	0.444	0.949	0.944	0.988	0.977	0.026	0.467
V48830	21-Jun-2001	Media law, 2nd reading (2nd try)	223	0.012	0.000	1.000	0.689	0.932	0.000	0.952	0.864	0.026	0.400
V49110	21-Jun-2001	Procedure for considering Labor Code	247	0.023	0.000	1.000	0.378	0.712	0.889	0.940	0.932	0.921	0.267
V51840	4-Jul-2001	Nadezhdin amendment (sets term limits for governors), 2nd reading	240	0.930	0.977	0.167	0.133	0.119	1.000	0.012	0.932	0.974	0.400
V52090	4-Jul-2001	Money laundering, 2nd reading	237	0.035	0.000		0.578	0.864	1.000	0.976	0.977	0.211	0.467
V52230	4-Jul-2001	Rates for calculating individual pensions, 2nd reading	230	0.012	0.000	1.000	0.400	0.881	1.000	0.964	0.977	0.000	0.400
V53370	6-Jul-2001	Minerals tax, 2nd reading	266	0.012	0.000	1.000	0.467	0.915	0.944	0.976	0.864	0.921	0.467
V54800	11-Jul-2001	Licensing business, 2nd reading	289	0.047	0.000	1.000	0.733	0.949	0.778	1.000	0.932	0.974	0.600
V55400	12-Jul-2001	Law on police (agreement comiss version)	236	0.163	0.326	1.000	0.689	0.966	0.778	0.964	0.023	0.053	0.667
V56710	13-Jul-2001	State pensions, 1st reading	255	0.000	0.000	0.917	0.556	0.678	0.722	0.988	1.000	0.816	0.533
V59270	14-Jul-2001	Land Code, 2nd reading	253	0.000	0.000	1.000	0.489	0.627	0.944	0.976	0.932	0.947	0.400
V60990	27-Sep-2001	Procuracy, 1st reading	242	0.233	0.349	0.000	0.556	0.593	0.944	0.976	0.114	0.947	0.533
V61300	28-Sep-2001	2002 budget, 1st reading	259	0.023	0.023	0.083	0.711	0.966	0.778	0.988	1.000	0.474	0.467

its members to vote the same way. The other two partners were far less unified. People's Deputy could deliver three-quarters of its membership less than
half the time, and Russia's Regions could muster 75 percent agreement only
20 percent of the time.

Table 3.3 indicates how closely factions were aligned with one another on
these thirty votes. Using a simple "party voting" measure, where the position
taken by a simple majority (50 percent plus one) of the members of a faction
is taken as the position of the faction, each faction's position is correlated
with that of every other faction. Majorities of Unity and People's Deputy
voted together twenty-seven of thirty times, so Pearson's r, the coefficient of
correlation, between their positions is .66. LDPR voted the same way as
Unity twenty-six of thirty times, so the coefficient is .64. People's Deputy
and LDPR were the most consistent voting partners of Unity on these votes:
neither OVR nor Russia's Regions was nearly as frequent a voting ally with
Unity; both in fact voted against Unity more often than they voted with it.
The communists and Unity never voted the same way, so the coefficient of
agreement is a perfect −1.0. Unity and SPS voted differently almost as often
as they voted together. Clearly, the coalition of the four had a considerable
distance to go before it could command a consistent and cohesive voting
majority. It was therefore in the interests of Unity and People's Deputy to
improve the coordination of the four core members of the government's
majority, and equally so for the government.

REMAKING THE FEDERATION COUNCIL

Putin's strategy for winning firm control of the Federation Council was quite
different. The law reforming the method by which its members were selected
provided a gradual transition to the new system. All the former governors
and legislative chairs were to rotate out of the chamber by the end of December 2001, but they could decide on the optimal timing of their departure in
order to arrange for their replacement. By October 31, 2001, nearly half
(eighty-five) of the members were newly appointed delegates, and by January
2002, nearly all were newly chosen. The new members were to be full-time
legislators, and many were experienced in regional and federal-level politics.
As soon as the rotation began, some of the new members positioned themselves as allies of President Putin and challenged Egor Stroev for leadership.
Stroev opposed forming any sort of group or faction in the Federation Council. The rules of the chamber do not provide for deputy factions, and several
previous attempts to form them had failed; more immediately, a strong pro-
presidential faction would undermine Stroev's ability to shape the terms of
bargains between the president and the chamber. However, the organizers of

Table 3.3. Interfactional Agreement Correlations on Thirty Key Votes, February–September 2001

		CPRF	APG	INDEP	LDPR	RR	PD	YAB	UNITY	SPS	OVR
CPRF	PC	1									
	Sig. (2)										
APG	PC	0.8292	1								
	Sig. (2)	0									
INDEP	PC	0.0364	0.0987	1							
	Sig. (2)	0.8487	0.6039								
LDPR	PC	-0.6407	-0.4886	-0.0987	1						
	Sig. (2)	0.0001	0.0061	0.6039							
RR	PC	0.2691	0.071	0.2789	-0.3752	1					
	Sig. (2)	0.1505	0.7093	0.1356	0.041						
PD	PC	-0.6667	-0.5528	0.2182	0.5528	-0.0673	1				
	Sig. (2)	0.0001	0.0015	0.2467	0.0015	0.724					
YAB	PC	-0.3152	-0.5584	-0.3268	0.202	-0.0053	0.0788	1			
	Sig. (2)	0.0897	0.0013	0.078	0.2845	0.9778	0.6789				
UNITY	PC	-1	-0.8292	-0.0364	0.6407	-0.2691	0.6667	0.3152	1		
	Sig. (2)	0	00.8487	0.0001	0.1505	0.0001	0.0897				
SPS	PC	-0.0334	-0.1914	-0.1166	0.1914	-0.1438	-0.0891	0.5898	0.0334	1	
	Sig. (2)	0.8609	0.311	0.5393	0.311	0.4483	0.6397	0.0006	0.8609		
OVR	PC	0.1961	0.2365	-0.1712	-0.0148	-0.343	-0.1307	-0.2164	-0.1961	0.0262	1
	Sig. (2)	0.299	0.2082	0.3657	0.9382	0.0635	0.491	0.2508	0.299	0.8907	

Note: PC = Pearson correlation; Sig. (2) = Sig. (2-tailed).
Number of key votes = 30.

Federation were not deterred. As the ranks of the group grew, they demonstrated their voting clout in a series of high-profile issues.

In January 2002, President Putin's advisors engineered a change in the way the Federation Council was governed. They proposed Sergei Mironov as chair, although he had not been closely associated with the Federation Group, and backed a new version of the Standing Orders that prohibited explicit party factions in the chamber. Close coordination between the Kremlin and the chamber is achieved through the weekly meetings between the chamber's first deputy chair and the committee chairs. At these meetings, the Kremlin's position on pending legislation is communicated, and the chamber's position is worked out. As a result, the chamber votes with remarkable efficiency to back the Kremlin on almost every issue: the chamber meets only one day every two weeks, speeding through dozens of bills each time, and providing large lop-sided majorities on almost every bill. Moreover, even on matters where many governors have registered their dissatisfaction or overt opposition, the Kremlin's influence is sufficient to ensure that members follow the president's line faithfully. Although members can be and sometimes are recalled and replaced, most governors appear to accept the political expediency of allowing their representatives to vote the president's line in the Federation Council as the price for giving them policy influence through lobbying on more particularistic issues.[9]

Thus, in both chambers, President Putin had helped to engineer the formation of standing majorities through which the presidential administration and government could bargain for their major legislative priorities, trading off privileged access to the Kremlin in return for reliable voting support.

RATIONALIZING POLICY DEVELOPMENT

Putin's effectiveness in dealing with the Federal Assembly also reflects close coordination between the two components of the executive in Russia: the presidential administration and the government. Under President Yeltsin the administration and government had not competed so much as they had divided responsibility; the president's staff tended to focus on political strategy and national security issues, leaving the development of much of the country's economic policy to the government, particularly after the initial wave of reform in the early 1990s had subsided.[10] As soon as Putin assumed the presidency, however, he began to organize a process for developing policy proposals that could be submitted to the Duma as draft legislation. He called upon think tanks to which he had ties from his service in St. Petersburg, including the Center for Strategic Planning (*Tsentr strategicheskikh razrabotok*) headed by German Gref. Gref's center became a central part of policy planning and development, sufficiently independent of the executive branch to be able to call upon experts and public figures as needed, but enjoying close access to Putin. One crucial aspect of the center's effort was to coordinate policy planning with the government. Government officials in a number of agencies, including those responsible for social welfare, were opposed to the liberal thrust of much of the Putin-Gref economic policy. For the most part, however, Putin's team succeeded in preventing them from blocking his policy initiatives by forming tacit alliances with sympathetic committees in the Duma. For one thing, government officials were brought into the working groups drafting much of the legislation, with the result that much of the legislative program was slow to form. For another, control of the key Duma committees in charge of the Putin team's priorities—budget, taxation, deregulation, judicial reform, pension reform, land reform, labor relations, and the like—was for the most part in the hands of the pro-Putin factions. A telling instance of the importance of committee jurisdiction control for the progress of legislation submitted to the Duma was the turf fight for control of the land code. In May 2001, the pro-Kremlin factions succeeded in transferring jurisdiction over the land code from the agriculture committee, which had been firmly controlled by the agrarian faction (allied closely with the communists) to the committee on property and privatization, whose chairman is a Unity deputy. Once the transfer occurred, the bill took the liberal form that the Kremlin desired and was quickly reported out for floor action.[11]

Putin made Gref minister for economic development and trade and assigned him a broad mandate for shepherding through the economic reforms. Gref continued to head the Center for Strategic Planning on an honorary basis and to draw upon its expertise and legislative drafting. Gradually Gref expanded his influence within the government, carefully lining up support from both executive-branch departments and important organized social interests. His ministry cultivated close ties with the Russian Union of Industrialists and Entrepreneurs (RUIE, headed since 1991 by Arkadii Vol'-skii) and other business groups, and encouraged them to submit its proposals on economic and social policy. The RUIE became an important source of influence and advice on tax policy, deregulation, and pension policy, for instance. Other government officials pursued a similar strategy of consultation with important affected social interests in developing legislation. Minister of Labor and Social Policy Pochinok helped to broker an agreement between the Employers' Association and FITUR (the Federation of Independent Trade Unions of Russia, the major umbrella association representing organized labor), over the terms of a new labor code. Dmitri Kozak, deputy head of the presidential administration, headed a working group of judicial specialists in drafting a comprehensive reform of judicial institutions. In some issue areas, the government has had to move slowly, as in the area of the reform of the housing-utilities sector. In most cases, the government and president have succeeded in finding mutually acceptable compromises with allies in the executive and legislative branches, particularly on distributive issues where the stakes are fungible. The Kremlin managers have demonstrated considerable skill in developing consensus within the executive branch and between the executive branch and major social actors before submitting legislation to the Duma. The Kremlin has been so successful in passing its legislative program not only due to its reliance on loyal members of parliament, but also due to careful preparatory work in minimizing opposition from within the state bureaucracy and important external interests.

Putin has also used the factor of intimidation to tame potential opposition. The procuracy has been used to harass and intimidate open and potential opponents, striking particularly at organizations and individuals associated with Boris Berezovsky and Vladimir Gusinsky and, in 2003, some senior figures in the Yukos group, including Mikhail Khodorkovsky himself. Putin has relied on the Security Council for some policy initiatives, as in the case of the package of decrees and laws on federal relations in 2000. The Security Council also developed the ominous "information security doctrine" in the summer and fall of 2001, which laid the foundation for a sweeping definition of the state's national security interests in the sphere of the media and telecommunications. In 2001, Putin's administration attempted to form a kind of overarching state umbrella organization to manage relations with all NGOs, although the president retreated from its initial conception and instead opted for a quasi-corporatist arrangement involving state recognition of social associations and institutionalized consultations. The law on parties, which Putin pushed through parliament with remarkable speed in 2001, indicated that Putin seeks to make the political arena more orderly, more regulated, more manageable, and less fragmented, although not to shut down political contestation entirely. His approach to policymaking combines paternalistic and authoritarian elements with democratic neo-corporatism, and it appears that his preferred model would be a state possessing relatively firm controls over the political arena and a market-oriented economic system operating under clear and well-enforced laws. His skill so far in enacting the legislative foundation for such a system suggests that he may achieve his goals.

CONCLUSION

President Putin has pursued a dual strategy in shaping the policymaking arena of parliament and parties. First, he has deployed police methods to deter and intimidate real and potential opponents by limiting the freedom of action of the media, by launching a series of espionage cases, and by selective high-profile criminal prosecutions against leading business figures. In such a climate, few politicians are willing to invest resources in building parties that openly challenge Putin. On the other hand, like Gorbachev and Yeltsin before him, he has acted to create a new institutional framework by bargaining off organizational rights to organized political interests in return for their support of his policies and power. Mikhail Gorbachev took the first steps by opening up the country to competitive elections in 1989 and allowing the plethora of informal political movements to channel their energies into contests for seats to the new USSR parliament that convened in that year. Once they were organized as parliamentary caucuses, he allowed them formal rights within the parliament and often called upon them for information and support. Likewise Yeltsin extended the practice of institutionalizing political factions within the interim RSFSR parliament in 1990–93, giving them wider formal rights in return for their support of his chairmanship. His successor as chair, Ruslan Khasbulatov, later went so far as to form a "Council of Factions" in the parliament, which he used when he needed to find a majority for a difficult decision. This experience in turn formed the basis for the new party-run model of governance in the Russian State Duma, itself the product of an electoral system that Yeltsin decreed into existence that gave half the seats in the Duma to candidates elected from party lists in a federation-wide electoral district. At each point, the leader sought to consolidate his own power by granting procedural, organizational, and electoral rights to partisan groups in parliament, whose leaders gained leverage thereby in attracting followers and invoking discipline. As a result, party development in Russia's parliament has outpaced party development in the country at large. The effect has been to regularize policymaking and give parliament a far greater opportunity to form majorities and speak with a collective voice than would be expected if parliament's development depended mainly on the far slower pace at which civil society has been forming. On the other hand, there has been no movement in the direction of increasing the accountability of the government to parliament. Quite the contrary—the consolidation of pro-presidential majorities in each chamber has only demonstrated the fact that neither chamber commands many independent political resources in either the electoral or regional arenas.

Nonetheless we should expect that Putin's strategy of building support within each chamber of parliament by building up institutionalized party organizations—a defined four-faction majority coalition in the Duma and a pro-Putin majority caucus in the Federation Council—will have consequences for the future. One possible direction of development is suggested by the continuing demands by the coalition of the four in the Duma to build a government of a parliamentary majority. The all-parties governance system in the past meant that no one faction bore any particular responsibility for either the maintenance or the policies of the government—even the previous "party of power," Our Home Is Russia. If there is to be a stable pro-Kremlin majority coalition in the future, it will stake further claims to influence over the government. Putin is undoubtedly too powerful and popular for the current coalition of the four to have much chance of pressing its case for now. If Putin weakens, however, and if the coalition succeeds in establishing reliable voting discipline, its ability to bargain for more rights for itself in determining the composition of the government will increase. Curiously enough, Putin himself alluded to this direction of development in his message to parliament in 2003, when he commented, "I have already said that I support a course for strengthening the role of parties in public life. And taking into account the results of the coming elections to Duma, I think it would be possible to form a professional, effective government relying on a parliamentary majority."[12]

Putin's dealings with parties and parliament have therefore had mixed effects. Some of the developments in the 2000–2003 period make the evolution of a French-style system of party government more likely; others undermine any such possibility. Putin's use of police methods against his rivals suggests that any steps expanding the power of independent political forces are taken purely at the pleasure of the authorities. Yet, one lesson from the record of the past decade in Russia's post-communist transition is that the institution-making that has resulted from short-term bargains between self-interested political leaders, at junctures when each side has something to offer and something to gain from agreeing on a new institutional arrangement, has been surprisingly long lasting.[13] Where new institutions have been produced by the stroke of a pen, as has frequently occurred, they have short shelf lives. But when actors have been in situations where they must negotiate with one another in order to obtain a preferred outcome, the result has been new institutions that last—and have serious and often unpredictable consequences for subsequent political development.

NOTES

1. G. A. Satarov et al., *Epokha Yel'tsina: Ocherki politicheskoi istorii* (Moscow: Vagrius, 2001), 385–6.

2. On the relations between Kremlin and Duma under Yeltsin and Putin, see Thomas F. Remington, "Putin and the Duma," *Post-Soviet Affairs* 17, no. 4 (November–December 2001): 285–308; Remington, "Taming Vlast': Institutional Development in Post-Communist Russia," in *A Decade of Post-Communism: The Fate of Democracy in the Former Soviet Union and Eastern Europe,* ed. Donald Kelley (Fayetteville: University of Arkansas Press, 2003); Remington, "Coalition Politics in the New Duma," in *Elections, Parties and the Future of Russia: The 1999–2000 Elections,* ed. Vicki Hesli and William Reisinger (Cambridge: Cambridge University Press, 2003); Remington, "The Evolution of Executive-Legislative Relations in Russia since 1993," *Slavic Review* 59, no. 3 (Fall 2000): 499–520; and Remington, "Majorities

without Mandates: The Federation Council since 2000," *Europe-Asia Studies* 55, no. 5 (2003): 667–91.

3. The bill reforming the method for selecting Federation Council members was initially rejected by the Federation Council on June 28, 2000. The chamber later passed a slightly modified version of the bill, however, on July 26, 2000, after an agreement commission made up of members of the two houses found a mutually acceptable compromise version of the plan.

4. On the manner in which majorities are formed in support of the Kremlin's positions, see Remington, "Majorities without Mandates"; also see L. V. Smirnyagin, ed., *Sovet Federatsii: Evoliutsiia statusa i funktsii* (Moscow: Institut prava i publichnoi politiki, 2003), esp. 443–53.

5. Deputies in the Duma are allowed to change affiliations at will. A deputy elected on a particular party's list may defect and join another parliamentary faction or group.

6. Polit.ru, April 17, 2001.

7. Polit.ru, April 18, 2001.

8. Polit.ru, September 24, 2001.

9. Remington, "Majorities without Mandates."

10. The recent collective memoir by Yeltsin's political advisors, *Epokha Yel'tsina*, provides extensive detail on the way the president's administration dealt with the government in policymaking. It is striking that the president allowed the government to take the lead in developing most of the country's economic and fiscal policy, sometimes agreeing to the government's requests for a decree to lend clout to a decision; in other cases, the government ignored Yeltsin's expressed wishes. See G. A. Satarov et al., *Epokha Yel'tsina: Ocherki politicheskoi istorii* (Moscow: Vagrius, 2001).

11. Polit.ru, May 17, 2001.

12. President's Message to Parliament, May 16, 2003 (accessed May 19, 2003), at www.kremlin.ru/text/appears/2003/05/44623.shtml.

13. Cf. Thomas F. Remington, *The Russian Parliament: Institutional Evolution in a Transitional Regime, 1989–1999* (New Haven, Conn.: Yale University Press, 2001); Michael McFaul, *Russia's Unfinished Revolution: Political Change from Gorbachev to Putin* (Ithaca, N.Y.: Cornell University Press, 2001).

Part Two

STATE AND SOCIETY

Chapter Four

Putin and the Media

Masha Lipman and Michael McFaul

In January 2004, two months before the end of his first term, 80 percent of the Russian people wanted Putin for president for another four years.[1] His re-election in March 2004 was a formality. It is ironic, therefore, that this most popular leader has orchestrated a comprehensive and sustained campaign to erode democratic institutions in Russia. Before Putin became president, Russian democratic institutions were already weak and unconsolidated.[2] During Putin's first tenure, democratization dramatically moved in a negative direction. Russian supporters of Putin refer to his regime euphemistically as "managed democracy," but one could very well flip the noun and adjective and call the current regime "competitive authoritarianism," given that nearly all political power has been concentrated in the Kremlin administration, and that government decisionmaking has been sealed from the public eye.[3] Since becoming president in 2000, Putin has continued an inhumane war in Chechnya, emasculated the power of the Federal Council (Russia's equivalent of the U.S. Senate), tamed regional barons who once served as a powerful balance to Yeltsin's presidential rule, reined in Russia's oligarchs through arrest and the threat of arrest, weakened the reach of independent political parties, and made the State Duma completely subservient to the Kremlin's interests.[4]

All of these antidemocratic actions were strengthened by one of Putin's most energetic campaigns—the elimination of independent or critical sources of information. Almost immediately after becoming president in the spring of 2000, Putin and his staff moved to weaken those media outlets independent and critical of the state. One of the leading indicators of a free society, an independent media, was the first to move in the negative direction under Putin. The move has been so fast that Freedom House has had to change its score for Russia, now labeling Russian media "not free." In its second annual Media Sustainability Index for Europe and Eurasia, International Research and Exchanges (IREX) reported that Russia had witnessed serious backsliding in freedom of speech, the ability of its citizens to receive a variety of independent news sources, and the quality of news and information its citizens receive.[5] Reporters Without Borders, which published their first worldwide freedom of the press index in 2002, ranked Russia 121 out of 139 countries assessed, just one ranking above Iran, and one of the worst performers in the post-communist world, even below Uzbekistan and Kazakhstan.[6]

The process of creating and sustaining Russian media not controlled by the state has never been only about democracy or politics. Those most involved in Russia's independent media outlets at the national level were never the most passionate defenders of democracy and human rights. Rather, they were profit seekers with questionable business ethics and controversial political agendas.[7] Their involvement, coupled with the specific economic context of post-Soviet Russian media, has served to cloud the cleavages between good and evil in the struggle for a free and independent press in Russia. Even after failing to identify "white hats" or "Sakharovs" in defense of Russia's independent media, we still conclude that the nature of Putin's policies has severely undermined one of Russia's most important democratic achievements of the last decade—a critical and independent press that acted, in some small way, as a check on state power. Although Russia's media tycoons may not have been ardent advocates of a free and independent press, their media outlets offered an alternative view, different from that of the state. Putin could have disciplined or brought to justice Russia's oligarchs without destroying their media empires. He did not. Instead, the Kremlin's exuberant campaign to crush these oligarchs also has squelched the free press in Russia by eliminating this alternative voice. The erosion of this vital institution will have long-term negative consequences for the future of Russian democracy.

PUBLIC/PRIVATE SPHERES IN POST-COMMUNIST RUSSIA

For most of the twentieth century in Russia, there was little space for political, economic, or social life independent of the state. The Soviet regime aimed to manage the economy, monopolize political activity, control the media, and destroy all independent associational life—and very nearly succeeded. To the extent that organized social or economic groups did exist outside of the family, they were atomized, apolitical, or illegal. At the same time, the Soviet system crowded private life with myriad social, political, and press organizations that mimicked their counterpart organizations in the West in name, but in practice helped to control society.

In the late 1980s, Gorbachev began to liberalize the Soviet political system. In the name of *glasnost*, Gorbachev allowed several newspapers, literary journals (the "thick" journals), and weekly magazines greater editorial license to criticize the Soviet system, especially its past. Gorbachev's *glasnost* gave birth to a new generation of independent-minded journalists and commentators. During the peak years of *perestroika*, writers at *Moscow News*, *Argumenty i fakty*, *Ogonyok*, and *Izvestiya* were ahead of the political class and civil society in leading the charge for democratic reform.[8] While still enjoying the economic benefits of state subsidization, new independent newspapers such as *Nezavisimaya gazeta*, *Kuranty*, and *Kommersant'* appeared for the first time. Liberalization of television was much slower. Only in the spring of 1991 did the Russian government succeed in compelling the Soviet state to give Russia its own television station, RTR.[9] Yet the general trajectory of more pluralism had even begun to penetrate electronic media by the end of the Soviet era. Significantly, however, the state—be it the Soviet Union or the Russian Republic—still owned or subsidized every major media outlet in Russia before the collapse of the Soviet Union in December 1991.[10] In other words, a paper like *Moscow News* could not have survived without assistance from the federal or local government. But because the state's leader, Gorbachev, tolerated a critical press, *Nezavisimaya gazeta* from the left and *Den'* from the right could publish critical articles of Gorbachev's government and without fear of closure.

After the collapse of Soviet communism and creation of an independent Russian state, Boris Yeltsin's reforms created new space for independent political, social, and economic activity. The first decade of post-communism in Russia was a period of freedom for the press, though the causes of this freedom were many. Yeltsin, at some fundamental level, appeared to value an independent press. He never intervened to mute criticism of himself or his government. Rhetorically, he lauded Russia's independent and critical media as an achievement of his democratic reforms. Early in his tenure, Yeltsin's government drafted and succeeded in passing some very progressive laws on freedom of the press. At the same time, during most of the early Yeltsin years leading up to the 1996 presidential campaign, Yeltsin and the press were allies against a common threat—a communist comeback.[11] This alliance likely was forged with no normative commitment to loftier principles of democracy, as the Yeltsin government was also weak. Fighting many political and economic battles simultaneously, the Russian state simply did not have the capacity to control the media. Even the state's own media—such as ORT, Russia's largest and most watched television network—was under the de facto control of a private actor, Boris Berezovsky.

Market reforms initially helped to stimulate still further the growth of media outlets not controlled by the government—including, first and foremost, television.[12] NTV, the first private television network, started by Vladimir Gusinsky in 1993, provided a source of information that was truly independent of the government and that reached beyond Moscow.[13] Defying government threats to its license, NTV earned its credentials as a serious news organization when it provided critical coverage of the First Chechen War. NTV also achieved a new level of post-Soviet professionalism, quality, and style that rival channels ORT (Channel 1) and RTR (Channel 2) lacked. News anchor Evgeny Kiselev became a national celebrity by producing and hosting *Itogi*, a Sunday-night talk show on politics. Before starting NTV, Gusinsky already had begun to publish his own daily newspaper, *Segodnya*. He also bought a stake in a popular radio station, Ekho Moskvy, and later founded a weekly magazine, *Itogi*, published in partnership with *Newsweek*, making Media-MOST a media powerhouse.

Other financial tycoons followed in Gusinsky's wake, believing that the media, especially television, was an important political tool.[14] Through an inside deal arranged by the Kremlin, Boris Berezovsky acquired part owner-ship and de facto control of ORT, Russia's largest television network.[15] Berezovsky also obtained a major stake in a smaller channel, TV-6. Moscow's mayor, Yuri Luzhkov, and his financial empire founded TV-Tsentr primarily as campaign tool for his (aborted) presidential bid in 2000. Russia's small group of financial houses and oil and gas companies also gobbled up most of the Moscow-based, mainstream daily newspapers.[16]

From afar, Russia's oligarchs may have appeared to be buying "private" media outlets and establishing independent media empires. Of course these outlets were biased, but at least they were private entities, which offered an alternative view to the state.[17] Yet even a decade after the collapse of commu-nism, the space for economic or political activity genuinely independent from the state was still very limited. The state—or more aptly in Russian, *vlast'* (the power)—was still the 800-pound gorilla in many sectors of Russian political and economic life. While the weakness of the Russian state was apparent in some sectors such as health, education, and security, the state was still a dom-inant actor in some strategic sectors, including the media. The Russian fed-eral state was still the majority shareholder in ORT and owned 100 percent of RTR, while regional heads of administrations still controlled the major television networks in their regions and subsidized most local print media. For periods in the 1990s, the state, and especially the Russian federal state under Yeltsin, did not exercise its property rights, creating the false sense of independence for some state-owned media outlets.

In contrast to ORT, RTR, TV-Tsentr, and many of Russia's national news-papers, Gusinsky's Media-MOST was the most financially independent media company in the 1990s. Different from other major media assets, Gusinsky's empire was not a privatized Soviet-era enterprise but was created from scratch, meaning the state did not initially own shares in his companies. But even Gusinsky acquired his initial capital from connections with the Moscow city government (his Most Bank served as the city's banker for years), then obtained additional control over Channel 4, on which NTV broadcast, as a reward for his cooperation with Yeltsin during the 1996 presidential election.[18] He then offered an equity stake to Gazprom, a largely state-owned gas company, to finance his expansion plans. Gusinsky also secured loans from several sources, including Gazprom and CS-First Boston.[19] Before the Russian financial crash in August 1998, Gusinsky's business plan and debt-to-equity ratios looked ambitious, but within reason. The crash, however, slashed the advertising market by two-thirds, from approximately $540 million to $190 million.[20] The crash also made Gusinsky's dollar-denominated debts significantly more expensive, compelling him in November 2000 to surrender more equity to Gazprom to retire some of these debts. This transfer of shares made Gazprom—or more specifically Gazprom's subsidiary, Gazprom Media—a 46 percent shareholder and left Gusinsky's Media-MOST with 49.56 percent of shares in NTV, with the balance, 4.44 percent, owned by an American investment company, Capital Research and Management Group.

Like any other sensible director of an ailing enterprise in Russia, Gusinsky pursued foreign investment as a strategy to avoid state control.[21] Although the details of the proposed deal remain murky, Ted Turner and a group of Western investors appeared ready to buy out Gusinsky's stake in NTV.[22] Turner's only condition was that the Russian government, now headed by Putin, agree that it would not interfere in the business or editorial affairs of NTV. Despite efforts from even the U.S. State Department, Putin never agreed to such an arrangement. He and his government resisted because NTV's problems were never just financial. They were also political.

GUSINSKY VERSUS PUTIN: A POLITICAL AND PERSONAL VENDETTA

NTV's editorial line regarding the Russian government has vacillated considerably throughout the 1990s. During the First Chechen War (1994–96), NTV reporters covered the war critically from within Chechnya. Although Russian federal commanders tried to limit coverage and denied reporters access to Russian troops, Russian journalists and NTV reporters in particular eventually exposed the brutal and ineffective military campaigns.[23] The coverage had a profound effect on Russian public opinion. By January 1995, only 16 percent of the Russian populace supported the use of force in Chechnya while 71 percent opposed the war.[24] Opposition to the war in turn fueled general disapproval of Yeltsin's presidency: 70 percent of those polled disapproved of Yeltsin's performance as president in September 1994, growing to 80 percent by January 1995.[25] To secure Yeltsin's re-election in 1996, his campaign officials believed that they had to end the war.[26] Thus, in April 1996, Yeltsin announced a cease-fire.

During the 1996 presidential campaign, NTV reversed course and supported Yeltsin in his re-election bid. In doing so, NTV joined forces with nearly every major media outlet in the country.[27] NTV's general director, Igor Malashenko, blurred the lines between the campaign and the media when he joined the Yeltsin re-election team without resigning from his television post. In providing unabashedly positive coverage for Yeltsin and very critical reporting of Zyuganov during the campaign, NTV reporters as well as journalists working for Gusinsky's *Segodnya* newspaper and his new weekly, *Itogi* (which began publication just before the presidential election), explained that they were protecting Russian democracy and, in particular, their survival as an independent media. If the communist Zyuganov became president of Russia, they argued that they would all be closed down.[28] For journalists concerned with preserving their independence, this election was considered a life-or-death matter. Yeltsin won, and the spectre of government seizure of non-governmental media was postponed (ironically until the next election).

After the 1996 presidential election, Gusinsky expected a payoff for his help during the campaign. Indeed, soon after the election he acquired full control of Channel 4 for NTV. He also hoped to acquire Svyazinvest, a telecommunications company that would dovetail nicely with his business interests in media.[29] Unlike the other oligarchs, Gusinsky did not acquire a major asset through the corrupt loans-for-shares program. Now he believed it was his turn, especially after his helpful work during the 1996 presidential election.

In the auction of Svyazinvest, Deputy Prime Minister Anatoly Chubais decided to change the old, corrupt rules of oligarchic privatization established (by himself) under the loans-for-shares program, and instead offered up Svyazinvest to the highest bidder.[30] Before Svyazinvest, competitive bidding had never occurred. Rather, every previous auction of a major company was an inside deal. Gusinsky was incensed that Chubais was now trying to change the rules, but he went ahead and made a bid anyway. Gusinsky teamed up with Boris Berezovsky and the Alfa group to raise the capital to acquire the company, but another team of investors, headed by rival oligarch Vladimir Potanin and his Western partner, George Soros, outbid Gusinsky by $16 million ($1.87 billion to $1.71 billion).

Chubais was elated with the process.[31] Gusinsky was furious and insinuated that Chubais had provided information about Gusinsky's bid to Potanin. Deploying his media as his weapon, Gusinsky set out to destroy Chubais and his reformist government. Berezovsky joined the battle and put his ORT— Russia's largest national television network—into action to besmirch Chubais and his allies.[32] Muckraking campaigns, encouraged by Berezovsky and Gusinsky, produced some embarrassing results for Chubais and his associates, including most damagingly a book contract for the Chubais group that paid five authors $90,000 each to write chapters for a book on privatization.[33] As a result of the book scandal, three of Chubais's closest associates were forced to resign from their government posts. Eventually Chubais himself had to leave.

The struggle between business giants for Svyazinvest, in which they shamelessly used their media to annihilate their enemies among economic reformers, had a tremendously detrimental effect not only on the stability of the Russian government, but also on Russia's media sector. This "information war" driven by selfish economic interests did irreparable harm to the professional ethics and solidarity among Russian journalists.

After the Svyazinvest scandal, NTV became increasingly critical of Yeltsin and his government, focusing in particular on corruption within the Kremlin's inner circle. NTV once again provided the only critical coverage of the Second Chechen War as it unfolded in the fall of 1999. This second war, however, was much more popular than the first military intervention, prompting Kremlin loyalists to call NTV an unpatriotic, pro-fascist (because they called the Chechen guerrillas fascists), pro-Western organization, which reported Russian military atrocities without devoting any coverage to violations of human rights carried out by Chechen guerrillas. Vladimir Putin, then prime minister, was offended personally by NTV's coverage and made his opinions known both to his colleagues in the government and to Gusinsky personally.[34]

In the run-up to the December 1999 parliamentary election, NTV did not support the government's candidates but gave much free airtime and positive coverage to opposition political parties, such as Fatherland and Yabloko. At the time, Fatherland leader Yevgeny Primakov was considered the only politician who might be able to seriously challenge Putin in the 2000 presidential elections. To their credit, especially compared to the other national television networks, NTV news editors allotted huge chunks of prime time to debates between parties and discussions among voters. Yet NTV did not endorse the Kremlin's party, Unity, in the parliamentary race nor back Putin in the March 2000 presidential election. Putin took notice.

After his landslide win in March 2000, Putin began to articulate a new approach toward the press and democratic institutions, one that differed qualitatively from that of Boris Yeltsin. Of course Putin endorsed the notion of a free press and the importance of democracy in principle. He repeatedly pledged allegiance to freedom of the press and readily admitted that freedom of the press is absolutely necessary in a modern society, and that if Russia aspires to become a modern society, it must ensure that the press is free. Yet his statements and speeches also revealed a poor understanding of these concepts and a lack of respect for their importance in the operations of the Russian state, economy, and society. In his first annual address (*poslanie*) to the members of the Russian parliament in July, Putin hinted of his mistrust of the press, claiming that "Sometimes [the media] turn into means of mass disinformation and tools of struggle against the state."[35] The Doctrine of Information Security issued several months later made it clear that state-owned media must dominate the information market, since only the state can provide the citizens of Russia with *objective* information about what goes on in Russia. The doctrine also pledged to battle disinformation coming from abroad.

When faced with crises that required action, Putin made clear his real attitude toward the disloyal press. Radio Liberty correspondent Andrei Babitsky was the first journalist to experience the wrath of Putin when Russian security services secretly arrested him in Chechnya and kept him incommunicado for several weeks. In March 2000, when Babitsky's whereabouts were still unknown, Putin claimed that Babitsky "worked directly for the enemy—for the bandits."[36] Putin made it very clear that there could be only one truth about the Chechen war. To publicly express an alternative view was considered traitorous. The following year, Anna Politkovskaya, a Russian journalist critical of Russia's military campaign in Chechnya, also came under pressure from the state and felt compelled to leave the country.

Putin also vehemently denounced those who criticized the way he and his government handled the crisis caused by the sinking of the *Kursk* submarine in August 2000. In an interview on RTR on August 23, 2000, Putin did not conceal his strong feelings toward his critics, asserting that they were responsible for the destruction of the Russian state, army, and navy.[37] It is against this background of statements and actions about the press by Putin that the campaign against NTV must be understood. Although NTV's financial woes made the company vulnerable, the state's campaign against the channel was simply *another* example of what happens to a news organization when it gets in the way of the Kremlin.[38] There was certainly a pragmatic desire by Kremlin officials (especially those responsible for Putin's re-election) for wanting to take control of the third-largest television network in the country and the only privately owned national channel. But Putin's personal hatred for Gusinsky and his "traitorous" opinions about the Chechen war should not be underestimated. According to Putin's definition of state interests, Gusinsky was the enemy of the state and therefore Putin's personal enemy.

Putin was too savvy and too concerned with his image in the West to be directly involved or to simply shut down NTV by force. Instead, those leading the campaign to seize NTV and dismantle Media-MOST pursued several different strategies over several months. One of these strategies was to threaten Gusinsky personally. The idea was to use the prosecutor's office to bring criminal charges against Gusinsky, intimidate him, and thus silence his media. The implementation of this criminal variant began with a raid on Gusinky's media office building in May 2000 by masked, gun-toting men who burst in under the pretext of a search. Gusinsky and his people were accused of various crimes, but no convincing evidence was ever presented, and the cases fell apart soon thereafter. In the months that followed the first raid, affiliate offices of Gusinsky's corporation were raided and searched dozens of times, proceedings were opened and closed, Gusinsky's employees were interrogated, and their apartments were searched. Eventually, in June, Gusinsky himself was arrested and then released three days later, but placed under house arrest.[39] A month later, on July 20, 2000, Gusinsky agreed to sign a secret deal to sell his controlling stake in Media-Most to Gazprom in return for his freedom. (His freedom was guaranteed in the notorious Protocol 6 signed by Minister of the Press Mikhail Lesin.) Six days later, Gusinsky signed the sales deal, was released, and immediately fled the country. Three of his closest associates soon followed him in exile, since they, too, feared arrest. Soon thereafter, information about the sale and the secret protocol became public. Gusinsky denounced these agreements as null and void, since they had been signed under duress. Thereafter, Gusinsky and Gazprom began negotiating again about debts and equity.

This ploy did not work. NTV continued to operate, and its coverage of Putin and his government was as critical as ever. Realizing that a strategy of intimidation through criminal charges had failed, the Kremlin placed greater attention on the "business variant." Media-MOST's largest creditor, Gazprom, moved to assert control over NTV. (The largest stakeholder in Gazprom is the Russian federal government.) A meticulous litigation campaign ensued. According to Russian weekly magazine *Kommersant-Vlast'*, for a period of two years, a court hearing involving Media-MOST was held every 4.3 days. Finally in April Gazprom succeeded in changing NTV's management. Boris Jordan, a former American investment banker, assumed the role of general director of NTV instead of the anchor Evgeny Kiselev, who had held that position.

The campaign against NTV caused public protest. A rally in downtown Moscow in defense of the network attracted 20,000 people, the largest showing of public activism for democracy since 1993. The following weekend, an estimated 15,000 people showed up. It looked as though NTV was winning the struggle for public opinion. But in fact, national polls suggested that "only four percent of the public regarded the NTV takeover as a state attempt to limit media freedom."[40]

Finally the government had to use force. In the predawn hours of April 14, the new managers assumed their offices at NTV's headquarters, accompanied by a newly hired security service. In response, the old NTV staff split allegiances. Kiselev and several dozen journalists and anchors went to TV-6, a channel owned by Boris Berezovsky, who by this time also had left Russia for fear of arrest. Others stayed behind to work for the "new" NTV, which has continued to broadcast but with a falling viewership.[41]

The assault against non-governmental media did not end with NTV. In the earlier debt negotiations between Gusinsky and Gazprom, Gusinsky relinquished a stake in each of his media assets, including his publishing house, Seven Days, which published *Segodnya* and *Itogi*. By the beginning of the year, Gazprom had enough shares in Seven Days to conspire with the president and shareholders of that publishing house to close *Segodnya* and oust the entire staff of *Itogi*. They did so on April 17, 2001. Like NTV, *Itogi* continues to be published, but with an entirely new editorial orientation. The first cover story of the new *Itogi* featured soccer, with no mention in the magazine of what had transpired the week before. *Newsweek* withdrew from the partnership with Seven Days, fully supporting the original staff of *Itogi*. The radio station Ekho Moskvy was the only survivor. As of this writing, it still retains an independent and critical editorial line. Still, it is fully at the mercy of powerful shareholder Gazprom, which makes it fully vulnerable to a Kremlin crackdown.

The destruction of Media-MOST took a lot of the government's time, money, and effort. Moreover, it cost Putin many an embarrassing moment during his foreign visits, when he was facing criticism for his crackdown on media freedom. In one especially notorious episode in June 2000, he was hounded with questions about Gusinsky's arrest in Moscow. Putin pretended he knew nothing about the matter and said he could not reach his Prosecutor General on the phone. But the Russian president remained firm in accomplishing his objectives. After the takeover of NTV, it gradually became clear that the government's goal with regard to the media was much more ambitious than eliminating a defiant tycoon and taming his media. The longer-term objective was to bring all national television networks back under state control.

This task was greatly facilitated by the fact that the majority of the Russian public did not regard the crackdown on the media as a violation of people's rights. Business and political elites were fragmented, and even liberal politicians would not stand up for Media-MOST. They chose to accept the government interpretation that the whole NTV/Media-MOST affair was a conflict of economic interests. Likewise, the journalistic community failed to show solidarity with their Media-MOST colleagues.

A LUTA CONTINUA: TV-6

Having devoted so much time and energy to wrestling NTV away from Gusinsky, the Kremlin faced an exasperating and humiliating outcome: the migration of many of NTV's staff to TV-6, which developed rapidly and successfully. Exiled oligarch Boris Berezovsky maintained his 75 percent share in the network and continued to finance the station from abroad. Although Berezovsky had little influence on the editorial policy of TV-6, he continued to make anti-Putin statements from exile, calling Putin a dictator and suggesting that he was also a criminal. Vladimir Gusinsky, though not a formal owner of TV-6, also loomed large behind the scenes. He maintained contact with the journalists who had come to TV-6 from NTV after the government takeover and, as a forced émigré in the West, continued to raise issues of freedom of the press in Russia.

TV-6 evolved as a network with national reach; its news content and editorial line remained independent of the Kremlin. By the fall of 2001 the former NTV team had managed to fully transform the channel's programming, turning it into a serious television business with highly professional news broadcast. They launched a few successful programs and were the first to produce a very popular "reality TV" show in Russia.

But TV-6 did not live long. In fact, the campaign against TV-6 began almost as soon as Yevgeny Kiselev's team came to work there. The weapons deployed were similar to those used against NTV. As in the NTV case from the previous year, the attack against TV-6 was disguised as a business affair. Using an obscure law that had never been invoked in Russia before, a minority stakeholder of TV-6 exercised its legal right to liquidate TV-6 (the stakeholder was a pension fund controlled by the giant oil company Lukoil, loyal to the Kremlin). Disappointingly, the vast majority of the Russian public paid no attention to the campaign against TV-6. Interested viewers understood that TV-6 was being attacked by the Kremlin for political reasons. Even some Kremlin supporters did not argue with Kiselev's statement that "This is an absolutely obvious political thing."[42] Yet few seemed to care.[43]

The court litigation, accompanied by a barely disguised involvement of the Kremlin administration, lasted for a few months. At the closing phase, Russia's first president, Boris Yeltsin, made an attempt to intervene and counter the attack on press freedom. In a rare television appearance, Yeltsin said firmly that TV-6 should not be liquidated. Even the Bush administration weighed in. U.S. State Department spokesperson Richard Boucher stated in early January 2002: "We continue to urge Russian officials to ensure that TV-6 gets a full hearing and ensure that press freedom and the rule of law can be best served by keeping TV-6 on the air."[44]

President Putin, who had kept silent all through the attack against TV-6, finally broke in to offer support to the TV-6 staff. Thus the TV-6 team faced the dilemma of either becoming yet another government-controlled media outlet or going out of business. They ultimately refused to take up the government's offer, and on January 22, 2002, TV-6 went off the air. The shutdown of TV-6 reverberated throughout the country, since 156 regional affiliates also lost their main source of programming that same day.[45] On Channel 6, where TV-6 used to broadcast, sports programming filled the void.

Immediately after closure, the TV-6 team began looking for a way to get back on the air. The government announced that on March 27, 2002, it would hold an auction for the rights to broadcast on Channel 6, so Kiselev decided to construct an offer. In February, a dozen prominent business tycoons, most with close ties to the Kremlin, formed a consortium to finance a new TV-6, soon to be called TVS.

In theory TVS was to become the last remaining privately owned national television network. But it was only nominally independent of the Kremlin. None of the dozen tycoons who had formed the consortium dared join without a thorough consultation with the Kremlin administration. They all checked and double-checked whether the Kremlin indeed did not mind them financing a television team whose "loyalty record" was not clean. According to Kiselev, abandoning Gusinsky and Berezovsky and trading financial support of exiled tycoons for that of the loyal and compliant ones was the only strategy for survival left for his team of journalists. But even the careful selection of the consortium members was not enough.

In the run-up to the March tender of the broadcasting license, Kiselev brought on new, unexpected allies to join his new company, Media-Socium, to insure victory. Most amazingly, former prime minister Yevegny Primakov and Arkady Volsky, the chief of the Union of Industrialists and Entrepreneurs, joined the Media-Socium team, allegedly at the request of government officials who were negotiating the future of the channel with Kiselev. Both men had much stronger loyalties to the Kremlin than Kiselev, prompting many commentators to conclude that Kiselev had sacrificed editorial independence for the chance to be on the air once again.[46]

Kiselev's team was certainly the best among other contenders of the tender, yet it was pretty clear that the tender had been prearranged: the matter was too sensitive for Kiselev's team to apply without a prior confirmation by the Kremlin that these journalists were indeed trusted to broadcast to a national audience.

After Media-Socium won the tender, Primakov stressed the need for "self-censorship" for the new company to succeed.[47] On June 1, 2002, the renamed TVS owned by Media-Socium did begin to broadcast on Channel 6, but the new station never recaptured the editorial edge of the "old" NTV nor developed a business plan for making the channel profitable. The tycoons who owned TVS were more anxious not to antagonize the Kremlin than to ensure that their network be properly managed. As Kiselev complained bitterly, someday the "Kremlin will thank [the TVS stakeholders] for eliminating a team of willful journalists who dared open their mouths against the authorities from time to time, criticize them and offer alternative opinion."[48]

Before long TVS became a management disaster. Feeble attempts were made by one or another of the rival tycoons to walk out from TVS, so that the remaining partners could figure out a more consistent business strategy. But no one ever put forth a plan for financial success. TVS was a business venture that none of the investors really had an interest in seeing succeed. On June 22, 2003, the government cut TVS off the air. The Kremlin was acting unlawfully, since broadcasting cannot be terminated without a court decision. In contrast to the approach taken in closing down NTV a few years earlier, those in Putin's administration no longer seemed to care about legality. By this time, they knew full well that no one would protest the closure. And they were right. TVS disappeared quietly.

By the summer of 2002, therefore, the government controlled all major national television networks. Even marginal television stations, such as Luzhkov's TV-Tsentr, became firmly loyal to the Kremlin, especially after the Moscow mayor joined Putin's party, United Russia. Anatoly Chubais, the CEO of RAU-UES and a leader of the liberal political party, Union of Right Forces, owned Ren-TV, which did maintain an independent editorial position, but the station had not developed serious news programming and currently enjoys only a fraction of an audience.

Yet even this level of control was not sufficient for the Kremlin authorities. In October 2002, Chechen terrorists held over 800 people hostage in a Moscow theater. Putin eventually ordered Russian special forces to end the standoff by gassing the entire building. Over one hundred were killed, and the "new" NTV (under Boris Jordan) reported it, asking tough questions as to why so many innocents were allowed to die. Putin ridiculed NTV's coverage of the hostage crisis as sensationalism designed to boost the station's ratings. Jordan was eventually forced to resign, sending a powerful message to all those working for government-owned and government-friendly media outlets about the limits of Putin's tolerance for criticism.

CONCLUSION

Even after all of the setbacks, Russia still has media outlets that are not controlled by the state. The printed press is still mostly privately owned and enjoys substantial freedom. Exiled tycoon Boris Berezovsky has even been allowed to maintain his ownership of Moscow dailies *Nezavisimaya gazeta*, *Novaya izvestiya*, and *Kommersant'*, while jailed oilman Mikhail Khodorkovsky has supplied funds to acquire control of *Moscow News*, the liberal Russian weekly paper. Russian oligarch Vladimir Potanin controls Prof-Media, which has large stakes in *Izvestiya* and the popular tabloid *Komsomolskaya pravda*. Novolipetsk Metallurgic Plant, headed by Vladimir Lisin, owns *Gazeta*, a daily newspaper started during the Putin era. The Communist Party and its affiliates control or have influence over a number of left-wing newspapers, including *Sovetskaya rossiya* and *Pravda*. The autonomy of some publications, such as *Argumenty i fakty* and *Trud*, are less clear; they may be privately owned but still loyal to the state. Moreover, some of the television journalists who had been staunchly defiant of the Kremlin and thus barred from working on television altogether have found jobs in print media and so far have been left alone by the Kremlin. Yevgeny Kiselev, who had been the leading news analyst and anchor on all three privately owned television networks taken over or shut down by the government, has taken the job of the editor-in-chief of *Moscow News*. An extremely popular television political satirist, Viktor Shenderovich, after finding out that he had been blacklisted and no TV network would put him on air, now has his piercing satire printed in one of the Moscow dailies. More than half a dozen Moscow dailies maintain a liberal editorial line and sometimes get fairly critical of the government, though even they avoid criticizing the president. Since these newspapers have low circulation—mostly in the dozens of thousands—the Kremlin administration does not have to worry about their influence over mass attitudes; moreover, 90 percent of Russian citizens report that their main source of political news is television.[49]

Smaller cable television networks, though mostly devoid of political content, are in operation, and private radio stations are in business. Ekho Moskvy, a relic of Media-MOST media group, managed to escape the fate of Media-MOST's other outlets and remains in business. It is a highly interactive radio station with a loyal and mostly liberal audience and strong political coverage. Just like liberal Moscow papers, Ekho Moskvy is in no way safeguarded against a government crackdown, especially since Gazprom remains its major stakeholder.

A few private political websites are in operation, some of them offering profound and insightful political analysis. It should be borne in mind, however, that Internet access in Russia is highly limited. As little as 5 percent have an opportunity to use the Internet on a regular basis.[50]

The Kremlin's success in shutting down critical media outlets at the national level has emboldened regional heads to take the same action against regional media critics, who are already small in number and weak in resources. In attacking non-compliant media, regional bosses rely on less sophisticated methods, and instances of direct censorship, harassment, and unlawful firing of journalists and editors are not at all uncommon.[51]

The Kremlin crackdown on electronic media has had a strong cautionary effect on most journalists and editors. Self-censorship has become common practice; those working in the media prefer not to antagonize the government, especially since the vast majority of the public does not demand an inquisitive press. In an October 2003 poll, 36 percent of respondents said tighter state control of the media is good for Russia, and only 25 percent believed it was bad; 24 answered that it made no difference.[52]

Cooperation with the government is a very important factor not to be underestimated when talking about constraints on the Russian media. Television managers cooperate willingly and easily with the Kremlin, and they do not see any problem with it. They are full-fledged and eager partners of the Kremlin and admired members of the social elite. Konstantin Ernst, the manager of the biggest Russian network, ORT, admitted that he spoke from time to time with Kremlin officials. Ernst said, "that's impossible," when asked in an interview what would happen if they disagreed over editorial policy. He said, "It's easy for me to work here because the Kremlin's foreign and domestic policy is always clear to me. . . . There's no mental difference between the majority view and government policy."[53] A similar kind of self-censorship occurs every day in the print press. Even staunch critics of the president are careful to pull their punches, for fear of suffering a fate similar to that of Gusinsky and his former colleagues.

The blow to Russian democracy more generally cannot be underestimated. As demonstrated most recently in the December 2003 parliamentary elections in Russia, competitive elections cannot occur without a pluralist and independent press.[54] Putin's party, United Russia, won a smashing victory in the December 2003 parliamentary elections, buoyed largely by Putin's 70 percent approval rating. Without question, however, the state-controlled media helped boost United Russia's vote total, while denying other parties national exposure. Likewise, corruption cannot be fought without a free press. Elected government officials cannot be held accountable to their constituents without a free press. And ultimately, Russia cannot become a normal European country without a free press. Putin continues to believe that these developments at home do not impact his foreign policy mission abroad. He has stated numerous times that he wants to see Russia become a full member of Western institutions, such as the G8, NATO, and the European Union. Today, however, these organizations do not accept applications from nondemocracies.

A growing economy and a better business plan will not be enough for the media to break free of state control. Under Putin's rule, property rights are insecure, and ownership can make only a limited difference; the state can effectively manage the editorial line even of those media that technically do not belong to it. The destruction of Media-MOST and the subsequent squelching of all television not controlled by the state revealed several other conditions necessary for a free press in Russia. First, Russia must develop an independent and uncorrupted judiciary that can defend not only state interests but minority shareholders' rights as well. When push finally came to shove, Gusinsky and his colleagues had no legal means to defend their interests within Russia because no court would stand up to the pressure of the state. In even starker fashion, the same was true for TV-6.[55]

Second, at least in the near future an independent media in Russia can only develop if the leadership in the Kremlin believes in the norms of free press and democracy more generally. For the foreseeable future, the state will continue to have enormous power over private, societal activity in Russia. In the wake of Putin's campaign against the media, Gorbachev's tolerance of and Yeltsin's commitment to an independent media are striking. Media were the first sphere where Putin unambiguously demonstrated that he is a proponent of a larger role for the state. He holds one gala press conference per year, which leaves no opportunity to ask pressing policy questions, and his press-man never holds open press events. Throughout the years of post-communist development, the Kremlin has never been so closed from the public as it has become under Putin. His comparison of journalists to intelligence officers also underscores his ignorance of the role that a free press plays in a demo-cratic polity.

Third, an independent press in Russia needs popular support. In a poll con-ducted in 2000, an overwhelming number of Russian voters—79 percent—answered that they considered freedom of the press to be important.[56] Yet few of these supporters of a free press believed that destruction of Media-MOST was such an issue.[57] A large plurality showed indifference to the cam-paign against TV-6. A solid 39 percent understood that the campaign against TV-6 was political, yet they did not seem bothered by that fact.[58] Unless there is public demand for an alternative, non-government, critical view, a journalist's mission is largely lost. Until Russian society values and is willing to defend an independent press as a basic institution of democracy, future media critics of the state will find it difficult to stay in operation.

NOTES

1. www.vciom-a.ru/press/2004011601.html.

2. On the weakness of Russian liberal institutions, see chapter 9 of Michael McFaul, *Russia's Unfinished Revolution: Political Change from Gorbachev to Putin* (Ithaca, N.Y.: Cornell University Press, 2001).

3. On these regime definitions, see Steven Levitsky and Lucan Way, "The Rise of Competitive Authoritarianism," *Journal of Democracy* 13, no. 2 (April 2002): 51–65. Diamond has already reclassified Russia as competitive authoritarianism. See Larry Diamond, "Thinking About Hybrid Regimes," *Journal of Democracy* 13, no. 2 (April 2002): 21–35.

4. For a complete accounting of these democratic reversals, see Michael McFaul, Nikolai Petrov, and Andrei Ryabov, *Between Dictatorship and Democracy: Russian Post-Communist Political Reform* (Washington, D.C.: Carnegie Endowment for International Peace, 2004).

5. www.irex.org/msi/.

6. www.rsf.fr/article.php3?id_article=4116.

7. David Hoffman, *The Oligarchs: Wealth and Power in the New Russia* (New York: Public Affairs, 2002).

8. On the emergence of civil society in the USSR, see M. Steven Fish, *Democracy From Scratch* (Princeton, N.J.: Princeton University Press, 1993); and Geoffrey

Hosking, *The Awakening of the Soviet Union* (Cambridge, Mass.: Harvard University Press, 1991).

9. Control over television was such a major issue for Russia's anticommunist forces before the collapse of the Soviet Union. One of the biggest demonstrations in downtown Moscow in 1991 was devoted to demanding a Russian television station. On Yeltsin's efforts to gain control of RTR, the Russian station, see Ellen Mickiewicz, *Changing Channels: Television and the Struggle for Power in Russia* (Oxford: Oxford University Press, 1997), 92–97.

10. Some political parties had their own newspapers, and a few small newspapers associated with human rights organizations published newspapers and newsletters with support from Western foundations. But the circulation of these kinds of publications was a tiny fraction of the state-controlled newspapers.

11. Michael McFaul, *Russia's 1996 Presidential Election: The End of Polarized Politics* (Stanford, Calif.: Hoover Institution Press, 1997).

12. Mickiewicz, *Changing Channels.*

13. On the channel's creation, see the detailed account in chapter 7 of Hoffman, *The Oligarchs.*

14. Floriana Fossato, "Russia: Changes Sweep Through Two TV Networks," RFE/RL, November 5, 1997.

15. Russian Public Television (ORT) gained control of the first national television channel in Russia through a presidential decree (no. 2133) on November 29, 1994, and began broadcasting on April 1, 1995. In the company's charter, fourteen organizations are listed as shareholders, including state institutions such as the State Property Committee of Russia, Ostankino Russian State Television, and Radio Broadcasting Corporation, as well as private companies such as Menatep, National Kredit, and Stolychny banks; Gazprom; and Berezovsky's own company, Logovaz. (See *Russian Public Television: Collection of Constituent Documents*, Moscow: ORT, 1995, 18.) The private companies purchased 49 percent of the new company and faced no competition for their purchase. Logovaz owned 8 percent of the shares, while the share of the state owners totaled more than 50 percent. Nonetheless, Berezovsky used side payments and bribes to gain control of the company's operations and editorial policy. See Paul Klebnikov, *Godfather of the Kremlin: Boris Berezovsky and the Looting of Russia* (New York: Harcourt, 2000), 159–61.

16. Mark Whitehouse, "Buying the Media: Who's Behind the Written Word?" *Russia Review*, April 21, 1997, 26–27; and Oleg Medvedev and Sergei Sinchenko, "The Fourth Estate—Chained to Banks," *Business in Russia* 78 (June 1997): 38–43.

17. On the distorting influences of private ownership on editorial lines, see Laura Belin, "Political Bias and Self-Censorship in the Russian Media," in *Contemporary Russian Politics: A Reader*, ed. Archie Brown (Oxford: Oxford University Press, 2001), 323–44.

18. Hoffman, *The Oligarchs.*

19. In Protocol 3, signed by Gusinsky and Gazprom-Media General Director Alfred Kokh on July 20, 2001, to authorize the transfer of Gusinsky's assets to Gazprom-Media (a protocol that Gusinsky later renounced), six different companies—CS-First Boston, Gazprom, Gazprombank, the city of Moscow, Vneshtorbank, and Eksimbank B—are listed as creditors. An initial CS-First Boston loan of $211

million due in March 2000 was taken over by Gazprom when Gusinsky failed to pay. The next CS-First Boston debt for $262 million was due in July 2001. The other non-Gazprom debts were not due until 2003 and 2009 respectively.

20. Celestine Bohlen, "Defining a Free Press: The Unique Evolution of Russian TV," *New York Times*, April 29, 2001, sec. 4, 4.

21. Gusinsky had wanted to secure foreign investors long before, which is why Capital Research was given an equity stake in his company.

22. Andrew Higgins, "Turner Sets Investment in Russia's Media-MOST," *Wall Street Journal*, January 22, 2001, A16.

23. Anatol Lieven, *Chechnya: Tombstone of Russian Power* (New Haven, Conn.: Yale University Press, 1998); and John Dunlop, *Russia Confronts Chechnya: Roots of a Separatist Conflict* (Cambridge: Cambridge University Press, 1998).

24. Fond obshchestvennoe mnenie (FOM), as quoted in *Segodnya*, January 28, 1995, 3. These numbers remained constant throughout the war. A fall 1995 poll conducted by FOM revealed that only 10 percent of the population supported the intervention, while 69 percent opposed. Fond "Obshchestvennoe mnenie," *Obshchestvennoe mnenie nakanune vyborov-95*, 3 (Moscow: October 25, 1995), 15.

25. Vserossiiskii Tsentr Izucheniya Obshchestvennogo Mneniya (VTsIOM) poll, as quoted in *Segodnya*, January 17, 1995, 2.

26. McFaul, *Russia's 1996 Presidential Election*.

27. Of course, press outlets owned by or loyal to the Communist Party did not endorse Yeltsin, but this was a small fraction of the media. Significantly, the Communist Party had no access to national television.

28. In frequent interaction with Russian journalists during the 1996 campaign, the authors heard this justification.

29. Like Gazprom, Svyazinvest had been created from hundreds of smaller entities to make it a viable private entity. It is the largest telecommunications company in Russia.

30. Chrystia Freeland, *Sale of the Century: Russia's Wild Ride from Communism to Capitalism* (New York: Crown Business, 2000); Hoffman, *The Oligarchs*, 433.

31. Hoffman, *The Oligarchs*, 437.

32. For details of the campaign, see Hoffman, *The Oligarchs*, 439–42.

33. The $450,000 was leftover funds from the 1996 campaign. The book contracts were a way to launder the money back to those who had been involved in the campaign. Chubais admitted to the scheme.

34. Vladimir Gusinsky, address at the National Press Club, Washington, D.C., May 3, 2001.

35. The speech can be found at president.kremlin.ru/events/200007.html.

36. *Kommersant*, March 10, 2000.

37. See his even more emotional statements quoted in *Kommersant-Vlast'*, 34, August 29, 2000.

38. NTV officials even dispute the company's alleged financial problems. See Chris Renaud, Finance and Strategic Director, Media-Most, "NTV Had No Financial Crisis," *Wall Street Journal Europe*, April 30, 2001.

39. Putin, in Germany at the time, claimed that he could not reach his chief prosecutor on the phone and argued that the prosecutors were acting independently of the

state. Yet, in a press conference, he displayed perfect knowledge of Gusinsky's credit history, exposing how intimately he was involved with the case.

40. Floriana Fossato, "The Russian Media: From Popularity to Distrust," *Current History* 100, no. 648 (October 2001): 343.

41. On certain issues such as Chechnya, the new NTV has provided more critical coverage of the Russian government than ORT or RTR, but the channel in no way resembles the old editorial line or qualitative journalism of the old NTV. See Peter Baker, "On NTV, Kremlin Is in Softer Focus," *Washington Post*, June 27, 2001, A18.

42. Press Conference with the TV-6 Director General Yevgeny Kiselev, Radisson Slavjanskaya Hotel, November 27, 2001, translated transcript provided by *Federal News Service*.

43. When asked about their reactions to the closing of TV-6, the biggest segment of the population—38 percent—expressed no emotion one way or another. See the VTsIOM poll results from January 25–28, 2002, at www.polit.ru/printable/469009.html.

44. Quoted in "Russian TV Station Ordered to Close," *Associated Press*, January 11, 2002. U.S. Ambassador to Russia, Alexander Vershbow, also spoke out in defense of TV-6. See "US Ambassador Concerned at TV's Independent Fate in Russia," *Interfax*, December 3, 2001.

45. Sabrina Tavernise, "Russia's Regional TV Stations Suffer as Nationwide Broadcaster Stays Dark," *New York Times*, January 28, 2002.

46. See Virginie Coulloudon, "Plus CA Change," and Laura Belin, "Has Kiselev Stepped on the Same Rake?" in *RFE/RL Political Weekly* 2, no. 10, April 2, 2002.

47. Ivan Chelnok, "Self-Censorship to Contribute to Democracy," Gazeta.ru, March 29, 2002.

48. Kiselev, June 18, 2002, as quoted in Laura Belin, "Russia's TVS: Another Failed Experiment in Private Television," RFE/RL Newsline, June 27, 2003, available at www.cdi.org/russia/johnson/7243–15.cfm.

49. See Timothy J. Colton and Michael McFaul, "Are Russians Undemocratic?" *Post-Soviet Affairs*, 18, no. 2 (April–June 2002): 91–121.

50. www.vciom-a.ru/press/2003120302.html.

51. In a 2003 Memo on Press Freedom, even the Human Rights Commission of the President of the Russian Federation raised concerns over the encroachments on media freedom in the regions. See www.gdf.ru/arh/file037.shtml.

52. www.vciom-a.ru/press/2003110402.html.

53. David Remnick, "Post-Imperial Blues," *New Yorker*, October 13, 2003: 78–89.

54. For the first time ever, the Organization for Security and Cooperation in Europe (OSCE) issued a critical preliminary report on Russia's 1999 parliamentary election, which stressed in part the media bias in the campaign period. See OSCE/PA (Organization for Security and Cooperation in Europe/Parliamentary Assembly) International Election Observation Mission, "Statement of Preliminary Findings and Conclusions, Russian Federation State Duma Elections, 7 December 2003." The full report is available at www.osce.org/documents/odihr/2003/12/1629_en.pdf.

55. In Putin's rule there have been repeated attempts to revise the Russian liberal media law passed in 1991. Uncommonly for Putin's Russia, the journalistic com-

munity has come out to oppose the revision. As of this writing, the old law remains in place, but the journalists are concerned that they may be unable to repel the new attacks that are sure to follow. See www.echo.msk.ru/interview/interview/14476.html.

56. See Colton and McFaul, "Are Russians Undemocratic?"

57. Strana.ru, April 27, 2001.

58. Office of Research, Department of States, "Russians Not Alarmed by Threats to Free Speech," No. M-2–02, January 8, 2002.

Chapter Five

Putin and Culture
Boris Lanin

The most striking feature of cultural life under President Vladimir Putin is the appearance of Vladimir Vladimirovich Putin as a figure and object of artistic communication, a process that he himself mediates, partly openly and partly in the shadows. Evidence of this control is the closure in February 2003 of the television program *Kukly* (puppets), the main satirical achievement of the 1990s. One can also point to the multiplication of songs about Putin and the sale of carpets, posters, and calendars with his image. These varied genres representing the "First Person" had not been seen in Russia since the era of Leonid Brezhnev (1964–82), though it should be noted that, as yet, the current level falls short of that seen under Brezhnev.

The inauguration of Putin on May 7, 2000, was itself a striking theatrical event. Putin strode energetically through Kremlin halls that were lined with dignitaries and soldiers dressed in new versions of tsarist-era uniforms. The ceremony was in stark contrast to the last inauguration of Boris Yeltsin, who staggered onto the stage for a mere twenty minutes. The anniversary of Putin's inauguration in May 2001 was marked by a public event organized by the youth movement Moving Together. According to police estimates, some 15,000 young people took part, not only Russians but also representatives from the capitals of Ukraine, Belarus, and Moldova. They were dressed in red, white, and blue soccer shirts (the colors of the Russian flag) adorned with the president's picture and the slogan "*Vse Putem!*" ("All OK!"). They marched from Slavanskyaya Square to Vasilevskii Bank, where they held a celebratory meeting amid banners proclaiming "Youth for the president!" and "Russia's Youth Squad: Trainer V. V. Putin."

The meeting adopted an appeal to Putin which noted inter alia that "the reforms begun by Vladimir Putin are a part of our present and give us hope for our future." The meeting closed with the participants holding hands and singing the Russian anthem. Most of the media reports on the event adopted an ironic tone. The next day's *Kommersant'* suggested that the organization Moving Together recruited members not by political appeals so much as promises of free Internet access and pagers. *Parlamentskaya gazeta* suggested, tongue in cheek, that they were attracted toward Putin because he personifies their moral code—he does not swear, drink, or use drugs. The reactionary *Sovetskaya rossiya* said that the event was inappropriate and a "provocation," detracting from the authority of the president. In 2002 Moving Together launched a protest campaign against the writer Vladimir Sorokin, condemning his 1999 novel *Blue Lard* as pornography (it features a sex scene with Stalin and Khrushchev). The campaign culminated in a ceremonial burning of his books in front of the Bolshoi Theater in June 2002. Critics began calling the group "*Putinomol*" (a word play on the Soviet Union's youth movement, the *Komsomol*) and "*Putin-Yugend*" (as in "Hitlerjugend").

In 2000 Putin restored the music of the old Soviet anthem as the official state anthem of the Russian Federation. The same year the Defense Ministry called for the reintroduction of compulsory military training in high schools as a key component of "military-patriotic education" of Russian youth. All of this can be seen as a window on the past. In the Kurshskaya promontory nature reserve, in Kaliningrad oblast, Putin stopped for lunch at a restaurant. The table where he sat has been turned into a place of pilgrimage. It is beribboned in red and gold, and visitors lay their hands on it, to draw energy.[1] In the northern village of Izborsk, the local authorities organized a "Putin tour" through the local open-air folk museum, which Putin had visited earlier in the year. The exhibits include a "wishing tree" where he had paused, and a stall where he bought a cucumber. The hill where Putin skied last year has been renamed in his honor. Ardent followers of Putin from around the country compose songs and poems, honoring his great deeds.

In 2001 Chelyabinsk law student Mikhail Anishchenko penned a song about the new Russian president, with the opening lines: "Tell me, Russia, why do you trust the president? And looking at him, don't you feel the tears start to rise, and your soul aches for him."[2] Klaus-Helge Donath, a journalist for the Berlin paper *Die Tageszeitung*, wrote an article about the ode to the president, provocatively titled "Kim Il Putin Lets Himself Be Celebrated," which suggested that the author was only "imitating patriotic feelings." Anishchenko unsuccessfully filed a court case, accusing the German publication of libel.[3]

Anishchenko was not alone. It appeared that penning "songs for the president" became quite a popular genre for "ordinary Russian people," successfully transposing the tradition from "ordinary Soviet people" of years past. August 2002 saw the appearance of the hit group Singing Together.[4] Their song "If Only I Could Find a Man like Putin," which reached the top of the charts, included the lyrics "One, like Putin, not to be fond of the bottle! One, like Putin, to love us! One, like Putin, not to offend us! One, like Putin, not to run away." It was written by Nikolai Petlyura, former press secretary of the Russian Supreme Court. The group was formed for the purpose of singing this particular song, which spread across the radio waves before it was available as a record. *Literaturnaya gazeta* published extracts of songs written by One Russia party members, including lyrics such as "Today Putin is the nation's hope that order will be restored."

Komsomol'skaya pravda carried a song which exulted: "Surely Putin is closest to God." The first street named after Putin appeared in the southern republic of Ingushetiya in October 2002, shortly after his fiftieth birthday. The village of Ol'geti, with thirty-seven homes, had been completely submerged in summer floods, but it was reconstructed thanks to federal funds. Ingush president Murat Zyazikov said that the authorities supported the villagers' request to name the settlement's main street in Putin's honor.

The Breget artistic workshop in Chelyabinsk started producing gilded pocket watches with Putin's face, and was surprised by the high demand for them, especially from government officials of all levels. In Saratov, some kindergartens reintroduced the tradition of "red corners" with portraits of Putin and local governor Dmitrii Ayatskov, along with the province's traditional loaf. Teachers solicit help from the children's parents to maintain the red corners in a semi-voluntary fashion.

There is already a statue of Putin on horseback, which is admittedly unlikely to get a wide audience: it was erected in a corrective-labor colony in Novgorod, carved from wood by a convict serving ten years for murder. The "state sculptor" Zurab Tsereteli, whose monstrous statues are scattered across Moscow, has not yet tackled the president, although he has noted that Putin has an "interesting face."

The Putin cult is most visible in his native St. Petersburg. The city is in the vanguard of Putinomania. One local sculptor is preparing a bronze bust. A local company has produced thousands of photographs of the leader and can barely keep pace with the demand. Viktor Yurakov, the self-styled "chief ideologist" of the local branch of the One Russia party, has mounted a campaign to win the hearts and minds of his fellow residents in support of Putin. In fall 2000 he arranged for the publication of 10,000 brochures for St. Petersburg elementary school pupils, providing a hagiographical account of Putin's life. The young Volodya, according to the brochure, "was never afraid and never misled anybody. His teacher realized that he was very talented." The pompous celebrations in 2003 marking the 300th anniversary of the founding of the city threw oil on the flames of Putinomania. The main project was the restoration of the Konstantin Palace in Strelna, on the outskirts of Petersburg, that will become a new presidential residence.

Perhaps it is premature to talk about the emergence of a presidential personality cult, but at least one can say that since he became president, considerable progress has been made in that direction. In addition to the multiple biographies and brochures, there are busts large and small, and portraits for all purposes. "The portraits come in different sizes, from desk-top to reception halls, depending on the rank and status of the official. The latest project is a 25 centimeter tall, 8 kilogram bust."[5]

Putin received symbolic gifts on his fiftieth birthday. In the unofficial Russian academy of jewelry arts, they prepared a copy of the Crown of Monomakh, the symbol of tsarist authority, lavishly decorated with sable fur, gold, and jewels, that was used to crown the Moscow prince in 1502.[6] One of the more unusual presents came from Bashkortostan, where former republican deputy prime minister Gabit Sabitov penned a three-page letter to the president in which every word begins with "p." It closes with the sentence "Through the whole planet they plant memorials of the World's Leading President, Putin."[7]

The latest addition to the genre was the opening, at the beginning of 2004, of an official Kremlin website (www.uznai-prezidenta.ru) for eight- to thirteen-year-olds, with text by Grigorii Oster, renowned for his tongue-in-cheek children's book *Bad Advice*. The interactive site includes questions such as "Who is more important, the president or mummy?" "Where does power come from?" and "Where are the limits of the president's patience?"

On the other hand, Putin is also the object of satirical humor. A group of well-known Petersburg writers associated with the Amfora publishing house—Pavel Kursanov, Vadim Nazarov, Sergei Nosov, Vladimir Rekshan, Aleksandr Sekatskii, and Il'ya Stogov—circulated in April 2001 an open letter to Putin in which they encouraged him to restore the Russian Empire with wider, "metaphysical" borders: "A grand goal does not by itself guarantee success, but an empire is guaranteed to succeed. In this connection it would be advisable to reintroduce the tsarist table of ranks as part of the Russian idea at state level."

THE STATE AND CULTURE

It was clear from the outset that the Putin administration regarded culture as merely "culture." The presidential pardons commission, headed by the writer Anatolii Pristavkin (who in Soviet times penned a well-known story about Chechnya), was disbanded on the grounds that it did not contain professional people. The members were mostly well-known writers and academics, such as the Bulgakov specialist M. O. Chudakova. They were trusted by the informal, "reading" segment of civil society. This kind of trust had no significance for the "Chekist minded" state officials. It is likely to be arbitrary and not subject to direction. But in Russia, literature had always seen itself as the representative of charitable forces, so the disbanding of the commission signaled to the reading public a reduction in "state mercy." For the state, it was almost a postmodern step, the dissolution of another hierarchy of authority.

A particular problem is the state of mass media and journalism under Putin. The situation is complicated by the fact that the Russian public is not quite used to the indirect method of expression and influence that Putin deploys. All previous rulers made clear their opinions about cultural issues. Stalin personally read through all the literary publications and watched all the films nominated for Stalin prizes. Nikita Khrushchev publicly denounced modernist painters as "pederasts." Under Brezhnev, there was tight control of writers, as was seen in the celebrated trial of Andrei Sinyavskii and Yuli Daniel, and the expulsion of (the then unknown) Joseph Brodsky and Alexander Solzhenitsyn. Even Mikhail Gorbachev gave out gold medals to the most loyal writers, secretaries of the Writers' Union such as Petr Proskurin, Georgii Markov, and Valentin Rasputin. But the Russian public had never before seen a ruler standing to the side while officials close to the ruler wielded the brute force of the law against the creative intelligentsia. Bans and repressive actions are disguised as "arguments among artists and professionals" from which state officials are at pains to distance themselves.

Viktor Shenderovich, the satirist and creator of the *Kukly* puppet show and discussion program *Itogo* for the independent television channel NTV, wrote: "Yes, and what is the relationship of the president of a superpower to these artists' quarrels? None whatsoever. But for some reason Vladimir Vladimirovich had at his fingertips the details of the case, the loans, the dates due, the interest rates. It's none of our business, but he happens to know. From time to time Putin repeats the idea of the independence of business and of the procuracy, not forgetting to gaze sincerely into the eyes of [newscaster] Svetlana Sorokina, who herself met the procurator leaving the presidential office as she headed in for a meeting with Putin."[8]

According to Shenderovich, "In May 2000 a senior Kremlin official made contact with one of the leaders of the Media-MOST company [that owned NTV] and presented a list of conditions which, if met, would mean the state would call off the 'attack' on the company. The conditions included changing the commentary on Chechnya, ending criticism of the Yeltsin 'Family' . . . but first on the list was the removal of the First Person from the *Kukly* puppet show."[9] Shenderovich lost his job after the closure of NTV and its successor station TVS.

That was the fate of the whole team of journalists working for Yevgenii Kiselev, a leading journalist who had been a guiding force on television throughout the whole Yeltsin era. The NTV station, which was owned by Vladimir Gusinsky, supported the parties opposing Putin in the 1999 parliamentary and 2000 presidential elections. He was to pay dearly for this: within months Gusinsky was forced out of the country, and in 2001 the station was taken over by the state-owned Gazprom company. At that point Kiselev's team was welcomed with open arms by the TV-6 station, owned by another oligarch who was in conflict with the Kremlin and who had fled the country—Boris Berezovsky. But after complaints from a minority shareholder (at the instigation of the Kremlin), that channel was declared insolvent and also shut down in January 2002. The Kremlin, not wanting to be seen as an enemy of the press, came up with a compromise. In June 2002 a coalition of Kremlin-friendly businessmen financed a new channel, TVS, which found a place for Kiselev's team. However, the channel ran up debts, and in the absence of anyone willing to cover them, the press ministry closed it down in June 2003. In this manner Kiselev's two-year odyssey came to an end, and the last remaining independent television station disappeared. It was clear that the Kremlin wanted to avoid any possible obstacles to its preferred outcome in the parliamentary elections that would happen six months later, and the presidential race six months after that.

Aleksei Venediktov, the chief editor of the country's last critical radio station, Ekho Moskvy, said that the closure of TVS meant "the appearance of a full state monopoly of television in Russia." The Russian mass media were divided into two groups. The first group comprised the national television channels, all more or less controlled by the state. The second channel, RTR, is directly state property. The first channel, ORT, formerly owned by Berezovsky, has had state representatives on its board since 2001. The state-owned Gazprom controls NTV. The "third button" carries a channel controlled by Moscow Mayor Yurii Luzhkov. TVS was replaced on Channel 6 by the Sport channel. The new presidential team acted decisively to bring to an end the era of media barons that had dominated the Russian political landscape in the second half of the 1990s.

The second group of media—newspapers and magazines, radio stations, local television channels—is mostly in the hands of private business. The *perestroika* years saw the rise of influential chief editors of print publications, who became virtually independent political players in their own right. Now the situation is completely different. The mass media have changed from being a public tribune to commercial operations. Among the more successful brands are some publications familiar from the Soviet times, such as *Moskovskii komsomolets, Argumenty i fakty, Komsomol'skaya pravda, Trud,* and *Izvestiya.* In contrast to the Gusinsky and Berezovsky operations, the media business continues to flourish, while avoiding conflicts with the authorities. Take for example the industrialist Vladimir Potanin, who bought *Izvestiya* and *Komsomol'skaya pravda.* His holding company, Prof-Media, has expanded to include more popular outlets such as *Sovetskii Sport* and *Avtoradio.* He has also bought outlets in cities where his industrial group Interros has a presence, such as Krasnoyarsk, Norilsk, and Murmansk. Another example is the Rodionov Publishing House, initially backed by the Imperial Bank, headed by Sergei Rodionov. The bank collapsed after the August 1998 crash, but the publishing house expanded beyond its initial business magazine *Profil* to include magazines such as *Kar'era* and *Moulin Rouge*, and even a new journal called *Politburo*. The Kremlin did not favor the old Journalists' Union, in part because it had supported Gusinsky, so they created a new organization, Media Soyuz, headed by former TV journalist Aleksandr Lyubimov.

Despite these trends toward state control, it would not be accurate to talk about a return to the past. There is simply more freedom of access to information now, especially thanks to new means of communication, from the Internet to cell phones. Above all, the new young generation does not want to be cut off from the outside world.

PUTIN'S LANGUAGE

Putin continues the tradition of Russian leaders taking liberties with language. He has not become as reckless as Nikita Khrushchev, but still his comment that terrorists should be "wiped out in the toilet" has continued circulating in the public arena since he uttered it in 1999. Also noteworthy is his blunt comment during his interview with CNN's Larry King—"It sank"—when asked what happened with the *Kursk* submarine. In a large Kremlin press conference he was asked a question about Boris Berezovsky, and he deadpanned, "Who is that?" Still darker humor was revealed in his comment at a meeting of Federal Security Service officers, that "the operation of the security service to place their man in the highest position in the country was successfully fulfilled." During the 2002 census, the television showed Putin answering the questions of a nervous young census taker. He told her that his profession was "public servant." On November 11, 2003, in Brussels, an exasperated Putin told an astonished journalist who was pressing him with questions about Chechnya, "If you want to become an Islamic radical and have a circumcision, I invite you to Moscow, because we are a multitalented country and have specialists there. I recommend that you have the operation done in such a way that nothing else will grow there." (The official Kremlin website, www.kreml.ru, carries a transcript of the press conference that does not include the exchange.)

LITERATURE

In September 2002, sociologists from the Komkon group released new research comparing cultural activities in different European countries. Russia turns out to be the cultural bulwark. For example, 63 percent of Russians expressed an interest in literature, whereas the European average was 40 percent. Theater-goers were twice as numerous in Russia, and those attending orchestral concerts three times as numerous as in Europe. While 38 percent of Russians claim to regularly visit art museums, the average for Europe was only 6 percent. Whatever the reliability of such data, they at least suggest the pull of culture on Russian identity, especially urban citizens.

The data show a turnaround in the publishing industry after a post-Soviet slump. The number of books printed fell from 1.3 billion in 1992 to 408 million in 1998, but rose to 600 million in 2002. The number of registered publishers exploded from 280 to 20,000, of which 5,000 are active. But half the market is covered by the top ten houses, and one-third by the top five.[10]

However, no striking new names have appeared in the Russian literary scene in recent years. Instead, there has been a flood of scandals. The most notorious is the "writers' affair" involving Vladimir Sorokin and Bayan Shiryanov (Kirill Vorob'ev). One part of the scandal developed when the Moving Together group organized a public book exchange in which people could drop off a copy of one of Sorokin's books and receive in its place a book by Soviet writer Boris Vasil'ev. They also published a brochure with pornographic extracts from Sorokin's book and organized a public burning of copies in front of the Bolshoi Theater. Sorokin sued the organization, but the Taganka district court threw out his suit. The court ordered Sorokin's publisher, Ad Marginem, to pay 75,000 rubles ($2,500) expenses, a decision that was upheld on appeal. Within a few months, the procurator dropped the case against Sorokin for spreading pornography, after evaluation of the publication by an expert commission (the usual legal procedure under article 242 of the Criminal Code on "the illegal spreading of pornography).[11]

At the same time, another investigation was under way of writer Bayan Shiryanov (the pseudonym of Kirill Vorob'ev), who wrote *Middle Pilotage* (Zebra E., 2002) and *Lower Pilotage* (Ad Marginem, 2001). The latter book received a warning from the Press Ministry, threatening to revoke the publisher's license, for its detailed description of drug-taking and invocation of post-drug euphoria. The Moving Together group accused him of pornography and encouraging drug use, and they staged a tomato-throwing of his picture. Vorob'ev sued the group for slander.[12]

The publishers defended the book by pointing out that it had been praised by well-respected writers such as Andrei Bitov and Boris Strugatskii. They had also taken precautions, such as including an afterword by a specialist from Doctors Without Borders, and selling the book in cellophane wrapping with a warning that it is not for readers under eighteen. Denying that the book gave precise instructions for drug-taking, the publishers argued that it in fact served to puncture the romanticism of drug-taking. They also noted that it is quite common to see hallucinatory passages in novels, such as the dream of Tatyana in Pushkin's *Evgenii Onegin* and the visions of Rodion Raskolnikov from Dostoevsky's *Crime and Punishment*. The publishers wrote: "The work of Bayan Shiryanov is an artistic text which in the Russian tradition addresses the plight of the 'fallen,' and clearly shows that drug-taking is an illness with deep social roots that requires serious analysis and not an 'administrative struggle' with sickness." The Press Ministry apparently agreed.

Nevertheless, in August 2002, Moving Together lodged a protest about *Middle Pilotage* with the Basmannoe police district, which began an investigation. They invited the Writers' Union and Gorkii Institute of World Literature to express their expert opinion. The union selected, *Soyuz Rossiiskikh Pisatelei*, is one of three existing writers' unions, and by no means the most progressive. Within a month, the union came back with a reply—that the author should be jailed. The letter, signed by secretary Nikolai Pereyaslov, warned that the portrayal of characters in the book "could undermine the cultural authority of our state and cause it considerable damage in the international arena." Subsequently, on September 27, 2002, a criminal case was opened against Vorob'ev under article 242 of the Criminal Code, and the legal machine was set in motion. However, the Gorkii Institute then came back with the opinion that the book was art, not pornography. On March 5, 2003, the Basmannoe police announced they were dropping the case, but the procurator intervened, insisting that if there were contradictory expert testimony, the case should continue. However, after the public interest faded, the case was quietly dropped.[13]

The critic and gallery owner Marat Gelman complained that an aggressive obscurantism was growing in society. "It appears that young people don't like the books by Sorokin, Pelevin and Erofeev. What, are they being forced to read them in school, like the writings of Brezhnev? What is the problem? Don't they have a choice? Why must a court forbid a writer to be published? Who defines that something has gone over the line? Do the early works of Pushkin fall into that category?"[14] Still, the only concrete result of the "writers' affair" was a surge in demand for books by Sorokin and Shiryanov.

Another scandal developed out of a strange situation that has arisen with regard to authors' rights in Russia. On top of the official printing of a book, there is a "gray" print run, the royalties for which are paid to the author in cash (and not declared for tax purposes). On July 23, 2003, the tax investigators showed up in the offices of the EKSMO publisher. A certain Lt. Col. Oleg Morozov said the investigation would be halted in return for a $1 million payment. The publisher contacted the police corruption unit, and Morozov was arrested in the act of taking the bribe. Despite that, the investigation of EKSMO for publishing excess "gray" books continued. At least, the size of the bribe that Morozov solicited showed that publishing is booming in Russia. And no wonder: the fourth volume of *Harry Potter* sold 15 million copies.

THEATER

It was after Putin's accession to power that musicals suddenly became popular in Russia. The first big success was the Polish musical *Metro*. The first home-grown musical, *North-East*, was extraordinarily popular. It was based on the novel *Two Captains* by Veniamin Kaverin, with bold heroes who live by the principle "Struggle and search, find and never give up." Many provincial families made trips to Moscow in order to see the show. It was this show that was the object of the terrible hostage-taking by Chechen terrorists in October 2002. The terrorist act not only led to the death of 129 hostages but it also killed off the show. In May 2003 the company left for a European tour, and the show did not return to the Moscow stage.

However, musicals became the most popular genre in the Russian theater. Great success was enjoyed by a Russian production of *The Hunchback of Notre Dame*, with lyrics by poet Yulii Kim, who returned from Israel to take advantage of the new market. There were also productions of *Chicago* and *The Witches of Eastwick* as well as a musical based on Ilf and Petrov's *Twelve Chairs*, and shows such as *Songs of Our Communal Flat* and *Songs of Our Courtyard* (in which the actors distribute salami and vodka shots three times during the performance). The theater crisis of the early 1990s seems to have been overcome, with the number of theaters in Moscow increasing from one hundred to 180. This is thanks in part to increased sponsorship from the mayor's office. The same is true of Petersburg. But elsewhere, provincial theaters are staggering into their second decade of hand-to-mouth existence.

CINEMA

The first modern, multiplex cinema opened in Moscow in 1996—the Kodak Cinemaworld. The movie market changed in 1999 with the appearance of two new companies, Karo-film and Five Stars. If in the early 1990s movie theaters were turned into car showrooms and furniture stores, the second half of the decade saw a revival of movie-going. September 2003 saw the opening of the first IMAX theater, with 3D projection. Ticket sales reached $110 million in 2002 and an expected $175 million in 2003.[15] The theaters show almost exclusively Hollywood movies. Even successful Russian movies such as *War* and *Brat-2* barely break even.

In September 2003, Andrei Zyagintsev's film *Return* won the Golden Lion at the Venice film festival. In previous years only two Russian directors had won the award: Andrei Tarkovsky for *Ivan's Childhood* (1962) and Nikita Mikhalkov for *Close to Eden* (1991). The young director Zyagintsev, barely known in Russia, had come to Moscow from Novosibirsk and worked as a janitor to get a free apartment. The film was self-financed, without any support from the state authorities. An even more remarkable artistic achievement was Aleksandr Sokurov's *Russian Ark* (2002), the first film ever to be shot in a single take—whose duration was 1 hour, 27 minutes and 12 seconds. On December 23, 2001, Sokurov took over the Hermitage Museum and arranged his actors to perform in a seamless series of scenes illustrating the history of Russia, filmed with a Steadycam moving from room to room. The film had its Russian premier in May 2003. It was a success in foreign art-house cinemas, earning a record $5 million.

Similar trends could be seen in the movie-making industry. Movies were made about the painful subject of the war in Chechnya. Aleksei Rogozhkin's masterpiece *Blockpost* (1998) can be compared to anti-war classics such as *Catch-22*. However, later films adopted a different tone, with Aleksei Balabanov's film *War* (2002) being regarded by some as anti-Chechen. Some even spoke about films being made according to government order, of director's desire to feed the emergent state mythology. The main hero and narrator of *War* is the soldier Ivan Ermakov, who escapes from Chechen captivity. He speaks some English, which saves his life when an English couple, John and Margaret, are also captured. John is freed in return for a two million pound ransom payment, and Ivan accompanies him, but is then himself subject to investigation for having killed innocent Chechen civilians. The scenes of the Chechen war are shown with shocking naturalism, and the episode where two Russian prisoners are beheaded is shown twice. It seemed clear that the impact of the film would be to fuel hatred of the Chechens and justify harsh actions by Russian soldiers and the Russian government.

The film also shows the absolute poverty of the Russian soldiers. To pay for his trip back to Chechnya to rescue Margaret, it is enough for Ivan to pay with his boots. On the other hand, the Chechen commander has a satellite phone and access to the Internet. A satellite phone features in the heroes' escape, with one character praising the quality of the connection.

Russian society is shown as unfair and hostile toward the upright and honorable hero. A KGB officer tries to steal the ransom money. Four friends of Ivan die—not in captivity, but in Tobol'sk. A Russian journalist asks John ridiculously naïve questions. There is the impression that intellectuals cannot stop the war, any more than one can turn back the clock. Directors typically search for the truth. But in such harsh times, truth lies not in mercy, but in the subject's perception of "justice." So John shoots the Chechen commander and uses the ransom money to pay for medical treatment for the Russian soldiers. It is noteworthy that there are dialogs between the protagonists, so this is not a straightforward action film. The hero cannot kill the villain until he has explained to him why he is going to shoot him. We learn that Aslan can name his family seven generations back, and all of them fought the Russians. What is Ivan doing in Chechnya? That is not the director's problem, for the situation has a logic of its own. The film *War* is very characteristic of the shift in mentality under way in Putin's Russia.

FACING THE FUTURE

At a June 2003 meeting of the State Council, held in St. Petersburg, Culture Minister Mikhail Shvydkoi laid out the parameters of future state policy toward culture.[16] Although he raised the possibility of "state orders" for major cultural projects, the main theme was encouraging business organizations to contribute to society through subsiding cultural projects. Already in St. Petersburg alone we have seen oligarch Vladimir Potanin buying Malevich's Black Square for $1 million and donating it to the Hermitage Museum, the Central Bank paying for the restoration of the Summer Garden, and Alfa Bank buying the communal apartment where poet Joseph Brodsky lived with a view to turning it into a museum.

In this way will culture and capitalism be unified, under Putin's leadership, in the new Russia. But this will inevitably mean shrinking freedom for media and self-expression, and will provide new challenges to Russian creative artists, to maintain their integrity in the face of the new conservative and imperial social trends.

NOTES

1. Strana.ru/worldwide/press/2001/05/08/989322475.html.

2. The full text was published on the Union of Right Forces website, February 12, 2001, at www.sps.ru/?id = 25035.

3. Robin Munro, "Ironic Article Lands Journalist in Court," *St. Petersburg Times*, February 26, 2002.

4. pravda.ru, December 12, 2002.

5. www.utro.ru/articles/2001050802023813028.shtml.

6. Julius Strauss, "So Glad It's Vlad," *Daily Telegraph* (London), October 9, 2002.

7. In the Russian: "*Po Planete postavyat pamyatniki Pervomy Prezidentu Planety Putinu.*"

8. V. Shenderovich, *Zdes' bylo NTV i drugie istorii* (Moscow: Zakharov, 2002), 36.

9. Shenderovich, *Zdes' bylo NTV i drugie istorii*, 26.

10. Denis Mater, "Fewer Books but a Whole Lot More to Read About," *Moscow Times*, June 6, 2003.

11. lenta.ru/culture/2003/04/24/sorokin.

12. lenta.ru/culture/2002/09/24/shiryanov.

13. vip.lenta.ru/fullstory/2003/03/13/bayan/index.htm.

14. lenta.ru/culture/2003/02/04/gelman/text.htm. For a lively review of the arts scene, see Gelman's website, www.gif.ru.

15. A. Starobinets, "My uzhe tam," *Ekspert*, September 15, 2003.

16. Olga Osinovskaya, "Arise, Ye Cursed and Defamed!" *Rosbalt*, January 6, 2004.

Chapter Six

Putin, Demography, Health, and the Environment

David E. Powell

On January 1, 1992, shortly after the Soviet Union collapsed, the population of the Russian Federation was 148,704,300.[1] Today, it has shrunk to 143 million, a decline of more than 5 million in a decade. Russia's overall mortality rate is the highest in Europe, and its birth rate is one of the lowest.[2] The decline in the birth rate and the rise in the death rate have proved to be a devastating combination. In fact, Russia (along with Ukraine) appears to be the first major country in history to experience such a sharp decrease in births versus deaths for reasons other than war, famine, or natural disaster.

In July 2000, in his first State of the Union address, President Vladimir Putin warned that Russia could lose another 22 million citizens over the next fifteen years and degenerate from superpower to third-world status. (Military leaders have already shifted from the term "superpower" to "great power" to describe the country.) "We are facing the serious threat of turning into a decaying nation," Putin declared.[3] Why this has happened, and how public health and population are interrelated, are the subject of this chapter.

THE SHRINKING POPULATION

In recent years, the total population has dwindled by about 0.7 percent annually; if this rate of loss continues, then the population will be cut in half within the next seventy years. The mortality rate currently is 50 percent higher than it was in the middle of the 1980s: some 7.7 million persons have died prematurely from heart disease, strokes, and other causes since the collapse of the Soviet Union. The birth rate has been halved as well.[4]

Currently, Russia's death rate exceeds its birth rate by 70 percent. These figures produce "natural" increases and decreases—that is, changes brought about solely by shifts in the numbers of births and deaths. But such statistics are not identical to the real expansion or contraction of the population. They leave out emigration from, as well as immigration into, the country. In 2002, the overall population loss was 900,000 (including a net in-migration of some 70,000 persons), and the Ministry of Economic Development and Trade expected an additional drop of 700,000 in 2003, another 700,000 in 2004, and 600,000 in 2005.[5]

In 2001, the government drafted a *konseptsiia* ("concept paper," similar to a British White Paper) entitled "Demographic Policy up to 2015," which pointed out that the "depopulation" of Russia is exacerbated by the increasing imbalance between younger and older population groups. The imbalance initially appeared in 1998, when, for the first time, the number of pensioners exceeded the number of children and teenagers. By January 1, 2000, the gap between these two groups was over one million. The aging of the population will inevitably lead to a deficit of the labor force and growing financial burden for the working population.[6]

The 2002 census revealed that the average age in Russia was 37.7 years, an increase of three years since the last census was taken in 1989. Children under the age of sixteen comprised only 18 percent of the population: they numbered 26.3 million.[7]

Furthermore, women are marrying later in life or choose not to marry at all. If they marry, they are less likely than their mothers were to have children, and if they have children, they generally are satisfied with one or at most two. Part of the problem here is the familiar one—crowded housing. The former Soviet practice of providing economic benefits each time a woman has a baby still exists, but the funds available today have been sharply reduced, and the bureaucratic obstacles confronting those who seek assistance are formidable.[8]

Projections of the situation in future years, offered by leading experts or authoritative institutions, are uniformly pessimistic. In March 2002, for example, Goskomstat (State Statistics Committee) predicted that by the end of 2050, the population would shrink by 30 percent, from 143.6 million to 101.9 million. This, Goskomstat said, was "the most probable forecast" of the country's demographic situation. But Goskomstat also offered "best-case" and "worst-case" scenarios: according to the former, the population will fall to 122.6 million by 2050, while the latter projected a drop to 77.2 million, a reduction of almost 50 percent.[9]

At about the same time, the Center for Demography and Human Ecology, part of the Russian Academy of Sciences' Institute of Economic Forecasting, prepared a similar set of population forecasts. The center developed twelve potential scenarios, all based on the assumption that the birth rate over the next fifty years will be somewhere between 1.3 and 2.0 children. This assumption appears to be rather optimistic, but conceivable under the right conditions. As for the death rate, none of the scenarios puts it any higher than the current rate, which is already very high by world standards. In the most optimistic variant, it was assumed that the death rate would decrease at a pace that, over a fifty-year period, would raise average life expectancy for men from the current fifty-nine years to seventy-seven, and for women from the current seventy-two years to eighty-three.[10]

These projections of life expectancy are followed by combinations of various estimates of total population. In the worst case (a low birth rate combined with a high death rate), the current population of 143 million Russian citizens would fall to 86.5 million by 2050. If the low birth rate continues but the death rate declines, the figure would be 103.3 million. If the birth rate increases but the death rate remains high, the population would be 94.5 million. Finally, if the birth rate increases and the death rate decreases, Russia's population would be 111.7 million. So not even the most optimistic forecast envisions the preservation of Russia's current population size, much less a natural increase.[11]

With male mortality four times that of females, the drop in the male population will be larger than that of the female population, and the female/male ratio will increase steadily. According to Goskomstat's "most probable" scenario, the male population will fall by 32.2 percent by 2050, while that of females will drop by "only" 27.4 percent. (Roughly 58 percent of sixteen-year-old males are likely to live to age sixty.) Even if people were inclined to marry, there would be a shortage of men, and the end result would be large numbers of unmarried women, an increased number of children born out of wedlock, and an overall decline in birth rates.

ISSUES IN PUBLIC HEALTH

The problems facing Russia's health care system are numerous and deep-seated. A partial list includes a drastic deterioration in medical services, shortages of medical supplies, a decaying infrastructure, poorly trained and demoralized physicians and nurses, the spread of infectious diseases (especially tuberculosis), stress, and so on. These are issues that have been examined before;[12] we focus chiefly on the downturn in demographic indicators, ecological threats, extremely high levels of alcoholism, and the growing problems of drugs and HIV/AIDS.

Falling Birth Rate

Russia's birth rate, which already was low, has dropped still farther since the final years of the Soviet Union. In 1990, it was 13.4 per 1,000 population, but by 1999, it had declined to only 8.3. In 2000, it increased to 8.7, and in

2002, it rose once again, this time to 9.8. Russian demographers expect the increase to continue, perhaps reaching 10.3 in 2005[13]—primarily because citizens born during the Soviet "baby boom" are reaching marriage age.[14] Still, in 1988, the average number of children born to women in the USSR was 2.2, while today it is only 1.2. Just to maintain the population by natural growth, that figure would have to increase to 2.1–2.2—a development that seems highly unlikely. Whether the relatively optimistic prognosis is warranted remains to be seen. Since 1998, the number of young Russian families with one child and the number with three or more children has declined. During the same five-year period, however, the number of families with two children remained stable.[15]

In addition, the number of children born out of wedlock has been rising steadily: in 1994, the figure was 275,800, or 19.6 percent of all newborns, and in 1995, it was 288,300, or 21.1 percent. In November 2001, Goskomstat reported, one-third of all babies were born to unwed mothers, a huge increase from 1992, when the proportion was only one out of seven.[16] More often than not, the women involved are young and unable to provide properly for their infants. Further compounding the problem is the aging of the citizenry: a smaller and smaller proportion of women are of childbearing age.

Over the course of the past decade, a million more people have died every year than were born. The low birth rate is attributable, in part, to many couples' conscious decision to limit themselves to one child, generally because of economic reasons. But surveys carried out by the Ministry of Health indicate that 5–6 million couples are unable to have children, more often than not because of the wife's inability to conceive or carry a child to term. Out of those who do become pregnant, only one in three eventually give birth. Although 10 percent of pregnant women have miscarriages due to health problems, 60 percent elect to have an abortion. Almost half make this choice due to financial difficulties, while another 20 percent make the choice because they do not see how they can provide adequately for a child or children. In Moscow, prenatal care from the early stages of pregnancy until delivery costs about $800–1,000; in regional centers the cost is $200–400, and about $100–165 in the more remote areas of the country. The government provides a one-time payment of 300 rubles (about $10) to assist those who seek treatment at a medical facility in early pregnancy—up to twelve weeks' gestation. The birth itself costs almost as much as the prenatal care, and there is no guarantee that payment will be followed by high-quality care. Aid to children of low-income families is 70 rubles (a bit more than $2) a month, and that sum is hardly enough to feed a child if a woman does not breastfeed her baby (30–40 percent of Russian infants are put on formula.)[17]

A leading Russian scientist, Nikolai Izmerov, noted in September 2003 that the nation's workforce had declined by 12 million persons over the previous ten years. Indeed, he added, the number of deaths due to "unnatural causes" (e.g., murder, suicide, motor vehicle and industrial accidents) corresponded to numbers in Russia a century earlier, and it was 2.5 times higher than the average for developed nations. Premature death is especially prevalent among males: the loss of the workforce among men is 5–7 times higher than among women. "If the current demographic tendencies continue," he concluded, "then by 2015 the workforce will be reduced by an additional ten million people."[18]

In the fall of 2003, however, the health ministry severely restricted the right of women to have an abortion for non-medical reasons after their third month of pregnancy. The number of circumstances in which the procedure would be permitted was reduced from thirteen to four. Today, a court must rule that a woman is unfit to be a mother, the pregnancy must be the result of rape, the father has to have died or be too ill to fulfill his parental obligations, or the mother must have been sentenced to a term in prison. Formerly, women could be guaranteed an abortion if they were unemployed, lacked adequate housing, were unmarried, already had a large family, already had a handicapped child, or had an income below the poverty threshold.[19]

For decades, Russian legislation on abortion was among the world's most liberal: women could have their pregnancy terminated until the twenty-second week after conception, and even later in cases involving serious medical problems. The number of abortions, which had been falling in recent years (chiefly because the number of pregnancies had dropped so sharply), is likely to drop still farther. In 1997, there were almost three abortions for every live birth; by 2002, the ratio had dropped to 1.3–1.[20]

The authors of the new regulations claimed to be acting out of concern for the health of mothers. But the social factors that most frequently impel women to terminate their pregnancy are, in fact, the ones that have been deleted from the new list. To quote one leading physician: "As a rule, women who want abortions are young girls under eighteen who missed the early signs of pregnancy or adult women who are poorly educated and unsophisticated and fail to care for themselves properly." The reasons they cite most frequently are "financial problems" or "not having a husband."[21] The ultimate outcome is likely to be a sharp increase in illegal abortions, gynecological complications, secondary infertility, and even death. Indeed, the most recent figures available (September 2003) indicate that only 32.1 percent of children in Russia under the age of eighteen are "healthy," while 16.2 percent have been diagnosed with chronic illnesses.[22]

Increase in Infant Mortality

In 1991, the year the USSR ceased to exist, infant mortality was 17.8 per thousand live births. By 1993, it rose to 19.9, and in 2001, it rose to 20.1.[23] In view of the difficult conditions prevailing in Russia today, numerous instances of premature births, low birth weights, extremely vulnerable infants, and a high rate of infant mortality are not surprising.

Both Soviet and Russian public health authorities used a highly idiosyncratic definition of the term "infant mortality" in order to minimize the extent of the problem. Deaths within the first week after birth frequently are listed as miscarriages, or the births are not even reported.[24] For example, only if they survive more than seven days do infants weighing 500–1,000 grams have to be officially registered at a government office. If such an infant is born alive but survives less than a week, the birth is not officially registered and is classified as a "late-term miscarriage." It is not included in infant mortality statistics—a clear violation of World Health Organization (WHO) practices.

Those infants who survive, however, remain at risk throughout their childhood. During the 1990s, the child mortality rate increased, reversing the trend toward progressively lower rates that started in 1948 (with a slight upswing in 1972–76). Russia's child mortality rate is now several times higher than that of the developed nations, and its rate of child mortality from lung diseases, accidents, and infections is tens of times higher. One study, carried out by the Center of Demography and Human Environment Center for Macroeconomic Forecasting, concluded that health care for mothers and children in Russia lags thirty to forty years behind that of the United States, Europe, and Japan.[25]

Decline in Life Expectancy

Life expectancy for both men and women in Russia is far lower than in any Western country. Among males, the change has been truly astonishing: the figure declined from 64.9 years in 1987 to 59 in 2003 (up from somewhere between 57.1 and 58.3 in 1995—different sources provided different figures). Today, the nation ranks 135th in the world in male life expectancy; among women, it is in 100th place. (For the past forty years or so, the nation's women have outlived men by about a decade, sometimes more; throughout this period, the male-female differential has been among the highest, if not *the* highest, in the world.) In August 2002, the Russian Academy of Sciences' Center for Demography and Human Ecology released population forecasts. The most optimistic variant predicted that life expectancy for men would rise from the current 58.6 years to 59.8, and for women from the current 72.1 years to 73.6. The life expectancy of Russians over age twenty-five is now lower than it was in the Russian Empire in the late nineteenth century, and there is every reason to expect the population to decline dramatically in future years.[26]

Ecological Threats

Environmental degradation is a worldwide phenomenon affecting both developed and developing countries. The situation in Russia, though, is so horrendous that one is tempted to say it can never be put right. Aleksandr Yanshin, a distinguished naturalist and a member of the Russian Academy of Sciences, addressed this theme in 1995. "Humanity," he said, "has so polluted the environment with wastes from industry and agriculture that nature has begun to take vengeance on human beings." Although Western nations had already begun to arrest the process of environmental deterioration—for example, by introducing new technologies, shifting economic priorities, and changing the mind-set of producers and consumers—"in our country, due to our *perestroika,* our lack of regulation and the chaos of our lives, we have ignored the demands of modern ecology."[27]

Russia, like other nations, is experiencing widespread pollution of the air and water, despoliation of the land, and contamination of its food. The government has also shown a cavalier attitude toward the creation and disposal of both nuclear and toxic waste. The damage done to certain rivers and lakes has reached tragic proportions, and industrial cities such as Magnitogorsk, Norilsk, and Novokuznetsk may actually be beyond repair. This situation, profoundly troublesome in its own right, has important consequences for the health of men, women, and children in every corner of the country.

In the early 1990s, two Western analysts, Murray Feshbach and Alfred Friendly Jr., were so struck by the magnitude of the problem, and so appalled by the indifference or impotence of the Russian authorities, that they coined the term "ecocide" to describe the situation.[28] Responsible officials in Russia agree. For example, in early 1994, the Interdepartmental Commission on Ecological Safety, an agency attached to the Russian Federation Security Council, declared that "the adverse effects of environmental pollution on public health" were "a genuine threat to national security." But neither the commission, nor the council, nor any of the ministers of environmental affairs, nor any of the president's advisors on ecological matters has been able to do much about it.

In the mid-1970s, a member of the Academy of Sciences predicted that by the year 2000, "not a single child will be born in our country without various defects." By 1996, the head of Gosepidemnadzor (the State Sanitary and Epidemic-Prevention Inspectorate), the agency that deals with national sanitary and epidemiological problems, indicated that 109 million people were living "in an unfavorable habitat, . . . areas where the amount of various pollutants exceeds maximum permissible concentrations at least ten-fold." In January 1997, the former minister for environmental affairs, Viktor Danilov-Danilian, offered somewhat more precise but equally horrific figures. He said that air pollution exceeded permissible levels in more than 200 cities with a total population of more than 60 million. In 120 of those cities, he went on, pollution levels were five times the permitted maximum.[29]

Two months later, health minister Tatiana Dmitrieva declared that about 40 million people were living in regions "with a level of atmospheric air pollution exceeding permissible standards by 5 to 10 times." Other sources suggest that the number of persons living in such areas is somewhere between 40 and 60 million. Although these figures are estimates, it is undeniable that few citizens of Russia—some put the number at only 15 percent of the nation's population—reside in areas that do *not* exceed these norms, and this percentage has been falling for years.

Numerous studies have demonstrated a strong link between environmental damage and health problems—ranging from runny noses to various forms of cancer. At the very least, toxic and carcinogenic emissions from industry, agriculture, power stations, motor vehicles, and nuclear waste disposal sites cause oxygen deprivation, coughing, watery eyes, dizziness, headaches, nausea, ringing in the ears, fainting spells, rapid heartbeat, high blood pressure, numbness in the extremities, irritation of the skin, disintegration of the mucous membranes of the eyes and lungs, and disruption of the nervous system and cardiovascular system. At worst, they cause radiation sickness, lung cancer, respiratory failure, and death. President Yeltsin's advisor on environmental affairs, Aleskei Yablokov, once suggested that polluting enterprises were responsible for about 30 percent of the overall illness rate of the population.[30]

Environmental pollution has had a particularly disturbing impact on the health of pregnant women and children. It is one of the principal reasons for the growing number of complications during pregnancy and maternal mortality that have been observed in Russia, and it contributes significantly to high rates of infant mortality and infant morbidity. For example, babies born near particularly "dirty" production facilities, or near toxic or nuclear waste disposal sites, are far more likely to experience retarded physical, psychological, and intellectual development than those who are born in cleaner areas. More generally, it has been said, "the principal cause of all serious children's diseases, pathologies and infant mortality is the unfavorable ecological situation as a whole."[31]

Air Pollution

Numerous studies have demonstrated a strong link between air pollution and health problems.[32] As an article in the newspaper *Vecherniaia Moskva* put it:

> the incidence of bronchial asthma, acute bronchitis, conjunctivitis, pharyngitis, and tonsillitis is 40–60 percent higher in areas with large amounts of air pollution [than it is in less polluted areas]. Children living in houses along the Garden Ring Road [in downtown Moscow] . . . experience six times the incidence of ear, throat and nose infections, and three times the incidence of bronchitis as children living [elsewhere in the city].

But the problem of air pollution is not confined to Moscow or other large cities in Russia. For example, the area near Murmansk, on the Kola Peninsula (in the northwestern part of the country), a place of almost pristine beauty only a few decades ago, has recently been described as "one of the most poisoned spots on earth—relentlessly transformed by Russian industry into a laboratory of ecological destruction."

The change is easy to explain: for years, two old and outdated nickel smelters have been emitting large quantities of heavy metals and sulfur dioxide into the air and damaging the surrounding countryside. Lung cancer, lead poisoning, and emphysema have reached epidemic proportions among workers in the mines and factories there, and more than 40 percent of all persons employed in industry suffer from respiratory diseases—five times the rate for the country as a whole. In a typical year, 20 percent of all workers in the region have to be hospitalized for such illnesses.

The same phenomenon—respiratory and other illnesses linked to "dirty" production facilities—occurs near aluminum plants, chemical plants, synthetic alcohol plants, pulp-and-paper mills, petrochemical installations, metallurgical combines, oil refineries, and production units manufacturing building materials, such as mines and gravel pits.

One of the most egregious examples of chemical pollution, which has done massive damage to both air and water, can be found in the city of Dzerzhinsk, located near Nizhnii Novgorod, 225 miles east of Moscow. In 1996, the environmental organization Greenpeace reported that a "choking red fog . . . cloaks the town and . . . people die young from chronic bronchial problems, cancer and poisoned livers." Some residents must wear gas masks in order to breathe. Greenpeace and the city environmental protection commission are trying to have Dzerzhinsk declared an ecological disaster zone. If they are successful, the city could stop paying federal taxes and use the money instead to provide medical treatment for its population.

The fall in industrial output might have been expected to lead to more or less commensurate reductions in pollution levels. But that has not proven to be the case. Beset by economic difficulties, unable to pay either their suppliers or their workers, and desperately anxious to cut costs, managers of industrial enterprises decided to reduce their spending on environmental protection. As a result, one journalist wrote in 1994, "the economic situation in the country has been aggravating the environmental situation."[33] To be sure, the cities of Moscow and St. Petersburg are beginning to experiment with programs calling on residents to separate their trash by type—glass, paper, aluminum, and plastic—as part of a recycling effort.[34] Much more needs to be done, however.

Water Pollution

As long ago as 1987, former USSR Minister of Health Evgenii Chazov pointed out that in 104 towns and cities, one-quarter of water for domestic use and one-third of that for industrial and office use had not been sufficiently purified. In almost all of the other sources of water, he went on, serious violations of the law were routinely recorded. But only a decade later, the situation had grown worse. Vladimir Chiburaev, head of the State Sanitary and Epidemic Prevention Committee, wrote in 1996 that 29.8 percent of all drinking-water samples "do not conform to the sanitary and medical standards that have been set, [and] another 26.6 percent fail to meet the required microbiological norms. The same can be said about 40 percent of all samples taken from other bodies of water and 10 percent of all subterranean-well samples."

At the beginning of the 1990s, specialists reported that approximately 28 million cubic meters of contaminated effluent were discharged into Russia's rivers, lakes, and reservoirs.[35] After rising for several years, the figure fell in 1997 to 58.9 million cubic meters, although the volume of pesticides and nitrates increased substantially. (The reasons for the drop in overall water pollution in 1997 are not clear.[36]) A large portion of the effluent—Goskomstat puts the figure at one-fifth, but other sources say it may be as high as one-third—undergoes no purification whatsoever. The remainder is seldom subjected to anything beyond primary treatment. In Kamchatka and Novgorod provinces, 66 percent of all sewage goes untreated; on the Chukchi Peninsula, the figure is 64 percent; in Perm, 48 percent. Moreover, 43 cities in Russia (4 percent of the total), 732 settlements (37 percent), and 146,000 villages (97 percent) have no systems that provide centralized disposal of sewage. To make matters worse, filters are in short supply, are out of order much of the time, and are not regarded by managerial personnel as important, at least in comparison with maintaining or increasing output.

Largely as a result of these circumstances, only a fraction of the nation's sources of drinking water—10–20 percent, depending on location—have water that meets official standards, even though these standards are usually quite modest. In almost all of the other sources of water, serious violations of the law are routinely recorded. In recent years, some Russians have taken to boiling their tap water as a precaution, and the more affluent have installed filters in their kitchens or begun drinking bottled imported water.

In 1997, Minister of Health Dmitrieva told a press conference that "almost half the inhabitants of Russia" use drinking water that is "far below the minimal standard requirements."[37] Clearly, the terms "almost half" and "far below" lack precision, but her point is nonetheless important. Large numbers of people are drinking substandard water, which inevitably does damage to their health. In Moscow itself, few of the nearly 3,000 industrial enterprises located in the city produce waste water that conforms to government requirements.[38] As a result, roughly one billion cubic meters of poorly treated sewage flow into the Moscow River each year. Every day, 17.5 tons of heavy metals are dumped into the capital's sewage system, and 3.8 tons of that make their way into the river. During thaws, the snow that enters the river has a zinc concentration that is 100 times greater than the permissible figure; for copper the concentration is 160 times, and for petroleum products it is 1,000 times greater than the maximum allowable.

More relevant for our purposes is the fact that in Moscow, as well as in other places around the country, dirty water has led to high rates of illness, including dysentery, cholera, typhoid fever, and viral hepatitis. But this list does not exhaust the range of illnesses attributable to water pollution. In many parts of the country, including Moscow Province, the concentration of iron in the water is so high that it leads to widespread liver and blood diseases and produces allergic reactions. High strontium levels are associated with the development of strontium-induced rickets, as well as brittle bones. Widespread discharges of heavy metals, chemical compounds, and various other toxic substances into the nation's rivers, lakes, and seas have also led to toxic and chemical poisoning and are responsible for various kinds of illness, paralysis, or even death. One high-ranking Orthodox Church clergyman, after viewing the oil, oil by-products, and assorted other debris fouling the Black Sea port of Novorossiisk, remarked in 1997: "Our once health-giving waters have turned into a source of disease."

Similarly, the city of Ulianovsk is said to be "facing a threat of environmental disaster." The threat comes from a dump of thousands of tons of galvanized waste (oxides of heavy metals which, if ingested, can lead to death), poisonous substances that for decades have been kept in rusted containers in the open air. The waste penetrates into subsoil waters and eventually flows into the Volga River. Because it looks like sand, residents sometimes use it as a building material.[39]

But the most horrifying example of water pollution is found at Lake Kaskovo, site of a chemical waste dump situated in Dzerzhinsk, 200 miles from Moscow. Greenpeace has described it as the most chemically polluted lake in the world. The 300,000 people living near it "enjoy" an average life expectancy of forty-two years. According to a description in a British newspaper, "Green slime oozes from charred toxic waste barrels onto the thin layer of orange ice covering Lake Kaskovo; passing birds that mistake the lake for water die as soon as they hit the surface; rivers feeding the lake are red and bubbling with poison; countless babies in the area are born with deformities."[40]

Hazardous Waste and Chemical Contamination

The Russian land itself has been badly scarred. In May 1996, Danilov-Danilian revealed that some 80 billion tons of solid waste had accumulated in the territory of Russia. Of this sum, he said, 1.6 billion tons were "a direct threat to human health and the environment." At that time, the country produced some 7 billion tons of waste every year, of which only 28 percent was recycled. The per capita share of hazardous waste was almost one ton (800 kilograms, or 1,760 pounds) a year.[41]

Pesticides, herbicides, fertilizer, and other products that are designed to increase agricultural productivity have also proven ecologically harmful. What we said earlier about the collapse of industry applies even more to the agricultural sphere: the nation's economic difficulties might have been expected to reduce the demand for pesticides and similar materials and thus ease the pressures on the environment. In fact, however, while the use of such products has diminished, Russia continues to use tens, if not hundreds, of different toxic chemicals (including DDT) that are banned in the countries where they are produced but have a large market in Russia because of their low price.[42]

In December 1989, the heads of the KGB, the State Planning Committee, and the Academy of Sciences declared that dioxin was so widespread that it posed "the maximum threat to the country." In early 1990, other parts of the Soviet leadership acknowledged that dioxin was "the most serious threat" to the country. But, as Feshbach has pointed out, "the government made every effort to keep this fact from the general public." In 1992, however, the State Report on the Environment termed dioxin pollution "a genuine threat" in a number of Russian cities.[43]

According to Greenpeace, almost 75 percent of Russia's territory has been contaminated by these substances. While the definitions used by the researchers lack precision (for example, at what point are concentrations substantial enough to warrant calling an area "contaminated"?), there is no doubt that a grave problem exists in many parts of the nation.

The health consequences of dioxin contamination are appalling. It is known to cause a wide range of diseases, including cancer, skin, liver, and kidney ailments, and birth defects. These phenomena appear to be especially prevalent in Dzerzhinsk. Describing the city as "one of the dirtiest cities in Russia, maybe even the world," Aleksei Kisilev (one of the authors of the Greenpeace report) has declared: "There is not a single healthy person there."

Kisilev and his colleagues found that the concentration of toxic agents in the groundwater is 50 million times higher than the norm, and the average life expectancy in the city is less than fifty years—forty-two for men, forty-seven for women. Similarly, an American news correspondent observed in 1997, "Cancer and respiratory diseases are widespread. Infant mortality rates are among the highest in Russia, and a shocking three-quarters of Dzerzhinsk's babies are born with birth defects."

Residents of the city eat vegetables they raise in their garden plots, just as others do elsewhere in Russia. What is special about Dzerzhinsk, however, is that many of the plots are less than a kilometer from the local chemical combine, and the soil in which potatoes and other basic foods are grown contains thousands, if not millions, of times the "safe" level of dioxins. Addressing himself to the city's residents, Kisilev warned: "You and your family may well face a future of depressed immunity, cancer, birth defects, liver damage, skin diseases and loss of reproductive capacity," as well as progeny with a higher than average incidence of birth defects.

Greenpeace and other non-governmental organizations (NGOs) have had only limited success in obtaining data about the level of dioxin contamination in Moscow. A 1993 study, however, revealed levels at or above the Russian tolerance limit in 7.7 percent of samples of Moscow drinking water. (The maximum figure acceptable in Russia, it should be noted, is 2,000 times higher than the one that applies in the United States and Germany.) But the highest concentrations of airborne dioxins in Moscow were found near waste incinerators. These are used to dispose of waste containing polyvinyl chloride, a widely used plastic that gives off dioxins when burned.

Garbage incinerators have also been linked to problems that only mothers and their babies experience. Thus, in 1991, one Russian specialist pointed out that the level of dioxins in the breast milk of nursing mothers in the capital "constitutes a danger for newborns. It is safer to feed them artificial formula." Unfortunately, tests have also shown a high antibiotic content in the sterilized baby formula produced by plants in Moscow that manufacture dairy products for infants.[44]

The soil in and around the capital is no less contaminated than its air and water. In the early 1990s, a research team investigating produce from three state farms serving Moscow found dangerously high levels of heavy metals. Carrot samples contained cadmium levels that exceeded permissible concentrations by a factor of between three and eight, and for beets the levels were ten to fourteen times the acceptable norm. The presence of zinc in beets was two to three times the maximum permissible concentration.

Partly because of this circumstance, the quality of foodstuffs consumed by Muscovites leaves much to be desired—and does great damage to the population's health. One study, carried out in 1993, found that 32 percent of all food products sold through the city's retail trade network "[did] not meet medical and biological requirements." Perhaps the most unhealthy food category is dairy products. Of the milk delivered to Moscow and sold by retail outlets, fully 80 percent did not meet official standards. As for dairy products in general—milk, cream, sour cream, and cottage cheese—a government inspection carried out in December 1992 showed that the capital's seven dairies were selling items with two to three times the allowable level of antibiotics and toxic elements (lead, zinc, and arsenic).

In areas of Russia with high dioxin levels, Greenpeace found, the public health situation was often catastrophic. In the city of Chapaevsk, the heavily polluted site of a large pesticide complex in Samara Province, the death rate is 30–35 percent above the general figure for the region. In another center of the chemical industry, Novocheboksarsk on the upper Volga, Russian experts put the overall level of sickness at 50 percent above that for the country as a whole. Infant mortality in Novocheboksarsk is about three times the Russian average, with congenital defects the main cause.

Nuclear and Chemical Weapons Waste

In 1995, Feshbach wrote that Russia was "awash with nuclear materials."[45] Today, in many parts of the country, especially those with military research centers, nuclear power plants, or nuclear storage facilities, the related problems of radioactive waste accumulation and how to dispose of it have assumed terrifying proportions. These materials represent a clear and present danger to the health, welfare, and safety of the population.

What has Moscow done to alleviate the danger? Most of this waste was simply dumped into the Baltic, Barents, Kara, and White seas (as well as the Sea of Japan), buried in the ground, and burned in open areas in Udmurtia, Chapaevsk, Gornyi, and the Aral Steppe. And what have the authorities done with the by-products left from the manufacture of weapons (especially those of a chemical or bacteriological type) that have been discarded, or from existing stocks that are currently in storage? Very little, it would appear. According to the Ministry for Environmental Protection and Natural Resources,[46] at least 160,000 tons of chemical weapons, much of it captured from or discarded by the Germans, may be buried in Russian seas. The ministry says that these substances currently pose "a grave threat to ecology and to people's health."

The Chemical Weapons Convention has been ratified by more than one hundred states, but Russia is not among them. Unless and until these weapons are destroyed, they will continue to represent a health hazard, even if they are not used for military purposes. One 20-kilogram shell containing a toxic agent can destroy half the population of a city of 700,000. For residents of Novocheboksarsk and other places where chemical weapons used to be produced, this is not a hypothetical threat.[47] According to N. Antonova, the former head of the Novocheboksarsk health department, "In 1994 and 1995, we experienced an increase in the rate of premature deaths from cancer and cardiovascular disease among employees at Shop No. 83 at Khimprom [the Chemical Industry Production Association]," where chemical weapons were produced. Half the workers were women, many of whom were pregnant. "Now nearly 500 children are suffering because their mothers worked 'in hazardous production conditions.' "

Medical examinations indicated a depression of the body's immune system at the cellular level, "a kind of chemical AIDS," to use Antonova's expression. Employees had been forced to put in twice as many hours a day as their counterparts in the West. And, according to one former plant employee,

"Even though the gas masks and rubber suits people wore in the shop were supposed to be destroyed after every shift, in our shop they were just rinsed off and used until they wore out."

The situation is indeed ironic. As a Moscow journalist put it in 1997, "Over the decades that Soviet chemical weapons were produced, stored and destroyed, they did not kill a single enemy soldier; at the same time, thousands of our fellow citizens have been disabled." Unfortunately, she added, "today we do not have any good destruction procedures, instruments, MPC [maximum permissible concentration] standards, or laws protecting the country's environment and its citizens."

The first Soviet plutonium production reactor in the Kyshtym Complex, once called Cheliabinsk-40, is also located in central Russia. Between 1949 and 1956, liquid radioactive waste was discharged directly into the nearby Techa River. It was there that a major nuclear accident, the "Kyshtym Disaster," took place in 1957. The incident involved the explosion of a container overflowing with liquid radioactive waste, and it resulted in the so-called eastern radioactive trail, extending over more than 1,000 square kilometers in Cheliabinsk and Sverdlovsk provinces. In the course of just one year, 260,000 people were exposed to radiation, and even today, people continue to die from radiation illness in Cheliabinsk Province.[48]

The inhabitants of nineteen nearby villages were evacuated after the disaster—some 8,000 men, women, and children. But most citizens continued to live in the contaminated area. Today, in villages along the Techa, background radiation is far above acceptable levels, and the riverbed "contains a whole store of radionuclides." In 1996, local residents contended that "Everyone is sick, and every day one or two people are buried." Similarly, medical staff at the Cheliabinsk Radiological Center asserted sarcastically that their patients "have earned a place in the Guinness Book of Records with respect to the quantity of strontium accumulated in their bodies."

Today, the areas that confront the greatest hazards from nuclear waste are to be found in the Kola Peninsula (in the northwestern corner of the country), in St. Petersburg, and in Siberia and the Far East. A particular problem is the nuclear materials stored on ships and submarines.

The Kola Peninsula In mid-1996, Norway's Bellona Foundation released a report on radiological contamination in Murmansk and Arkhangelsk *oblasty*. These two provinces, which are located on the Kola Peninsula in northwest Russia, have the highest concentration of nuclear reactors (most of them military) in operation on the globe. According to the report, 182 such plants are currently functioning, and 135 are no longer in use; together, they constitute 18 percent of all the reactors in the world. Bellona also found that thirteen reactors, including six with their fuel assemblies still installed, had been dumped into the Kara Sea. Indeed, by mid-1996, between 3.1 million and 9 million curies of radioactive waste had been thrown into the Pacific

Ocean and the Kara, Barents, and Baltic seas—twice as much as the combined total from the rest of the world.[49]

The Russians have found it exceedingly difficult either to discard or process all that waste.[50] What they have done to date consists largely of placing it in various containers, most of which are corroding and thus putting citizens living or working nearby at risk. For example, at the Radon radioactive waste disposal site, 30 miles outside Murmansk, 400 cubic meters of low-level radioactive waste lie "buried in eight manholes secured by rusting padlocks and a barbed wire fence with holes big enough to walk through." In an interview with a visiting journalist, the facility's chief engineer revealed astonishing ignorance about the dangers literally lurking beneath his feet. He dismissed the concern expressed by local environmentalists that rain seeping through the top of the manholes might contaminate the groundwater supply. "Offering to open the lids of the disposal chutes to prove the radiation is not dangerous, he claims a stiff vodka is the best shield against contamination."[51] One can find occasional press reports of workers at nuclear dump sites on the Kola Peninsula being exposed to radiation that exceeds normal levels.[52]

St. Petersburg and Its Environs Nuclear waste stored in the Arctic and elsewhere represents a danger to the health not only of Russians but of their neighbors as well. The same is true of another on-land storage site, known simply as "Building No. 428," part of the nuclear power facility at Sosnovy Bor, on the outskirts of St. Petersburg. Located a mere 50 miles north of the Hermitage Museum and only a hundred yards from the Gulf of Finland, it is in no better condition than the plants farther north on the Kola Peninsula. Unlike its northern counterparts, however, it is situated next to a city of 5 million people.[53]

Water seeping into the building is causing cracks in its interior and exterior walls as well as the roof. In some places, "repairs" consist of filling holes with bricks. While this would be undesirable in any industrial structure, Building No. 428 is being used as a storage site for roughly 22,000 spent fuel assembly rods from the four obsolete and dangerous reactors of the Leningrad Nuclear Power Plant. These and other wastes are stored in a way that should shock both friends and foes of nuclear power: in some hallways, unsorted radioactive waste simply sits in plastic bags.[54]

The storage facility is full, and it is also falling apart. The water in its cooling pools is becoming more and more radioactive. Between May and November 1996, concentrations of Cesium-137 in it increased a hundred-fold. Even more alarming, water from the cooling pools themselves has been seeping into the groundwater under the building.

Virtually all of the nuclear power plants operating in the region are poorly maintained and have deteriorated in major ways. In addition, large quantities of nuclear waste have accumulated throughout the region. All of this led Marrti Ahtisaari, the former president of Finland, to describe the situation as "a time bomb for all of us" in the Baltic region. Ahtisaari asserted that 70–80 percent of all the pollution found in the Baltic Sea could be attributed to St. Petersburg alone.[55] (The city of St. Petersburg, together with Leningrad Province, which surrounds the city, also pours large quantities of untreated, non-nuclear waste into the Baltic Sea.)

Nuclear Materials aboard Vessels   Decommissioned ships, standing off-shore or alongside quays in major ports, are being used as repositories for spent atomic fuel.[56] This practice dates back to 1957, when the nuclear reactor aboard the Soviet icebreaker *Lenin* overheated and the ship was declared unusable. During the 1960s and 1970s, the fuel was removed and placed on board a transport vessel known as the *Lepse*—a few kilometers from the center of Murmansk, a city of 440,000 people. It remains there today, nothing more than a storage facility for 624 spent fuel assemblies. Because its cargo is so hazardous, the *Lepse* has been called "a ticking atomic bomb."

What can the authorities do to reduce the risk? Most of the waste materials are enclosed in steel containers, where the possibility of leakage—or even an explosion—grows with each passing day. Removing them for disposal elsewhere is both difficult and dangerous, not to mention expensive. But the need to act is pressing. The hold of the fifty-year-old *Lepse* is said to be so contaminated that it will not be safe for human contact for tens of thousands of years. According to Bellona, radioactivity on the ship's bridge is two or three times normal background levels.

Out-of-service nuclear submarines represent an additional problem. As of 1996, a total of eighty-eight such ships belonging to the Russian Navy's Northern Fleet were tied up in harbors near Murmansk. By November 1997, their number had grown to ninety, and today there are about one hundred.[57] Some are in very poor condition: one estimate says that 75 percent of them represent an immediate danger to the population of the entire region. The reactors on board many of these ships are filled with spent nuclear fuel, which the fleet does not have the money to remove. Although cooling mechanisms on the submarines are still operating, they could break down at any time. If this were to happen, the result could be an explosion and widespread radioactive contamination.

The same dangerous situation exists near Vladivostok, in the Russian Far East. As the place where the Soviet Pacific Fleet was based, the city was "protected" by a heavy concentration of ships, including scores of submarines. In 1993, the Russian Navy was severely criticized for dumping the radioactive waste from nuclear submarines into the Sea of Japan. Although officials promised to end the practice, they have not done so. In addition to continuing to dump nuclear waste into the sea, the navy has also been "drowning" decommissioned submarines in the same area.

Russian authorities may have the expertise, but they do not have the money to deal with the problem of nuclear waste storage and disposal. Moscow now wishes to dismantle the entire decommissioned submarine fleet, but it would cost hundreds of millions of dollars to do so. Lacking such funds, for years technicians managed to disassemble only five or six vessels annually. As of 1997, a total of sixteen of the nation's 156 retired nuclear submarines had been fully disassembled, and another hundred were scheduled to be dismantled by 2000. Today, more than 60 percent of the mothballed submarines still have fuel in their reactors, making them particularly prone to accidents.[58]

With the assistance of the American and Norwegian navies, Russia is trying to find better ways to dismantle its nuclear submarines, store solid radioactive waste, develop new technologies for treating liquid radioactive waste, and reduce the volume of all such material. Norway, Finland, Germany, the United States, and Russia have agreed to help improve radioactive waste treatment at the Murmansk Shipping Company, which is responsible for maintaining the security of the various ships which carry reactors aboard decaying vessels. The Russian Ministry of Atomic Energy claims to be recycling nuclear submarines "at an accelerated pace in recent years"—up from the former two or three annually to fifteen or twenty, "with financial assistance from foreign investors."[59]

To deal with the most urgent matter, the situation on board the *Lepse*, two European companies (SGN Eurysis of France and AEA Technology of the United Kingdom) have presented a number of innovative proposals for removing the waste. Provided with the equivalent of $9.7 million by a consortium of Nordic countries along with France and the European Commission, the two firms are exploring the possibility of using robots to do the job. Germany, too, is investing in the recycling of nuclear-powered submarines withdrawn from the Russian Navy.[60]

Alcohol Abuse

The excessive use of alcoholic beverages continues unabated and still has an adverse effect on the country's population. One cannot help but agree with Walter D. Connor, an American sociologist who in 1972 posited the existence of a Russian "drinking culture" that, "because of its extreme permissiveness both on quantity to be imbibed and on the situation and locations in which drinking is accepted or encouraged, leads to heavy drinking and frequent drunkenness."[61]

Official statistics put the annual per capita consumption of absolute alcohol (i.e., 100 percent or 200-proof alcohol, a statistical construct rather than the beverage of choice) at 15 liters, or 16.5 quarts. This figure includes the entire population, not just those over the age of eighteen, which means that the "drinking-age population" consumes approximately 30 quarts of absolute alcohol—or some 75 half-liter bottles of 80-proof vodka—each year. It also appears to include not only legally distilled beverages, but also illegal *samogon*, or "moonshine."

Since alcohol contributes to population mortality both directly (as in cases of alcohol poisoning and certain other diseases) and indirectly (when alcohol aggravates already existing health problems), it is not possible to put a precise figure on the number of deaths that alcohol consumption "causes" or to which it contributes. Dr. Aleksandr Nemtsov of the Institute of Psychiatry has noted that about one-fifth of all persons who die with a diagnosis of cardiovascular disease had alcohol in their blood at the time of death, and the blood of 11 percent of the men and 3 percent of the women contained a "lethal amount" of alcohol. According to Nemtsov, the number of lives lost because of alcohol consumption is 500,000–700,000, and alcohol is "responsible" for 30 percent of all deaths.[62]

According to a survey on substance abuse among minors, carried out by the Russian Health Ministry, alcoholism "is getting younger in Russia, with teenagers being introduced to alcoholic beverages at the age of 13–14, on average," and with three in every four fifteen- to sixteen-year-olds "consuming alcohol on a regular basis."[63]

Studies indicate that the consumption of bootlegged or low-quality liquor causes greater health damage and leads to a more severe form of alcoholism. At the same time, of course, high-quality alcoholic beverages, if consumed to excess, may be equally destructive, although the pace of destruction is slower.

Russian commentators say that alcoholism has increased significantly since the unraveling of the USSR, but it is extremely difficult to obtain accurate figures on the number of alcoholics and on how much they or other Russians drink. According to Nemtsov, the average annual level of alcohol consumed in 1999 was 14.6 liters per person, twice the level recorded in 1990. In 2003, Natalia Rimashevskaia, director of the Russian Academy of Sciences' Institute for the Study of Social and Economic Problems of the Population, said the official figure was 16.5, but in view of the recent effort to wean people from vodka and have them switch to beer (a campaign which has increased beer consumption without affecting vodka consumption), the true number "may well be approaching the 20-liter mark."[64] Official data suggest that there are 1,500–2,000 alcoholics per 100,000 people, but many specialists say the true figure is three or four times higher.[65] There is all but universal agreement that per capita consumption is higher in Russia than in any other country in the world.

Nemtsov calls alcohol "the main culprit" in the decline in life expectancy in Russia, especially among males; corroboration comes from a study which found that two-thirds of all men age twenty to fifty-five who died were drunk at the time of death.[66] In Russia, alcoholism and the diseases associated with it are the third leading cause of death; only cardiovascular diseases and cancer take more lives. In fact, given the close correlation between heavy drinking on the one hand and cardiovascular problems and cancer on the other, many medical specialists are inclined to rank alcoholism first or second. Some have even termed alcoholism "the great killer," noting that the life expectancy of an alcoholic is typically ten to fifteen years lower than that of a non-drinker or social drinker.[67]

Some analysts contend that the the poor quality of alcoholic beverages available today (especially illegally produced *samogon*) contributes even more to health-related problems than does the quantity of beverages consumed. In 2001, some 37,824 people died of accidental alcohol poisoning—largely because they consumed contaminated vodka. The figure for 2000 was 33,979, which means that the death rate per 100,000 persons rose from 23.5 in 2000 to 26.2 in 2001.[68] In 2002, the most recent year for which data are available, the number of Russians who died of alcohol poisoning rose to about 40,000—a striking contrast with the United States, where a few hundred persons die of this cause annually.[69]

Drug Abuse

The remarkable upsurge in the use of illegal drugs over the past decade or so has fueled Russia's health problems and exacerbated its demographic crisis. Since 1999, the number of "drug users" has been put at "close to 2 million,"[70] 3–5 million,[71] 3 million,[72] and 2.5–4 million.[73]

The number of "drug addicts" has been said in recent years to be 3 million,[74] "at least 3 million,"[75] "more than 1.5 million,"[76] "over 3 million,"[77] "at least 2.5 million,"[78] and 4 million.[79] Various figures have been offered for the number of users, abusers, or addicts being treated—or simply "registered" with public health or police agencies. In August 2002, a health ministry official declared that the non-medical use of drugs and psychotropic substances had "skyrocketed more than 20-fold in 10 years."[80] A year later, a Duma deputy leading the fight against drugs said that almost 3 percent of the population were "registered drug addicts" (*narkomany*). The head of the Ministry of Health organization designed to combat HIV/AIDS responded skeptically, saying that the "real number" was six to eight times higher.[81]

Confusion about the meaning of these various figures stems heavily from the sloppy use of language: Russian sources often fail to distinguish between drugs and narcotics; drug use, drug abuse, and drug addiction; and injecting drug use (IDU) and other forms of drug abuse. Thus, a February 2000 report by the health ministry's chief expert on drugs, indicating that some 230,000 "drug addicts" are hospitalized annually in Russia,[82] leaves unanswered the question of how many other "addicts" remain unhospitalized.

Whatever the real number of drug users, including IDUs, in Russia, it is clear that public health and internal affairs officials regard the increase in drug use as threatening social stability and even national security. On June 26,

2002, for example, Nikolai Solovev, first deputy secretary of the Russian Security Council, said that drug trafficking is "more than a threat to the country's national security."[83] On the same day, a member of the "expert group on drug issues" declared: "The drug abuse problem in Russia is a direct threat to the security of the country, individuals, families and society."[84]

Of particular concern is the upsurge of IDU, fueled primarily by cheap heroin that is placing many more drug abusers at risk of contracting HIV/AIDS. The Customs Service contends that heroin, which enters Russia largely from Central Asia, has become "the unconditional leader of the Russian drug market."[85] However, groups frequently share syringes or needles to inject "Russian heroin," a cheap homemade mixture of liquid opium and vinegar or acetic anhydride. The substance often has a cloudy, muddy color; to clarify it, users add several drops of their own blood to the "communal" pot from which they all partake. They then inject it into their own bodies, along with HIV or traces of any other communicable disease present in the group. Until very recently, roughly 90 percent of all new HIV infections were brought on by sixteen- to twenty-nine-year-old IDUs.[86]

Sexually Transmitted Infections

Russia has experienced a veritable explosion of sexually transmitted infections (STIs), a development with horrendous consequences, especially to young people. In April 2002, a leading physician noted: "When we were studying 30 years ago, we did not come across congenital syphilis. We first encountered it 10 years ago. Now students do not regard this as anything very much out of the ordinary." The result is seen, in part, in the huge number of birth defects afflicting Russian infants: in 2001 alone, 14,000 of the 20,000 children who died before reaching their first birthday lost their chance to survive because their mothers suffered from one or another STI.[87]

The largest risk group for STIs is made up of children and teenagers, the principal "beneficiaries" of the sexual revolution. The incidence of syphilis among girls under the age of fourteen increased 140 times during the period 1990–97, and it continues to rise, though at a slower pace. Indeed, a leading doctor contends, "It is not prostitutes but adolescents who constitute the largest risk group for syphilis."[88]

Between 1990 and 1994, the number of cases of syphilis rose eight-fold, from five to forty cases per 100,000 persons, while the incidence of gonorrhea grew by a factor of ten. Perhaps the most important factors explaining these developments are the "sexual revolution" and "the impoverishment of the population and a pronounced stratification into very rich and very poor." Not only have the latter led to feelings of hopelessness, but "impoverishment is what made women hit the streets. The main reason for engaging in prostitution is the impossibility of earning money in any other way, and the need to feed one's children." According to data gathered in Moscow, one of every four prostitutes working in the capital has children.[89]

HIV/AIDS

Between January 1, 1987 (when the AIDS virus first appeared in the USSR), and December 31, 2000, a total of 83,054 individuals were diagnosed as HIV-positive.[90] In 2001, the total registered cases doubled, reaching 177,354 at the end of 2001.[91] In August 2002, Vadim Pokrovskii, head of the Federal Center for the Prevention and Treatment of HIV/AIDS (the AIDS Center), put the figure for registered HIV-positive citizens at 206,000,[92] and at the end of September 2003 it had risen to "more than 250,000."[93]

But the figure for those "registered" with the state is misleading. Experts acknowledge that to determine the actual number of HIV-positive individuals, some sort of multiplier—suggestions cluster around six to ten—must be used, since those persons most likely to become infected avoid contact with the authorities. In particular, IDUs who are susceptible to arrest simply because they use drugs evade testing. WHO puts the "true number" of Russian infections at seven to ten times the figure for those officially registered,[94] while Pokrovskii uses a multiplier varying between six and ten. In July 2002, when reporting that 205,000 cases of HIV had been registered, he added that the total number infected "could be eight to ten times higher."[95] On July 5, 2002, the *real* number who were HIV-positive was said to be 1.2 million.[96] Today, the figure one encounters most frequently is 1.5 million—some 650,000 more than can be found in the United States, a nation with a population twice that of Russia. According to Pokrovskii, despite years of public health authorities focusing on "screening" the population, only 16 percent of all citizens have, in fact, been tested for HIV.[97]

More important, Russia has the world's highest rate of growth for new HIV cases—although the rate allegedly has begun to decline.[98] It is unclear whether the slowdown is real or the authorities are underreporting new cases. In 1996–2001, the number of new infections increased on average by 2.4 times annually; in 2003, the incidence of *recorded* HIV cases is unlikely even to double.[99] In January 2001, Pokrovskii predicted that there would be 2 million cases by the end of the year; by 2005, he suggested the total could reach 5 million.[100] More recently, he has suggested that by the end of the current decade, somewhere between 5.4 and 14.5 million would be infected—possibly 10 percent of the population.[101]

We have already noted that roughly 90 percent of all new infections were attributed to IDUs, but Russian analysts recently have detected a change. In July 2001, First Deputy Minister of Health Gennadi Onishchenko declared that "Heterosexual transmission of AIDS is increasing."[102] In 2000, people infected by male-female intercourse represented roughly 6 percent of all new cases (Pokrovskii puts the figure at 4.7 percent); in 2001, the number had grown to 12 percent, and reports for the first nine months of 2003 ranged as high as 40 percent.[103]

Data from Samara Province suggest that the number of new cases attributable to sexual transmission may, in fact, turn out to be far higher. In October 2003, the province statistical office noted that the number of women in Samara infected with HIV as a result of sexual contact has risen from 2 percent in 1998 to 50 percent in the first three-quarters of 2003. According to the head of the province public health department, doctors "now expect a significant rise in the number of people infected with HIV."[104] The situation in other regions likely will parallel that of Samara.

In Russia, as in America, early initiation into sexual activity, having multiple sex partners, practicing unsafe sex, and being an IDU are powerful risk factors for contracting HIV. One study of Moscow secondary school students, carried out in the mid-1990s, found that 34.9 percent of all sexually active youngsters had had four or more sex partners, and 5 percent were IDUs. "Given the incubation period of up to ten years from the onset of the HIV infection to full-blown AIDS," the investigators observed, "many HIV infections were introduced by sexual practices during adolescence."[105]

Although high-quality condoms are now widely available nationwide (a dramatic change since the Soviet era), few men use them. A recent survey of fifteen- to eighteen-year-olds in St. Petersburg found that 40 percent of sexually active students had never used a condom.[106] Another investigation, carried out among students in vocational schools, determined that "only 12 percent consistently used condoms and 74 percent rarely or never used condoms during sex"; 58.3 percent had not used a condom the last time they had sexual intercourse.[107]

Perhaps 25 percent of female sex workers are IDUs;[108] other sources put the number of prostitutes in Moscow and Volgograd who are IDUs at 25–35 percent.[109] Toward the end of 2000, the AIDS Center suggested that 15 percent of the 70,000 sex workers in the capital were HIV-positive. This led Arkadiusz Majszyk, the UN representative in Moscow, to say, "that is 15 percent of the 70,000 women who will be out there tonight. Which means their clients get it and pass it on to their families, and back to other prostitutes, and so on." Now, of course, after homosexuals, bisexuals, prostitutes, and IDUs have been infected, the virus is moving into the general population. It is confined largely to young people: Onishchenko has said that 70–80 percent of all carriers are between the ages of fifteen and twenty-nine.[110]

While both men and women are carriers, the government is increasingly concerned about young males about to undertake military service or already serving in the armed forces. During the first nine months of 2003, for example, approximately 5,000 young men were rejected for military service because they were HIV-positive, while another 500 soldiers were discharged from the service because they contracted the virus while serving.[111]

Still, the government spends very little money on HIV/AIDS education and prevention. In 1996, the Ministry of Health received no funds to carry out such programs. In 1997, the federal budget called for a mere $8 million to be spent on AIDS prevention and treatment, and in 2002, Russia's entire anti-AIDS budget came to about $6 million, of which $3.3 million were assigned to treat those with full-blown AIDS. Pokrovskii estimated that these funds were enough to finance the treatment of 300 individuals, while another "several dozen people [were] being treated at their own expense."[112] In September 2003, he asserted that three to four thousand citizens needed treatment, but the budget would permit only 300–500 individuals to receive proper medication. (He added that $65 million would be required annually for treatment and prevention programs, while the federal budget for all AIDS-related efforts came to less than $4 million.)[113]

For the period 2002–06, public health agencies have allocated 2.7 billion rubles ($90 million) to fight AIDS ($24.5 million from the federal budget and $65.5 from regional and local authorities). This includes a modest amount for medicines, enough to treat about 1,500 persons with HIV or AIDS. If implemented, the plan would entail a considerable increase in expenditures—to an average of $18 million a year. Still, as one health publication put it, "treatment [of HIV/AIDS] remains a luxury."[114]

In October 2003, Russia signed an agreement with the World Bank; according to the terms of the loan, the bank will lend Russia a total of $150 million to combat both tuberculosis and AIDS. The project proposed by the bank will increase three-fold the total sum assigned by the Russian government to deal with the emerging epidemic.[115] Only two months later, the Global Fund made a five-year grant of $89 million to several NGOs in Russia to combat HIV/AIDS. The groups, both Russian and Western, will focus their energies on prevention programs directed at young people and, to a lesser extent, on treatment.[116]

Although Moscow's political will to deal with the situation seems insubstantial, Russian and foreign non-governmental organizations have tried to curb the spread of HIV. There are programs that provide sex education, support for infected individuals; needle-exchanges, and distribution of free condoms. Attempts to carry anti-drug and anti-AIDS messages to youngsters through the mass media have been fewer: they have encountered resistance from the Russian Orthodox Church and other conservative institutions or politicians

CONCLUSION

The depopulation of Russia seems destined to worsen in the coming years, with major implications for the military, labor force, personal and societal health, and even national security. Relatively few people have died of AIDS—analysts put the figure at about 5,000 to date. Lacking antiretroviral drugs, virtually all those who are HIV-positive will die within a decade. The government has shown almost no political will, an indispensable prerequisite for slowing the spread of the disease. Neither the politicians nor religious leaders, who are highly influential regarding such issues as sex education, condom distribution, and needle exchanges, seem willing to take the necessary measures to lead their country out of the cul-de-sac in which it finds itself. The record with respect to drug and alcohol abuse, smoking, and the spread of disease is equally discouraging. At the same time, passivity and fatalism are pervasive among the general population. As the head of one Russian NGO put it in 2003, "People are used to thinking that health is the responsibility of doctors, not a result of their [own] behavior."[117]

The situation with respect to mental health and its treatment also contributes to Russia's health crisis. Approximately 7.5 million citizens seek psychiatric help annually. The incidence of psychoses increased 92.3 percent, schizophrenia 29.2 percent, and mental disorders as a whole by 41.5 percent over the past decade. Every year, roughly 60,000 people commit suicide, and two-thirds of these cases are regarded as a consequence of some sort of mental disorder. Treatment facilities and, more generally, government support are grossly inadequate.[118]

One journalist has described Russia's mental hospitals as places that are "reminiscent of orphanages as shown in horror movies. There is no money to treat or feed patients." They are, she went on, "miserable and squalid, are so overcrowded, and their patients . . . so starved that fainting at their sight is a natural reaction." Although the principal reason behind this circumstance is a combination of government indifference and a lack of funds (which may, in practice, be one and the same thing), officials tend to place the blame on other, darker forces. For example, according to the director of Moscow's Scientific Research Institute of Psychiatry, "All our efforts come up against the opposition of the Scientologists, who have found a way into the State Duma. . . . The deputies who had pledged support now refuse to talk to us."[119]

Similarly, the chief doctor of St. Petersburg's largest psychiatric hospital has pointed to the allegedly nefarious efforts of a charitable organization known as the Civil Commission on Human Rights—linked with the Church of Scientology. He asserts, "They distribute enormous numbers of leaflets with the same content: 'Mental hospitals must not be given a kopeck, for psychiatrists are murderers and their medicine is poison.'" In point of fact, some mental institutions, finding themselves without the money to treat (or even to feed, clothe, and house) patients, have simply released them. The journalist mentioned above has pointed out that food rations in psychiatric hospitals "are rather reminiscent of torture by hunger"; furthermore, all but

a handful of them "cannot afford modern pharmaceuticals, while old preparations [that are still used] often injure patients, rather than cure them."[120]
To be sure, Russia is now in its fourth year of economic growth, and the
nation possesses an educated and skilled labor force, as well as a community
of scientists, who could ameliorate the medical problems that have led to the
demographic crisis. It is not inconceivable that the self-destructive habits that
literally consume many Russians can be alleviated. What is needed is leadership, money, and the recognition that the situation in the sphere of public
health is doing untold damage. Russians sometimes are accused of thinking
only in the short term, but a long-term perspective is indispensable. If current
trends continue, the number of Russians will decline; they run the risk of
being overrun by predatory neighbors or submerged by more efficient economies, and Russia may literally find itself on the Endangered Species List.

NOTES

1. *Demograficheskii ezhegodnik Rossii* (Moscow: Goskomstat, 2000), 19.
2. *Novye izvestiia*, July 17, 2001; RosBusiness Consulting, August 14, 2002.
3. Cited in Murray Feshbach, "Russia's Population Meltdown," *Wilson Quarterly* 25, no. 1 (Winter, 2001): 15.
4. Rosbalt Press Service, October 16, 2003.
5. RosBusiness Consulting, August 14, 2002. In recent years, net in-migration
has fallen dramatically. In 1997, immigration compensated for more than 45 percent
of natural attrition, but in the first ten months of 2001, the figure was below 8 percent. See *Vremia MN*, January 10, 2002. The numbers today are negligible in comparison with the early post-Soviet period.
6. *Rossiiskaia gazeta*, August 4, 2001.
7. *Russkaia liniia* (St. Petersburg), October 29, 2003.
8. See pravda.ru website, March 19, 2002.
9. This section is based on ITAR-TASS, March 16, 2001; *Rossiiskaia gazeta*,
August 3, 2001; and Interfax, March 27, 2002.
10. *Novye izvestiia*, February 28, 2002; RosBusiness Consulting, August 14, 2002.
11. *Novye izvestiia*, February 28, 2002. More recently, a prominent demographer
predicted that the country's population would be 100 million in 2050. *Novye izvestiia*, October 9, 2003.
12. See, e.g., Mark G. Field and Judyth L. Twigg, eds., *Russia's Torn Safety Nets*
(New York: St. Martin's Press, 2000).
13. RosBusiness Consulting, August 14, 2002.
14. *Moscow Times*, June 25, 2003.
15. *Moskovskaia pravda*, October 29, 2003.
16. *Rossiiskaia gazeta*, November 24, 2001.
17. *Argumenty i fakty*, July 23, 2003.
18. Rosbalt Press Service, September 5, 2003.
19. *Izvestiia*, August 19, 2003.

20. ITAR-TASS, September 8, 2003.

21. *Izvestiia*, August 19, 2003.

22. Interfax, September 10, 2003.

23. *Demograficheskii ezhegodnik Rossii*, 183; U.S. Central Intelligence Agency, *World Factbook*, available at the CIA website.

24. This section is drawn from *Meditsinskaia gazeta*, July 3, 2002.

25. *Moskovskaia pravda*, October 31, 2003.

26. *Novye izvestiia*, February 28, 2002; RosBusiness Consulting, August 14, 2002. *Moskovskii Komsomolets*, August 15, 2002, provides slightly different numbers for current life expectancy. See also *Novye izvestiia*, October 9, 2003.

27. *Pravda*, January 25, 1995,

28. Murray Feshbach and Alfred Friendly Jr., *Ecocide in the USSR* (New York: Basic Books, 1992). See also Murray Feshbach, *Ecological Disaster* (New York: Twentieth Century Fund Press, 1995), 70–71; and David E. Powell, "Environmental Problems in Moscow," in *The Soviet Empire Reconsidered*, ed. Sanford R. Lieberman et al. (Boulder, CO: Westview Press, 1994).

29. For more recent complaints about air pollution in major Russian cities, see ITAR-TASS, September 19, 2003, and October 13, 2003.

30. Although his meaning was clear, his language and his use of mathematics were considerably less so. His exact words were, "our health depends on the environment by approximately 30 percent." *Rossiiskaia gazeta*, June 9, 1994.

31. *Novaia ezhednevniaia gazeta*, September 6, 1995.

32. The following is derived from Feshbach and Friendly, *Ecocide*; Feshbach, *Ecological Disaster*; and Powell, "Environmental Problems in Moscow."

33. *Selskaia zhizn*, March 12, 1994.

34. *Moscow Times*, October 9, 2003.

35. Siberia, once a land of pure water, seems to have experienced unusually heavy damage. In Tiumen and Tomsk provinces, as well as in the Khanty-Mansi and Yamal-Nenets Autonomous Regions, water pollution exceeds accepted levels by a factor of ten.

36. *Segodnia*, December 3, 1997.

37. That same year, Gosepidemnadzor made much the same point, announcing that the only drinking water available for half the country's residents is "of poor quality"; *Segodnia*, December 3, 1997.

38. The following discussion relies on Powell, "Environmental Problems in Moscow."

39. *NTV*, September 18, 2003, as reported in BBC Monitoring Service, September 18, 2003.

40. *Sunday Times* (London), December 16, 1996.

41. ITAR-TASS, May 20, 1996.

42. *Selskaia zhizn*, March 12, 1994.

43. This and the following paragraph rely on Feshbach, *Ecological Disaster*, 70–71.

44. This discussion of the capital's ecological difficulties is taken from Powell, "Environmental Problems in Moscow."

45. Feshbach, *Ecological Disaster*, 19. The following discussion relies on pp. 19–21 of this volume.

46. Interfax, December 7, 1995.

47. This section is drawn from *Izvestiia*, October 17, 1997, and *NTV-Mir*, reprinted in BBC Monitoring Service, October 21, 2003.

48. This paragraph and the one that follows rely on *NTV*, July 15, 1996, in U.S. Foreign Broadcast Information Service, FBIS-TEN-95–008, and *Segodnia*, March 31, 1997.

49. Colin Woodard, "A Terrible Communist Legacy," *Transition*, July 26, 1996. For an earlier report on Bellona's reaction to plans to dispose of submarine reactors in the Kara Sea, see *Izvestiia*, March 23, 1994.

50. For details, see *Nezavisimaia gazeta—regiony*, October 2003, and the *Independent* (London), October 23, 2003.

51. *Financial Times*, September 13–14, 1997, and BBC Monitoring Service, October 15, 2003.

52. See, e.g., *Moscow Times*, September 25, 2003.

53. For Finnish expressions of concern about toxic waste at Sosnovy Bor and plans to assist Russia in improving conditions, see *Chemical News and Intelligence*, October 14, 2003.

54. *St. Petersburg Times*, November 18–24, 1996.

55. *Financial Times*, November 25, 1996. The former president went as far as to call the threat posed by Russian pollution Finland's greatest security problem. As he put it, "I would be much happier if I could clean up the Baltic and swim in the sea than join NATO."

56. The following discussion is drawn from *Financial Times*, September 13–14, 1997, and *Stolichnaia vecherniaia gazeta*, October 2, 2003.

57. *Moscow Times*, September 25, 2003.

58. A member of the Russian Academy of Sciences has stated: "Such a submarine may leak radioactivity and its reactor may spin out of control, leading to an uncontrolled chain reaction."

59. BBC Monitoring Service, April 22, 2003.

60. BBC Monitoring Service, October 10, 2003.

61. Walter D. Connor, *Deviance in Soviet Society* (New York: Columbia University Press, 1972), 39–42. Quotation on p. 41.

62. *Izvestiia*, October 1, 2003.

63. This paragraph and the one that follows are derived from *RIA-Novosti*, September 1, 2003.

64. *Novye izvestiia*, October 9, 2003.

65. For further evidence to support this hypothesis, see *Izvestiia*, July 31 and August 6, 1997, and *Segodnia*, August 7, 1997.

66. *Pravda*, January 25, 1995.

67. See N. Ia. Kopyt, *Profilaktika alkogolizma* (Moscow, 1986); I. N. Piatnitskaia, *Zloupotreblenie alkogolem i nachalnaia stadiia alkogolizma* (Moscow, 1988); Boris M. Segal, *The Drunken Society* (New York: Hippocrene Books, 1990), 329–46; Stephen White, *Russia Goes Dry: Alcohol, State and Society* (Cambridge: Cambridge University Press, 1996); and numerous articles in the medical journal *Zdravookhranenie Rossiiskoi Federatsii*. Some years ago, a leading Soviet jurist argued (exaggerating for effect) that the destructive force of alcoholism could only be compared with that of nuclear

weapons. See Iu. M. Tkachevskii, *Pravovye mery borby s pianstvom* (Moscow, 1974), 174.

68. See RIA Oreanda at www.rambler.ru/db/health/news.html (July 2, 2002).

69. *Izvestiia*, September 27, 2003.

70. *Nezavisimaia gazeta*, August 16, 2002.

71. *Segodnia*, May 26, 1999. The Ministry of Health added, however, that the actual number could be as much as 50 percent higher. See *Voprosy narkologii*, 1999, no. 1.

72. Interfax, February 21, 2001.

73. Interfax, April 10, 2001.

74. Interfax, August 6, 2002.

75. Interfax, December 28, 2000.

76. Interfax, July 8, 2001.

77. Interfax, March 19, 2002.

78. *RIA Novosti*, May 23, 2002.

79. Izvestia.ru website, June 26, 2002.

80. *Rossiiskaia gazeta*, June 26, 2002.

81. *Novye izvestiia*, September 30, 2003.

82. Interfax, August 6, 2002.

83. Izvestia.ru website, June 26, 2002.

84. See *Rossiiskaia gazeta*, June 26, 2002.

85. Interfax, June 26, 2002.

86. Interfax, June 26, 2001. Almost none of them are provided with "serious treatment," however. State medical institutions lack the funds needed to do a proper job, which means that only wealthy people get proper medical attention—usually in private clinics located abroad. *Moscow Times*, February 27, 2002.

87. Russian Public Television (ORT), 2002, reported in BBC Monitoring Service, April 15, 2002.

88. *Nezavisimaia gazeta*, February 13, 2002.

89. See David E. Powell, "The Problem of HIV/AIDS," in Field and Twigg, *Russia's Torn Safety Nets*; and U.S. National Intelligence Council, *The Global Infectious Disease Threat and Its Implications for the United States* (Washington, D.C.: U.S. Department of State, 2000).

90. Interfax, March 11, 2002.

91. *New York Times*, July 21, 2002.

92. Interfax, August 6, 2002.

93. *Farmatsevticheskii vestnik*, September 30, 2003.

94. Interfax, August 6, 2002.

95. ITAR-TASS, July 31, 2002.

96. *Trud*, July 5, 2002.

97. *Novye izvestiia*, September 30, 2003.

98. *Izvestiia*, October 16, 2003.

99. See, e.g., *Izvestiia*, October 16, 2003; *Vremia novostei*, November 28, 2002; and *Farmatsevticheskii vestnik*, September 30, 2003.

100. *Trud*, July 5, 2002.

101. *Novye izvestiia*, September 30, 2003.

102. ITAR-TASS, March 13, 2001; Yuri A. Amirkhanian et al., "AIDS Knowledge, Attitudes, and Behavior in Russia: Results of a Population-Based, Random-Digit Telephone Survey in St. Petersburg," *International Journal of STD and AIDS* 12 (2001): 50–57.

103. *Novye izvestiia*, September 30, 2003; *San Francisco Chronicle*, July 28, 2002.

104. *Nezavisimaia gazeta*, October 6, 2003.

105. Wayne W. Westhoff et al., "Sexual Risk-Taking by Muscovite Youth Attending School," *Journal of School Health* 66, no. 3 (1996): 102.

106. I. Lunin et al., "Adolescent Sexuality in Saint Petersburg, Russia," *AIDS* 13 (1999): 741–49.

107. Seth C. Kalichman et al., "The Emerging AIDS Crisis in Russia: Review of Enabling Factors and Prevention Needs," *International Journal of STD and AIDS* 11 (2000): 71–75.

108. *Zhurnal mikrobiologii, epidemiologii i immunobiologii* 1 (January–February, 1999): 102–4.

109. Cited in *Drugs, AIDS, and Harm Reduction: How to Slow the HIV Epidemic in Eastern Europe and the Former Soviet Union* (New York: Soros Foundation, Open Society Institute, 2001).

110. *Moscow Times*, September 11, 2003.

111. *Novye izvestiia*, September 30, 2003.

112. ITAR-TASS, July 31 and August 1, 2002. Elsewhere, Pokrovskii has said that 500 of the 2,500 individuals with full-blown AIDS are receiving "adequate treatment." ITAR-TASS, July 31, 2002.

113. *Novye izvestiia*, September 30, 2003. The World Health Organization estimates that 10 percent of the officially reported 250,000 HIV-positive citizens of Russia are receiving "adequate treatment." *Izvestiia*, October 16, 2003.

114. *Farmatsevticheskii vestnik*, September 30, 2003.

115. ITAR-TASS, October 8, 2003.

116. AIDS-Infoshare website (in Russian), December 14, 2003.

117. *Moscow Times*, October 8, 2003.

118. *Izvestiia*, October 3, 2003.

119. *Izvestiia*, October 3, 2003.

120. *Izvestiia*, October 3, 2003.

Part Three

THE ECONOMY

Chapter Seven

Putin and the Economy

James R. Millar

In April of 2001, after a little more than a year in office as president, Vladimir Putin's First Annual Address to the Federal Assembly stressed his commitment to stability. His aim was to calm public expectations of a continuation of the turbulent and revolutionary character of the previous decade under President Yeltsin. Public apprehension, he said, was based on:

> [T]he well known logic that revolution is usually followed by counter-revolution, reforms by counter-reforms and then by a search for those guilty of revolutionary misdeeds and by punishment, all the more so since Russia's own historic experience is rich in such examples. But I think that it is time to say firmly that this cycle has ended. There will be no revolution or counter-revolution. Firm and economically supported state stability is a good thing for Russia and its people and it is long since we learnt to live according to this normal human logic.

A little more than two years later, on May 16th, 2003, President Putin's State of the Nation address spelled out his dream of what Russia could and should become:

> Russia should be and will be a country with a developed civil society and stable democracy. Russia will guarantee full human rights, civil liberties and political freedom. Russia should be and will be a country with a competitive market economy, a country where property rights are reliably protected and where economic freedom makes it possible for people to work honestly and to earn without fear of restriction.

If one judges Putin by these official statements, he is clearly a leader committed to democratization, civil society and the development of a competitive market economy. He also appears to subscribe to the principles of political and economic stability and to gradual reform as well. Putin's actions, however, have been more ambiguous, and his commitment to the institutions necessary for the attainment of democracy and market economics less than wholehearted.

The performance of the Russian economy on Putin's watch since 2000 has been the best since 1992, when radical reforms were introduced by Boris Yeltsin and Yegor Gaidar. GDP grew by more than 9 percent in 2000. Inflation was tolerable, about 21 percent, and official reserves of gold and hard currency increased from about $13 billion to $28 billion. The recovery from the financial crisis of 1998 was due largely to an increase in the price of oil exports, the favorable effect of the 1998 devaluation of the ruble on domestic industry, and the negative impact of higher prices on imports. The recovery continued in 2001 and 2002, but at the lesser rates of 5 and 4.3 percent respectively, and inflation declined to 15 percent. Prospects for 2003 are for steady rather than faster growth, despite Putin's pressure to average 8 percent. Real average wages, however, increased 7.8 percent in 2000 and another 25.9 percent in 2001. Real wages remain almost 20 percent below the level of 1998, and the benefits provided by the cheaper ruble continue to diminish over time. Moreover, another oil price boost is highly unlikely. Indeed, prices may decline. In fact, recently Russia has been increasing oil production and exports, thereby undercutting OPEC attempts to maintain the world market price of oil products.[1]

President Vladimir Putin can view economic developments with some satisfaction, therefore, but it must be tempered by the fact that the price of oil is not controlled by Russia and cannot be credited to his administration. Moreover, the devaluation of the ruble took place before Putin became president. There is no assurance, therefore, that the relatively happy current state of the economy can be sustained for long, especially since economic issues have not been given high priority on Putin's action list. Yet, the promotion of domestic and foreign investment is critical if Russia is to sustain an acceptable rate of growth and modernization. Progress toward these goals is unlikely until reforms in corporate governance, secure legal protections of property rights, protection from economic corruption and predation, and rational land tenure systems are established. Admittedly, none of these ends will be easy to accomplish in Russia, but progress has been much slower than is necessary to avoid a decline in growth rates and stagnation in industrial modernization.

Putin's main efforts to date have been devoted to achieving political stability, maintaining the territorial and political integrity of Russia, the projection of Russia's influence into the former Soviet republics and allies, and the reestablishment of domestic *poryadok*, or order. Of these goals, the last appears to have had priority, as one might have expected of a former officer in the KGB. The vigorous pursuit of *poryadok* has led democratic forces in Russia and abroad to worry that Putin is seeking to undermine Russia's fragile democracy and establish an autocratic state. In his early tenure, Putin has focused more upon accumulating power than upon its exercise. This is a sign of insecurity in a leader who, above all else, intends to remain in power. Is there a real possibility that Putin could reestablish a variant of Stalinism and, with it, a return to central planning? Or will he press more firmly for the continuation of market reforms? The answer lies partly in an examination of the fundamental trends in Soviet-Russian history and partly in a resolution of the thus far ambiguous character of Putin himself.

THREE WHO UNMADE A REVOLUTION

> Hegel remarks somewhere that all facts and personages of great importance in world history occur, as it were, twice. He forgot to add: the first time as tragedy, the second as farce. Men make their own history, but they do not make it just as they please; they do not make it under circumstances chosen by themselves, but under circumstances directly encountered, given, and transmitted from the past. The tradition of all the dead generations weighs like a nightmare on the brain of the living.
>
> —Karl Marx, "The Eighteenth Brumaire of Louis Bonaparte"[2]

Putin has inherited from Nikita Khrushchev, Mikhail Gorbachev, and Boris Yeltsin an intermittent but long and consistent policy of de-Stalinizing the Soviet social system. His actions and prospects for action are necessarily constrained by those prior efforts. A Putin seeking to be Stalin would be the farce to the Stalinist tragedy. It would be a mistake, therefore, to evaluate Putin's ambitions and prospects in the light of Yeltsin's heritage alone. The stage for de-Stalinization was set by Khrushchev. Gorbachev played Hamlet. And Yeltsin brought down the curtain. As the quote from Marx above suggests, these men made history, but they did "not make it just as they pleased." Things turned out quite differently than any of them expected. Let's examine what this tradition portends for Putin.

Nikita Khrushchev

After a brief struggle for power with Georgie Malenkov and a period of collective leadership, Khrushchev revealed himself as a determined reformer of the system he inherited from Stalin. Interestingly, the years of Khrushchev's rule (1958–64) were years of optimism and high confidence in the future of Soviet socialism. The Soviet consumer experienced a rising standard of living. The camps of the Gulag began to be emptied out of prisoners, and, although the "fear" was not eliminated from private lives, it was diminished significantly, especially the fear of mass, widespread repression. Soviet industry was growing apace. The space program had great successes, and Soviet science prospered generally.[3]

Nikita Khrushchev was clearly a true believer in the promise of socialism and its ultimate victory on the world stage over capitalism. It was just a matter of time. The spread of communism to Eastern Europe and China appeared to support this optimism. However, all was not well. Stalin's legacy of repression threatened elite party members as well as the population at large. Khrushchev sought through his reforms to end the terror, to revitalize and purify the Communist Party, and to invigorate the economy. Khrushchev's expectations were dashed by reality. His economic reforms produced short-term gains, but failed in the long run to ensure sustained growth. There were numerous attempts to improve the incentive system for enterprise managers and workers. The so-called Kosygin reform of 1965 was, in fact, a carryover from Khrushchev's era. It was the end of Khrushchev's efforts, not the beginning, it turned out, of Brezhnev era reforms. Leonid Brezhnev lacked enthusiasm for fundamental economic reform and thus the Kosygin reform had no discernible long-term impact. As one astute observer noted, the effort to reform industrial management became merely a treadmill, continually repeating itself, going nowhere.[4]

Khrushchev's attempt to invigorate agricultural production was equally unsuccessful. A case study in the irrationality of Soviet economic thinking, the Virgin Lands program expanded cultivation, especially of grains, by one-third. The idea was to enhance the production of feed grains so that livestock herds and thus meat consumption could be greatly increased. Grain production did go up, but only in the short run. A large portion of the land brought under cultivation could not be maintained and had to be abandoned at great cost. One of Khrushchev's last acts was to authorize the import of grain from the United States and the West in order to continue to support the larger herds of beef animals. It would have been more rational for the USSR to import meat directly, because livestock in both the United States and Europe converted grain into meat much more efficiently than could poor quality Soviet livestock herds.

In any case, Nikita Khrushchev was removed from power in a palace coup in October 1964, and the impetus to reform diminished rapidly thereafter. His most lasting impact, however, was to initiate the process of de-Stalinization at the Twentieth Party Congress. He sought to undercut political opponents and disassociate the Communist Party of the Soviet Union (CPSU) from the worst of Stalin's crimes, but criticism of Stalin was limited to the years after 1934. Achievements such as collectivization and the rapid industrialization drive remained off limits to serious criticism until well into the 1980s. This was partly to protect himself and his colleagues from complicity in Stalin's crimes, but also to affirm the principal institutions of the Soviet system: central planning, emphasis upon heavy industry, collectivized agriculture, and comprehensive state ownership and management of productive assets. This was the core of Soviet socialism, and Khrushchev had no intention of undercutting it. He hoped instead to shift priorities toward the consumer and to attain a rate of growth of gross domestic product (GDP) that would catch up with the United States before the end of the twentieth century.

The embarrassing outcome of the Cuban Missile Crisis and the perception that Khrushchev was pursuing too many "harebrained" domestic reform projects and destabilizing the party bureaucracy led to a palace coup in 1964. His successors, Leonid Brezhnev and Alexei Kosygin, and then Brezhnev alone, did not continue the reform effort with the same vigor as Khrushchev. The CPSU and its leadership lapsed into a bureaucratic, self-satisfied, and self-rewarding pattern of behavior. The Brezhnev years have quite rightly been labeled the era of stagnation. The leadership grew long in the tooth, and the legitimacy of the party was badly eroded. Meanwhile, the economy suffered a loss of dynamism. A rise in the price of oil, thanks to OPEC, along with an increase in the world price of gold, increased state revenues and reduced the pressure for economic reform. In fact, our best measurements reveal that most economic indicators began to show declining rates of growth in about the middle of the 1970s. The downward trend continued into the 1980s and confronted Brezhnev's successors with stark alternatives. They could allow a very disappointing slow rate of economic growth to continue and abandon the goal that Khrushchev had set of "catching up with and surpassing" the United States in economic power and well-being, or they could carry out wide-ranging, deep economic reforms that would restore the rates of growth that the Soviet Union achieved in the 1950s and 1960s.

Mikhail Gorbachev

Mikhail Gorbachev and his political allies viewed themselves as "children of the Twentieth Party Congress." They were young men at the time of Khrushchev's anti-Stalin speech, and it left an indelible mark on their political consciousness. In this sense, Gorbachev's innovations of *perestroika* and *glasnost* were rooted in Khrushchev's reforms. In introducing these policies Gorbachev had no intention of undermining the planned economy or the CPSU. Instead, Gorbachev and his circle of advisors genuinely believed initially that an adjustment here and an improvement there and a limited opening to market forces and the world economy could provide for a gradual improvement in economic performance and strengthen the party. It is true that Gorbachev used the word "revolution" early on in his speeches, but it is also perfectly clear that he did not have a real revolution in mind. However, as he ran into resistance and unanticipated fragmentation of the Soviet Empire, his reform efforts became more frantic and ambiguous. In the end, "*glasnost*" led to the repudiation of the party as the sole repository of political power; "*pere-stroika*" brought about the collapse of the system of central planning and a decline in economic performance; "democratization" fostered ethnic separatism; and the "new thinking" in foreign policy led to a rollback of communism in Eastern Europe. In each case, developments outdistanced the expectations of the reformers and careened out of central control.[5]

Gorbachev was more successful initially in controlling the transformation of the political process. No doubt this reflected his greater skill and interest in the art of political maneuver and the fact that political processes depend so largely upon personal relations and personality, at which Gorbachev excelled. Reforming the economy proved more intractable than political liberalization because the distribution of gains and losses that economic reform entailed were much more diffuse and uncertain than those associated with the redistribution of political power. Almost everyone had something to lose, whether it was privileged access to deficit commodities, or job security, or personal savings, while possible gains had to be viewed as highly uncertain and therefore highly discounted. It was naturally much more difficult to establish a consensus with the public much less with the elite, which was divided on ideological grounds as well. Ed Hewett wrote in November 1989, "Mikhail Gorbachev is writing a textbook on the political economy of transition—the first textbook of its kind."[6] Unfortunately for Gorbachev, his book had an unhappy ending.

The critical turning point for Gorbachev on economic reform came in mid-1990, when he rejected the radical S. S. Shatalin plan for conversion of the Soviet economy into a market-oriented economy in 500 days.[7] Although it was patently unrealistic, the Shatalin plan crystallized as no previous document had done the fundamental issues confronting economic reform. Gorbachev responded:

> They want to take a gamble. Let everything be thrown open tomorrow. Let market conditions be put in place everywhere. Let's have free enterprise and give the green light to all forms of ownership. Let everything be private. Let us sell the land, everything. I cannot support such ideas, no matter how decisive and revolutionary they might appear. These are irresponsible ideas, irresponsible![8]

The Shatalin plan assumed that political power would rest ultimately with the constituent republics of the USSR. All powers of the Kremlin would be derivative, and its economic base would depend upon the revenues and authority the republics would be prepared to cede to the central government. The Shatalin plan assumed that all forms of property would stand on a completely equal footing in the new economy. There would be no legal distinction made for socialist property. The plan also called for dismantling the institutions of central planning completely. Acceptance of the Shatalin plan, then, meant that Gorbachev would have to be prepared to accept the possible dissolution of the USSR and abandonment of belief in the superiority of socialist property and of socialism itself. This was more than he could stomach, and it was the end of Gorbachev the reformer. Reform was spinning out of control and threatening to become revolution. Henceforward, Gorbachev shunned all change, even in quite modest forms, and sought economic and political stability that would conserve the union against separatist ethnic forces. Gorbachev became the Hamlet of political and economic reform. As a child of the Twentieth Party Congress, he could not be Stalin. His few attempts at repression were too weak and failed. But he could not abandon Soviet socialism or the USSR either. Gorbachev's reform objective had been much more modest and conservative. It was best expressed by his first economics minister, Abel Aganbegyan: "*Perestroika* must carry Soviet society to a qualitatively new state, when thanks to the advantages of socialism we will surpass the capitalist countries in productivity, and other indicators of cost-effectiveness, in quality of production and the level of technology."[9]

Clearly Gorbachev had exactly the same goal as Khrushchev. When it could not be achieved without abandoning socialism, Gorbachev was stymied. Indecision led ultimately to the failed coup by party hard-liners in August 1991, and the rise to full power of Boris Yeltsin.

Gorbachev's place in history is secure, however, because he thoroughly de-Stalinized the USSR. He took Soviet society back as nearly as the arrow of time permits to the origins of the Stalinist system, back essentially to Vladimir Lenin's New Economic Policy of the 1920s. The year 1934 no longer remained as the limit for criticism of Soviet institutions. In criticizing and limiting the power of the central economic ministries, proposing substantial, if still restricted, private ownership of productive assets, retail outlets and dachas, he had traveled well beyond Khrushchev, if less far than his erstwhile radical economic advisors wanted. In this sense Gorbachev was a true heir of the Twentieth Party Congress.

Gorbachev took one enormous step that Khrushchev would not. Although Khrushchev was a reformer, he was not prepared to lose the post–World War II empire in East-Central Europe. Thus he put down the 1953 disturbance in East Germany, crushed the Hungarian revolution, and built the Berlin Wall. Gorbachev's "new thinking" in foreign policy allowed him to disassociate domestic reform and maintenance of Soviet power in Eastern Europe, a connection over which domestic reform had repeatedly stumbled. The Brezhnev doctrine was abandoned and the consequences accepted, even though they turned out much more definitive and anti-Soviet than Gorbachev and his ministers anticipated.

On August 19, 1991, Mikhail Gorbachev was made a prisoner in his villa in the Crimea, where he had gone for vacation. An eight-man "state emergency committee" had been formed of highly placed party and military men with the intention of carrying out a coup against the Gorbachev government. It sought to halt the reform process, to forestall opening the Soviet Union to the global economy, to restore to the Communist Party monopoly control of politics, and to preserve the command economy. Within forty-eight hours the coup had failed and the members of the committee were in disgrace. James Billington, the Librarian of Congress, was in Moscow on those days and present at the White House, where the decisive defeat of the coup took place. He recently reported: "It was unexpected, it really hasn't been adequately explained since. After all, most of the five and a half million people in uniform, the largest uniformed force at one command in the history of the world, was stared down by 150 armed people in the Russian White House."[10]

Boris Yeltsin

The coup elevated Boris Yeltsin, who had been elected president of the Russian Federation (RSFSR) the previous spring, to unanticipated political heights. The image of Yeltsin standing defiantly on a tank in front of the White House remains the prime emblem of the resistance. As president of the RSFSR, the largest and most important republic of the Soviet Union, Yeltsin was in a position to take political advantage of the failed coup. He was unique among experienced Soviet party officials in two respects. He had been a stout supporter of *perestroika* and *glasnost* as party chief for Moscow and as a member of the Politburo, but he had been alienated from Gorbachev and the Communist Party as a result of political differences. Dismissal from his positions of power and authority had led to a nervous breakdown and, in the end, repudiation of the Communist Party of the Soviet Union. As a result he had no brief for the party and was prepared to destroy it. Second, as president of the RSFSR he was willing to break up the USSR in league with other republic leaders and thereby unseat its president, Gorbachev. Yeltsin's own self-interest, then, was consistent with the final and complete destruction of the USSR and the Stalinist social system. The factors that caused Gorbachev to hesitate in the face of radical reform did not deter Yeltsin from bringing the curtain down once and for all on Soviet communism and the Soviet Union.

Yeltsin sought out radical economists who would thoroughly undermine the command economy. It was teetering on the brink of collapse in any case. Inflation was soaring, the stores were empty and the federal budget was out of control. Under the influence of Yegor Gaidar and several Western economic advisors, he was persuaded to introduce what is known as "shock therapy" in January 1992.[11] His advisors assured him that the economy would decline sharply as prices were freed from controls and central planning abandoned, but an upturn could be expected in nine months. The close kinship of shock therapy with the Shatalin plan is obvious, but the latter was actually better reasoned and structured and more gradual as well. Yeltsin plunged where Gorbachev had hesitated—perhaps with good reason. However, it took almost nine years, not nine months, for the economy to turn up again. The economic depression of those years was deeper and more devastating than any in recorded peacetime period anywhere.[12] In the process the basic institutions of the Stalinist model of the Soviet economy, which were created in the crucible years of 1928–32, were completely abandoned. These institutions formed a true system in the sense that each component part depended upon all of the rest. They consisted of the five-year plan: centrally set, hyperambitious, physical-quantity monthly and annual targets; central supply allocation of priority commodities and services, the collective and state farms; strict controls over labor and residential mobility, heavy reliance upon welfare entitlements and subsidized consumption, egalitarianism in wage policy, and special incentives for members of the elite. Before 1992 was out these institutions had disappeared, and it is highly unlikely that such a combination could ever be restored in Russia. Yeltsin abolished the Communist Party too, and confiscated its assets. It reappeared subsequently only in much modified form as one party among many others.

The severely negative economic consequences of shock therapy for the majority of Russian citizens soured most on market reform and created political opposition to further reforms in the Duma and in the various republics of Russia. As a result, the process of creating new market institutions under Yeltsin was fraught with obstacles, and the process remained incomplete when he passed power to Vladimir Putin. Today many large-scale industries have been privatized, but many also remain either state owned or owned in part and dominated by the state. Privatization created a tiny class of very wealthy individuals, known as the oligarchs, and a large portion of the population became destitute. Market institutions are in place for the most part, but many need regulation or restructuring. The banking system remains weak and needs reform. Investment opportunities in Russia are so few and so risky that foreign capital fears to enter and domestic capital takes flight. However, the central bank and the state budget are now operating with greater sophistication than ever, and, as was mentioned earlier, export earnings, principally on oil, and the cheap ruble have stimulated the economy to its best performance in more than a decade. However, much remains to be done to turn the Russian economy into a market economy that can produce sustained growth and satisfactory performance.[13]

CONTINUITY AND CHANGE: PUTIN'S OPTIONS

The continuity of policy from Khrushchev through Gorbachev to Yeltsin, both in what they attempted and what they tried to avoid, is clear. It is also obvious that together they unmade the Bolshevik Revolution. Like Humpty-Dumpty, the Soviet Union as it existed cannot be put back together again by Putin or anyone else. The evidence is that Putin can be taken at his word when he states that he seeks, "Firm and economically supported state stability." That does not, of course, rule out autocracy, but it does imply a conservative approach to further economic reform—that those efforts will be incremental and based on consensus. It is also consistent with stagnation as a reaction to the hectic series of changes and mistakes that have characterized the last decade or so, just as Brezhnev sought stability and found stagnation following Khrushchev's riot of reforms.

During the difficult early days of shock therapy a Russian babushka was interviewed on TV. She was asked what she hoped would happen. "All we want," she said, "is to live in a normal economy like everyone else in the world." What did she mean by a "normal economy?" It can be defined in the first instance as an economy in which the everyday citizen can form reasonably assured expectations of the future. That means an economy where personal savings decisions can be made with confidence that they will not be confiscated by inflation or by the state, one in which daily necessities can be expected to be available in stores all day every day, employment will not fluctuate wildly, and plans can be made for the more distant future, such as for education for one's children, or for retirement, with reasonable certitude. A normal economy is one in which citizens may gauge the degree of risk associated with various economic options with some accuracy and therefore choose the risk profile he or she prefers. In this sense, the Russian economy today approximates the "normal economy" the babushka wished for, but it remains highly sensitive to volatile global raw material prices, especially for oil, and it is not attracting the volume of domestic and international capital investment required to ensure sustained economic growth. To achieve these ends additional reforms are necessary, but they need not be made in a radical fashion. The greater danger is that in the quest for political stability and continuation in office Putin will fail to achieve the reforms necessary to sustain a normal level of economic performance. It is already clear that the approach of elections for the Duma in Fall 2003 and for the presidency in Spring 2004 is inhibiting economic reform and fostering competition for economic assets and advantages.

An examination of economic reform efforts of the twenty-five independent countries that emerged from the collapse of the Soviet Empire indicates that success or failure has been determined by three major factors. First, and perhaps most important, has been a strong, unambiguous commitment to economic reform. The most successful states have been those that wanted desperately to escape Soviet power. They have sought successfully to link their fortunes to Europe, especially the European Union (EU). Second, the more successful reformers are those that had experienced a period of independent existence as states before falling under Soviet influence. A complementary interpretation would be that these states practiced the Soviet economic model for a shorter period of time and could draw upon past experience with market institutions. Third, progress in economic reform, as measured by the European Bank for Reconstruction and Development (EBRD), and in democratization, as measured by Freedom House, are highly correlated. The Pinochet model, in which political authoritarianism is used to force market reform, has not offered any promise in Central and Eastern Europe or in the former Soviet states. Alternation of power between different political parties and shared political power between the executive and the legislature appear to have produced the best economic results.[14]

As has been the case for the leaders of the other former republics of the USSR, except in the Baltic states, Yeltsin's commitment to economic reform was never constant, and it diminished over the years of his erratic and increasingly autocratic rule. Sixty years of central planning would be difficult to overcome with the greatest determination and consistency, so it is not surprising that Russia remains stuck halfway to market reform, a stark example of the failure of Pinochetism in this region. In fact, a recent survey of Russia's business elite revealed that only 27 percent consider Russia to have a marketing economy. Thirty-nine percent said that Russia is still a command economy, and 21 percent reported that the economy is equally split between command and market.[15] Vladimir Putin remains something of a mystery. Is he a cautious but ultimately determined reformer seeking step-by-step change based on consensus with the Duma and the population at large? His statement on Russia Day 2001, a celebration of ten years as a republic, might be interpreted in this way: "Everything we endured over the past decade, all our experiences, successes and failures, shows one thing—any reform only makes sense when it serves the people."

Or is Putin primarily concerned with maximizing political power in order to maintain his position? Putin has talked like a true reformer, but his actions have been more ambiguous. His presidency has benefited from two windfalls: a rising and relatively high price of oil and the devaluation of the ruble in the financial crisis of 1998. Unfortunately, he has not used this breathing space to push economic reform vigorously. He has been more concerned with hushing up critics, burnishing his image, and seeking to project Russian influence in the former republics of the USSR, among old Soviet allies in the Middle East and East Asia, and on the world scene. With a few exceptions the oligarchs remain in place, economic and bureaucratic corruption and crime remain almost untouched, and capital flight continues.[16]

At the outset of his presidency, Putin indicated that he planned to reduce the political and economic power of the wealthy individuals known as oligarchs, who had benefited so greatly from the highly inequitable privatization of Soviet industry and natural resources. Thus far two of the most prominent and vocal oligarchs, Boris Berezovsky and Vladimir Gusinsky, have been thoroughly undermined. Gusinsky has lost his media empire, and Berezovsky has gone from kingmaker (for both Yeltsin and Putin) to political outcast. Putin's motive, however, appears to have had less to do with economic power than with the desire to quiet criticism of his policies by their media enterprises. Subsequently, Putin engineered the removal of Rem Vyakhirev, who had been CEO of the giant natural gas monopoly Gazprom since 1992, and replaced him with a longtime Putin loyalist, Aleksei Miller. Vyakhirev was a variant type of oligarch, one appointed essentially by the central government to manage the huge, partly private, partly state enterprise. In replacing Vyakhirev, Putin strengthened his hand in many respects because Gazprom is such an important cash cow for the budget. This change will represent a major economic advance, if indeed Miller manages Gazprom more efficiently and does not use access to its great wealth mainly to enrich himself, which remains to be seen. The remaining oligarchs have been lying low and staying out of visible politics. This was apparently in conformity with Putin's policy toward the oligarchs when he came to power. They could retain ill-gotten wealth as long as they stayed out of politics—except, of course, to back and fund Putin's own leadership.

YUKOS

On July 2, 2003, Platon Lebedev, co-owner of Russia's largest oil company, Yukos Petroleum, was arrested and taken from his hospital bed to prison and charged with malfeasance in a privatization scheme during the halcyon days of privatization under Yeltsin. His partner, Mikhail Khodorkovsky, was also questioned and put on notice. This development was a great surprise, a bolt of lightning striking two oligarchs out of a clear blue sky. The company has been highly successful and is regarded as a model of transparency and good management consistent with best Western practice. And during the first half of 2003, the Russian economy performed at a high level, with GDP growth on the order of 7 percent, strong government revenues, reduction in external debt and tolerable inflation. Economic conditions appeared to be highly positive for continued economic growth and stability. The Russian business community, foreign investors and political analysts have therefore struggled to explain the willingness of Putin's government to risk economic turmoil by what appeared to be a renewed targeting of several oligarchs.

Most observers assume that the move against Yukos and its leaders was related to the forthcoming elections for the Duma and the Presidency, but just how remains debatable. Did Khodorkovsky and Lebedev engage too freely in politics, supporting possible political opponents of Putin and his supporters? Or is there a renewed internecine battle over control and ownership of previously privatized, highly lucrative extractive industries? It is probably too early to tell, and especially since Putin himself has remained noncommittal and apparently not directly involved in the struggle.

What is clear, however, is that privatization of the Russian state's prime, large-scale industries, which took place in the mid-1990s under Yeltsin, may not be irreversible. Three-fourths of the Russian population at large believes, correctly in fact, that the handful of Russian billionaires acquired their riches illicitly for a song, thanks to their political connections. And they also think that those privatizations should be reversed. Many of Putin's old former KGB colleagues and current civil servants agree, and may hope to benefit personally should privatization be reconsidered. Politically, reversal of privatization, or perhaps only picking off a couple of oligarchs, would resonate favorably with the voting public. Economically, however, this is a dangerous course to pursue.

After the fact, and especially five to ten years after the fact, de-privatization poses a true dilemma for the leadership: Legitimacy of private ownership and protection of property rights in general versus popular demand for an equitable distribution of property that was, under the Soviet state, public property. Failure to ensure the protection of property rights would be certain to jeopardize productive investment both domestic and foreign. Why make long-term investments in plant and equipment if, sometime in the future, they may be expropriated? On the other hand, a dozen or so Russian citizens became billionaires overnight not by providing valued goods and services to customers, but by virtue of strategic political contacts. The strong belief of Russian citizens that privatization was unfair also tends to undermine public support for private ownership and enterprise. Worst of all, the process of de-privatizing and re-privatizing might very well lead to another unacceptable outcome: the substitution of government bureaucrats and Putin's cronies for the current oligarchs. The best outcome would be a deal that limits (e.g., taxes) earnings and wealth of the oligarchs without depriving them of control of their enterprises. Alternatively, Putin may be satisfied that his point has been made to the oligarchs about staying out of partisan politics, if, in fact, his is behind the attack. In any event, once he is re-elected it may be possible to resolve the problem of the oligarchs without damaging the economy. It is not clear at this point, however, how likely that outcome is.

Opposition to the privatization of urban and rural land was sufficiently broad and deep to prevent it during the Yeltsin years. He issued several decrees regarding land tenure, but they had little effect. The notion of private ownership of land ran against long-held views in pre-revolutionary Russia and Soviet practice. Legislation passed by the Duma in October 2001 declared that urban land, which comprises about 5 percent of all land area in Russia, is now open to private, and possibly even foreign, ownership. Implementation, however, may prove gradual and frustrating. Urban land has been controlled historically by mayors and regional leaders for local purposes and personal profit. They will be reluctant to surrender the power and revenue it represents, and they will be able to use a number of strategies to frustrate and delay urban land privatization.

Provision of legislation permitting private ownership of rural land was delayed for another year due to violent opposition based on historical and ideological grounds. Agricultural land has been treated as commons or as communal property in Russia for as long as there are any records, and most peasants preferred such a designation. Arable land, in particular, was always allocated to those who would apply their own labor to it, and it was reallocated when not so utilized. Another concern has been that privatization of rural land would wind up as inequitably owned as occurred to urban industry, with the oligarchs claiming a disproportionate share. Even so, President Putin managed to encourage the Duma to pass a Land Act that permits private ownership of rural land, but it is hedged in many ways to prevent foreign ownership, protect local farm and town interests and slow large-scale acquisition. Until both urban and rural land become clearly subject to private tenure and may be traded on markets like other commodities, both domestic investment in agriculture and foreign direct investment in Russia in general will be inhibited.[17]

More problematic, there is no single systematic economic program in place. In fact, two quite distinct initiatives circulated a few years ago at the highest levels of the Russian government. Thus far, apparently, Putin has not decided which to adopt, if either, but they illustrate conflicting tendencies in state economic policy. The plan that has received the most attention was prepared under the auspices of Minister of Economic Development and Trade German Gref. The Gref plan attempted to prescribe developments through the year 2010. The plan has undergone countless revisions and amendments at various levels and departments of the government. Curiously in this respect, it has certain earmarks of Soviet-era Five-Year Plans, and it may have met the same fate—to be announced with great fanfare and then forgotten. One of Putin's other prominent economic advisors, Andrei Illarionov, has criticized it harshly as insufficiently reformist (read liberal) and unrealistic. Perhaps the Gref plan has been used as a general guideline for economic policy, but the public cacophony of voices from a variety of economic advisors and policymakers, including Gref, Illarionov, Kasyanov, and Anatoly Chubais, makes that doubtful. Economic policy seems to be made on an ad hoc basis when it is made consciously at all. One thing is clear: despite Putin's carefully projected image in other arenas, economic policies have not been bold, coherent, or decisive.

The other plan, also prepared at Putin's insistence, was not published officially. It was drawn up under the auspices of Viktor Ishayev, governor of Khabarovsk, by a group of "leading economists," or so it was reported. Entitled

"Strategy for Development of the State to the Year 2010," it was presented to the Russian State Council in November 2000.[18] Although billed as a "supplement" to the Gref plan, reports indicate that the two are fundamentally different and impossible to reconcile. According to Jonathan Tennenbaum of the Executive Intelligence Review, the document is based upon the reviews of the nineteenth-century German economist Friedrich List and Russia's own nineteenth-century economist and prime minister, Sergei Witte. That may be the case in a general sense, but what it recalls more vividly is the Soviet practice of resource mobilization. This approach requires a strong state and a leading role for the state in the mobilization process. This is necessary, the report claims, because the middle class in Russia is not large enough to generate the savings required for significant breakthrough to high rates of growth. Without high rates of growth, the standard of living of the great mass of the population cannot be elevated sufficiently.

> Reaching the proposed level of consumption dictates the need for high rates of growth of the real productive sector of the economy, which in turn depends on achieving a 'break-out' in terms of investment. This means a "forced increase in capital investment" on the order of 8–9 percent growth per year, as well as state support for key sectors, including agriculture and infrastructure areas such as electricity, which are not able to generate the required rates of investment themselves.

The document goes on to give the state primary responsibility for the direction of investment. It was to judge investment opportunities not on the basis of profitability but in terms of the benefit of the industry and its products to the economy as a whole, whatever that means.

The Ishayev plan naturally brings to mind Stalin's program of forced industrialization in the 1930s. In fact, it could be read as calling for the creation of "capitalism in one country," that is, attempting to build a modern economy using entirely or mainly only domestic sources. It is not a plan that relies on market institutions, and it appears to shun foreign investment. The changes it calls for in the way of the banking system, investment policy, wage policy, and so forth represent an implicit restoration of the institutions of Soviet central planning. If attempted, the outcome would be either a tragedy or a farce.

According to reports, President Putin asked to have the Gref and Ishayev plans integrated (harmonized), an impossible task because they rest on different and irreconcilable foundations. Once again, Putin may have been simply postponing a decision on differing courses of action. Or, perhaps he simply does not understand economics and the different ramifications of the two plans. In this case, he would be avoiding a decision because he cannot be confident of the outcome, and, if so, he resembles Gorbachev in the last years of his reign, where, like Hamlet, he could neither move back to Stalinist methods nor forward to the possible abandonment of socialism. Of course Putin, in this instance, may simply be acting as a typical bureaucrat in the absence of decisive instructions from above. If so, this is not a promising outlook for successful economic reform in Russia under his presidency. There is no one else to give them.

Before the September 11 terrorist attack on the World Trade Towers, Putin's foreign policy actively sought to restore economic and political relations with the Soviet Union's old allies: Iran, Iraq, Cuba, and North Korea. He was strengthening relations with China. Foreign Minister Ivanov also stated that the "near abroad," Russia's term for the former republics of the USSR, falls within Russia's sphere of influence. The implication is clear: Putin was seeking to reestablish Russia's dominant position in the region and, to the extent possible, restore the Soviet empire through energy dependency, aggressive military exercises, showing the flag, and minatory behavior in the Caspian region. With the exception of China, the countries that Putin has been reaching out to are either global outcasts or economic basket cases. It appears to be an alliance of losers. This policy, if continued, was potentially a costly one internationally and economically. An attempt to attain hegemony over the former Soviet republics would represent a serious drain on Russia's military and economic resources. So is the interminable war in Chechnya.

Putin's positive response to the terrorist attack on the United States and to President Bush's declaration of war on international terrorism tempered his attempt to create an alliance to counterweight America as the sole remaining superpower in the world. Not only has he moved sharply back toward the Western camp, he has acceded to U.S. action in Afghanistan and, more surprisingly, to the placement of U.S. troops and other military assets in Uzbekistan and elsewhere in Central Asia. Putin will ultimately have to choose between attempting to create a "multipolar" strategy and becoming a junior partner in the international alliance against terrorism. The U.S. invasion of Iraq has sharpened this contradiction in policies.

CONCLUSION

Viewed in historical perspective, Putin appears to have more in common with Brezhnev than with his more decisive, risk-taking predecessors. Khrushchev, Gorbachev, and Yeltsin risked their positions in attempts to de-Stalinize the Soviet Union. Putin can retard, but cannot reverse that long historical process. It would take an ideology, a mass party and a fearless sense of purpose, none of which exists today. The long process of bringing the Soviet Union, and then Russia, back into the world economy has featured radical changes and long pauses with some backtracking. Putin's rule seems to be more pause than reform to date, and that is, incidentally, what the public wants, too. Revenue from overseas oil sales has given him the luxury of a pause, as was true for Brezhnev too.

The outlook for economic reform and continued economic growth over the next several years is positive, but only marginally so. Khrushchev tried unsuccessfully to make Stalin's economic system work better without Stalin. Gorbachev sought to reform the Soviet socialist economy, to make it more humane and more responsive to the popular will by introducing certain elements of democracy and of a market economy. His efforts failed. Yeltsin led a revolution that destroyed the coordinates of the Soviet planned economy and attempted to replace it quickly with the most liberal of market institutions. The revolution achieved partial success. The planned economy was totally destroyed, but the revolution had disastrous consequences for the population at large as it was captured by the *nomenklatura* and ground to a halt halfway to workable markets. Putin is now leading a partial restoration of Russia, a pause in the radical changes that have been taking place since *perestroika* and *glasnost* were introduced in the 1980s. In this sense the transition is over, but, of course, a good deal remains to be done to complete market institutions.

The state committees, such as the Gosplan, and the other institutions of central planning have disappeared, but public surveys both before and since the collapse of the Soviet economy reveal that very substantial majorities expect the government to provide price stability, job security, free medical care, free public education through college, subsidized housing, and cheap transportation. Similarly, the majority has repeatedly indicated a strong preference for public ownership of railroads, airlines, heavy industry, communications, banks, and other large-scale enterprises such as defense industries. Moreover, many enterprises, both private and public, still operate like company towns and have yet to rationalize employment practices.[19] The Russian economist Nikolay Shmelev aptly pointed out that it had taken "three generations" to build the "insane asylum" that was the Soviet economy and that it would take at least three more to escape from it. To escape fully will require changes in both the thinking and the behavior of citizens and leaders alike.[20]

Although Russia is not now a candidate for accession to the EU, its institutional structure can be expected to shape Russian economic and legal institutions to a substantial degree in the future. In fact, the EU is much more likely to influence economic reform and development in Russia from here on out than are the International Monetary Fund (IMF) or the World Bank, both of which have been associated with major policy failures in Russia and other transition economies. The EU is an important trading partner and likely to become increasingly important over time, if only because Russia is such a critical source of energy supplies to Europe. Russia also trades with East-Central Europe, and many of these countries are either on the path to accession in the EU or hope to be in the near future. The EU has spelled out in chapter and verse just what a country needs to do to harmonize its institutions with those of Europe. Russia is certain to be influenced both directly and indirectly to do the same. This is the most optimistic outlook for the future of capitalism in Russia in the next decade regardless of who is president.[21]

As many observers have noted, the criteria for accession to the EU are essentially the same as the requirements for a successful transition to a market economy. Accession indicators that are used to determine eligibility for membership include measures of the extent of large-scale and small-scale privatization, of success in restructuring enterprises to harden budget constraints, rationalize production and employment, and improve corporate governance. The indicators also seek to measure the degree to which markets are competitive, prices have been liberalized, and import and export restrictions have been eliminated. In addition, banking and other financial institutions are evaluated against international standards of regulation and performance. Basically, the accession process involves modeling the aspiring economy upon the most successful members of the EU and moving toward the model in stepwise fashion.

Countries are scored on each of the eight principal indicators on a scale ranging from one for little progress to four + for achieving standards and performance typical for advanced industrial countries. According to my own rough estimate, Russia's scores today range from a two, for example, on large-scale privatization and corporate governance, to a three + on price liberalization and foreign trade and exchange system policies, for an overall score of three or three − . These scores would not be sufficient to earn Russia membership in the EU, but they are indicative of the progress that has been made in market reform since 1991. The long-run outlook for Russia is therefore positive if Putin's and subsequent governments continue to press consistently for gradual reform and avoid foreign policy adventures and domestic distortions caused by corruption and an ambiguous commitment to joining the global economy.

It does not necessarily follow that the market economy that is developing in Russia will be any more successful than many other late-developing market economies, such as Brazil, Mexico, or Argentina. Stop-go economic policies have been endemic in much of Latin America and elsewhere because economic reform runs into resistance from the public and also from the elite members of society. The adverse consequences of stopping reform eventually generate another round of reform, which, in turn, generates public resistance. Escaping from this circular process of reform and reaction is Russia's challenge in the long run. Catching up with the developed economies, or even catching up with the more successful economies of East-Central Europe, is not likely in the foreseeable future. Instability of the global economy may pose problems also. As Marie Lavigne concludes: "The countries in transition do know where they want to go. We are all on the same boat; we know how to make it float but we don't know how to steer it."[22]

Russia has yet to decide definitively where it wants to go, but it has little choice in the long run to do other than to join the world economy in the "boat." The alternative, autarky, failed miserably. The sooner the leadership commits to joining the global economy as a fully fledged market economy, the better off Russia and the Russians will be.

NOTES

1. Secretariat of the Economic Commission for Europe, *Economic Survey of Europe 2001*, no.1 (New York and Geneva: United Nations, 2001), 109–20; WEFA Group, Emerging Europe Economic Outlook, Second Quarter 2001 (Eddystone, Pa.: DRI-WEFA, 2001), 3.3–3.15; *World Economic Outlook* 2, first quarter 2002 (Eddystone, Pa.: DRI-WEFA, 2002), 9.3–9.4.

2. Lewis Feuer, ed., *Marx & Engels* (Garden City, N.Y.: Anchor Books, 1959), 320.

3. Gertrude E. Schroeder, "Post-Soviet Economic Reforms in Perspective," in *The Former Soviet Union in Transition*, ed. Richard F. Kaufman and John P. Hardt for the Joint Economic Committee, Congress of the United States (Armonk, N.Y.: M.E. Sharpe, 1993), 65.

4. James R. Millar, *The ABCs of Soviet Socialism* (Urbana: University of Illinois Press, 1981).

5. James R. Millar, "Perestroika and Glasnost: Gorbachev's Gamble on Youth and Truth," in *The Soviet Economic Experiment*, ed. Susan Linz (Urbana: University of Illinois Press, 1990), 269–88.

6. Ed A. Hewett, *Is Soviet Socialism Reformable?* The Ernest Sturc Memorial Lecture, November 8, 1989 (Washington, D.C.: SAIS, Johns Hopkins University, 1989), 1–16.

7. S. S. Shatalin et al., *Transition to the Market, Parts I and II* (Moscow: Cultural Initiatives Foundation, 1990).

8. James R. Millar, "Prospects for Reform: Is (Was) Gorbachev Really Necessary?" in *Europe in Transition: Political, Economic, and Security Prospects for the 1990s*, ed. J. J. Lee and Walter Korter (Austin, Tex.: Lyndon B. Johnson School of Public Affairs, 1991), 76.

9. Abel Aganbegyan, *The Economic Challenge of Perestroika* (Bloomington: Indiana University Press, 1988), 226 (italics added).

10. *Johnson's Russia List*, #5403, August 21, 2001.

11. Yegor Gaidar, *Days of Defeat and Victory* (Seattle: University of Washington Press, 1999).

12. James R. Millar, "The De-development of Russia," *Current History: A Journal of Contemporary World Affairs* 98, no. 630 (October 1999): 322–27.

13. James R. Millar, "Can Putin Jump-Start Russia's Stalled Economy?" *Current History: A Journal of Contemporary World Affairs* 99, no. 639 (October 2000): 329–33.

14. James R. Millar, "The Post–Cold War Settlement and the End of the Transition," Presidential Address, *NewsNet, The Newsletter of the AAASS* 41, no. 1 (January 2001): 1–5.

15. Office of Research, U.S. Department of State, "Opinion Analysis," Washington, D.C. (March 6, 2003).

16. James R. Millar, "The Russian Economy: Putin's Pause," *Current History: A Journal of Contemporary World Affairs* 100, no. 648 (October 2001): 336–42.

17. Sophie Lambroschini, "The Government's Uncertain Role in Land Privatization, Part 1," *RFE/RFL Daily Report*, February 9, 2001.

18. Jonathan Tennenbaum, "The Ishayev Report: An Economic Mobilization Plan for Russia," *Executive Intelligence Review* 28, no. 9 (March 2, 2001).

19. James R. Millar, "Empire Envy and Other Obstacles to Economic Reform in Russia," *Problems of Post-Communism* 45, no. 3 (May/June 1998): 58–64.

20. James R. Millar, "The Economics of the CIS: Reformation, Revolution or Restoration?" in *The Former Soviet Union in Transition*, ed. Richard F. Kaufman and John P. Hardt for the Joint Economic Committee, Congress of the United States (Armonk, N.Y.: M. E. Sharpe, 1993), 34–56.

21. James R. Millar, "The Post–Cold War Settlement."

22. Marie Lavigne, *The Economics of Transition: From Socialist Economy to Market Economy*, 2d ed. (New York: St. Martin's Press, 1999), 280.

Chapter Eight

Putin and Agriculture

Stephen K. Wegren

Similar to the rest of Russian society and economy, Russia's agricultural sector is in transition. However, the transition is considerably different from the transition experienced during the years Boris Yeltsin was president. The transition under Putin is one from a period of radicalism to a period of consolidation, stability, and moderation. That is to say, the "loud revolution" of the Yeltsin years—during which privatization was pursued as a mobilization campaign—are over, replaced by a "quiet revolution" under Putin. While Putin's revolution is quiet, the policies being pursued today will shape domestic and international agrarian relations for decades to come. Putin's new stage has signaled that the politics of confrontation have ended. Conservatives, who tried to block reform efforts under Yeltsin, have lost. Conservatives have been marginalized and seen their influence diminish for two reasons: first, their platforms, which were often anti-market, went against the tide of history, and so perhaps their cause was doomed to fail; and second, Putin has significantly moderated agrarian policies by deradicalizing them and showing a sensitivity to agrarian interests in a way Yeltsin never did. At the same time, new groups of rural actors and new issues are emerging. Taken together, Putin's "quiet revolution" and new realities are providing Russia with a more stable foundation for future development in the agricultural sector.

THE YELTSIN LEGACY

In the early 1990s, Russia undertook an agrarian revolution, based on the privatization of large farms and land, that was expected to make agriculture operate on market principles and improve domestic food production and quality. In addition, it was believed that a healthy agricultural sector would contribute in significant ways to economic growth. The dramatic changes

141

which characterized the transition from a Soviet to a post-Soviet agricultural system involved the withdrawal of the post-Soviet state from regulation over production, delivery, and processing of food. By the end of the Yeltsin period, a short list of structural change included:

1. ending of planned production.
2. ending of obligatory procurements and delivery to procurement points.
3. removal of federal regulation over wholesale food trade.
4. relaxation of federal regulation over purchase prices.
5. removal of federal regulation over input prices.
6. decline of federal production subsidies to farms.
7. removal of federal consumer subsidies at the retail level.
8. change in predominant channels of food trade, with most food trade now channeled through private markets.
9. liberalized import and export rights to large farms and private farmers.
10. removal of job security from farm employees, who now may be fired for incompetent work or for economic reasons.

While change in the agrarian sector was dramatic during the 1990s, original reform goals and expectations were largely frustrated.[1] Food production fell precipitously—declining to about 50 percent of 1990 levels by late decade—farm productivity declined, farm debt and unprofitability soared, food imports increased significantly, leading to concerns about the nation's food security, and domestic output from the agricultural sector contracted, leading to a reduction in its contribution to GDP from about 14 percent at the beginning of the 1990s to about 7 percent at the end (in a significantly smaller economy). Declines in animal stocks during the Yeltsin years exceeded those of Stalin's collectivization. Under Yeltsin, the amount of agricultural land under cultivation declined, land reclamation virtually ceased, and harvests fell. In 1998, the harvest was only 47.9 million tons, the worst harvest since the early 1950s.[2] By the later years of the Yeltsin era, the combination of extraordinarily bad harvests and the financial collapse of the ruble in 1998 led to regionally imposed price controls on food products and Western food aid to prevent starvation in certain regions.[3] Thus, when Putin assumed the presidency in Russia, the agricultural situation was bordering on catastrophic.

NEW BEGINNINGS IN AGRARIAN POLICY

During the first year of the Putin presidency (during part of which Putin was acting president, January–May 2000), two main changes occurred regarding agrarian policy in contrast to the Yeltsin years. First, there were clear indicators that the revival of food production was considered a priority strategic policy direction. In February 2000, a national conference on the problems of the agroindustrial complex was held in Krasnodar kray. More than 1,000 specialists, scholars, food producers, heads of ministries, and department heads attended, as did Acting President Putin. In his speech to the conference, Putin stated: "Our first-order task is to raise the volumes of food output to the levels they were at the end of the 1980s–beginning of the 1990s and to appreciably reduce the country's food dependence on imports."[4]

Shortly thereafter, the administration unveiled its long-term policy goals in agriculture. On July 27, 2000, the outlines of a program entitled "Basic Directions of Agrofood Policy to 2010" were presented to the cabinet by Deputy Prime Minister and Minister of Agriculture, Aleksey Gordeev (August 1999–present).[5] The speech given by Gordeev summarized the program, positing three broad tasks: (1) develop and strengthen market conditions in the rural economy; (2) stabilize food production; and (3) achieve the first two tasks in the shortest time possible.[6] Specifically, when presenting the new program, Gordeev indicated that the highest priority goals of agricultural policy consisted of:

1. improving the financial status of agricultural enterprises through debt reduction and increased budgetary allocations, allowing them to expand production.
2. using custom and tariff policies "to ensure the income growth of domestic food producers," and allowing domestic producers to compete with foreign imports.
3. regulating the grain market, using "the entire arsenal possessed by the government," including customs and tariff regulation, commodity intervention, and through the use of commodity purchase intervention.
4. "perfection" of credit organizations and the dispersion of subsidized credits.
5. improving the stock of agricultural machinery and changing the process of leasing agricultural machinery.

Thus, after years of indifference during the Yeltsin era, the condition of Russian agriculture once again became important to policymakers. In an interview in mid-2002, Gordeev mentioned that "the President *constantly* assigns special attention to the problems of the agro-industrial complex, keeping in his field of vision all the basic questions that are connected to providing the country with food"[7] (emphasis added). The rediscovered importance of the rural sector does not mean that agricultural interests receive everything they want or that all needs are satisfied. Far from it, as is illustrated by the fact that the country in 2002 spent approximately as much on food

imports as was allocated from the federal budget to support domestic producers. It is not uncommon for rural interest groups to write an open letter to
President Putin, published in the agricultural press, requesting more
resources. Nonetheless, it is clear that the goal of agrarian policy under Putin
is to create an economic environment supportive of domestic producers.

This new course is evidenced by two examples. First, in 2002 a special program for the social development of the countryside was passed that intends
to improve infrastructure, housing, education, communications, and the provision of electricity, gas, and hot water to rural communities during the
course of the next few years.[8] While the passage of a program for the social
development of the countryside is hardly unique, it did coincide with an
upturn in resource flows from the federal budget to rural areas. A second
example of the reversal of indifference toward agriculture is seen by the state's
intervention in the grain market for the purpose of "regulating" the grain
market to the advantage of grain producers. During the Yeltsin period, grain
producers suffered first from continued state control of purchase prices during 1992–93, and thereafter from a "price scissors" in which the price of
production inputs such as fertilizers, machinery, fuels, and spare parts
increased in price at many times the rate of increase in grain production.
Under Putin, however, the state purchased grain as a way to prevent domestic
prices from dropping too far as a result of "excess" supply, and in this way
created a system of price support for grain producers. Following the 2002
harvest, for example, the Russian government expended nearly 5 billion
rubles on the purchase of grain from domestic producers.[9] The intent is to
store the grain in elevators to support prices during a period of excess supply,
and to disperse grain from these reserves during periods of shortage.

The second main change from the Yeltsin period has been an emphasis on
large farms to lead Russia's agricultural revival. The post-Yeltsin government
has deemphasized the importance of private family farms and instead priori-
tized the revival of food production on large farms. From the beginning of
the Putin administration, Minister of Agriculture Gordeev has spoken out
repeatedly that the future of Russian agriculture, and the main food producer
for the nation, will be large farms. For example, at an agricultural conference
in Moscow oblast in late February 2001, Gordeev stated that the policy of
attempting to destroy large farms in the early 1990s "had a negative influence
on the course of reform." Gordeev continued that at the present time "no
one should doubt the priority of large producers over small ones."[10] In an
article appearing in mid-2001, Gordeev criticized previous agrarian policy as
lacking "a scientific basis."[11] He instead argued that "the Russian experience
witnesses the fact that the future of agriculture is large enterprises and the
vertical integration of agroindustrial organizations."[12] The policy reorienta-
tion toward large farms is supported by the passage of a law in mid-2002 on
the rejuvenation of agricultural enterprises, providing for the restructuring of

farm debt and introducing a process for the enterprise to avoid bankruptcy.[13] Thus, unlike during the Yeltsin era, Putin's agrarian policy supports large farms, which are seen as the most important element of agricultural revival.

NEW AGRARIAN POLITICS

Putin has benefited from a level of rural support that Yeltsin never had. This support is evident through voting data, voting characteristics of rural voters, and the emergence of new agricultural interest groups. Each are discussed in turn in this chapter, but first it is useful to survey the nature of rural politics during the Yeltsin period.

At the beginning of economic reform in Russia, logic would hold that those with the most privilege during the Soviet era would be most resistant to reform. As reforms unfolded, the assumption by many analysts was that:

> those in a privileged position in the old system would be very reluctant to support a radical economic reform that threatened the old institutions or that exposed workers to sharp price increases and unemployment. . . . The larger the city, the better the living conditions. . . . Life in small towns and villages in the provinces seemed a throwback to decades ago. . . . For all these reasons, if privilege were the crucial factor, those living in large cities should have been disproportionately conservative. Those living in small towns and the countryside should have advocated radical change because they were especially disadvantaged.[14]

With the introduction of democratization and competitive elections in the Soviet Union and then Russia, however, it became clear that the base of political support for the Communist Party was not the voter who resided in large cities, but rather the voter in small towns and the countryside. The importance of the rural vote in the reemergence of the Communist Party in Russian politics was evident in the Duma elections in 1993, 1995, and 1999.

In Russia's first three Duma elections, only the Communist Party managed to increase the percentage of the vote it received from party lists. A key component of the revival of the Communist Party was the rural vote. The electoral performance of the Communist Party and its candidates is shown in Table 8.1, with special attention paid to the importance of the rural vote to Communist Party electoral performance.

The data in the table are based upon electoral results from twenty-three oblasts, krays, and ethnic republics in three economic regions in European Russia (nationally, Russia has eighty-nine oblasts, krays, and ethnic republics). These twenty-three regions have a southern location and are agriculturally rich. Although their populations are statistically urban (as is Russia as a whole, with 72 percent of the population considered urban), the economies of these regions are heavily agricultural and these regions are the primary

Table 8.1. Electoral Support for Communist Candidates in Duma Elections, 1993, 1995, and 1999 (party list only)

	1993 Duma Election	1995 Duma Election	1999 Duma Election
Total number of votes for Communist Party and percentage of total party list vote	6,666,000 (12.4%)	15,432,963 (22.3%)	16,195,569 (24.29%)
Of total votes for Communist Party, number and percentage of votes from southern regions[a]	2,681,773 (40%)	8,372,491 (54%)	5,825,229 (36%)
Percentage of vote in Moscow city received by Communist Party	11.03%	14.8%	11.77%
Number of regions won by Communist candidates (88 possible)[b]	4	63	32
Percentage of party list seats received by Communist Party	14%	44%	30%
Total number of seats obtained by Communist Party from party list (225 possible)	32	99	67

Sources: Author's calculations from election data; and www.rusline.ru.
[a] Southern regions are defined as republics, oblasts, and krays within the Central Black Earth, Volga, and Northern Caucasus Economic regions.
[b] Chechnya is excluded from the calculations.

agricultural producers for the country. More so than any other regions, these oblasts, krays, and ethnic republics comprise the "red belt" of the rural south because of their support for Communist candidates.

In these three Duma elections, as the data show, a disproportionate percentage of electoral support for Communist candidates came from southern regions. These twenty-three oblasts, krays, and ethnic republics produced 40 percent of the total Duma vote for Communist candidates in 1993, 54 percent in 1995, and 36 percent in 1999, thereby significantly exceeding the percentage of votes the Communist Party received nationally. Conversely, urban support for Communist candidates was weak, reflected by the poor showing in Moscow in those three elections.[15]

While rural support for the Communists has been significant, there are signs that such support declined in the 2000 presidential election, shifting significantly to Putin. Electoral results for the 1996 and 2000 presidential election are compared in Table 8.2. The table uses the same twenty-three regions that were used in Table 8.1.

At the macro regional level, the data show that a significant shift in support

Table 8.2. Electoral Distribution of Votes for Presidential Elections, 1996 and 2000

	1996 Votes for Yeltsin	1996 Votes for Zyuganov	2000 Votes for Putin	2000 Votes for Zyuganov	Decline for Zyuganov, 1996–2000
Total number of votes/ percentage of votes won	40,203,948 (53.8%)	30,102,288 (40.3%)	39,740,434 (52.9%)	21,928,371 (29.1%)	−8,173,917 (−11.2%)
Of total votes, number and percentage from southern regions[a]	13,827,884 (34.4%)	14,936,328 (49.6%)	15,776,158 (39.7%)	9,483,552 (43.25%)	−5,452,776 (−6.4%)

Sources: Author's calculations from election data; www.rusline.ru; Christopher Marsh, *Russia at the Polls: Voters, Elections, and Democratization* (Washington, D.C.: *Congressional Quarterly,* 2002), 67, 83, 92; and *Itogi vyborov 19 Dekabrya 1999 goda po regionam: chislo i protsent golosov za federal'nye spiski* (Moscow: Panorama, 2000).

[a] Southern regions are defined as republics, oblasts, and krays within the Central Black Earth, Volga, and Northern Caucasus Economic regions. Chechnya is excluded from the calculations.

occurred away from Zyuganov and toward Putin in the 2000 presidential election, indicated by an increase in the number of votes Putin captured in these red-belt regions and an increase in the percentage of his total vote that came from these regions. Conversely, comparing the 1996 election with the 2000 election, Zyuganov experienced a decline in the number of votes—more than 8.1 million overall—of which 5.4 million came from these twenty-three red-belt regions. This shift in support is significant because it means core red-belt regions support Putin's mandate to rule instead of opposing it, as happened with Yeltsin. Further, rural support provides a basis for accommodation and legislative achievement. Whereas under Yeltsin a sharp and distinct north/south electoral cleavage characterized electoral politics, under Putin that cleavage appears to be diminishing. Survey data from five regions further demonstrate rural support for Putin at the individual level, shown in Table 8.3.[16]

The data in Table 8.3 show that rural voters gave Putin a strong majority of support across a spectrum of social characteristics: both genders voted for Putin; all age groups voted for Putin; all educational levels voted for Putin; all income categories, including the very poorest, voted for Putin; and the employed and unemployed voted for Putin. It is especially noteworthy that the rural poor and rural unemployed support Putin and not Zyuganov—it is precisely those two groups that are targeted by the Communist political platform.

Thus, to sum up rural mass politics, we have seen that under Yeltsin the

Table 8.3.   Social Characteristics of Rural Voters in Five Regions,
2000 Presidential Election

	For Putin	For Zyuganov
Total percentage in five regions[a]	68.4%	15.8%
Male	65.3%	19.55
Female	69.9%	13.9%
Age 18–29	62.8%	5.8%
Age 30–39	73.2%	7.3%
Age 40–49	72.2%	13.9%
Age 50–59	70.4%	18.5%
Age 60 +	65.7%	21.4%
Husband's education 0–6 years	60.4%	25.0%
Husband's education 7–9 years	65.6%	20.4%
Husband's education 10–11 years	66.5%	12.8%
Husband's education 12 + years	71.6%	14.3%
Per capita income 0–762 rubles per month	69.8%	6.9%
Per capita income 763–1524 rubles a month	66.2%	17.9%
Per capita income 1525–2286 rubles a month	69.2%	21.2%
Per capita income 2287–3048 rubles a month	70.0%	22.5%
Per capita income 3049 + rubles a month	78.4%	8.1%
Employed	54.7%	9.4%
Unemployed	69.6%	16.3%

Source: Survey data, 2001.
Note: Rows do not add to 100% because "other candidates," "vote against all," and "did not vote" are not included.
[a] The five regions are Belgorod oblast, Volgograd oblast, Krasnodar kray, Novgorod oblast, and the Republic of Chuvashia.

Communist opposition drew considerable support from southern agricultural regions. There was a distinct cleavage in electoral politics that cut across urban/rural and north/south lines. Under Putin, rural support for Communist candidates has declined, shifting toward Putin. Putin is popular across various socioeconomic variables, including, age, education, and income, for which the disadvantaged commonly support Communist candidates.[17] At the mass level, therefore, Putin has enjoyed considerable rural support and is likely to continue to do so.

If mass political support is one important factor in the new agrarian politics, elite politics is another. Under Yeltsin, the primary rural political interests were the Communist Party of the Russian Federation (CPRF), the Agrarian Party of Russia (APR), which is a conservative party and in many ways a mirror of the Communist Party except it draws support from rural dwellers, and the private farmer association called AKKOR.[18] The Communist Party and the Agrarian Party were opposed to Yeltsin's agrarian reforms, and AKKOR, while pro-reform, remained politically weak throughout the 1990s, unable to exert much influence in the countryside or on national politics. As the 1990s came to a close, the Communist and Agrarian parties saw their rural strength diminish, as both suffered from internal divisions and political infighting. In the CPRF, splinter groups spun off from the main organization, thereby dividing constituent loyalties. The leadership experienced a nasty fight in mid-2002 when it was outmaneuvered by Putin and forced to resign the CPRF's committee chairmanships in the Duma. In the APR, the leadership of Mikhail Lapshin, the leader of the party since its founding in 1993, was challenged, and calls for a leadership change became increasingly vocal.

While the two traditional political parties with ties to the countryside experienced dissension and division, two important developments were occurring. The first was Putin's introduction of moderate economic policies that essentially coopted some key elements of conservatives' policy platform, for example, the program on social development of the countryside and the law on the rejuvenation of agricultural enterprises (see also the section on agrarian economics below). The second important development was the emergence of a rural interest group that is moderate and loyal to the Kremlin, not oppositionist as had been the CPRF and APR.

In May 2002, the founding congress of an organization called the Russian Agrarian Movement (*Rossiyskoye agrarnoye dvizheniye*, or RAD) was held, electing Minister of Agriculture Gordeev as its chairman. Unlike the CPRF and APR, RAD has access to President Putin, indicated by his meeting with leaders of RAD following its opening congress. As an outcome of that meeting, Putin instructed the government to consider a number of proposals designed to protect domestic producers from "unfair" foreign competition.

In an interview, the deputy chairman of RAD, Valentin Denisov, described RAD as neither a leftist nor rightist organization, but rather as an organization working "for the unification of all those who contribute their participation and responsibility for the creation of a highly effective agro-industrial complex, for ensuring the food security of the country, for the revival of the countryside, and for the creation of a worthwhile life for the peasantry."[19] Denisov further indicated that RAD was ready to work with other political organizations such as the APR, AKKOR, or the Agroindustrial Union. He cautioned that RAD's program must not become the "traditional" plea of "give us financial resources," or "give us a normal legislative base." Most of all, he warned that the program should not become the "fruit of creative groups of Muscovites," and should not become an organization of "agrarian bureaucrats."[20]

Whether RAD can be successful, or whether it represents the further splintering of agrarian interests, remains to be seen. On the one hand, with Gordeev as leader, RAD will enjoy access to the Kremlin, and implicitly the organization is the primary intermediary between the government and the countryside by being the mouthpiece for rural interests and in turn supporting state policies. On the other hand, cooperation with other rural interest groups and parties remains problematic, as previously existing organizations are unlikely to be willing to subsume their goals and constituencies to a new organization that claims to unite all agrarian interests—a claim made as well by the APR and the Agroindustrial Union. When RAD was first formed in mid-2002, Lapshin indicated that the APR was ready to cooperate.[21] However, by the end of 2002, signs of discord became evident, and press reports indicated that Lapshin felt his leadership position was threatened by the emergence of RAD.[22]

NEW AGRARIAN ECONOMICS

Since the financial collapse in 1998, the situation in agriculture has improved considerably. Gross agricultural output, measured in ruble value, averaged 5.5 percent growth annually for four consecutive years (1999 through 2002). Harvests have rebounded and provide Russia with enough grains to meet domestic needs and rebuild stocks; Russia also became an exporter of grain, selling more than 9 million tons of wheat abroad in 2002.[23] As a result of the improvement in domestic production, food imports declined and farm profitability improved.[24] To be sure, part of the rebound is due to luck—a string of years with good weather, which is always a crucial variable. At the same time, it is necessary to acknowledge the importance of the components of Putin's "quiet revolution" in economic policy toward agriculture. As alluded to above, economic policy is multifaceted, including measures to rebuild and improve rural infrastructure, and state intervention to regulate the food market by offering price support. Putin's strategy to support domestic producers and revive Russian agriculture, in particular large farms, is best understood by a discussion of policies toward food imports and measures to rejuvenate agricultural enterprises with financial assistance.

Food Import Policy

International food trade policy under Yeltsin was relatively open. Import tariff rates were comparatively low, on average about one-half the world average. For example, in the European Union, some tariffs on specific food imports can reach 200 percent.[25] Worldwide, agricultural tariffs averaged 40 percent in the late 1990s.[26] In contrast, under Yeltsin, aggregate Russian import tariffs were only about one-half of world levels, and many food tariffs did not exceed 10 percent.

During the Yeltsin years, the composition of Russian imports changed, due in large part to the significant decline in animal herds, which reduced demand for feed grains and thus the need for grain imports. As a consequence, Russia imported much less grain in the 1990s than it had during the 1980s, representing a reversal of previous trends.[27] Measured in dollar value, meat imports became the most important food import. Moreover, during 1992–98, food imports increased as a percentage of total food supply, in particular for meat products. From 1992 through 1997, total meat imports increased 440 percent; poultry meat increased over 2,500 percent, pork imports increased by nearly 500 percent, and beef imports increased by almost 245 percent.[28] Meat imports rose from 8 percent of domestic supplies in 1992 to 30 percent in 1997. Following the collapse of the ruble in August 1998, meat and poultry imports declined significantly in the third and fourth quarters of 1998, and overall fell to 25 percent of total supply for the year. However, in 1999, meat imports (not including poultry) surpassed their pre-crisis levels, in part due to food assistance from the United States and the European Union.

Thus, thanks to an open trade policy, during the 1990s Russia spent as much, if not more, on food imports as was allocated to the agricultural sector in the federal budget. The sum of imports as a percentage of total food supplies reached its peak in 1997. In that year, Russia spent $13 billion on food imports. Thereafter, the sum of imports as a percentage of total food supplies declined to 20 percent in 1998 and to 17 percent in 2000.[29] However, even in 2000, an estimated $7.5 billion was spent on food exports. In comparison, in 2001, which witnessed a large increase in funds allocated to agriculture, less than $1 billion from the federal budget was assigned to support domestic producers.[30] In 2002, Russia spent $8 billion on food imports.

In the late 1990s, food import policy began to change as concerns about the nation's "food security" permeated the political landscape. Advocates of national food security support higher trade barriers in the form of tariffs or even import quotas in order to protect domestic producers. Today, it would be fair to conclude that "food security" is part of the everyday political dialogue among policymakers and has become a cornerstone of the nation's food policy. Minister of Agriculture Gordeev has a track record of supporting protectionist measures. For example, Gordeev argued prior to becoming minister of agriculture that "food security of the Russian Federation is a component part of its economic security."[31] It is a theme that he has repeated many times since becoming minister of agriculture.

The origins for a more restrictive food import policy are several-fold. One of the strongest proponents for more protection of domestic producers was former Minister of Agriculture Viktor Semenov (March 1998–May 1999), who advocated a system of higher tariffs and quotas on imported food products that compete with Russian products, and lower tariffs on products that Russia did not grow.[32] Semenov's views echoed those of agrarian conservatives, who since 1995 were vocal advocates for Russian food security. Over time, concerns over food security spread to agricultural academic institutes, the printed media, and finally politicians. These voices responded to increasing imports and the relatively open foreign trade policy pursued by Russia since market reforms began.

Beyond the Ministry of Agriculture, there is significant bureaucratic support for protection of domestic producers. Advocates for food security draw support from large farms and private farmers, from food-producing regions, from food processors, from various agricultural interest groups such as the meat, grain, sugar, and poultry unions. In addition, political parties and movements such as the APR and more recently RAD support protectionism.

Finally, Putin himself supports less open food import policies. Almost immediately after Putin became acting president, tariffs on many types of poultry, meat, and fish were changed.[33] A few days later, Putin remarked that tariffs on imports should be used not only to protect domestic producers, but also to stimulate production of high-quality products.[34] Subsequently, Putin has repeated on numerous occasions the theme that the country needs to reduce imports and become more food self-reliant. The use of custom and tariff policies to protect domestic producers was included as a plank in the government's ten-year agricultural program to 2010.[35] Ironically, Russia has become more protectionist under Putin as agricultural production has rebounded, as interest in investing in the agricultural sector has increased, and as Russia negotiates over entry into the World Trade Organization (WTO).

Russia has four main food unions, each representing a certain category of food production or processing. The four are the Sugar Union, the Meat Union, the Poultry Union, and the Grain Union, each of which has a permanent bureaucratic structure and a chairman. Individual producers or processors voluntarily join a union relevant to their economic activity. In this way the unions act similarly to peak associations in Germany. These unions support trade protectionism, as noted above, and each union has benefited from government policies.

Sugar interests (and now the Sugar Union) were among the first to receive protection for their producers.[36] In February 2000, the Russian government imposed an import quota of 3.5 million tons on sugar, and also levied import tariffs ranging from 10–45 percent on sugar imports, depending on the time of the year.[37]

The meat and poultry unions also have received protectionist measures. The outbreak of foot and mouth disease in England forced the Russian government to impose a ban on meat imports from the United Kingdom in February 2001. This ban was expanded in March 2001 to all countries stricken with foot and mouth disease, and later expanded again to include all meat and meat products from European Union nations, Eastern Europe, and the Baltic states.[38] As the epidemic receded, the ban was lifted at the end of April 2001 and in early May for countries that had not experienced foot and mouth disease. The ban on meat and dairy products was continued only for the Netherlands and the United Kingdom.

Aside from restrictions generated by concerns over disease, in July 2001 the Ministry of Agriculture proposed a quota on imported beef, pork, and poultry, with high custom duties of 50–100 percent on any imports above the quota. During early 2002, Russia and the United States engaged in a mini–trade war over chickens, with Russian banning their import over alleged sanitation and health violations.[39] Most analysts believe that the real reason was retaliation over U.S. tariffs on Russian steel exports. The sanitation issue was eventually settled and the United States regained access to the Russian market, but it was not the end of the dispute.

In December 2002, the Russian Ministry of Agriculture proposed to reduce meat and poultry exports by about one-third in 2003 by imposing import quotas and tariffs.[40] In January 2003, the government imposed higher tariffs on meat imports above the government-defined quota (similar to the action taken in 2001).[41] For importation of poultry meat, strict quotas were enacted that especially affected the United States, the single largest exporter of poultry meat to Russia.[42] In February 2003, the Ministry of Agriculture revoked, without explanation, all import licenses for meat and poultry. Minister of Agriculture Gordeev was quoted as saying that "Western companies want to gain ground on the Russian market, and we should take steps to curb these aspirations."[43] Importers had to reapply for permits, a process that took several months to complete. In May 2003, Gordeev visited the United States and signed a memorandum on agricultural cooperation, and poultry imports resumed in July 2003. However, U.S. exports remained limited by the import quotas.[44]

Finally, the Grain Union has not benefited from direct import quotas or tariffs, primarily because grain imports have comprised such a small percentage of the nation's grain supplies—no more than 3 percent in any one year since 1994—so there has been little reason to erect trade barriers.[45] However, the Grain Union has lobbied for and received advantageous rates for the transportation of grain from one region of Russia to another; and benefits from a range of other indirect support measures that help make Russian grain cost-competitive with foreign imports.

Although protectionist measures help the revival of Russian agriculture and benefit domestic producers, they call into question Russian entry into the World Trade Organization, which Putin has made a priority. The goal of WTO entry clashes with his more restrictive food import policies. Negotiations continue but have stalled, primarily over the pricing of domestic energy and the restrictive agricultural trade policies discussed above. In general, the United States supports Russian entry, but the optimism of early entry has faded. Expectations of Russian entry during 2003 were dropped. The stark reality is that membership is likely to require lower import tariffs and less protection for Russian agriculture, a fact that worries Russian agro-economists and policymakers because agriculture is one of the sectors most vulnerable to foreign competition. While Russia has made significant progress in meeting the provisions for WTO entry in other policy spheres, there has been little evidence that Russia is willing to lower trade barriers in agriculture in order to meet the conditions for WTO entry.[46]

The Financial/Credit System and Policy

There is a consensus among analysts of Russian agriculture that the financial system has had two main shortcomings: (1) the lack of a strong agricultural bank to issue credit to producers, and (2) a "soft" credit policy that helped weak and unproductive farms remain in existence.[47] The importance of credit to agricultural producers cannot be overstated and is a key factor influencing the financial health and productive potential of the agricultural sector. One Russian analyst summarized the situation thusly: "a network of banks which specialize in serving agriculture is missing. Commercial banks do not have the experience and the knowledge necessary for working in agriculture."[48]

In an effort to reform the financial/credit system of Russian agriculture, in mid-March 2000, Acting President Vladimir Putin signed instructions for the creation of a new agricultural bank, called Rossel'khozbank.[49] The bank was registered in April 2000 and received its license to conduct banking activities in June 2000. By September–October 2000, the new bank received its first state credits and began operations, finishing its first year of operation with a 3.4 million ruble profit, growing to 340 million rubles in 2002. By mid-2001, Rossel'khozbank had thirty-four regional branch offices; in 2002, it had 200 branch offices throughout the regions of Russia. Unlike with other banks, most of the business activity of Rossel'khozbank comes from agriculture, an estimated 75 percent. In 2002, Rossel'khozbank distributed over 5 billion rubles in credit, an increase from the 4.6 billion rubles distributed in 2001. During its first two years of existence, Rossel'khozbank distributed credit primarily to enterprises, not individuals. For example, in 2002, the chairman of the bank, Aleksandr Zhitnik, indicated that food-producing enterprises received 48 percent of credits distributed, food processing plants 23 percent, organizations involved in the sale of agricultural produce 17 percent, and agricultural repair enterprises 3 percent.[50] However, in early 2003, it was announced that Rossel'khozbank would begin to make loans to individuals as well, which means that private farmers will become eligible to participate.[51]

The second area in need of reform has been the nature of credit policy itself. During the early years of reform, agricultural credit and credit policy were essentially unchanged from the Soviet era. The reasons for this were that the state continued to require deliveries of agricultural produce to it during 1992–93 and farm gate prices were controlled by the state as well. Agricultural credits were channeled through a central state-owned bank called Agro-prombank (later renamed Rossel'khozbank, until its demise after the financial crisis of 1998). By 1994 it was necessary to replace the Soviet system of agricultural credit, which was based upon subsidized interest rates. A lending bank would receive a concessionary interest rate from the Central Bank, and would then in turn lend credit to a farm at a higher interest rate. However, with high inflation, and with it, higher interest rates, all parties were hurt. Banks were repaid with devalued rubles (when they were repaid at all—it was not uncommon for lending banks not to receive the subsidy from the Central Bank, and the state often did not pay producers for their deliveries, which affected farms' ability to repay credit debt.) Moreover, as the cost of funds changed, the Central Bank changed the interest rate paid by the borrower, even in mid-loan. The effect was that no borrower could accurately calculate the true cost of any credit loan. The uncertainty of borrowing was a key factor in decreasing farm output, as farms were unable to fund production expenses on their own and were unwilling to take on high interest debt that was economically disadvantageous.[52]

Thus, starting in 1995, a commodity credit system was introduced, whereby farms were allocated "credit" (a balance sheet to purchase inputs from local distributors) to be repaid in kind by the end of the year, plus interest. In reality, low repayment rates by farms resulted because purchase prices were not sufficient to cover production costs. Eventually, rural commodity credit debt was converted to state bonds, which added to the financial burdens leading up to the August 1998 crash of the banking system and default on internally held debt.

In mid-2000, a new credit system was announced by Gordeev. The new system provides subsidized interest rates to purchase needed inputs or to fund operations, instead of providing subsidized inputs as in the recent past. The new credit system took effect for the 2001 sowing season. In this new system, state credits (money) are transferred to Rossel'khozbank (and other banks, including Sberbank and other Moscow banks), which then provide loans directly to food producers at higher interest rates, from which the bank derives a profit.[53] The federal budget includes a budget line (a preferential credit fund) for the subsidization of seasonal loans.

The goal of the system is to increase the effectiveness of the agricultural credit system, give banks a profit incentive to participate, and at the same time provide the seasonal support that food producers need. One of the main differences between the previous system and the new system is attention to the ability of the debtor to repay the loan. Aleksandr Zhitnik, the head of Rossel'khozbank, explained that because the monetary resources of the bank are limited, "we provide credit only after a careful investigation, a deep analysis of the economy in each enterprise-loanee. I am able to say that such an approach is justified. During the past year the rate of overdue loans is less than one percent of our credit portfolio."[54]

CONCLUSION

This chapter has argued that Putin has undertaken a "quiet revolution" in agriculture. Gone are the days of radical agrarian reform and the indifference to the agricultural sector that characterized the Yeltsin years. Putin has reversed the Yeltsin legacy in a number of important ways, introducing policies that will shape agrarian relations for years to come. Among the main goals of Putin's "quiet revolution" in agriculture has been to stabilize the rural sector, much as he has attempted to stabilize society after the tumultuous Yeltsin years. Putin has benefited from higher oil revenues and increased tax collection, which have allowed him to increase state support to the agricultural sector. At the same time, his pragmatism has paid off by addressing concrete problems that affect domestic food production. For these efforts he is to be applauded: the agricultural economy as a whole has produced positive growth rates for four consecutive years.

In terms of agrarian politics, we have seen how Putin enjoys a level of mass support from rural dwellers in a way that Yeltsin never did. This support cuts across age, gender, education, income, and employment status. The new realities of rural support for Putin mean that a realignment of electoral support is under way, requiring the Communist Party to search out new bases of support. Moreover, at the elite level, the Kremlin-backed RAD has emerged as a viable alternative to those who are disillusioned with the policies and leadership of the APR and Communist Party, and who see brighter prospects in cooperating with the Kremlin rather than confronting it.

In agrarian economics, Putin has moved decisively toward a less open trade regime by increasing tariffs and using import quotas on certain products. Restrictive trade measures are an integral part of the overall strategy to support domestic producers, revive domestic production, and ensure the nation's food security. Complementing protection from foreign competition has been the reform of the agricultural credit system. A new state agricultural bank has been created, which distributes credit to domestic producers. Credit policy now gives preference to strong, productive farms and, more recently, to individuals who are able to use credit effectively and repay the loan.

Although the rural sector of Russia remains plagued by numerous problems, some of which are not easily addressed by state policy, there is more reason to be cautiously optimistic about Russian agriculture under Putin than at any time in recent history.[55] Agriculture is once again a priority of policymakers, and Putin has moved pragmatically to stop the decline in agriculture and to revive domestic production. As a result, the agricultural sector, which appeared to be simply hopeless a few short years ago, has rebounded from its nadir under Yeltsin.

NOTES

This chapter is based upon a previously published article entitled "Russian Agrarian Policy under Putin," *Post-Soviet Geography and Economics* 43, no. 1 (January 2002). The author thanks V. H. Winston and Son, Inc., for permission to use some material from that article.

Some of the research in this chapter was supported by the National Council for Eurasian and East European Research, contract number 816–14g, under the authority of a Title VIII grant from the U.S. Department of State. The author alone is responsible for the views expressed.

1. See David J. O'Brien and Stephen K. Wegren, eds., *Rural Reform in Post-Soviet Russia* (Washington, D.C.: Woodrow Wilson Center Press and Johns Hopkins University Press, 2002).

2. *Sel'skoe khozyaystvo v Rossii* (Moscow: Goskomstat, 2000), 57.

3. See Stephen K. Wegren, "The Russian Food Problem: Domestic and Foreign Consequences," *Problems of Post-Communism* 47, no. 1 (January–February 2000): 38–48.

4. *Krest'yanskiye vedomosti*, no. 7 (February 14–20, 2000): 2.

5. The basic directions of the program and agrarian policy are also summarized in interviews with Gordeev in *Sel'skaya zhizn'*, July 25, 2000, 1; August 24–30, 2000, 1, 4; December 7–13, 2000, 1, 3; and January 30, 2001, 1, 2.

6. The new program was designed to replace the previous program, "Federal Special Purpose Program for the Stabilization and Development of the Agroindustrial Production during 1996–2000," which had been largely ignored and was ineffective.

7. *Sel'skaya zhizn'*, July 25–30, 2002, 3.

8. "O federal'noy tselevoy programme 'Sotsial'noye razvitiye sela do 2010 goda,'" *Sobraniye zakonodatel'stva Rossiyskoy Federatsii*, no. 49 (December 9, 2002): 11441–497.

9. *Krest'yanskiye vedomosti*, nos. 1–2 (January 1–31, 2003): 2–3.

10. *Krest'yanskiye vedomosti*, nos. 9–10 (March 1–15, 2001): 2. For additional coverage of the conference, see *Sel'skaya zhizn'*, February 27, 2001, 1.

11. A. Gordeev, "Za effecktvnoye agroproizvodstvo i kachestvennuyu produkt-siyu," *APK: ekonomika, upravleniye*, no. 5 (May 2001): 6.

12. A. Gordeev, "Za effecktvnoye agroproizvodstvo i kachestvennuyu produkt-siyu," 5.

13. "O finansovom ozdorovlenii sel'skokhozyaystvennykh tovaroproizvoditeley," *Sobraniye zakonodatel'stva Rossiyskoy Federatsii*, no. 28 (July 15, 2002): 7121–130.

14. Jerry F. Hough, Evelyn Davidheiser, and Susan Goodrich Lehmann, *The 1996 Russian Presidential Election* (Washington, D.C.: Brookings Institution, 1996), 5–6.

15. The same general pattern is evident with regard to presidential elections. In both the 1996 and 2000 presidential elections, the rural southern vote far exceeded the percentage of the national vote obtained by the Communist candidate Gennady Zyuganov. In 1996, for example, Zyuganov received 40 percent of the vote nationwide. About one-half of the vote came from the twenty-three rural regions. Likewise, in 2000, Zyuganov received 29 percent of the national vote, but 43 percent of his

vote came from the rural south. Therefore, it is clear that the rural southern vote has been a major component in the resiliency of the Communist Party.

16. A discussion of the methodology for the survey may be found in Stephen K. Wegren, David J. O'Brien, and Valeri V. Patsiorkovski, "Winners and Losers in Russian Agrarian Reform," *Journal of Peasant Studies* 30, no. 1 (October 2002): 1–30.

17. Timothy J. Colton, "Determinants of the Party Vote," in *Growing Pains: Russian Democracy and the Election of 1993*, ed. Timothy J. Colton and Jerry F. Hough (Washington, D.C.: Brookings Institution, 1998), 75–114; and Yitzhak Brudny, "Continuity or Change in Russia Electoral Patterns? The December 1999–March 2000 Election Cycle," in *Contemporary Russian Politics*, ed. Archie Brown (Oxford: Oxford University Press, 2001), 154–78.

18. For a survey of these groups and their policy stances, see Stephen K. Wegren, "Rural Politics and Agrarian Reform in Russia," *Problems of Post-Communism* 43, no. 1 (January–February 1996): 23–34.

19. *Krest'yanskiye vedomosti*, nos. 31–32 (September 23–29, 2002): 7.

20. *Krest'yanskiye vedomosti*, nos. 31–32 (September 23–29, 2002): 7.

21. *Krest'yanskiye vedomosti*, nos. 25–26 (June 21–30, 2002): 2.

22. *Krest'yanskiye vedomosti*, nos. 37–38 (November 4–December 15, 2002): 2.

23. *Krest'yanskiye vedomosti*, nos. 5–6 (February 16–28, 2003): 2.

24. *Krest'yanskiye vedomosti*, nos. 3–4 (February 1–15, 2003): 2.

25. S. Pilaev, "Ob obespechenii prodovol'stvennoy dostatichnosti naseleniya Rossii," *Ekonomist*, no. 7 (July 1998): 25.

26. "World Trade: Fifty Years On," *Economist*, May 16, 1998, 22.

27. Grain imports were a fraction of the levels during the late Soviet period. For example, during 1981–85, the Soviet Union imported an average of more than 40 million tons of grain a year; during 1986–90, it imported an average of more than 35 million tons annually, or roughly 15 percent of total grain availability.

28. Calculated from data in FAO databases atapps.fao.org.

29. A. Gordeev, "Sostoyaniye i perspektivy poizvodstva prodovol'stviya," *Ekonomist*, no. 5 (May 2001): 4.

30. *Krest'yanskaya rossiya*, no. 13 (April 2–8, 2001): 1.

31. A. V. Gordeev, A. I. Altukhov, and D. F. Vermel', "Prodovol'stvennaya bezopasnost' Rossii: sostoyanie i meri obespecheniya," *Ekonomika sel'skokhoziyaystvennykh i pererabatyvayushchikh predpriyatiy*, no. 10 (October 1998): 10.

32. V. Semenov, "Novyi kurs agrarnoi politiki," *Ekonomist*, no. 1 (January 1999): 14. See also *Sel'skaya zhizn'*, July 25, 2000, 1.

33. *Krest'yanskiye vedomosti*, no. 1 (January 1–9, 2000): 2.

34. *Krest'yanskiye vedomosti*, no. 3 (January 17–23, 2000): 2.

35. A. Gordeev, "Stabil'noye i dinamichnoye razvitiye APK—pervostepennaya zadacha," *APK: ekonomika, upravleniye*, no. (November 2000): 10.

36. In May 2001, the founding meeting of the Sugar Union was held in Moscow. The founding members included twenty-five different organizations. Among the founding members was Rossel'khozbank, and the state-licensed grain purchasing agent, Roskhleboprodukt. *Krest'yanskiye vedomosti*, nos. 19–20 (May 16–31, 2001): 3.

37. The general import tariff for processed sugar is 30 percent. However, special

seasonal tariffs of 45 percent are levied in January and June. The general import tariff for raw sugar is 5 percent. There was a "temporary special tariff" imposed in May 2000. In addition, there are seasonal tariffs of 45 percent levied in January and 40 percent levied in June. See E. Serova, *Rossiyskaya ekonomika v 2000 gody: tendentsii i perspektivy*. Moscow: Institute of Economics during the Transition Period, 2001. Section 2.4, table 11, available at www.iet.ru/trend/2000/2000.html.

38. *Krest'yanskiye vedomosti*, nos. 13–14 (April 1–15, 2001): 2. Previous to the March 2001 decision, imports of meat and milk products were prohibited from Argentina, Mongolia, and China.

39. Several ministries and committees have responsibility for ensuring that food imports meet sanitary and health criteria: the Ministry of Health, the Ministry of Trade, the State Tax Service (to ensure state monopoly on alcohol production), the State Bread Inspectorate, the State Customs Committee, the State Committee on Standards, and the Veterinary Service of Russia. In addition, there is a Veterinary Inspectorate within the Ministry of Agriculture. These organizations have the authority to refuse acceptance of a specific cargo, and to issue broader prohibitions of foodstuffs from specific nations. For example, in April 2000, the Veterinary Service of Russia prohibited the importation of meat and animal feed from China, South Korea, Vietnam, and Japan. *Krest'yanskiye vedomosti*, no. 15 (April 10–16, 2000): 3.

40. *Krest'yanskiye vedomosti*, nos. 37–38 (November 4–December 15, 2002):4; and nos. 39–40 (December 15–31, 2002): 2.

41. *Krest'yanskiye vedomosti*, nos. 1–2 (January 1–31, 2003): 2.

42. Resolution no. 48, "O merakh po zashchite Rossiyskogo ptitsevodstva," January 23, 2003, available at www.agronews.ru/.

43. Article from www.NewYorkTimes.com, February 1, 2003.

44. The import quotas reduce poultry imports to 744,000 tons annually for three years. The United States remains the primary exporter to Russia, allowed to export 553,500 tons. Previously, Russia imported well over one million tons of poultry meat annually, of which the United States supplied more than 80 percent.

45. I. Terent'ev, "Sostoyaniye i perspektivy APK," *Ekonomist*, no. 4 (April 2000): 87, 90.

46. For a discussion, see *Johnson's Russia List*, #7192, May 22, 2003, item number 9 on WTO accession.

47. R. N. Cherniy, "Problemy formirovaniya effektivnoy finansovo-kreditnoy sistemy po obsluzhivaniyu APK," *Ekonomika sel'skokhozyaystvennykh i pererabatyvauushchikh predpriyatiy*, no. 9 (September 2000): 24–26.

48. O. K. Yastrebova, "Kredit, finansy i investitsii v sel'skoye khozyaystvo," *Byulleten'*, no. 3 (July-October 2001); available at www.iet.ru/personal/agro/newslet/bullet9/left.html 2001.

49. *Krest'yanskiye vedomosti*, no. 12 (March 20–26, 2000): 2.

50. *Sel'skaya zhizn'*, June 18, 2002, 2.

51. Regional banks that had been operating for at least two years and were profitable would be allowed to take on individuals as clients. *Krest'yanskiye vedomosti*, nos. 1–2 (January 1–31, 2003): 2.

52. It should be remembered that during 1992–93, even though interest rates charged to farms were below the inflation rate, purchase prices for food products

lagged the inflation rate and price increases in other branches of the economy. In short, prices paid by farms were increasing faster than the prices they received for their production. In addition, the state was chronically in debt to producers for the food sold to the state, so farms were hurt by a double squeeze.

53. For more detail on how the system works, see *Krest'yanskiye vedomosti*, nos. 13–14 (April 1–15, 2001): 4.

54. *Sel'skaya zhizn'*, June 18, 2002, 2.

55. For a survey of the problems in Russian agriculture and the ability to solve them, see Stephen K. Wegren, Vladimir R. Belen'kiy, and Valeri V. Patsiorkovski, "The Challenge of Rural Revival," in *Russia's Policy Challenges: Security, Stability, and Development*, ed. Stephen K. Wegren (Armonk, N.Y.: M. E. Sharpe, 2003), 222–49.

Chapter Nine

Putin and the Oligarchs

Peter Rutland

Politics, like nature, abhors a vacuum. With the collapse of the USSR, a huge void of political and economic power opened up in the post–Soviet Union. Key institutional structures such as the Communist Party and the central planning system were dismantled, and the new entities that emerged in their wake (the presidential administration, the State Committee for the Administration of State Property, regional governors) were hard-pressed to expand their effective zone of control.

In the chaos of transition, power shifted from formal political institutions to informal networks of influence among individuals who had political connections or economic resources at their disposal. While market forces penetrated large sections of economic activity, the Russian economy was only partially marketized by the liberalization reforms. A whole parallel barter economy sprang up, accounting for perhaps half of all business-to-business transactions.[1] The interface between polity and economy was mediated by corruption and mutual favors, instead of political orders as under the old regime.

The rise of the oligarchs was unexpected and unpredicted. Nobody watching the tentative *glasnost* reforms of 1986 would have predicted that ten years later thirty-something billionaires would be bankrolling a presidential election campaign with rock concerts, direct mailings, and pop jingles. As the economic controls were gradually loosened under Gorbachev, journalists noted the appearance of bright young entrepreneurs, making money by importing personal computers or selling phone directories. But no one would have imagined that these people would become owners of large swathes of Soviet manufacturing industry, or would push up the price of villas on the Spanish Riviera. Rather, they were portrayed as heroic but somewhat comic figures out of an Ilf and Petrov novel of the roaring 1920s; part of Russia's rich history of eccentrics.[2]

161

There were bigger stories to pursue in 1989–92: the fall of the Berlin Wall; the titanic duel between Gorbachev and Yeltsin that led to the collapse of the Soviet Union; and the dramatic decision to free prices in January 1992. The reformers hoped that the lifting of economic controls would lead to a surge of entrepreneurship, while the privatization program, involving the distribution of vouchers to all citizens, would produce a "popular capitalism" with ownership distribution among the general population. However, the voucher privatization was hijacked by incumbent directors, who used it to turn their de facto control over their enterprises into de jure ownership, while the expected surge of entrepreneurship in the newly freed private sector failed to materialize. Although about one million small businesses were registered, their development was choked off by bureaucratic regulation on one side and mafia extortion on the other.

Russia's raw capitalism threw up a new class, not of small entrepreneurs, but of powerful oligarchs. The first important signal that the Russian transition had gone badly off track came, curiously enough, in a short newspaper article by an American diplomat in November 1995.[3] Thomas Graham argued that Russia was in fact ruled by a small number of individuals, loosely allied into rival "clans" that were jostling for the ear of the all-powerful president. Yeltsin's crushing of the Congress of People's Deputies in October 1993 had removed the last major challenge to presidential rule. But Yeltsin lacked the power, and the inclination, to rule as a dictator. Instead he was pulled this way and that by cliques of influential advisers—the security apparatus, represented by head bodyguard Aleksandr Korzhakov; the economic reformers, led by Anatoly Chubais; the gas lobby, represented by Victor Chernomyrdin; the military-industry complex, whose advocate was Oleg Soskovets. Real power lay with these individuals, and not with the formal democratic institutions—parliament, the courts, political parties. Russia had dismantled an autocracy, but instead of rule by the many (democracy) it had arrived at rule by the few (oligarchy).

The "clan" metaphor did not quite catch on. It sounded a little archaic and mysterious; and it overstated the extent to which the individuals involved had a group loyalty and identity. People seemed more comfortable with the idea that power was being wielded by clearly identifiable individuals. Hence, by 1996 the favored term was "oligarchs." The word was first used by Aleksandr Privalov of *Ekspert* magazine, who started a regular poll of elites, publishing rankings of who were seen as the most influential political and business figures.[4]

The oligarchs fell into two overlapping groups.[5] One contingent included officials formerly in the middle or upper reaches of the Soviet *nomenklatura*, who managed to negotiate the transition to capitalism and stayed in charge of organizations which were no longer in state ownership, or at least no longer under effective state control.[6] Examples include the natural gas giant

Gazprom, the electricity monopoly Unified Energy Systems or EES, the railways ministry, and the coal conglomerate Rosugol. Even the Central Bank itself can be seen as an autonomous player, since it pursued a fairly independent monetary policy, indulged in all sorts of dubious accounting practices, and rewarded its top officials with lavish salaries.

The second, and more visible, group were young businessmen who had grown rich during the process of market reform.[7] Some of them came from academia, some from the criminal world. Most of them made their initial capital in business start-ups in the late 1980s, mainly through trade or banking operations spun off from state-owned enterprises. Alfa Group, Inkombank, Menatep, Rosprom, SBS-Agro, and Rossiiskii Kredit all had their origins in enterprises formed under the auspices of the Communist Party of the Soviet Union (CPSU) or its youth branch, the Komsomol. Vladimir Potanin's Oneksimbank came out of the foreign trade ministry, but grew into the most extensive and diversified of the oligarchic holdings.[8] Only Vladimir Gusinsky's MOST and Boris Berezovsky's Logovaz can be regarded as relatively independent start-up operations. The oligarchs expanded their scope by gaining control of companies during the voucher privatization launched in 1992.[9] A few years later, a small group of favored insiders bought lucrative state assets such as Norilsk Nickel or the Tyumen Oil Company at giveaway prices during the notoriously corrupt loans-for-shares auctions of 1995.

The leading oligarchs united in their efforts to ensure the re-election of Boris Yeltsin in 1996, after which several of them directly joined the government. The oligarchs had much to offer the Yeltsin administration: energy, leadership, organizational skills, Western contacts, and above all lots of cash. Their most important political asset was control over the main media: print, radio, and television. Most of these media outlets were making huge losses, but they enabled the oligarchs to convert money into political power. The media gave them the power to mould public opinion, to make or break reputations, and to shape elite perceptions and policy debates. The path was blazed by entrepreneurs such as Vladimir Gusinsky and Boris Berezovsky, but they were followed by mainstream oil companies and banks. Gusinsky's MOST Bank founded NTV television and the newspaper *Segodnya* in 1993, by 1996 Berezovsky had control over the TV stations ORT and TV-6 and papers *Nezavisimaya gazeta* and *Novye izvestiia*. Potanin's Oneksimbank controlled the papers *Komsomol'skaia pravda*, *Izvestiya*, *Russkii telegraf*, and *Ekspert*.[10] Another political asset was the private security services that each magnate assembled. Apart from providing physical protection, such services gathered intelligence (*kompromat*) which could be used to discredit rival oligarchs or uncooperative politicians. In return the oligarchs grew fat from government favors: export and import licenses, soft loans, the right to handle government accounts ("authorized banks"), government contracts, lax taxation, and first claim on assets to be privatized.

In the spring of 1997, the liberal wing of the government tried to launch a second wave of reforms, raising utility prices and cracking down on corruption. Deputy Prime Minister Boris Nemtsov started attacking the oligarchs in the name of "popular capitalism." But the reforms were blocked by an unholy alliance of business interests, regional governors, and the communist opposition. There was no constituency in favor of raising utility prices, and cheap energy seemed vital for domestic political tranquillity. Subsidized fuel suited some oligarchs very well (especially the metals producers), and those whom it harmed (the oil and gas companies) were compensated through tax breaks and permission to pocket the lion's share of their export earnings. In the summer of 1997, the oligarchs started feuding over how to divide the spoils in the next wave of privatization—most notably, the telecommunications monopoly and the remaining state-owned oil companies. By September the fighting—in the form of personal attacks and corruption allegations in rival newspapers—was so intense that Yeltsin called the six leading bankers to a meeting and persuaded them to declare a truce.[11]

Crony capitalism, it seemed, was here to stay. The reform process was stalled in midstream.[12] Powerful leaders had a vested interest in preserving the status quo, and there was no significant coalition of groups with a stake in further reform. Ordinary citizens were dissatisfied but felt powerless. The economy had been sufficiently liberalized to enable the oligarchs to enrich themselves, but not so much as to expose them to effective competition (from foreign companies, for example). They showed little interest in the creation of effective legal and regulatory institutions, which could threaten their power and independence. The downside of this partial reform was that economic output fell for seven years in a row, while investment declined even more precipitately. One reason for the slump in investment was that the property rights of the new owners were precarious, and could be challenged by a rival clan, or by the state, at any time.

The rise of the oligarchs was a striking and unexpected development in post-Soviet Russia, but the fact that business elites exercise political power is hardly unusual in a global and historical perspective. In that broader comparative context, what is striking about contemporary Russia is how important a role is still played by the state, and in particular by the presidential apparatus. Russia is still quite a way from a Latin American model, with "all power to the oligarchs."

THE AUGUST CRISIS

The key turning point in Russia's economic evolution in the 1990s was the August 1998 financial crash. The crisis was caused by two erroneous policies. First, the government borrowed money to defend the ruble at an exchange rate that was overvalued against the dollar, and second, it issued $40 billion of short-term debt to cover its yawning budget deficit instead of trying to cut government spending. Russia was also struggling to meet payments on $150 billion of foreign debt and was kept afloat only by $80 billion in annual earnings from oil, gas, and metals exports. The 1997 Asian financial crisis caused a slump in commodity prices; Russia's trade surplus eroded; and international investors panicked. In August 1998 the Russian government defaulted on its debts, the ruble lost 75 percent of its value, and most private banks collapsed, wiping out much of the savings of Russia's nascent middle class. The oligarchs were seriously weakened by the August 1998 financial crisis. Many went bankrupt, and the survivors were even more dependent on financial assistance and other favors from the state. A few banks survived the crisis and were able to strengthen their position as a result (such as Alfa Bank and SBS-Agro). The oil, gas, and metals producers were generally unaffected.

At the insistence of the State Duma, in September the conservative Yevgeny Primakov was appointed prime minister, and he launched anticorruption probes against some of the oligarchs, notably Boris Berezovsky. Berezovsky's holdings included Aeroflot, the auto company Logovaz, and oil interests. He also had effective control over Russian Public Television (ORT). Berezovsky was close to Yeltsin's daughter Tatiana Diachenko: his network of contacts in the Kremlin was known as "the Family."

Primakov's anticorruption campaign led to his own dismissal by Yeltsin in March 1999. He subsequently joined forces with regional leaders, Moscow Mayor Yuri Luzhkov and Tatarstan President Mintimer Shaimiev, to mount the most serious political challenge yet to the Yeltsin establishment—the Fatherland/All Russia (OVR) alliance. To meet this threat Yeltsin installed Vladimir Putin, the head of the Federal Security Service (FSB), as prime minister in August 1999. From his new position, Putin oversaw the launch of the second Chechen war, in retaliation for terrorist bombings and raids on Dagestan. The war drew broad public support, and Putin showed himself to be a competent and effective leader.

Kremlin aides launched the Unity party to challenge OVR in the December 1999 State Duma election. Berezovsky's media rallied to the Kremlin cause, with the ORT channel launching blistering attacks on Luzhkov and Primakov. The campaign worked. Unity finished second with 23 percent of the vote, only just behind the Communists, and Fatherland/All Russia was placed third with 13 percent.

On December 31, 1999, the eve of the new millennium, Yeltsin resigned and appointed Putin acting president. Putin then set about preparing himself for the March 2000 presidential election. The main challenger, as in 1996, would be the anemic and uncharismatic Communist stalwart, Gennadiy Zyuganov. Key figures from Berezovsky's clique stayed on in the Kremlin. The only leading figure to be let go was Yeltsin's daughter, Tatiana Diachenko.

Most notably, Putin reappointed Aleksandr Voloshin, the éminence grise of the Berezovsky clan, as chief of staff of the presidential administration, a pivotal position controlling access to the president. Allegations repeatedly surfaced over the next two years about Voloshin's financial machinations at Sibneft and the AVVA auto concern back in 1994–95, but Putin has kept him on.[13] The financial linchpin of the Family, Pavel Borodin, was appointed to head the Russia–Belarus Union. This post granted him diplomatic immunity, which was useful given that on January 26, 2000, he was indicted by Swiss prosecutors for money laundering during his time as Kremlin property chief.[14]

Already by February 2000 it was clear that Putin was headed to certain electoral victory, so Russia's political and economic elite was lining up to support him. Berezovsky gave out the impression that he personally had been the architect of Putin's rise to power.[15] This seemed to be confirmed by a February government decision to allow the Berezovsky-allied Sibneft oil company to merge with Oleg Deripaska's Sibal to form a company that would control 70 percent of Russian aluminum production. However, one week before the election Putin sent a warning signal. Speaking to Radio Mayak on March 18, he attacked the oligarchs who have been "merging power with capital" and declared, "Such a class of oligarchs will cease to exist." With state and private media rallying to his cause, Putin's approval ratings continued to rise, carrying him to a first-round victory over Zyuganov.[16]

PUTIN IN CHARGE

At the time of his election, Putin was widely regarded as a tool of the Family with no independent standing or room for maneuver. These skeptics underestimated Putin's ability to use the authority vested in him as acting—and then elected—president to chart his own course.

Yeltsin's penchant for political reshuffles and aversion to the routine tasks of government had produced administrative chaos. Putin wanted to restore a stable chain of command, but it was not clear whether he had the administrative experience or the team of loyal cadres to pull this off.

The officials in the government and presidential apparatus were divided into three rival groupings in the spring of 2000:

1. "The Family"—Chief of Staff Aleksandr Voloshin, Prime Minister Mikhail Kasianov, Railways Minister Nikolai Aksenenko, Procurator-General Vladimir Ustinov, Energy Minister Viktor Kaliuzhnyi, Atomic Energy Minister Yevgenii Adamov, Science Minister Valerii Kirpichni-

kov; plus other figures outside government such as former Yeltsin aide Valentin Yumashev and MDM-Bank head Aleksandr Mamut.

2. "The Petersburg Liberals"—Economics Minister German Gref; Deputy Prime Ministers Aleksei Kudrin and Viktor Khristenko; Dmitrii Kozak, deputy head of the presidential administration in charge of legal reform; Antimonopoly Minister Ilya Yuzhanov; presidential economics advisor Andrei Illarionov, and Anatolii Chubais, the architect of Yeltsin's privatization program who had become head of the electricity monopoly EES in 1998.[17]

3. "The Security Men"—Security Council Secretary Sergei Ivanov, FSB head Nikolai Patrushev, Viktor Cherkessov (deputy head of FSB), Defense Minister Igor Sergeev, Deputy Prime Minister and defense industry chief Ilya Klebanov, Interior Minister Vladimir Rushailo, Igor Sechin, the head of the presidential chancellery; Viktor Ivanov, the deputy head of the presidential administration; Viktor Zolotov, the head of the Presidential Security Service.

A significant proportion of both the liberals and security men (*siloviki*) were acquainted with Putin from St. Petersburg, where he had spent most of his career. His four years in Moscow also enabled him to forge some links with the Kremlin apparatus and with the FSB and other security ministries.[18] But generally it was thought that the St. Petersburg team (both its liberal and security wings) were not sufficiently experienced and influential to really pose a threat to the political and economic establishment that had emerged in Moscow under Yeltsin's rule. The continuation in office of staff chief Voloshin and Premier Kasianov signaled to many that the Family was still calling the shots.

Putin apparently had good working relations with all three groups in his administration, and wanted to delineate duties more clearly in order to stamp out factional conflicts—something that Yeltsin had actually encouraged as part of his "checks and balances" style of rule. There was no immediate purge of ministers after Putin took over. It was widely reported that the Family had dissuaded Putin from appointing his first choice for procurator general, Dmitrii Kozak, in favor of Vladimir Ustinov. But the expected open warfare between rival clans fighting for the spoils of the new administration failed to materialize. Instead, Putin initially turned his attention to reining in the power of the regional bosses who, like the oligarchs, had grown fat during the Yeltsin era.

THE MEDIA CRACKDOWN

One oligarch who remained outside the broad tent that Putin had erected was Vladimir Gusinsky, whose media outlets had backed the wrong horse (the OVR alliance of Primakov and Luzhkov) in the 1999 Duma election. Gusinsky's television channel, NTV, ran into financial problems after the August 1998 crash, and the government refused to help out. NTV ended up borrowing $400 million from the Gazprom corporation (still 40 percent state-owned and closely tied to the Kremlin). Putin grew increasingly displeased with NTV's objective coverage of the war in Chechnya. Another bone of contention was NTV's puppet satire show *Kukly*, which portrayed Putin in a variety of unflattering scenes. (At the end of May 2000 *Kukly* agreed to drop the Putin puppet.)

These tensions boiled over in the aftermath of the presidential election. Masked tax and security police staged a dramatic raid on Gusinsky's Media-MOST offices in downtown Moscow on May 11. Media-MOST was not only a media company, it also ran an extensive private security service that snooped on business and political rivals to gather *kompromat*. On June 13, Gusinsky himself was arrested and locked in the infamous Butyrka prison, on vague charges dating back to 1998 involving the privatization of a small Petersburg company called Russkoe Video. He was released three days later, after an international outcry. Putin was on a state visit to Spain and Germany at the time, and he neither endorsed nor condemned the arrest. Gusinsky, who was also the president of the World Jewish Congress, was a highly visible international figure.

In July Gusinsky made a secret deal with Press Minister Mikhail Lesin and the head of Gazprom-Media, Alfred Kokh, under which he agreed to cede control over NTV in return for the cancellation of its debts to Gazprom and the dropping of criminal charges. Gusinsky was allowed to leave the country, and in September, from the safety of Gibraltar, he publicly denounced the deal. Lesin was reprimanded by Prime Minister Kasianov for making the obviously illegal deal, but was not fired. In November Gusinsky reluctantly agreed to allow Gazprom-Media to take control over NTV.

During the summer months a number of other oligarchs also felt the hand of the state on their shoulder. Vladimir Potanin's Interros, Anatoly Chubais's electricity monopoly EES, and the Tyumen Oil Company were all accused of irregularities during their privatization, while LUKoil, auto giant AvtoVAZ, Gazprom, and Roman Abramovich's Sibneft were all subject to tax inspections. None of these probes led to any actual arrests or legal actions, but they served their purpose of warning the oligarchs. Polls suggested that the Russian public were either indifferent to these struggles or sympathetic with Putin: 44 percent expressed approval, and only 6 percent expressed concern about his moves against the oligarchs.[19] In a bid to calm the waters and consolidate his position, on July 28, 2000, Putin met with twenty-one leading businessmen in the Kremlin.[20] In contrast to previous meetings between Yeltsin and select oligarchs, this time it seemed to be the president laying down terms to the oligarchs, rather than the reverse. Also noteworthy was the absence of some key figures from the meeting. Gusinsky, Berezovsky, and Sibneft's Abramovich were not invited, and Chubais declined to attend. The outcome of the meeting was a bland statement that the state would cooperate with businesses "whose actions function in the state's interests." Putin was signaling that the age of the oligarchs was over, but in reality it was business as usual for those who were willing to avoid mounting a political challenge to Putin. Putin made no serious effort to reverse the corrupt privatizations of previous years, nor to overhaul the sweetheart deals under which the oligarchs reaped rich dividends from exporting Russia's natural resources.

The oligarchs seemed content with or perhaps resigned to the new order, at least once Gusinsky had been released from jail. At the June meeting, Putin advised the oligarchs to join the Russian Union of Industrialists and Entrepreneurs (RSPP), a rather staid organization representing traditional state-owned factories headed by a Gorbachev-era functionary, Arkadii Volskii.[21] In this way, he would be able to put his negotiations with the oligarchs on a firmer, more institutionalized footing.

Apart from Gusinsky, the other oligarch in Putin's sights was Berezovsky. On May 31, 2000, Berezovsky published an open letter denouncing Putin's plans to revise Russia's federal structure and weaken the power of regional leaders. In June, under pressure to repay a $100 million loan from state-owned Vneshekonombank, Berezovsky announced that he was ready to transfer his 49 percent stake in the television company ORT back to the state. On July 14, procurators interviewed Berezovsky in connection with Aeroflot's foreign currency accounts. In a curious move, Berezovsky gave up his seat in the State Duma on July 19 (a post which gave him immunity from prosecution) and tried to create a political movement in opposition to Putin. He recruited a handful of intellectuals and movie stars to sign his manifesto, "Russia at the Crossroads," which was published on August 9, but there was no public response. In October, Berezovsky was again questioned over the Aeroflot case, and he was forced to vacate the state-owned villa near Moscow that he was renting for $300,000 a year. In November he went into exile. However, exile was not necessarily a safe haven for the oppositional oligarchs. On December 12, 2000, Spanish police arrested Gusinsky, acting on an Interpol warrant filed by Russian prosecutors. Gusinsky was released on bail, and on December 26 a Moscow court dismissed the fraud case against him.

In the midst of the NTV crisis, leading businessmen from the RSPP issued a statement disowning Berezovsky, stating, "We view the attempt of big business to monopolize control over the country as the worst mistake of the past decade. The same goes for the attempt to force its will on the government through the use of controlled media."[22] On January 24, 2001, Putin held a second meeting with the oligarchs. Those attending included Oleg Deripaska, head of Russian Aluminum. Deripaska had just (November 2000) managed to acquire, in a hostile takeover, 25 percent of the auto giant Gorkii

AZ in Nizhniy Novgorod. Interestingly, the same month Deripaska was uninvited from the Davos World Economic Forum, following the filing of a suit by three Western companies accusing him of making death threats.[23] Later in 2001, Deripaska married the daughter of Valentin Yumashev, Yeltsin's ghostwriter and former head of the presidential administration. Yumashev in his turn married Yeltsin's daughter, Tatiana Diachenko.

Although some saw Putin's summer offensive against the media barons as signaling the end of the oligarchs, Putin's crackdown was limited to those who mounted an open political challenge to his rule. Critics saw Putin's moves against Berezovsky and Gusinsky as targeting not so much those individuals themselves, but the relatively critical and independent media that they controlled. They viewed it as part of a systematic campaign to limit free speech and reassert state control over the media. Indeed it is clear that the main targets of Putin's campaign were those oligarchs who had used their wealth to create media empires. Putin's defenders argued that it was appropriate for Putin to end the manipulation of the media by the oligarchs, and that it did not necessarily mean that he was an enemy of democracy.

THE RETURN OF THE CLAN WARS

Putin kept the Family appointees in place during his first year in office, but in March 2001 he dismissed most of the top security officials he had inherited from Yeltsin and replaced them with his own people, many drawn from the "Petersburg Chekists."[24] Defense Minister Igor Sergeev was replaced with Sergei Ivanov, a former KGB official and close Putin ally. Vladimir Rushailo, a Family appointee, replaced Ivanov as head of the Security Council, and Petersburg politician turned Unity party leader Boris Gryzlov took over from Rushailo as interior minister.

However, this shuffling of the security apparatus did not touch the Family. Through the rest of 2001, observers argued that the various Kremlin factions were waging a bitter, but hidden, struggle for power. It was assumed that a victory for the Chekists over the Family could pose a serious threat for the oligarchs as a whole.[25] Presidential economic adviser Andrei Illarionov openly stated in December 2001 that the power struggles under Putin "are no less vicious than they were under President Yeltsin."[26] These battles within the administration did not directly involve the oligarchs, however. As one editorial cynically observed: "No one is competing with the president for power; all are competing for a place under his right heel."[27] Yet Natalia Astrakhanova argues that "the president doesn't hold the controlling interest in Russia Inc. There are many shareholders in this corporation; making decisions acceptable to everyone is difficult, and making decisions fast is altogether impossible."[28] Inessa Slavutinskaia argued that "the people from St. Petersburg want the financial channels of the Railroads Ministry, Alrosa and the State Customs Committee, which are all still controlled by the Family."[29]

A new wave of anticorruption investigations was launched in 2001 by the procurator's office and the Duma's Audit Chamber—but behind them observers saw the hand of the "Petersburg Chekists." However, Svetlana Babaeva warns against oversimplifying and polarizing the Kremlin intrigues. "The concepts of 'St. Petersburg team' and 'family' are flexible, because too many changes have taken place in Russia. It is not a geographic location, it is rather a way of thinking. It is a system of recognition, of telling 'us' from 'them.' "[30]

Putin did recruit some loyal executives from St. Petersburg and placed them in key national companies.[31] Most notably, on May 30, 2001, he ousted the long-standing head of Gazprom, Rem Viakhirev, and replaced him with a young economist from Petersburg, Aleksei Miller, who had spent six months as deputy energy minister. Gazprom's $15 billion exports make it Russia's largest cash earner and the second largest company after Unified Electricity Systems (EES). It has more than its share of scandal, with new revelations surfacing in 2001 about its Enron-like transactions with subsidiary Itera.[32] Similarly, Sergei Zivenko was parachuted into the alcohol manufacturer Rosspirtprom and Valerii Yashin into the telecom holding company Svyazinvest. Putin even brought in people he had known in East Germany (Andrei Belianinov and Sergei Chemezov) to head the newly merged arms export companies.[33]

In the absence of major reform initiatives from the Kremlin, business elites had little to complain about. At their third meeting with Putin on May 31, 2001, the main grouse seemed to be the continuing requirement that 75 percent of dollar earnings be exchanged into rubles.[34] Of the twenty-two men at the meeting, nine came from the oil and gas sector, six from metals and engineering, six from banking, and only one from a high-tech company. The most sensitive political decision was the setting of export duties on oil and natural gas.[35] Finance Minister Kudrin and Central Bank chief Gerashchenko argued for higher rates to enable Russia to meet its foreign debt repayments, while the energy bosses pleaded for more profits to finance investment.[36] A new unified tariff body, the Federal Energy Commission, was created to fix prices in all the natural monopolies. Its head, Grigorii Kutovoi, was seen as a member of the Family, hostile to Chubais's pleas to raise electricity prices, but approving higher rates for Gazprom.[37] Chubais devised an ambitious program to split EES into twenty regional divisions and divide its generation and transmission businesses, in a bid to separate out the profitable sides of the operation. This plan was attacked by regional elites fearful of losing their cheap power, and even by foreign owners of EES shares, who feared being cheated. Chubais managed to hold on to his position as head of EES, thanks to his long-standing ties with Gref and Kudrin, Putin's leading economic officials.[38]

Meanwhile, it was largely business as usual for the oligarchs. In the course of 2001 there were ownership conflicts over major regional companies such as Rospan, Ust-Ilim combine, Karabash, and Kuzbassugol. Ironically, the new 1998 bankruptcy law opened up new opportunities for rivals to tie up the assets of companies they coveted, by filing suit for bankruptcy often in corruption-prone provincial courts. Major companies such as Severstal, Gazprom, Mosenergo, LUKoil, and Transenergo found themselves entangled in such proceedings in 2001.[39] Vladimir Potanin's Interros group bought a 34 percent stake in Novolipetsk Metal Combine, the third largest steelmaker, but was not able to win full control. He did however manage to block George Soros's efforts to restructure Svyazinvest.[40] In general, an OECD study concluded, "There is no unified economic space, or level playing field in Russia" for foreign investors.[41] Projects were undermined, for example, by the sudden withdrawal of phone frequencies or changes in rail tariffs, plus many "unforeseen hurdles" such as negotiable regional taxes.

Ekspert magazine continued to track the rise and fall of various oligarchs. The end of 2001 saw the decline of Sibneft's Abramovich (who had retreated to the post of governor of distant Chukotka) to be replaced at the head of the list by Victor Gerashchenko, the head of the Central Bank (a post he had held in the Soviet Union). The rising figures on the list were not independent players, but those with close ties to the Kremlin: Sergei Pugachev (Mezhprombank), Leonid Reiman, Vladimir Kogan.[42]

MEDIA WAR, PART TWO

The struggle against the independent media of Gusinsky/Berezovsky continued in 2001.[43] In April 2001, Gazprom-media took over NTV, and looked around for new owners.[44] Moves by foreigners such as Ted Turner to bail out the station were rebuffed, and in mid-May 2001, Yevgenii Kisilev and his team of talented journalists quit NTV and moved to TV-6, taking with them key commentary programs like *Itogi* and *Glas naroda*. Boris Jordan, an American banker and associate of Chubais, became the new chief of NTV, and the channel has managed to retain a degree of its professional integrity.

Attention then shifted to the Moscow-based TV-6 channel. Berezovsky owned 37 percent of MNVK, which operates TV-6, and in 1999 the station head Eduard Sagalaev sold him another 37 percent. LUKoil-garant, the oil giant's pension fund, owned 15 percent. The arrival of the Kisilev team at TV-6 prompted LUKoil-garant to sue, presumably at the Kremlin's instigation, although claiming that as the company was making losses and not paying dividends it should be liquidated. In November the Moscow Arbitration

Court threw out the LUKoil-garant case, but this decision was reversed on appeal to the federal arbitration court on December 29. TV-6 was ordered closed on January 11, 2002, shutting down the last non-state-controlled TV station in Russia.[45] TV-6 had reached 80 million viewers through 156 regional affiliates, so the impact of the closure would be felt beyond Moscow.[46]

After lengthy negotiations, in June 2002 Kisilev's team of respected journalists was allowed to continue broadcasting as TV Center (TVS), under the supervision of a board of a dozen pro-Kremlin businessmen headed by ex-premier Yevgeny Primakov. At the same time a group of independent journalists were awarded the license to continue broadcasting the independent radio station Ekho Moskvy. However, in June 2003 the media ministry also shut down TVS. TVS was behind in paying its bills, and the oligarchs bankrolling the station, Deripaska and Chubais, did not want to continue losing money, and did not see any political benefits from maintaining this independent voice. The Kremlin's quashing of independent television in Russia seemed complete.

The London-based Berezovsky continued to wage war on the Putin administration. In 2002 he sponsored a book and a TV documentary accusing the Federal Security Service (FSB) of planting the apartment bombs that killed 300 Russians in September 1999. He also produced a lively movie, *Oligarch*, loosely based on some fictionalized elements of his own career, which showed at cinemas throughout Russia. In summer 2002 Berezovsky boasted that he was ready to put $100 million into the new Liberal Russia Party. He even gave money to radical nationalist Aleksandr Prokhanov, although the Communist Party (KPRF) rejected his offer of support.

HUNTING SEASON

One utility that had ridden the storms of transition fairly successfully was the railways ministry, MPS. Trains somehow managed to run on time, and more or less made a profit, using revenues from freight customers to subsidize passenger travel. MPS head Nikolai Aksenenko was widely tipped as a possible successor to Prime Minister Kasianov. However, on October 22, 2001, criminal charges were filed against Aksenenko, charging him with illegally spending $2.3 million on apartments for his deputy ministers.[47] The charge stemmed from an investigation by the parliament's Audit Chamber, headed by ex-premier Sergei Stepashin. The MPS was also under investigation for hiding $1.9 billion revenue in off-budget funds, and failing to pay $370 million in federal taxes. Aksenenko was replaced by Gennadii Fadeev, who had previously served as railroads minister from 1992 until 1996.

In December 2001, prosecutors arrested the director of Gazprom subsidiary SIBUR, Yakov Goldovskii, and two assistants and charged them with embezzling 2.6 billion rubles (US$90 million). The arrests sent shock waves through the business community: a delegation from the Russian Union of Industrialists and Entrepreneurs spent two hours with Procurator-General Vladimir Ustinov, seeking assurances that a witch-hunt of businessmen was not in the offing.[48] They were probably not reassured by Putin's comments in a January 14 interview in France, where he said, "It so happens in Russia that a man who drinks too much vodka and beats up his neighbor is jailed as a hooligan, and man who stole a sackful of potatoes is jailed as a thief. On the other hand, the men who embezzled capital running into tens or hundreds of millions are viewed as politicians."[49]

THE OLIGARCHS IN THE REGIONS

During the Yeltsin years, attention was riveted on the clashes between oligarchs struggling for the commanding heights of the national economy, in major privatization deals that were decided in Moscow. Under Putin, attention has shifted to the role of oligarchs at the regional level. From the beginning, of course, oligarchs had a strong presence in the regions, since that was where their mines and oil fields, their smelters and steel mills were located. In most cases, it was mutually beneficial for business leaders and regional governors to work in tandem. The former would finance the governor's election campaigns, would pay local taxes, and would invite the governor and/or his cronies into lucrative business ventures. In return, the governor would provide a political "roof" (*krysha*) for the entrepreneur. The governor could use his influence over the regional police and courts to protect businessmen from challenges to their property rights (such as creditors seeking payment) or from worker unrest. In 1996, Gazprom was the only major corporation to run its own candidates in gubernatorial elections in ten regions—winning only in Yamal-Nenets Autonomous Okrug. More typical was for a corporation to "domesticate" the governor—witness Siberian Aluminum and Aleksei Lebed in Khakassiia or Severstal and Viacheslav Pozgalev in Vologda.[50] Corporations also had some interest in placing their people in local legislatures.

In some cases there was more than one important business located in a region, which could lead to fierce battles between rival elites. For example, in the oil-rich Nenets Autonomous Okrug in 2001, Severnaya Neft backed the incumbent governor Vladimir Butov, beating off a challenge from a LUKoil-sponsored candidate. In Murmansk, Norilsk Nickel, the MDM bank, Severstal, and Menatep-Yukos began competing for influence. Some governors, most notably Yurii Luzhkov in Moscow, have managed to forge corporate structures of their own which can stand up against outside rivals. The controversial Governor Yevgennii Nazdratenko had created such a power base in Primorskii krai, in Russia's Far East. Once Putin had engineered his removal in 2001 (he was "promoted" to minister of fisheries), Severstal and Evrazkholding moved in, buying shares in the province's major ports.

Robert Orttung notes that "Russia's richest businessmen are much more powerful than its governors, so the appearance of these big businesses in the regions puts severe constraints on what the governors can do in their own region."[51] Increasingly, as the decade wore on one saw businessmen looking to move directly into political office, sponsoring their own candidates or even running for governor themselves. In 2000 Roman Abramovich, the head of Sibneft and Siberian Aluminum, got himself elected governor of the impoverished province of Chukotka, on the shores of the Bering Sea.[52] This baffling move was driven by a sudden attack of altruism, and/or a desire to take time out from the snake pits of Moscow. Abramovich was not alone, however. Norilsk Nickel director Aleksandr Khloponin was elected head of the equally remote Taimyr republic; Yukos director Boris Zolotarev became head of Evenkiia; and in January 2002 the head of the diamond monopoly Alrosa, Viacheslav Shtyrov, was elected president of Sakha.[53] Putin's reform stripping governors of their seats in the Federation Council created a new opportunity for businessmen to seek appointment as senators. Some see the potential for a powerful coalition of regional leaders and business magnates lining up to constrain Putin's authority.[54]

Another interesting development in recent years has been the emergence of new regionally based conglomerates as successful metals producers plough back their profits into buying upstream manufacturing plants—unlike the financial-industrial groups of the mid-1990s, which were typically put together by Moscow-based banks. Hence 2001 saw Aleksei Mordashov, director of the Severstal steel mill in Cherepovets, acquiring the Ulianovsk and Zavolzhskii auto plants, the UGMK (Magnitka) metals combine, and Kuzbasugol coal mine.[55] Similarly Deripaska's Rusal bought Nizhniy Novgorod's Gorki AZ auto plant, Avtobank and insurer Ingosstrakh.

THE BATTLES CONTINUE

By 2002 oligarchic capitalism seemed firmly entrenched in Russia, and optimists were hoping that the age of oligarch wars was over. A study that Peter Boone and Denis Rodionov of Brunswick UBS Warburg released in mid-2002 concluded that eight conglomerates together control 85 percent of the shares in the top 64 firms in Russia. The "big 8," they argued, "have successfully lobbied for radical tax reform, land privatization, state recognition of property rights and a realignment of foreign policy toward the West. It is in their interests to ensure a stable political regime and conservative financial policy."[56]

However, the leading oligarchs remained vulnerable to further assaults, especially if they sought to turn their economic muscle into political influence at national level. The continuing crisis over Chechnya, symbolized by the bloody hostage-taking in the Nord Ost theater in downtown Moscow in October 2002, strengthened the hand of the security bosses in the Kremlin, and they had no great love for the oligarchs. And in preparation for the December 2003 State Duma elections, the Kremlin was putting a lot of effort into building up the United Russia party, a project that could be derailed if the oligarchs decided to back rival political parties.

The year 2002 closed with the controversial privatization of Slavneft, the sixth largest oil company in Russia and one of the few still in state hands. In spring 2002 Sibneft and the Tyumen Oil Company (TNK), working together, began quietly buying blocks of shares in Slavneft subsidiaries, and there followed a series of ugly boardroom battles. In May Slavneft president Mikhail Gutseriev was ousted by a shareholders' meeting called at the initiative of Prime Minister Mikhail Kasyanov, and replaced with Yuri Sukhanov, a vice-president who had recently joined the company from Sibneft. In December all 75 percent of the company's shares that the state owned were sold to TNK and Sibneft for $1.86 billion, in an auction in which they were the sole bidders. Other companies such as LUKoil and Surgutneftegaz were persuaded to withdraw their bids, and the Chinese National Petroleum Company was barred from participating. The Slavneft deal was reminiscent of the infamous "loans for shares" arrangements in 1995. It seemed to be business as usual for the oligarchs with ties to Premier Kasyanov.

Sibneft was headed by Roman Abramovich, a 36-year-old with close ties to Berezovsky and to Kasyanov. *Forbes* declared him the second richest man in Russia, with assets of $5.7 billion. Abramovich astonished soccer fans by buying London's Chelsea football club in June 2003 in a deal costing more than $200 million.

Russia's richest man, 39-year-old Khodorkovsky (worth $8 billion) was also becoming increasingly visible. His company, Yukos, adopted Western corporate governance practice, put Westerners onto its board, and mounted an ambitious campaign of philanthropy and public relations in Western capitals. In April 2003 Yukos announced that it would merge with Sibneft in a $14 billion deal that would create the world's fifth-biggest oil company. This came just two months after British Petroleum said it was going to spend $6.75 billion on a joint venture with TNK. Yukos signed a declaration of intent to build their own export pipeline to China—in competition with a state-backed project. In addition, Khodorkovsky boasted of his willingness to spread money around the centrist and opposition parties in the Duma. The former head of taxes at Yukos, Vladimir Dubov, entered the Duma in 1999 and became head of its tax committee. In 2002 Dubov introduced an amendment capping export duties on reined oil products that cost the government $400 million.[57] All in all, Khodorkovsky seemed positioned to make a serious political and economic challenge to the bloc of Gazprom-LUKoil oligarchs loyal to the Kremlin.[58]

It was not long before the oligarchs' opponents struck back. During his regular meeting with leading businessmen in February 2003, Putin delivered what seemed to be a warning to Khodorkovsky, hinting that it might be time to reinvestigate the privatization of the oil companies in the mid-1990s. Khodorkovsky had triggered this threat by disputing the legality of state-owned Rosneft's acquisition of the Severnaya Neft oil company.

In May 2003 a major scandal erupted when a centrist think-tank published a report authored by Joseph Diskin warning that the oligarchs were executing a "crawling coup" against President Putin.[59] Diskin argued that key oligarchs, particularly Khodorkovsky, had lost faith in Putin and the system of presidential rule in general. Having invested heavily in buying the political loyalty of parliamentarians and of governors out in the regions, these oligarchs allegedly wanted to introduce a more parliamentary system of rule, with a government and prime minister selected by a parliamentary majority. The report produced a firestorm of controversy. Observers noted that the report was strangely silent about certain businesses, such as LUKoil and Gazprom, while vigorously attacking Khodorkovsky.

The plot thickened the next month. On 23 June investigators arrested half-a-dozen senior police officials on grounds of corruption. Then on 2 July prosecutors arrested Platon Lebedev, co-owner of Yukos and another of Russia's newly-minted billionaires. He was accused of malfeasance in the long-forgotten privatization of a fertilizer company. There were more raids in search of evidence of tax evasion in the offices of Yukos and its partner, Sibneft.

Putin stayed above the fray, neither condoning nor condemning the investigations. He said in June 2003, "I am absolutely convinced that the much talked about equal distance between various business representatives and the authorities has been achieved in our country in the past few years. Today, those who disagree with this position, as they used to say, 'are no longer with us.' "[60] Observers argued that Putin was trying to maintain a balance between the security and business wings of his administration.[61]

At the height of the Yukos affair, Putin scored a major success, securing passage of a reform of the electricity giant EES, Russia's largest company and a lynchpin of the country's energy-dependent economy. In March 2000 EES head Anatolii Chubais proposed an ambitious program to separate EES's generation and transmission operations, and split the power stations into dozens of companies that would be auctioned off. Critics feared that the best companies would be sold off to Chubais cronies, as in the 1995 loans-for-shares auctions. The leading skeptics were the foreign investors, who held 30 percent of EES stock, and oligarchs who had also been buying up EES shares. Chubais came back with a revised plan, to be phased in over five years, that increased state control and guaranteed the rights of the existing shareholders.

Electricity prices would have to increase, since the current tariff was not enough to replace aging capital stock. EES wanted to double the price paid by residents, but the government kept the annual increase to 14 percent, roughly the general rate of inflation. Despite public protests about the rate increases that were already being introduced in some regions, the reform bill passed the decisive second reading in the State Duma in February 2003, and was signed into law in May. Thus Putin was able to shield the unpopular Chubais and secure the passage of a much-needed and complex structural reform.

CONCLUSION

Putin's crackdown against the media barons consolidated the power of the Kremlin but did little to alter the structure of oligarchic capitalism in Russia. Contrary to the hopes of the communists, there was no mass reversal of privatization, no top-level convictions for theft and corruption during the loans-for-shares and other scandals. Despite his background as a seventeen-year KGB veteran, Putin was apparently comfortable with the idea of an economy based on private ownership and market pricing. He was even, apparently, comfortable with the type of crony capitalism that had emerged in Russia. Aleksandr Tsipko argues that "[j]ust as under Yeltsin, Russia is still ruled by a group of oligarchs via their protégés in the president's administration, the government and the security services."[62]

Putin's outlook on life had been transformed during the years 1989–95. As head of the department working with foreign investors in the administration of the reformist mayor of St. Petersburg, Anatoly Sobchak, Putin learned the ropes of doing business in the new Russia. He was a pragmatist, not a zealot: neither a zealot for anticorruption, nor a zealot for market reform. He had no desire to roll back the market reforms that had been put in place under Yeltsin, but nor did he have any desire to disrupt the status quo with further change. Rather, the direction of Putin's reforms would be to streamline procedures and regularize the legal–administrative framework: to routinize what had previously been managed by informal norms and relationships.[63] The new philosophy was summed up by Gleb Pavlovskii, the architect of Putin's election campaign, who related how Putin told a private meeting with businessmen that "[t]hey could keep what they had already stolen, but now they had to play clean, pay taxes, make investments and stay out of politics."[64]

In his first years in office Putin did not develop a serious plan for dismantling the power of the oligarchs as a class. Reform efforts were concentrated on controlling the regional leaders, and plugging some of the legal and administrative gaps in the architecture of the new state (tax law, land code, labor code, judicial reform, etc.) Measures that aroused public anxiety, such as reform of the financially strapped pension fund and public utilities, were postponed. It's not clear whether the slow pace of change is because Putin does not understand the need for further reform, or because he still lacks the political authority to carry it out.

NOTES

1. Alena V. Ledeneva, *Russia's Economy of Favours: Blat, Networking and Informal Exchanges* (Cambridge: Cambridge University Press 1998); David Woodruff, *Money Unmade: Barter and the Fate of Russian Capitalism* (Ithaca, N.Y.: Cornell University Press, 1999).

2. For an amusing account, see Craig Copetas, *Bear Hunting with the Politburo* (New York: Simon and Schuster, 1991).

3. Thomas Graham, "The New Russian Regime," *Nezavisimaya gazeta*, November 23, 1995.

4. Olga Romanova, "News," *Vedomosti*, January 29, 2002.

5. Sergei Peregudov, "Corporate Capital in Russian Politics," *Polis* 6, no. 4 (2000).

6. David M. Kotz and Fred Weir, *Revolution from Above: The Demise of the Soviet System* (New York: Routledge, 1997); David Lane and Cameron Ross, *The Transition from Communism to Capitalism: Ruling Elites from Gorbachev to Yeltsin* (New York: St. Martin's, 1999).

7. For journalists' accounts of life among the oligarchs, see Rose Brady, *Kapitalizm: Russia's Struggle to Free Its Economy* (New Haven, Conn.: Yale University Press, 1999); Chrystia Freeland, *Sale of the Century: Russia's Wild Ride from Communism to Capitalism* (New York: Crown Business, 2000); Paul Klebnikov, *Godfather of the Kremlin: Boris Berezovsky and the Looting of Russia* (New York: Harcourt, 2000); Matthew Brzezinski, *Casino Moscow: A Tale of Greed and Adventure on Capitalism's Wildest Frontier* (New York: Free Press, 2001).

8. Tatiana Lysova, "Reform of the Oligarchs," *Ekspert*, March 18, 1998.

9. Interview with Uralmash head Kakha Bendukidze, "Russian Business: What Kind of Life," *Ekspert*, January 21, 2002.

10. Laura Belin, Floriana Fossato, and Anna Kachkaeva, "The Distorted Media Market," in *Business and the State in Contemporary Russia*, ed. Peter Rutland (Boulder, Colo.: Westview Press, 2001); Yelena Rykovtseva, "No Unity within Russia's Matryoshka Media," *Russian Journal*, August 10, 2001.

11. Dmitrii Pinsker, "Anti-Davos in Moscow," *Itogi*, September 23, 1997.

12. Joel Hellman, "Winners Take All: The Politics of Partial Reform in Post-Communist Transitions," *World Politics*, no. 50 (January 1998): 203–34.

13. "Informed sources say that leaving Voloshin alone for at least a year was one of the agreements between Yeltsin and Putin when the matter of succession was discussed." Inessa Slavutinskaia, "Aleksandr the First," *Profil*, no. 21 (May 5–11, 2000).

14. Andrew Higgins, "Swiss Money-Laundering Probe Finds a Kremlin Link," *Wall Street Journal*, July 23, 2001.

15. One specific indicator of their familiarity was that Putin, then head of the FSB, attended Berezovksy's wife's birthday party in February 1999, a time when he was facing corruption charges.

16. Peter Rutland, "Putin's Path to Power," *Post-Soviet Affairs* 16, no. 4 (December 2000): 313–54.

17. Thanks to Oleg Kharkhordin for clarification on the composition of this team.

18. Ivan Trefilov, "Muscovites Swell the Ranks of the People from St. Petersburg," *Vedomosti*, no. 45 (July 2–4, 2001).

19. VTsIOM poll, July 20–25, 2000.

20. Inessa Slavutinskaia, "Liberalissimo," *Profil*, August 7, 2000.

21. They included Kakha Bendukidze, Oleg Deripaska, Aleksander Mamut, Vladimir Potanin, Mikhail Fridman, Mikhail Khodorkovsky, and Anatoly Chubais. Aleksei Germanovich, "Tycoons Will Repent," *Vedomosti*, February 14, 2001.

22. Aleksei Germanovich, "Submission," *Vedomosti*, February 15, 2001.

23. Jamestown *Monitor*, January 25, 2001.

24. The Cheka was Lenin's secret police. This group is also known as the "ghosts" and "oligarchs in uniform." Konstantin Smirnov, Andrei Bagrov, "Putin's Warriors," *Kommersant-Vlast*, no. 45 (November 2001); Konstantin Smirnov, "Winter Hunt," *Kommersant-Vlast*, no. 48 (December 2001).

25. Kirill Rogov, "Snake Eating Its Own Tail," at www.polit.ru (last accessed December 7, 2001); Boris Vishnevsky et al., "Equidistance in Different Directions," *Obshchaia gazeta*, June 7–13, 2001.

26. Yelena Tregubova, "Things Will Get Worse," *Kommersant*, December 21, 2001.

27. *Novaia gazeta*, December 25, 2001.

28. Natalia Astrakhanova, "Natural Clan Selection," *Ekspert*, no. 46, December 2001.

29. Inessa Slavutinskaia, "It Takes a Clan to Expel a Clan," *Profil*, no. 46 (December 2001).

30. Svetlana Babaeva, "Relatives versus the St. Petersburg Team," *Izvestiya*, November 29, 2001.

31. Yulia Latynina, "A Muzzle for the Oligarchs," *Novaia gazeta*, no. 93, (December 2001).

32. Anna Raff, "Gazprom Takes PwC Audit to Heart," *Moscow Times*, August 1, 2001. After Gazprom in export revenues in 2000 came oil companies LUKoil ($5.7 bn), Yukos ($5.2 bn), Tyumen NK ($3.5 bn) and Tatneft ($2.6 bn), followed by Rusal ($2.2 bn) and Norilsk Nickel ($2.2 bn). Alla Startseva, "Ten Firms Have 40% of Exports," *Moscow Times*, July 19, 2001.

33. Ol'ga Gladkova, "Putin's Obscure Followers," *Argumenty i fakty*, no. 47 (November 2001); Viktor Litovkin, "Jammed Weaponry," *Obshchaia gazeta*, June 7–13, 2001.

34. Almira Kozhakhmetova, "Obedient Oligarchs Go to the Kremlin," *Novye izvestiia*, June 1, 2001; Boris Kagarlitsky, "No Magnate Storms in Sight," *Novaia gazeta*, June 7–14, 2001; Denis Prokopenko, "Putin Promises Oligarchs to Liberalize Hard Currency Legislation," *Nezavisimaia gazeta*, June 1, 2001.

35. Aleksandr Tsipko, "Putin's Power Hierarchy Sinks into the Sand," *Prism* 7, no. 3 (March 2001).

36. Stanislav Menshikov, "Budget Battles to Start," *Moscow Tribune*, June 1, 2001.

37. Vladimir Ustinov, "Tariff Increase Unavoidable," *Vedomosti*, January 28, 2002.

38. See the Chubais interview "Happy New RAO EES," *Profil*, no. 44 (November 2001).

39. Bulat Stolyarov, "Oligarchs Are Judged," *Vedomosti*, October 4, 2001.

40. Yurii Granovskii, "Potanin ubil Mustcom," *Vedomosti*, June 20, 2001.

41. *Investment Environment in the Russian Federation*, May 2001 at www.oecd .org/daf/investment/fdi/russia.pdf.

42. Andrei Grigoriev, "Twelve and a Half," *Kompaniia*, no. 1 (January 2002). On Pugachev, see Oleg Lurie, "Putin Likes Skiing," *Novaia gazeta*, November 26–28, 2001.

43. Christian Caryl, "Twilight of the Oligarchs," *Newsweek International*, February 5, 2001.

44. Denis Shevchenko, "The Kremlin and the Opposition," *Rossiia*, July 10, 2001; Andrei Zolotov, "Six Months On, NTV Still up in the Air," *Moscow Times*, October 15, 2001.

45. "Economic Swan Lake," *Ekspert*, January 28, 2002.

46. Floriana Fossato and Anna Kachkaeva, "Russian Provincial Broadcasters to Suffer Most in Moscow TV Battles," *New York Times*, January 24, 2002.

47. Bulat Stoliarov, "Aksenenko Retreats," *Vedomosti*, October 23, 2001; Andrei Savitskii, "Kremlin Ghosts," *Nezavisimaia gazeta*, November 29, 2001.

48. Mikhail Kozyrev, "Imprison and Defend," *Vedomosti*, January 29, 2002.

49. Cited in *Kommersant*, January 17, 2002.

50. Nataliya Zubarevich, "Russia's Big Businesses in Regional Elections," *Russian Regional Report 7*, no. 4 (January 30, 2002).

51. Robert Orttung, "Money and Power in Putin's Russia," *Russian Regional Report 7*, no. 2 (January 16, 2002).

52. Elena Dikun, "Abramovich's Golden Hills in Chukotka," *Prism 7*, no. 9 (September 30, 2001).

53. Pavel Isaev, "Fusion of Oligarchs and Governors," *Russian Regional Report 7*, no. 2 (January 16, 2002).

54. Valerii Fedorov, Vladislav Sakharchuk, "Horn of Plenty for Regional Leaders," *Vek*, no. 24 (June 22, 2001).

55. Yuliia Bushueva, "Unfortunately, I Am from Petersburg," *Vedomosti*, October 4, 2001.

56. *Moscow Times*, 23 August 2002.

57. Gregory White and Jeanne Whalen, "Why Russian oil is a sticky business," *Wall Street Journal*, 1 August 2003.

58. Catherine Belton, "Berezovsky: Oligarchs of the world unite," *Moscow Times*, 9 July 2003.

59. Joseph Diskin, "An oligarchic coup is being prepared in Russia," Council for National Strategy. On the web at: www.kprf.ru/projects/economy/admin/12412 .shtml. "Oligarch-conspirators," *Stolichnaya vechenyaya gazeta*, 29 May 2003.

60. Transcript of 20 June press conference from kremlin.ru, in Johnson's Russia List #7233, 21 June 2003.

61. Olga Kryshtanovskaya, "Putin's people," *Vedomosti,* 30 June 2003.

62. Aleksandr Tsipko, "The Family Takes Control of Domestic Politics," *Prism 7,* no. 9 (September 30, 2001).

63. A. Nikolskii, "State Regulation of the Economy," at www.polit.ru (last accessed September 5, 2001).

64. Frederick Kempe, "On the Russian Front, President Putin Advances," *Wall Street Journal Europe,* March 21, 2001.

Part Four

MILITARY AND SECURITY

Chapter Ten

Putin and Military Reform

Dale R. Herspring

From all appearances, Putin has become serious about military reform. This does not mean that the reader should expect radical or revolutionary changes. Indeed, as Lilia Shevtsova pointed out in her recent book on Putin, whereas Boris Yeltsin was a revolutionary, a man who destroyed the pre-existing communist political system, Vladimir Putin is a bureaucrat, a man who considers his primary task to bring stability to Russia.[1] The problem, however, is whether this bureaucrat will remain primarily a "stabilizer" or whether he is prepared to move closer to reform by becoming a "transformer; a pioneer reorganizing for the first time in history the way Russia is ruled."[2]

Before continuing, something about Putin, the politician: five factors characterize Putin's approach to politics.[3] First, as noted above, Putin is a bureaucrat. Putin believes that the leader at the top should be able to set the system's parameters; once having done so, he would prefer to leave policy implementation to the bureaucrats, but he recognizes that the bureaucracies often work to subvert a political leader's wishes. This is especially true of the military, which tends to be very conservative and live in the past. Generals and admirals often like doing things "the old way." Getting them to accept a new way of doing things generally means imitating Lenin's famous dictum of "two steps forward and one step backward." Forcing a bureaucracy to change is a slow, frustrating process, but Putin believes that such organizational structures can only be changed by continually pushing them, by gradually changing the structure, attitudes, and personnel in the bureaucratic system. Given its highly bureaucratized nature, Putin fully understands that it cannot be turned upside down as the Bolsheviks did the tzarist army during the civil war. He has to work with what is available. This is why those observers (including this writer) who expected Putin and his hand-picked defense minister, Sergey Ivanov, to take the kind of "bold" decisions necessary to

185

make military reform a reality in a relatively short period of time were mistaken. Bold decisions are not part of Putin's leadership style.[4]

Putin's second characteristic is respect for Russian political culture. While he may be seen as a "Westernizer" of the Peter the Great type by many in the West, he believes that it would be wrong to force the Russian military (or any other part of Russian society) to mimic the West. He wants to move the Russian military closer to the kind of system found in the West, but he is smart enough to know that in the end, it will continue to have its Russian idiosyncracies.

The third factor that characterizes Putin's leadership style is his ideological approach to dealing with policies. When he was a KGB officer, his primary goal was to find a way to solve problems. If a liberal idea would "work," fine; he would accept that. If a conservative approach worked better, he was ready to accept that approach as well. The result: he is pragmatic, and flexible when it comes to policy issues.

Fourth, Putin is *not* a long-term planner. He lives in the here and now, just as he did in the KGB. This helps explain why he has not come up with a long-term plan to reform the military (or any other part of the Russian polity)—other than to push the somewhat vague concept of military professionalism. He does not conceptualize problems or answers; rather, he takes whatever the situation will permit—and that includes retreating on occasions, but always pushing for the vague idea of a professional military.

Finally, and much to the frustration of many Western observers and policymakers, Putin is cautious when it comes to making changes. His decision-making approach tends to be incremental. He knows he does not have enough power to make all the changes that Russia desperately needs at once. The country is in too bad shape for that approach. Nevertheless, he also knows that if Russia is to survive, it must change. The state must be rebuilt if it hopes to handle the country's problems in an efficient manner. It is also worth noting that Putin will take advantage of events—as he did with the September 11, 2001, terrorist attacks against the United States—to get the military to do what he wants, but in the end, he is the opposite of a Khrushchev with his "hair-brained" schemes. Putin is more the tortoise than the hare (and we all know that in the end, it was the tortoise that won the race). He takes one small step at a time, always pushing the system to change, but backing off if bureaucratic resistance gets too strong.

Before going into the kind of changes Putin has been making in the military, let us turn to the situation the Russian military finds itself in as Putin is in his third year in office.

PROBLEMS IN THE RUSSIAN MILITARY

One could easily write a book just on the problems in the Russian armed forces. This chapter does not go into this topic in great detail.[5] Nevertheless, it would be helpful for the reader to understand just how serious the situation is at present. In January 2003, for example, one writer pointed out that hazing continued to be a major problem: "Of course, hazing has not disappeared. Instead, it has worsened in many cases. The Defense Ministry steadfastly refuses to consider plans to create a professional non-commissioned officer (NCO) corps, but as long as there are no professional NCOs, grandfathers will remain indispensable as an organizing force in the barracks, and officers will continue to permit hazing."[6] In fact, the chief military prosecutor noted that the list of 316 officers who had been convicted of bullying the previous years included "one general who beat up a colonel."[7]

Then there is the question of training—vital to every military. In May 2003, it was noted that from 1992 until the year 2000, the military did not have any combat training—because of a lack of funds. Insofar as pilots were concerned, they were receiving only six to eight hours per year, far below the 150 or so that NATO requires of its pilots.[8] This means that Russia now has a whole group of mid-level officers who have had little or no hands-on training (except for those who have served in Chechnya). The result is, "It is not possible to make professionals of them in a couple of years."[9]

Then we have cases of senior military officers complaining about the weapons systems they have. For example, General Yuri Grishin, the deputy commander of the air force, complained that the air force will not get new planes until 2010. In the meantime, it will have to "fly planes that are 20 to 40 years old."[10] Or take the airborne forces. According to their commander, General Georgy Shpak, "Outmoded BMD-1 and BTR-D vehicles, adopted into the armament in 1969 and 1974 respectively, make up the bulk of the inventory. Up to 80 percent of them have been operated for fifteen years or more."[11] And the situation in the Navy is just as bad. To quote the Commander of the Black Sea Fleet, Admiral Vladimir Komoyedov, "Our Navy has been going downhill for a long while, gaining speed each year. A few years more and there may be an invisible process in about 5–7 years; we simply won't have any ships left. At least, ships that are moving."[12] And if that were not enough, in August 2003 the Defense Ministry announced that military procurements would be cut in 2004.[13]

The military also has very serious problems both with crime and with the quality of draftees it gets twice a year. To begin with, desertion is becoming a way of life in many units. To quote one observer, "Soldiers are deserting because they see no chance of a normal human existence for themselves either in or after the Army."[14] The military claims about 5,000 desert every year.[15] The number of suicides has also increased. "Last year, 70 soldiers, warrant officers, and officers committed suicide, whereas this year this figure is 89."[16] The generals blame desertions on the commanders—who often pay little attention to what is going on in units, preferring to let the "grandfathers"

exercise discipline—discipline that often results in rapes, beatings, and sometimes even death.

The situation among draftees—necessary as long as conscription exists—is
not much better. The deputy chairman of the Defense Committee, Nikolay
Bezborodov, complained that "12 percent of young men drafted for active
military service consume alcohol on a regular basis and 8 percent have taken
narcotics." Furthermore, "The educational level of soldiers is not high.
About 7 percent have only primary education, over 30 percent do not have
secondary education, and 40 percent had not worked or studied before they
joined the army. The soccer fans who rampaged in Moscow are some of the
youth drafted for active military service."[17] To make matters even more difficult, only "10.3% of those eligible for military service will actually be called
up in 2003."[18] Why? For a number of reasons: deferments, medical problems
(some attested to by physicians who were bribed), criminal backgrounds,
drug use, and alcoholism, among others.

Finally, it is worth noting that crime is out of control in the Russian military—and not just among enlisted personnel. Officers, including some very
senior officers, are also involved. In one case, for example, a general in charge
of the food supply for the internal troops in Siberia was charged with stealing
more than one million rubles that were intended to purchase food for Russia's already underfed troops.[19] And the situation is not improving.

> In 2001 alone the Chief Military Prosecutor's Office recorded 1.1% more crimes
> than in 2000. One in every two crimes committed by servicemen falls into the
> serious or particularly serious categories. Most often they are committed in a
> drunken state: The number of crimes of that kind increased 26% in the year,
> while those involving weapons grew 25%. The number of murders increased by
> an average of 7% and instances of deliberately causing serious damage to health
> by 4.5%[20]

The question is, why is the military faced with these problems? Is it just
because of a lack of funds, as some of the generals and admirals claim? Or is
it an integral part of the kind of military structure that Russia has at present?
There are serious structural problems. For example, NCOs (as the term is
understood in the West) do not exist, and rather than get involved in dealing
with junior enlisted personnel the way that American or British NCOs do,
officers avoid the problem. The result: brutality at the unit level.

The list of examples could go on, but by now the reader has an idea of just
how bad the situation is within the Russian military. Indeed, it is questionable
that this military has the ability to go to war. After all, the performance of the
Russian armed forces in Chechnya has been miserable. Corruption, brutality,
and an inability to bring this "war" to a close are all signs of just how bad
the situation has been.

So what does this mean insofar as Putin is concerned? To suggest that he is not aware of the problems noted above would be naïve. He is very aware of them, and he knows that something must be done to deal with them. Putin cannot afford to ignore and starve the military the way that Yeltsin did. It is important to him both as a force for protecting the country and as an influential political institution within the Russian polity.

PUTIN AND STRUCTURAL CHANGES

If there is a term to describe Putin's approach for dealing with the military's problems, it could be called "muddling through." Being the bureaucrat he is, Putin has avoided the glossy frontal assault on the military's problems that some of his critics have suggested he follow.[21] Instead, as he has in other areas, he has overseen a number of small steps, leading up to the introduction of the most important step, the Military Reform Plan approved by him on June 1, 2003.

To begin with, the Russian military now has only three services where it once had five. Second—and Yeltsin deserves credit for this—the size of the Russian military shrank drastically under Yeltsin. The military that Russia inherited from the USSR numbered 2.7 million. By January 1, 2001, they were down to 1,365,000. In addition, the 600,000 troops that were stationed outside of Russia were brought back to the homeland, causing very serious dislocation problems—no housing, no place to put them. In some cases, they were resettled in Siberia—in tents, at −30 degrees in the dead of winter!

As one might expect, Putin adopted a cautious approach in dealing with the military. On May 27 and August 17, he set up commissions to look at problems within the military. Their findings were placed on the agenda at Security Council sessions in August and November 2000. The proposals were approved by the Security Council and dealt with the development of the military up to 2010. They included a broad range of issues, such as improving management of the military, increasing combat readiness, improving the defense industrial complex, upgrading the status of servicemen, increasing financial assistance to the military, improving command and control.[22] The key point in comparing Putin's approach with the various reform plans that were put forth during Yeltsin's time (even if he only gave them minimal support as well as the plan put forth by the Union of Right Forces—SPS) is that Putin's plan read more like a laundry list of items that needed to be fixed. There was no grand master plan. Instead, like the problem solver he is, Putin preferred to look at specific problems and see what could be done to deal with them one at a time.

Then Putin closed down two of Moscow's three overseas bases—Lourdes in Cuba, and Cam Ranh Bay in Vietnam. When asked why Moscow chose to pull back by closing these bases, even though some senior military officers were opposed, Defense Minister Ivanov replied that they were too expensive.

> The use of the Lourdes base cost us 200 million dollars a year. It is true that Cuba owes us 20 billion dollars but when we raise the question they look surprised, pretending not to understand. Cuba will never repay this debt. But we kept pumping money into the Lourdes base and what did we get from it? The base was built in the 1960s as a tracking station. It was a different world and the base brought practical information results. Almost a half century has passed. A logical question arises: Do we need today what was good 40 years ago? And do we need it for $200 million a year? . . .
>
> As for Cam Ranh Bay, in the past 15 years everything that could be stolen there was stolen and the rest broke down. The base was actually used for refueling our ships but they called at it only two or three times in the past ten years.[23]

The important point to note here is that there was no effort on Ivanov's part to explain Moscow's decision as part of a grand design. Instead, he suggested that Putin was given a cost-estimate analysis that indicated that Moscow was not getting its money's worth—so the bases were closed.

The reader should not get the impression that Putin and his administration were looking at military reform in isolation. By no means. Putin was savvy enough to understand that the military did not live in isolation. He probably would have agreed with one writer who argued that military reform referred to "a set of political, economic, legal, strictly military, military technical, social and other measures carried out at certain times and aimed at a quality transformation of the state's military organization."[24] In other words, whatever was done in the military had to be seen against the backdrop of Russian society as a whole. But a grand plan? As time would show, Putin would accept an interrelated framework for military reform, but only after a lot of bureaucratic battles and compromises had produced something that made sense as a way to bring the Russian military into the twenty-first century.

On May 11, 2001, a commission Putin had formed presented him with proposals on social problems faced by military personnel. Based on this report, Putin placed a priority on reforming the pay and allowances system as well as achieving pension reform and improving housing and medical services. In October, Putin chaired a session of the Security Council that focused on the military-industrial complex. It resulted in increased focus on the need to reform the military-industrial complex from the old Soviet model to a new, more competitive one. Finally, on November 27, 2001, Putin chaired another Security Council meeting that looked at the issue of mobilization readiness. It is also worth noting that in 2001, Putin succeeded in raising the military budget to 380.5 billion rubles. Another 34.6 billion was allocated for pay and allowances as well as for repayment of the ministry's outstanding debts.[25] The point here is that throughout the year, Putin pushed the bureaucracy to look at a wide variety of military-related issues. He was clearly *not* ignoring the topic.

Given his tendency to work within the various bureaucracies, it was not surprising that Putin waited for the military to provide him with a proposal for changing its form of technical support—a plan that was delivered on November 1. This was followed by another proposal to reform the military-educational complex in July of 2001. Suggestions on how to handle military personnel were sent to Putin as well. He approved them on November 16. It was also at this time that he ordered the military to come up with a plan to fill certain positions with servicemen serving on contract. The idea was to experiment with one or two units in order to "determine more precisely the nature and scope of measures and the outlays necessary for converting them to the contract method of manning with servicemen."[26]

The generals agreed that a volunteer, professional military was in many ways preferable to what they had when it came to combat. On the other hand, there were many who wanted to keep the old system—it provided free labor (i.e., conscripts) to help build dachas for officers. Then there were those who believed that the country needed young men who had been socialized in the Russian military—it made for more patriotic citizens.

At this point it should be noted that the Defense Ministry was not the only one to come up with a plan for reforming the military. The Union of Right Forces under the leadership of Boris Nemtsov also had its own version. According to this plan, the army would be transformed into a professional military almost immediately. Pay would be increased significantly to attract contract soldiers who wanted to serve. At the same time, conscripts would serve only six months, and instead of working in the fields and building dachas for generals, they would be trained as specialists and then sent to the reserves. Indeed, supporters of this approach even worked out the numbers for the transition.[27]

Before discussing the Pskov experiment, it should be noted that the idea of contract service in Russia was not invented by the Putin administration. Contract service began on December 1, 1992, and targeted soldiers with certain specialties, who were offered two- and three-year contracts. The program was gradually expanded until on April 11, 1996, the chief of the Russian Defense Ministry's Planning and Mobilization Directorate stated that there were 270,000 contract soldiers in the military, many of them the wives of officers who joined because it was impossible to live on an officer's salary.[28]

Unfortunately, this experiment was a failure. In fact, during the 1993–95 time period, some 50,000 resigned, primarily for financial reasons.[29] For example, a contract serviceman earned 278,000 rubles. However, the average wage in Russia in September 1995 was about 550,000 rubles, including supplements. The subsistence minimum per person in Russia at that time was 300,000 rubles, and in some regions it was two or three times that.[30]

The situation did not improve. For example, in 1997 the chief of recruitment observed that, given the dangerous conditions and low pay faced by many contract soldiers, a person who volunteered for contract service "would either be one of the long-term unemployed or someone who has already poisoned his mind with alcohol."[31] And even those who joined quickly left. According to the same officer, in 1997, "some 30,000 contract soldiers had left the army so far" that year, while "only 15,000 had enlisted."[32] In February 2001, it was reported that "49.9 percent of contract servicemen have an income lower than the official subsistence minimum."[33] And it was clear that the army was still not attracting the kind of quality individuals it sought as professionals. Those who joined were often "the most unfortunate layers of the population, that part least prepared for market conditions, and on the other hand, young people not easily adaptable to barracks life."[34]

During his 1966 presidential campaign, Boris Yeltsin promised to end conscription by the year 2000. However, as was often the case with Yeltsin, he failed to factor in the economic costs involved or follow through on his promises. The bottom line is that while a professional military may be popular among the populace, and while such individuals do a better job in combat, it is more expensive. Considerably more expensive. As one Russian general put it, "A Conscript costs us 17,900 rubles a year, while a professional soldier costs 32,000 rubles. A professional army would require the corresponding infrastructure, which also would cost a lot. It's not realistic now."[35] Or as another senior Russian general put it in 2001, "because of the lack of funds it will not be possible for Russia to build a fully professional army for at least the next five years."[36]

The Pskov experiment was controversial, and opposed by most of the country's senior military officers. They complained (rightly) about the costs involved, and they worried about its impact on the combat readiness of the Russian Army—not a very serious concern given the horrible conditions it was in. Something had to be done, and it had to be more than a case of throwing money—which the country did not possess—at the problems.

Recognizing the bureaucratic problems he faced in dealing with the military, but convinced that he had to keep pushing the generals and admirals if he hoped to get anything done, Putin decided to carry out what was labeled an "experiment." The idea was to fully professionalize the 76th airborne division based at Pskov, to see how realistic the idea of professionalizing the military would be. The experiment began on September 2002 and was to last a year. In this case, the recruitment criteria would be different. Contracts would make it very clear that the contract serviceman would be expected to serve in difficult/dangerous combat areas such as Chechnya. In addition, the individual had a right to housing—something new for enlisted personnel in the Russian Army. One author argued that the basic salary for a soldier would have to be increased to 4,000 rubles a month if the army hoped to attract contractees.[37]

According to some observers, the military was out to "sabotage" the experiment from the beginning.[38] For example, on September 28, 2002, the chief of the General Staff, General Anatoly Kvashnin, visited the Pskov division and announced that "no one intended to give apartments to the soldiers."[39] As a result, forty-eight soldiers who had previously signed contracts submitted requests for discharge.

The major problem faced by those who wanted the experiment to succeed was how to make military service attractive. As far as the 76th division was concerned, the experiment was failing. It was supposed to attract 2,600 contract troops, but by the first part of October, it had only recruited 749 candidates, and of them, "four hundred passed the medical exam, and two hundred and fifty signed a contract."[40] Indeed, by November, the experiment had stalled because of a lack of volunteers. The division was only able to attract about 600 young men—in a unit that required 1,630. Clearly something had to be done.

In response to the situation in Pskov, the Union of Right Forces suggested that the pay (which was being held at 3,000 rubles) for soldiers should be raised to 4,000–4,500 rubles a month. Furthermore, they recommended that officer pay should be increased by 40–50 percent.[41] They further proposed that soldiers who signed a contract should be given free tuition if they decided to continue their education when their time of service was over, and that conscription be ended—immediately!

Putin was well aware of problems such as those at Pskov. For example, the Russian government held a meeting on November 26. At this meeting, Putin stated that he had a "generally positive" outlook on the changes under way in the military—a clear sign that he expected further movement toward a professional military. By this point, the generals were proposing that the transformation go through three stages. The first, the Pskov division, was to end in 2004. The second, according to Ivanov, was to cover a period of seven years. The goal was to have 50–60 percent of soldiers and sergeants serving on contract. The third stage was left undefined: "It is planned that all armed forces will be manned with 'contractees' during the third stage."[42] There were problems with this staged approach, however. The second stage would end after Putin left office—just what many critics believed was the generals' goal: wait Putin out.

Apparently feeling strong enough to begin to take on the generals, Putin and Ivanov began a campaign to bring together the outlines of a serious military reform program. First, Putin stated on November 29, 2002, that in the future Moscow would place primary reliance on professional soldiers, not conscripts, to fight the country's wars.[43] Then, speaking to journalists,

Defense Minister Sergey Ivanov stated that priority would be given to recruiting individuals to serve in the airborne troops, the 42nd Motor Rifle Division, as well as the Naval Infantry. In addition, he came up with the figure of 166,000 for contract soldiers. This "applies to the 92 subunits in a permanent state of combat readiness which 'will form the basis of a professional army.'"[44] For the first time, Ivanov was drawing the outlines of what would become a mixed force, but with some units dedicated to front-line combat while others became reserve units. By the end of 2002, commentators were suggesting—for the first time—that the government might have turned the corner in introducing changes in the military. The branches of the services were now down to three, but it was obvious that even 4,000 rubles a month would not be enough to attract soldiers to serve on contract. Putin promised to address the pay issue—to continue pay raises until military service became attractive.

April 2003 would become a key month for reform in the Russian military. Indeed, if one day can be singled out as the most important one, it would be April 24. On this day the government endorsed a long-term reform plan that, when compared to what the generals were asking for a year earlier, made it clear that the pressure Putin had been putting on them was sufficient to force them to make some compromises. The structure of this reform plan can be divided into five parts.

1. *Conscription—from two years to one?* The most controversial proposal was how long conscripts would serve. Almost no one wanted to serve as a conscript in the Russian military. But the military needed bodies. Should service by conscripts be limited to one year? This was a critical issue for the Kremlin. The bottom line was rather simple. The Duma provided so many ways to get deferments (e.g., university enrollment) that only about 11 percent of eligible Russian men were available to be drafted—and many could not be drafted because of health, drug use, or criminal background. Furthermore, draft evasion had become a national sport in Russia; some paid doctors to say they were unqualified, while others simply refused to show up for induction.

The initial defense ministry reform plan represented a move toward the kind of military Putin desired. For example, Ivanov suggested that the Defense Ministry was "prepared to consider the question of reducing the length of compulsory military service from two years to one."[45] Assuming such a program were adopted, the first six months would be spent at a training center. During the second six months, the conscripts would be attached to a regular unit. The units to which they would be attached would not be the "permanent-readiness" units made up of professionals, but second-line units. By the end of April, it was beginning to sound like a firm decision had been made on the reduction of service as the deputy chief of the General Staff stated that, beginning in 2008, service time would be reduced to twelve months. At the end of six months, conscripts would have an opportunity to sign a contract. Indeed, it was clear that Putin came down hard on the military on this one—forcing them to agree to a finite date (while he was still in office) on which conscription would end.

2. *A Bifurcated Army?* Assuming the plan proposed in April and approved in June 2003 is put into effect, Russia will have two different armies. On the one hand, it will have professionals. Within five years, Ivanov stated that ninety-two units made up of ground forces, airborne troops, and marines will be all-volunteer. All together this will mean ten divisions, seven brigades, and thirteen regiments; a total of 166,000 soldiers. This process will start in 2004.[46] Thus, units serving in the North Caucasus will be transferred to contract soldiers during 2004–05. Then, during the period from 2004–07, the entire military will be modified so that those units on "permanent standby," those which "substantially affect the combat readiness of the country," will become fully staffed with soldiers serving on contract.[47] The rest of the military would be made of junior officers who would train those conscripts who decided to leave after the first year. In essence, Russia would have a front-line military force capable of being deployed at a moment's notice and a reserve force useful in the event of a national emergency.

3. *A Foreign Legion?* Given how desperate the Kremlin was for manpower, it decided to reach out to citizens (mostly Russians) living in the Commonwealth of Independent States (CIS). Individuals who volunteer to serve in the Russian military will be given accelerated citizenship (they will only have to wait three instead of five years) if they serve as contract soldiers. Priority will go to those individuals who have "military professions or previous military training."[48] There will not be a "foreign legion." All CIS volunteers will be integrated with regular Russian troops, and the language of command will be Russian.

4. *Women in Combat?* In the past, women have been relegated to support roles such as medical or administrative positions, although some have been permitted to serve in units such as the Strategic Rocket Forces.[49] The mere fact that the Russian Army is opening up positions for women which will permit them to serve "in combat roles" is a clear indication of just how bad the manpower problem has become.

5. *NCOs?* Moscow understands on one level that it is desperately in need of the kind of NCOs that exist in the West. As part of the military reform plan, they intend to institute special training for them. The hope is that with a well-trained NCO corps, Moscow will be able at long last to do something about the seemingly eternal hazing problem. Not only will introducing an NCO corps mean a major change in the way the Russian military looks at matters—that is, it will require officers to delegate authority, something that they have never done—it will also require higher salaries. For example, at present conscripts make about $3 a month. Low-ranking officers make an

average of $75 per month, while an estimated 20,000 non-commissioned officer positions remain unfilled.[50] In addition to raising salaries and delegating authority, the Russian military would also have to make major changes in its over-bloated officer corps.

PAYING FOR THE TRANSFORMATION

This process will not be cheap. It was estimated that implementing the transformation of the military to this mixed professional/conscript armed forces would cost 135 billion rubles ($4.34 billion), with the majority of the money going to paying wages and creating the kind of infrastructure (e.g., housing, schools, medical facilities) that is critical to the maintenance of a professional military.[51] In order to ensure that sufficient funds to pay for this experiment were on hand, Putin set money aside in the 2004 budget that was to be approved by June 1. To get an idea of how difficult this problem will be, it is worth noting that in 2003 alone, 14.7 of all government spending (333 billion rubles) was for national defense—and that did not include the cost for security.[52] If the two are taken together, one-third of Russia's state spending goes to defense and security. So coming up with an additional 135 billion rubles will not be easy. Indeed, on April 24, 2003, Prime Minister Mikhail Kasyanov approved less than one-third of Defense Minister Sergei Ivanov's 138 billion ruble supplemental budget request, reducing it to 30 billion rubles.[53]

In spite of these actions, Boris Nemtsov and his party continued to challenge the Putin government, arguing that Putin had sold out to the military. He told Putin that if the military did not accept his party's proposal (in lieu of the longer, phased approach advocated by the military), his party "will work to obtain the resignation of Defense Minister Sergey Ivanov." Putin's response was to suggest "to Nemtsov that he calm down and keep trying to find a common language with the defense minister."[54] During this meeting—which was attended by a wide variety of government officials—senior military officers argued that Nemtsov's plan would radically reduce the size of the military in two years and not leave it with a new recruitment mechanism.

Showing the importance he attached to it, Putin made military reform one of the three issues he singled out for special attention in his State of the Union address on May 16. To begin with, he noted that Moscow "will continue to form a permanent, professional rapid reaction force." As far as conscription was concerned, Putin was categorical, observing that it would be reduced from two years to one in 2008. He also reiterated the government's plan to provide preferential entry into Russian institutions of higher education for those who serve three years, and he repeated Ivanov's promise to grant accelerated citizenship to individuals from the CIS countries who served in the Russian military.[55]

ATTACKS ON THE GENERAL STAFF

One of the techniques that Putin successfully used to push the military in the direction he wanted—if not to change their attitudes—was to seize on events to move matters in the direction he favored. The first such event was the September 11, 2001, attack by Al Qaeda on the Twin Towers in New York City and the Pentagon in Washington, D.C. Of all the events that took place in 2001, few shook the Russian military more than this attack by terrorists. While Putin may be a turtle in his tendency to push matters through the bureaucracy, he showed that he was also able to seize on such situations and use them to his advantage. Putin believes very strongly that good relations with the United States are key to Russia's economic and political recovery. The 9/11 attack was a perfect opportunity to improve U.S.-Russian relations.

Putin was the first foreign leader to call President George W. Bush, and he made it clear that he was prepared to help in any way. The Russian military, however, was not particularly forthcoming. Their suspicion vis-à-vis the West and NATO was still very strong. As a result, Putin called the senior generals together on September 24, just before he traveled to Bush's ranch in Crawford, Texas. At this meeting, Putin laid down the law, informing Moscow's generals and admirals that it was time to recognize that there had been a major change in the country's security policy. And the generals got the message. Shortly thereafter, the Kremlin dropped its opposition to the presence of U.S. forces in Central Asia and became very helpful in providing the United States with intelligence information relative to the conflict in Afghanistan. Furthermore, the defense ministry toned down its opposition to things like greater cooperation between Russia and NATO.

The situation was similar when a large helicopter—that was clearly overloaded—crashed and killed all on board in Chechnya. Heads rolled. Then came the attacks within Russia on Russian civilians, as well as terrorist acts abroad. Putin seized on this event—perhaps to keep the military off guard—and demanded that the Russian armed forces adapt so that they could fight terrorism on a global scale. As Putin put it, terrorism "is increasingly becoming a factor of global policy and, therefore, the Armed Forces should be oriented primarily to oppose this phenomenon."[56] In practice, this meant the army had to "develop operational plans and train personnel to secure important objects and to storm them if they are captured by terrorists."[57] In fact, a Russian general writing in October 2002 underlined just how out of date the Russian military was.

The most effective way to fight terrorists in cities is not the broad-scale military operations that are being conducted in Chechnya today; it is focused work by agents to identify and forestall terrorist acts. The main thing is to obtain information about preparations for terrorist operations in time. Of course, if there had been such information, measures would have been taken. But you cannot assign special forces detachments to every theater. Therefore the role of all the special structures who are getting information about the terrorists and their plans unquestionably increases.[58]

Like a good soldier, General Kvashnin, the chief of the General Staff, followed up a month later, ordering all "military units and garrisons to submit contingency plans for the prevention of terrorist attacks."[59] From a bureaucratic standpoint, this meant that Putin had the generals and admirals just where he wanted them. He had come up with a new task, and they were at a loss on how to respond because their military was not structured to deal with this new threat. They would have to change structure, and when that happened, it would become more difficult to oppose the president on other issues.

Then, to make matters even worse for the generals and admirals, there was the American invasion of Iraq. If anything, the speed and effectiveness of the American assault on Iraq stunned the country's military leaders. As Pavel Felgenhauer put it,

Russian generals were expecting another prolonged so-called non-contact war, like the one against Yugoslavia in 1999, in Afghanistan in 2001 or the first gulf war in 1991, when a four-day ground offensive was preceded by a 39-day air bombardment. It was believed that the Americans were afraid of close hand-to-hand encounters, they would not tolerate the inevitable casualties.[60]

The situation looked more bleak from the military's standpoint when it became known that three Soviet-period generals had visited Baghdad prior to the American attack and purportedly given the Iraqis advice on how to resist the American attack—an event that suggested the Russian military had underestimated how far behind the Americans it was technologically. Insofar as Putin's relationship with the military was concerned, it was a gift from heaven—a clear call for major change. "The Russian army should immediately draw lessons from the Gulf War. . . . A key conclusion that we should draw is [that] the obsolete structure of the Russian armed forces must be changed."[61] Or as a member of the Duma put it, "The Iraqi war has proven once again that a volunteer contract force equipped with state-of-the-art weapons and using modern tactics can fulfill any task."[62]

The bottom line was that these developments made it very clear that change was a necessity, and permitted Putin to push the issue through at the April 24 meeting. On July 10, 2003, the cabinet formally approved the

Defense Ministry's reform proposal. Under it, about 49 percent of the Russian military will be serving on contract by 2007, while the time served by conscripts will be lowered to one year. In his press conference, however, Defense Minister Ivanov warned that a fully professional military "was still many years away."[63]

CONCLUSION

Given how many times we have heard comments from the Kremlin suggesting that military reform was just around the corner, it is difficult to take these latest changes seriously. Skepticism is clearly warranted. Will these changes under way be enough to create a new kind of armed forces? It is hard to say. The jury is still out. On the other hand, it is worth noting that there are still some serious problems facing Moscow's political and military leadership.

To begin with, the experiment at Pskov was far from successful. It still lacks about 2,000 volunteers. The recruitment plan is only 22.5 percent completed. And there are problems inside the unit itself. "For 62 percent of service members, expectations from contract service had not been met, and for 91 percent of these it was owing to the low level of pay and allowances. . . . In addition . . . 72 percent of service members are dissatisfied with the social and living conditions of service, partly because of the lack of housing." This led Colonel General Georgiy Shpak to ask that the recruitment period that was supposed to end May 1, 2003, be extended to October 1, 2003.[64]

Then there are problems when it comes to attitudes on the part of military personnel toward the country's leadership. A recent survey by the National Public Research Center (VtsIOM) of professional soldiers in Moscow (done in May 2003) indicated that the "military does not trust its leaders; none of the present heads of the Defense Ministry and General Staff won the approval of more than 5% of the respondents."[65]

There are also problems with the institution of NCOs. Discussing this topic with Russian officers one comes away with the impression that while they understand the term, they attach a totally different meaning to it. They still cannot grasp the conceptual idea behind an NCO. The idea of delegating authority to the degree that Americans and British do seems beyond them. When Russian naval officers visited an American ship in Norfolk some years ago, for example, the commander of the Northern Fleet asked how many men serviced a particular missile mount on board a U.S. ship. When he was told that a twenty-year-old petty officer second class was in charge of both maintenance and firing the weapon, the Russian could not believe what he was hearing. He told this author that in the Soviet Navy, two officers would be used, one to maintain the weapon and one to fire the weapon. Yet this kind of delegation of authority is critical if the Russians hope to attract volunteers to man their NCO corps in this day of high technology.

One of the key questions facing Putin is the old one—money. His critics are right; he must raise salaries if he hopes to attract volunteers. Furthermore, he must provide the "creature comforts" that are so much a part of a professional, volunteer military. So far, the military does not have the 138 billion rubles it needs to implement the program.

So where does that leave military reform in Russia? In this writer's opinion, Putin has pushed the military farther toward reform during the last year than in the previous twelve years since the collapse of the USSR, when it comes to pushing the outlines of a military reform program. It is always possible that the military will outlast him, as many have suggested. However, if the plan put forward on April 24, 2003, approved in June, and endorsed by the Duma on July 24 is implemented, the Russian military will have a different structure—a professional military backed up by a reserve force. In this regard, it is important to again emphasize that the Russian military is being pushed hard to change by events such as Iraq, the new fight against terrorism, and recognition on its own part that it can no longer compete in the world of modern combat. A military made up primarily of conscripts cannot fight the kind of war the U.S. fought in Iraq. If it wants to be competitive with Western military, it must change, and present indications *suggest* that Putin will continue to push (even if he retreats now and then) until the military begins to make the necessary serious structural and perhaps even attitudinal changes.

NOTES

1. Lilia Shevtsova, *Putin's Russia* (Washington, D.C.: Carnegie Endowment for International Peace, 2003), especially chapter 3.

2. Lilia Shevtsova, "Putin's Dilemma: To Stabilize or Transform?" *Moscow Times*, January 13, 2003, in Johnson's [Russia] List, January 14, 2003.

3. Dale R. Herspring, ed., *Putin's Russia: Past Imperfect, Future Uncertain* (Boulder, CO: Rowman & Littlefield, 2002), 259–62.

4. See, for example, Stephen Blank, "This Time We Really Mean It: Russian Military Reform," *Russia and Eurasian Review* 2, no. 1 (January 7, 2003); Roger N. McDermott, "Putin's Military Priorities: Modernization of the Armed Forces," *Insight* 3, no. 1 (2003); Dale R. Herspring, "De-Professionalizing the Russian Armed Forces" (London: Palgrave, 2002), 197–210; Dale R. Herspring, "Putin and the Armed Forces," in Dale R. Herspring, ed., *Putin's Russia: Past Imperfect, Future Uncertain* (Boulder, CO: Rowman & Littlefield, 2002), 155–75; Peter Rutland, "Military Reform Marks Time," in Peter Rutland, "Russia in 2002: Waiting and Wondering" for *Transitions Online* (www.fol.cz).

5. A number of articles and chapters discuss these problems. See, for example, Zoltan Barany, "Politics and the Russian Armed Forces," in Zoltan Barany and Rob-

ert G. Moser, *Russian Politics: Challenges of Democratization* (Cambridge: Cambridge University Press, 2001), 175–214; Herspring, "De-Professionalizing the Russian Armed Forces."

6. Yelena Shishounova, "Defence Chief Briefs Putin on State of Military," January 9, 2003, gazeta.ru, in Johnson's List, January 9, 2002, 12.

7. "Russian Chief Army Prosecutor on Bullying, Draft Problems, Bribes, Specific Cases," *Rossiyskaya gazeta*, June 6, 2003, www.dialogselect.com/intranet/cgi/present, June 13, 2003.

8. "Chief of General Staff Urges More Money, Training for Russian Armed Forces," *Rossiyskaya gazeta*, May 14, 2003, in Johnson's List, May 15, 2003, 22.

9. "Chief of General Staff Urges More Money, Training for Russian Armed Forces," 24.

10. "Russian Air Force Command Worried about Aging of Aircraft," ITAR-TASS, March 26, 2003, in WNC@apollo.fedworld.gov. WNC Military Affairs, March 27, 2003.

11. "Russian Military Continues to Decay While Few Projects Are Funded," *Trud*, January 18, 2003, in WNC@apollo.fedworld.gov. WNC Military Affairs, February 11, 2003.

12. "Admiral Komoyedov on Future of Russian Navy, Views on CINC Navy Kuroyedov, *Tribuna*, October 30, 2002, in WNC@apollo.fedworld.gov. WNC Military Affairs, October 30, 2002, 4.

13. "Defense Ministry Says Military Procurements to Be Cut in 2004," *Monitor*, August 11, 2003.

14. "Russian Expert Mulls Political, Social Reasons for 'Never-Ending' Army Desertion," *Rossiyskaya gazeta*, June 19, 2002, in WNC@apollo.fedworld.gov. WNC Military Affairs, June 20, 2002, 1.

15. Anna Badkhen, "Hard Times for Russia's Reeling Military," *San Francisco Chronicle*, December 2, 2003.

16. "Vladimir Georgiyev, "The General Staff Releases Crime Statistics," *Nevavisimaya gazeta*, July 12, 2002, in Johnson's List, July 12, 2002, 14.

17. "Russian MPs Say Army Desertion Mirrors Criminal Trends in Society," ITAR-TASS, June 18, 2002, in WNC@apollo.fedworld.gov. WNC Military Affairs, June 19, 2002.

18. "Only 10.3% of Those Eligible for Military Service Will Actually Be Called Up," *Rosbalt*, April 10, 2003, in Johnson's List, April 10, 2003, 25.

19. . "Security Council Amending Military Reform Plans Again," *Nezavisimaya gazeta*, June 4, 2002, in Johnson's List, June 8, 2002, 25.

20. "Russia: Former Military Prosecutor Cited on Army's Ills," *Izvestiya*, June 15, 2002, in WNC@apollo.fedworld.gov. WNC Military Affairs, June 18, 2002.

21. For example, Pavel Felgenhauer suggested to this writer in 2002 that Putin could do anything with the military he wanted, "he is the president, and they will obey."

22. See "Russia: Survey of Military Reform in the Russian Federation," *Yadernyy kontrol*, April 19, 2002, WNC@apollo.fedworld.gov. WNC Military Affairs, September 6, 2002, 5.

23. "Defence Minister Sergei Ivanov about Iraq, UN, NATO and the Russian

Army," *Komsomolskaya pravda*, April 2003, Nos. 58–59, in Johnson's List, April 3, 2003, 27–28.

24. "Russia: Survey of Military Reform in the Russian Federation," 1.

25. "Russia: Survey of Military Reform in the Russian Federation," 8.

26. "Russia: Survey of Military Reform in the Russian Federation," 10.

27. "Major Clash Shaping Up Between Rightist Politicians and Military Chiefs on Military Reform," *Obshchaya gazeta*, December 13, 2001, in WNC@apollo.fedworld-.gov. WNC Military Affairs, December 17, 2001.

28. "Staffing Levels in the Russian Army," *Monitor*, April 11, 1996.

29. "Conversations without Middlemen," *Moscow Television*, September 14, 1995, in FBIS, CE, September 18, 1995, 21.

30. *Krasnaya zvezda*, September 12, 1995.

31. "Russian Army Struggles with Contract Service," *Monitor*, October 15, 1997.

32. "Russian Army Struggles with Contract Service."

33. "Soldiers Face Major Housing Shortages," *RFE/RL Daily Report*, February 24, 2001.

34. "More on Russian Defense Concept: Military Reform," *Monitor*, August 14, 1998.

35. "Russia's Army Still Mired in Conscript Crisis," *Russia Journal*, April 24–30, 2000, in Johnson's List, April 27, 2000.

36. *Monitor*, June 27, 2001.

37. "Russia: Problems, Including Low Pay, in Converting 76th Airborne Division to Unit of Contract Soldiers," *Rossiyskaya gazeta*, August 16, 2002, in Johnson's List, August 21, 2002, 2.

38. Pavel Felgenhauer, "Leaking, Lobbying, Looting," *Moscow Times*, July 18, 2002, in Johnson's List, July 18, 2002, 5.

39. "Russia: Scandal Brews over Military Reform, Pskov Contract Service Experiment," *Moskovskiye novosti*, October 8, 2002, in WNC@apollo.fedworld.gov. WNC Military Affairs, October 10, 2002.

40. "Litovkin: 'Political Games' Doom Contract Service Experiment in 76th Division." *Vremya*, October 8, 2002, WNC@apollo.fedworld.gov. WNC Military Affairs, October 24, 2002.

41. "Litovkin: 'Political Games' Doom Contract Service Experiment in 76th Division."

42. "Russian Defense Minister to Address Government on Military Reform," ITAR-TASS, November 20, 2002, in WNC@apollo.fedworld.gov. WNC Military Affairs, November 21, 2002.

43. "Russia's Putin Says Professional Soldiers, Not Recruits Should Fight in 'Hot Spots,'" *Moscow Interfax*, November 29, 2002, in WNC@apollo.fedworld.gov. WNC Military Affairs, December 2, 2002.

44. "Russian Defense Minister Outlines Professional Army Timetable," ITAR-TASS, December 20, 2002, in WNC@apollo.fedworld.gov. WNC Military Affairs, December 23, 2002.

45. "Russia Considers Reducing Conscription from Two Years to One," ITAR-TASS, April 24, 2003, in WNC@apollo.fedworld.gov. WNC Military Affairs, April 25, 2003.

46. Simon Saradzhyan, "Core of Army to Go Contract by 2008," *Moscow Times*, November 22, 2002, in Johnson's List, November 22, 2002.

47. "Government Sides with Generals over Military Reforms," gazeta.ru, April 24, 2003, in Johnson's List, April 24, 2003, 11–12.

48. "Defense Ministry Sets Requirements for Contract Soldiers from CIS," ITAR-TASS, May 22, 2003, in WNC@apollo.fedworld.gov. WNC Military Affairs, May 28, 2003.

49. See Dale R. Herspring, "Women in the Russian Military: A Reluctant Marriage," *Minerva* 15, no. 2 (Spring 1997): 42–59.

50. "Russia Recruits Army Volunteers," *Atlanta Journal-Constitution*, January 5, 2003, in Johnson's List, January 5, 2003, 15.

51. Simon Saradzhyan, "Army's Plan for Reform Wins Out," *Moscow Times*, April 25, 2003, in Johnson's List, April 25, 2003. Other estimates went higher, for example to 138 rubles. "Russian Defense Minister on Military Reform," ITAR-TASS, April 25, 2003, in WNC@apollo.fedworld.gov. WNC Military Affairs, April 28, 2003.

52. "Russia Gives Priority to National Defense in 2003 Budget," Interfax, June 13, 2002, in Johnson's List, June 13, 2002. Apparently, the budget was raised to 344 billion rubles.

53. "Government Slashes Military Chiefs Reform-Funding Request," *RFE/RL Report*, April 25, 2003.

54. "United Russia Puts Active Support Behind Military Reform," *Tribuna*, May 16, 2003, in WNC@apollo.fedworld.gov. WNC Military Affairs, May 28, 2003.

55. "Russia Pledges to Follow Through on Delayed Military Reform," *AFP*, May 16, 2003, in Johnson's List, May 17, 2003.

56. "Russia's Putin Says Armed Force Should Focus on Opposing Terrorism," ITAR-TASS, November 26, 2002, in WNC@apollo.fedworld.gov. WNC Military Affairs, November 27, 2002.

57. "Defense Minister to Prepare Army for War Against Terrorism," *RFE/RL Report*, November 5, 2002.

58. "Russian General, Senator Reviews Needs in War Against Terrorism," *Rossiyskaya gazeta*, October 31, 2002, in WNC@apollo.fedworld.gov, November 7, 2002, 2.

59. "General Staff Orders Troops to Be Ready for Terrorist Attacks," *RFE/RL Report*, December 11, 2002.

60. "The Elite's Feeling the Heat," *Moscow Times*, April 10, 2003, in Johnson's List, April 10, 2003.

61. BBC Monitoring, "Russian Army Reform Should Draw On Gulf War Lessons—Expert" April 10, 2003, in Johnson's List, April 10, 2003, 23.

62. Maria Golovnina, "Russia Speeds Up Army Reform, Analysts Skeptical," April 15, 2003, Reuters, in Johnson's List, April 15, 2003.

63. "Russia Creeps Slowly Towards Fully Professional Army," *AFP*, July 10, 2003, in Johnson's List, July 14, 2003.

64. "Lessons Learnt from Russian Armed Forces Contract Experiment—Defense Minister, *Krasnaya zvezda*, May 29, 2003, in Johnson's List, June 3, 2003, 34.

65. "The Military Doesn't Like Its Leaders," *Nezavisimaya gazeta*, June 4, 2003, in Johnson's List, June 4, 2003, 14.

Chapter Eleven

Putin and Russia's Wars in Chechnya

Jacob W. Kipp

Over the past decade Chechnya has become the great defining issue of Russian statehood and the test of Russian military power. Conflict there did
much to undermine the tenure of one president and became the distinguish-
ing element in another president's march to office. Since 2001, President
Vladimir Putin has linked the endgame of the conflict in Chechnya with Russian participation in a broad, antiterrorist coalition. In the wake of the events
of September 11, Putin chose to redefine the former conflict to fit within the
latter. This was not a particularly onerous task because Putin had long been
describing the war in Chechnya as a campaign against bandits and terrorists.
As early as March 2001, the Russian government sent to the UN Security
Council a memo making an explicit linkage between elements of the
Chechen resistance and Osama bin Laden's Al Qaeda organization in
Afghanistan, and describing a network of camps that included at least 2,560
Chechens serving or training with the bin Laden organization.[1]

In a September 24, 2001, address to the Russian people, Putin announced
his support for the war against terrorism. Labeling the attacks barbaric, Putin
offered Russian support for the antiterrorist struggle.[2] He noted that Russia
had long called for a unified effort against international terrorism, had been
battling it in Chechnya and Central Asia, and was now ready to take an active
part in a multilateral coalition against it. "Russia has not changed its stance.
Surely, we are willing now, too, to contribute to the antiterror cause. As we
see it, attention must turn primarily to enhancing the role of international
institutions established to promote international security—the United
Nations and its Security Council."[3] On specific cooperation in the Afghan
theater of military operations, Putin pledged Russia in five areas: intelligence
sharing between security services, air passage over Russian territory for
"humanitarian cargo" in support of antiterror operations, use of Moscow's
good offices to secure access to the airfields of its Central Asian allies, engage-

ment of Russian forces and facilities in international search and rescue operations, and closer relations and greater assistance to the Rabbani government and Northern Alliance forces. Putin put Minister of Defense Sergei Ivanov in charge of coordinating the intelligence sharing and practical cooperation with the antiterrorist coalition.[4]

As he pledged support for the antiterrorism coalition, Putin also addressed Chechnya in a manner that tied the two topics directly to one another. "As we see it, Chechen developments ought not to be regarded outside the context of efforts against international terrorism." This was clearly a marker on the table. Putin noted the historical peculiarities of the Chechen conflict that made it a distinct part of the struggle against terrorism and then appealed for the misguided and/or misinformed to lay down their arms.

> That is why I call all paramilitaries and self-styled political activists urgently to sever whatever contacts with international terrorists and their organizations; and to contact official spokesmen of federal ruling bodies within 72 hours to debate the following: the disarmament procedure of the paramilitary groups and formations, and arrangements to involve them in peacetime developments in Chechnya. On behalf of federal authority, Victor Kazantsev, envoy plenipotentiary of the President of the Russian Federation to federal district South, which incorporates Chechnya, has been authorized to affect such contacts.[5]

Putin's challenge was to make peace with those Chechens who were willing to seek a political arrangement within the Russian Federation as opposed to the creation of an Islamic state or a Jihad against Russia. Since then, the fighting has continued and evolved. Terrorism and repression within Chechnya continue, but spectacular terrorist actions have also targeted Moscow itself, including the tragic hostage incident in the fall of 2002 at the Nordost Theater, with the associated loss of life among the civilian hostages, and the bombing incident at a rock concert in the summer of 2003. The Russian press devoted considerable attention to the appearance of "black widows," Chechen women and girls willing to give their lives in revenge attacks upon Russian civilian and military targets. Russian security services identified these "kamikazes" with attacks inside Chechnya, in the Russian south, and in Moscow and stated that they operated under the direction of Shamil Basayev.[6] On the Russian side, throughout 2002 there were claims of progress in counterinsurgency operations and calls to strike at foreign bases of Chechen/Islamic terrorists, especially those in Georgia's Pankisi Gorge. In the summer and fall of 2002, these calls took place against a backdrop of incidents along the Chechen-Russian border. While the United States, which had deployed Special Forces to train Georgian Army units for antiterrorist actions, warned against any action that would compromise Georgian sovereignty, it also recommended that the Georgian government take its own actions to deal with the threat.

In late 2001 the Putin administration briefly sought and then abandoned negotiations with President Aslan Maskhadov's rebel government on terms that amounted to surrender for the rebels. One commentator categorized Putin's call for such negotiations an exercise in "political metatechnology" (*metatekhnologiia*) that reframed the Chechen question and laid the foundation for a fresh approach to ending the conflict.[7] In this context, the failure of negotiations served to reinvigorate "regularization" through efforts to strengthen local organs of power and improve their performance in the sphere of law enforcement and by economic development. According to Putin, the main task before the Russian government in Chechnya was to deny to terrorists the use of its territory to destabilize Russia and conduct attacks upon its borderlands.[8] In place of negotiations the Kremlin turned toward the regularization of Chechnya via constitutional reform, economic recovery, and the election of local officials and a Chechen president. This strategy was in keeping with Putin's commitment to rebuilding the authority and power of the central state. In late March 2003, with fighting still ongoing, Chechens voted for the new constitution, which proclaimed: "the territory of the Chechen Republic shall be united and indivisible and shall be an inalienable part of the territory of the Russian Federation."[9] According to some observers, Chechens voted for peace in confirming the constitution, but peace did not come. The rebels vowed to continue fighting and rejected the vote as Moscow's manipulation. The population remains demoralized and trapped between the insurgents and the Russian military and intelligence services. In early October 2003, facing almost no opposition thanks to the Kremlin's interventions, Akhmed Kadyrov was elected president of Chechnya in an election notable for high turnout and the absence of Western observers of the voting.[10] The U.S. State Department responded to Kadyrov's victory by questioning the fairness of the election. Richard Boucher observed that the exit of all viable challengers to Kadyrov's candidacy and the overt control of Chechen media by pro-Kadyrov forces made the elections appear neither fair nor free.[11] For the rebels, Kadyrov was simply a traitor to their cause. The deep roots of this conflict and the proclaimed objectives of the opposing sides have made for a protracted conflict that is difficult to resolve. On May 9, 2004, Kadyrov was assassinated during Victory Day celebrations when a bomb exploded at a Grozny stadium.

A nation in a region of many nationalities, the Chechens have emerged as the most formidable challenge to the sovereignty and territorial integrity of the Russian Federation. Moscow came to view a Chechen victory as a geopolitical "domino" that would subject the Russian Federation to the same forces of disintegration that had torn apart the Soviet Union. The Chechens' struggle, which has combined a call for national self-determination and a revival of Islam, pitted a small but proud and warlike nation against a state struggling to redefine itself after seven decades of communism. At the heart of the conflict remains the question of Russia's relations with those nations brought into the tsarist empire by force of arms and subjected to repression by the most ruthless totalitarian methods.

The Yeltsin administration, having invoked Russian nationalism to bring about the end of the Soviet Union, found its sovereignty challenged by a nation of less than a million people and sought to thwart Chechen self-determination by force in 1994. After a year and a half of inconclusive warfare and fragile cease-fires, the Yeltsin government waited until after the second round of the presidential election to renew fighting, only to be embarrassed by the Chechens' recapture of Grozny on the same day as Yeltsin's inauguration. An infirm president was forced to accept a cease-fire and the withdrawal of Russian forces from Chechnya in August 1996.[12] With an armistice and a five-year period to negotiate a political settlement, both sides watched law and order deteriorate in the region and began preparing for renewed hostilities. Chechen rebels with a radical Islamic ideology took to exporting their insurgency beyond Chechnya into multiethnic Dagestan on the southern border of the Russian Federation and Azerbaijan.

In September 1999, in response to Chechen armed incursions into Dagestan, Moscow renewed hostilities. Under the leadership of a new prime minister, Vladimir Putin, it embarked upon the systematic pacification of Chechnya by brutal military assault and mass repression. Putin staked his own rise to power on military success in Chechnya, and between his appointment as acting president and his election, Russian forces captured the flattened Chechen capital, Grozny. The uneven struggle, however, continues, pitting regular Russian troops and paramilitary formations against Chechen Mujahadeen. The Chechens cannot expel the Russians and the Russians cannot prevent Chechen raids and terrorist actions. This struggle is a manifestation of what Samuel Huntington has described as a "clash of civilizations." Like other such conflicts, it has its roots in the history of the interactions between the protagonists, Russians and Chechens, and how they define themselves and the "other."[13] Many Chechen fighters have embraced an Islamic revival to foster internal solidarity and to mobilize a broader struggle across the region. It is the region itself that defines the clash.

Since the border conflicts of the nineteenth century, the Islamic peoples of the Caucasus have posed a stark challenge to Russian state builders. Russian writers—Pushkin, Lermantov, and Tolstoy—understood that the mountain warrior was different. A challenge to Russia's imperial pretensions, he was the Other who could be admired for his bravery and ferocity but never tamed. The cleavages—cultural, religious, geographic, political—run deep.

By the time Vladimir Putin took charge of the Russo–Chechen War there was a long legacy that shaped the parameters of the conflict. Putin would have to operate within a well-delineated context that would dictate his course of action. Insofar as he defined his own political future and Russia's national

recovery in terms of a strong, stable, centralized state, Chechen independence could not be accepted, only imposed, and certainly not by the Chechen
resistance alone.

THE CHECHEN THEATER
OF MILITARY OPERATIONS

Geography

Chechnya is a small, landlocked, autonomous republic within the Russian
Federation. Covering an area of 6,000 square miles, an area slightly smaller
than the state of New Jersey, and with a population of about one million
before the present round of fighting, Chechnya has been an area of confrontation between Imperial Russia/Soviet Union and the Chechen nation for
several centuries. It is surrounded on three sides by Russian territory—on the
north by Stavropol' Krai, on the west by Ingushetiya, and on the east and
south by Dagestan.

Chechnya has one international frontier—to the south with Georgia. Two-
thirds of the country north of the Terek River is open steppe; the land south
of the Terek is dominated by the foothills of the Caucasus Mountains that
stretch east to west across the region. Chechnya has limited oil production,
but part of the pipeline system to carry oil from Baku, Azerbaijan, to the Russian Black Sea port of Novorossiysk is located in Chechnya, giving the region
a role in the politics of the emerging Great Game of Caucasian, Caspian, and
Central Asian oil, gas, and pipelines.

History: The Chechens and Islam[14]

Steppe and mountain, Cossack and mountaineer, Christian and Muslim, soldier and warrior, oppressor and bandit—these dichotomies describe the conflict between Russians and Chechens. Former Chechen president Aslan
Maskhadov, a colonel who served in the Soviet Army, described the current
war as the continuation of a four-century struggle: "Here, the Chechen people are fighting Russia. Russia does not want to clarify its relations with
Chechnya. For this reason, the war has been continuing for more than 400
years."[15] This is no exaggeration, since the struggle between Russians and
Muslims of the Caucasus began in the seventeenth century. That unequal and
bitter struggle has defined their mutual relations and the Chechens' sense of
their place in the world. The protracted and episodic nature of the contest
has had a profound impact on the character of the Chechen nation, its social
organization, and self-perceptions. For the Chechen, clan loyalty and per-

sonal freedom gave meaning to a warrior culture that sets the nation apart from the Cossack settlers north of the Terek River. South of the Terek is the hill country that rises steadily to the peaks of the Caucasus. These mountains stretch 650 miles from the Caspian to the Black Sea and form a natural rampart separating Europe from Asia. The Arabic language and Islamic faith gave Chechens access to a literate world that linked Chechen culture to a greater identity. Chechens embraced the religion brought by Muslim missionaries and made it their own. By the eighteenth century most of the peoples of the Caucasus, with the exception of the Georgians and Armenians, were Muslims. Islam provided the basis for alliances with the many other Islamic peoples of the region in their struggle with Orthodox Russia.

Clan life in a Chechen mountain village (*aoul*) revolved around raising sheep and raiding. The fortified stone villages were located on high peaks. The clans practiced the blood-vendetta (the *kanli*) where no offensive against clan honor could go unpunished, and feuds could go on for generations. Only the strong survived. Chechens continue to identify their nation with the wolf, the embodiment of elemental freedom. To supplement their meager existence, Chechen warriors frequently raided north of the Terek, carrying off goods, animals, and slaves from Cossack settlements. Horsemanship, marksmanship, and personal bravery defined a warrior's place in the clan. As the Russian frontier leaped across the steppe and toward the Terek, the imperial government in St. Petersburg turned its attention to the intractable mountain people.

Tsarist Intervention and Chechen Resistance

Under Catherine II, Russia defeated the Crimean Tartars, vassals of the Ottoman Empire, and began to push Russian settlements into the North Caucasus, extending serfdom into the new lands. The vehicle of that control was the Russian Imperial Army, setting in motion a conflict between soldiers of the regular army and Chechen warriors. Catherine II deployed Russian troops to revenge the defeat of a Russian column south of the Terek and made war against a coalition of mountain Islamic peoples, including Chechens, led by Sheikh Mansur Ushurma. The Russian advance culminated with the capture of the Black Sea Ottoman fortress of Anapa and the Sheikh himself in 1791.

After the Napoleonic Wars, Russia renewed its advance south. The Russians established fortress settlements at Grozny, Khasav-Yurt, and Mozdok to provide bases of operations. General Aleksei Yermolov, the first Russian commander in the protracted war that ensued, set the tone for an uncompromising and unforgiving struggle of extermination. Confronted by a barren and dry steppe north of the Terek River, Russian forces set their operational line east-west and set about building up a chain of fortress settlements on the

Terek that would block raids from the south and provide the foundation for campaigns against the mountain villages to the south. That conflict defined the myth of Chechen nationhood by linking the protracted struggle to a charismatic leader, Shamil, and to national and religious self-determination.

In the 1820s a profound spiritual movement swept the Chechens and other Islamic peoples of the North Caucasus, led by Mullah Muhammad Yaraghi, a scholar and Sufi, who set out to establish a Koran-based social order which embraced the "*Naqshbandi* Way." Those who accepted the mystical path of enlightenment known as Sufism, became the disciples, *murids*, of the mullah. He called for the suppression of customary law and the blood feud and the establishment of the *Shari'ah*, or Islamic law. In keeping with Islamic tradition, he preached temperance. His followers included Qazi Mullah, an Avar from Dagestan. In 1829 Qazi Mullah preached a *jihad* (holy war) against the Russians as the final stage of the revival. He warned: "Your marriages are unlawful, your children bastards, while there is one Russian left in your lands!"[16] The Islamic scholars of Dagestan gathered at Ghimri, and, acclaiming him imam, pledged their support.

The Russians responded to this threat by co-opting some clans with concessions and using military power against the resistance. Like the Yeltsin government a century and a half later, Nicholas I's agents had only limited success in this policy of divide and rule. Ultimately, the Russian military faced two wars in the North Caucasus: in the west against the Cherkess people and in the east against the peoples of Dagestan, Chechnya, and Ingushetia.[17] The eastern struggle produced a Dagestani warrior and imam who would embody the Chechen myth of resistance.

Shamil Imam (1796–1871), an Adar noble of Dagestan, joined the resistance led by Qazi Mullah. Shamil fought heroically in the defense of Ghimri in 1831. Wounded in the fighting, Shamil escaped capture, as he would on many later occasions. Proclaimed imam in 1834, he rallied the peoples of the east Caucasus to resist the Russian advance. Supported by the *murids*, Shamil checked Russian power for almost three decades and built an Islamic state to prosecute a guerilla war, relying upon the impenetrability of the forests and mountains of the Caucasus to protect his force.[18] Undeterred, the Russians made war on the Chechen population, striking at the *aouls*. While they could not level the mountains, the Russians could and did cut back the forests to allow their columns to move against the fortress settlements. For a brief moment during the Crimean War it appeared that Shamil might get Western support for his struggle, but following the war, Shamil was isolated from outside support and forced to surrender to General Alexander Bariatinsky in 1859. The war ended in 1864 with a Russian victory.[19]

From the beginning, Russian rule in the North Caucasus had been imposed by force and was thus maintained. When war broke out with Turkey in 1877, Chechens joined an armed uprising, which was suppressed by the tsarist authorities. In the early twentieth century some of Chechnya's leading families emigrated to Turkey and thereby created a Chechen diaspora. In the chaos that overtook Russia after 1914, the empire collapsed, with much of the non-Russian periphery seeking self-determination. On May 11, 1918, the North Caucasus peoples declared the formation of the Republic of the North Caucasus Federation under the sponsorship of the Central Powers. Germany's defeat and the outbreak of civil war in southern Russia turned the North Caucasus into a battleground for Reds and Whites. The Reds supported the independence of the region as part of their struggle with the Whites and in the hope of using Islam against the imperial powers. The Whites found support among the Russian Cossack populations living on the steppe and resistance among the Chechen mountaineers. In Bolshevik propaganda Shamil became a revolutionary and symbol of resistance to imperial rule. However, after the civil war the Bolsheviks sent the Red Army into the region, overthrew the existing order, and annexed it in 1922.

Stalinism and Chechnya

Joseph Stalin, the Bolshevik commissar of nationalities and a Georgian, adapted the class struggle to the traditional policy of divide and rule. Soviet federalism provided a national veneer to a centralized state controlled by the Communist Party that sent Russians to staff the key party posts within the various republics.[20] However, the Chechens again proved a difficult people to subdue. In 1929 they revolted against collectivization, and for a decade Chechnya was rife with revolt and repression. Soviet propaganda now cast Shamil as a class enemy. Soviet interest in Chechnya grew with the development of its oil fields and the arrival of Russians to manage the oil industry.

During World War II, when the German Army advanced into the Caucasus, there were more signs of Chechen unrest and collaboration with the enemy. In late February 1944, Lavrenti Beria's NKVD carried out Stalin's "solution" to the Chechen Question—mass deportation of Chechens to Central Asia. Over 70,000 of the 450,000 Chechens expelled died during transit or upon arrival. Chechnya ceased to exist. The exile became the defining event for succeeding generations of Chechens.[21] In 1957 Nikita Khrushchev decreed that the Chechens could return to their ancestral homelands. Chechnya and Ingushetia were joined administratively into the Chechen-Ingush Autonomous Republic. This arrangement joined the rebellious Chechens with the traditionally loyal Ingush in a clear continuation of Moscow's policy of divide and rule. Inside Chechnya, Soviet officials made their own arrangements with local clans while keeping an uneasy eye open for signs of resistance to Communist rule.

THE FIRST CHECHEN WAR OF THE
RUSSIAN FEDERATION, 1994–96

Road to War

When Mikhail Gorbachev embarked on his ill-fated attempt to save the Soviet system via *glasnost* and *perestroika*, Chechen nationalists saw an opportunity to attain national self-determination. Then in the chaos and collapse of the Soviet Union, Boris Yeltsin led a resurgent Russian Federation and championed greater self-rule within the Union republics. In his political struggle for control of Russia, Yeltsin encouraged the national republics within Russia to seek greater autonomy. The Chechens exploited this opportunity. In late November 1990, a national Chechen conference, including delegates representing all ethnic groups in Chechnya, convened in Grozny. The conference declared the independence and sovereignty of Chechnya and its secession from the Soviet Union. On November 27, 1990, the soviet of the Chechen-Ingush Republic unanimously dissolved the union of Chechnya and Ingushetia and declared their independence and sovereignty.

General Major Dzhokar Dudaev quickly emerged as the leader of the self-proclaimed Chechen government. Dudaev, the first Chechen officer to reach the rank of general, had served in Afghanistan and commanded a strategic bomber unit in the Baltic. In June 1991, Chechen and Russian nationalism moved in lockstep against Soviet power as Yeltsin won 80 percent of the vote in the Chechen-Ingush returns from the Russian presidential elections. In the aftermath of the August coup of 1991 and the collapse of efforts to reform the Union, Chechens voted for independence and elected General Dudaev as president by an overwhelming majority. The Yeltsin government proved quite ineffective in countering these moves, and their ham-handed tactics again convinced most Chechens that whoever was in power in Moscow was an enemy of self-determination. In December 1991, the Soviet Union collapsed when the presidents of Russia, Ukraine, and Belarus voted to abolish the Union. Now Chechnya was a matter to be resolved by the Yeltsin government in Moscow and Dudaev's government in Grozny.

At this juncture as the struggle for Chechen independence began, Moscow was weak, and Grozny drifted into chaos as crime and corruption grew at a staggering pace. Yeltsin viewed Chechen independence as a threat to Russia's territorial integrity and sovereignty and a magnet for other disgruntled Caucasian peoples chafing under Russian rule. Initially, the Yeltsin government paid little attention to the Chechen problem. Dissolving the Soviet system, trying to create a viable Russian government, and transforming the economy through privatization and marketization were given top priority. The Chechens, thanks to corrupt and incompetent Russian officials, seized large quantities of Soviet arms left in Chechnya. Dudaev distributed the arms but did not create an effective regular military.

The Yeltsin administration, having invoked Russian nationalism to bring about the end of the Union, watched Chechen separatism under General Dudaev become an effective challenge to Moscow's rule. While the Dudaev government managed to gain control of most of the Soviet weapons left in Grozny, it did not create an orderly or stable government. Chechnya sank into a morass of crime and terrorism that adversely affected Russian economic and political interests. The Russian population of the republic began to leave. At first, the government tried to build an alliance with disgruntled Chechens, who opposed Dudaev's increasingly arbitrary and corrupt government. However, in 1994, fearing that Yeltsin's rival and former speaker of the overthrown Russian parliament, Ruslan Khasbulatov, would emerge as leader of that opposition, the Yeltsin government attempted to overthrow Dudaev's regime by covert action, with disguised Russian military personnel spearheading the attack on Grozny. When this attempt failed, the government resorted to force of arms in December 1994. While invoking the threat of instability in Chechnya to justify intervention, the Yeltsin government sought to present military intervention as something less than a war. The intervention was to involve a peacemaking mission (*mirotvorchestvo*) that would restore "constitutional order" and require that the Russian forces deploy to separate the warring "factions" and de facto reestablish Russian sovereignty in Chechnya. Yeltsin and his advisors wanted to use military power to awe the Chechens but not to fight a protracted partisan war. The problem was that once the black operation had failed, they had no plausible explanation for their "peacekeeping intervention."

That plan began to unravel in late November 1994 when Russia-sponsored, anti-Dudaev Chechens mounted an assault on Grozny and were badly defeated. In spite of the qualitative and quantitative decline in Russian conventional military power and the defeat of their covert attempt to overthrow Dudaev, the Yeltsin government did not anticipate serious or effective military resistance from the Chechens, either Dudaev's troops or a popular insurrection. Competent military professionals did warn the government regarding the condition of Russian forces and the danger of underestimating Chechen resistance. General Edvard Vorob'ev turned down the position of theater commander when Minister of Defense Pavel Grachev refused his request for additional time to prepare Russian forces for the operation. Grachev, an airborne commander with experience in Afghanistan, dismissed these concerns and did not provide sufficient or timely leadership in the preparation of the forces for combat, which he treated as another contingency operation, like those that Soviet and Russian forces had been engaging in since 1989. Indeed, speaking of a *coup de main* to take out Dudaev's government, Grachev had estimated one airborne brigade and two hours to finish the task. Russia's military leadership gravely underestimated the risks of a popular uprising in support of Chechen independence. The Yeltsin govern-

ment made the common mistake of reinforcing failure with tragic consequences. Rather than redrafting their plans with the failure of the anti-
Dudaev opposition to take the city, they stuck with their peacekeeping operation and went into combat in the dead of winter with forces unprepared for
combat.

Confronted with a failed covert operation, Yeltsin's government sought to
use force to recover from the disaster. The political leadership, while eager
for a military solution, was unable to provide a plausible explanation for the
use of force in Chechnya and was still suffering from a serious challenge to
its credibility after its ill-judged support of a Russia-sponsored faction in
Chechnya. Denials of Russian involvement gave way to admission of "volunteers" and then to reports of active recruiting of military personnel by the
Federal Counter-Intelligence Service (FSK) for the opposing force's unsuccessful assault on Grozny. When the Security Council voted to overtly deploy
Russian forces to Chechnya, Boris Yeltsin absented himself from the public
eye, leaving it to others to explain his administration's course of action and
rationale. The First Chechen War never invoked broad public support, and
the Russian media, with few exceptions, critically questioned the government's account of the campaign.

The Assault on Grozny

In early December 1994, three Russian columns—made up of composite
units and numbering at most 23,000—began their advance on Grozny from
three directions: northeast, west, and east. The slow pace and uncoordinated
nature of the Russian advance allowed the Chechens to organize their
defense. Ad hoc detachments defended the presidential palace and took on
the advancing Russian columns in a series of ambushes. With the Russian
advance stalled, the Chechen defenders organized strong points, which over
time became three concentric defensive belts around the presidential palace.

The total number of defenders, regular Chechen troops, volunteer detachments, and foreign mercenaries numbered between nine and ten thousand
under Colonel Aslan Maskhadov, Dudaev's chief of staff. By the last day of
December, Russian forces were in position to begin their occupation of
Grozny, advancing as though Grozny was a Russian city. In fact, many Russian residents of the capital had already fled and others were already fearful
because of Russian air attacks upon the city. The Chechen population was
united in the struggle against the Russian assault. In the course of their
advance into the city, the Russian columns were ambushed by Chechen
fighters. The Chechens operated in small ten to twelve-man mobile groups
fighting from building to building and making good use of off-the-shelf commercial communication equipment. Unprepared for the demands of urban
combat and suffering from poor coordination and intelligence, the Russian

attackers had 1,500 casualties on the streets of Grozny during the New Year's Day battle. Of 120 BMPs (armored personnel carriers) that advanced into the city, over 100 were destroyed by enemy action. The attacking forces lost twenty of twenty-six tanks in the initial assault. Humiliated by the initial success of the Chechen defense of Grozny, the Russian Army and Internal Forces fought a month-long, bloody battle to take the city, and began the pacification of the countryside.[22]

Pacification and Its Failure

The Chechens conducted a successful withdrawal from the city and then mounted protracted partisan warfare in the countryside. General Anatoliy Kulikov, the commander in chief of internal troops, was given the task of pacification. Russian soldiers occupied more villages but could not uproot the insurrection. Failing to impose their will or find a viable Chechen faction that would serve as Moscow's agent, the Russians began negotiations to end the conflict. Meanwhile, morale and discipline among the Russian forces in Chechnya, which had been low to begin with, declined further.[23] Thanks to bad field sanitation, an outbreak of viral hepatitis, much like those suffered by Soviet troops in Afghanistan, decimated the Russian forces in Chechnya.[24] On the one hand, low morale and lack of discipline led to widespread excesses against the civilian population, turning every village into a source of Chechen intelligence. At the same time, it facilitated transfers of arms for cash between Russian troops and the Chechen rebels. On the other hand, relations between regular army units and units of internal troops deteriorated rapidly. Russian media provided in-depth and largely accurate accounts of the fighting. When Shamil Basaev's band raided the village of Budennovsk in Stavropol' Krai ninety miles inside Russia and took hostages at the local hospital in June 1995, it was the Russian media that depicted the government's incompetent response, turning Basaev into an international figure, and further discrediting the Russian government's cause. As a final straw, the government failed to free hostages held by Basaev, and was forced to negotiate their release while permitting the escape of the Chechen detachment.[25] A major shake-up in the Russian power ministries followed this disaster. Prime Minister Viktor Chernomyrdin initiated negotiations to end the fighting.

Chechen forces continued to conduct raids and terrorist attacks against Russian troops and mounted assassination attempts against Russian officials in Chechnya. In October 1995, the Chechens carried out a bombing attack against General-Lieutenant A. Romanov, seriously wounding the MVD commander and chief Russian negotiator. While the Russian authorities concentrated on trying to create an alternative Chechen government and to carry out the normalization of life in Chechnya—symbolized by Chechnya's participation in the federation's parliamentary elections in December 1995, the

Chechens regrouped their forces and mounted daily attacks against Russian posts and convoys. They carried out daring raids into Grozny itself. In January 1996, Salman Rudaev mounted a major raid against Russian forces at Kizliar in Dagestan. Rudaev's band broke off their attack upon the Russian units there and fell back upon the village, where they took civilian hostages. Following negotiations with Dagestani authorities and the release of some of their hostages, Rudaev's fighters were given buses and safe passage to the Dagestani frontier with their remaining hostages. After failing in their initial attempt to capture Rudaev's contingent, Russian special forces found themselves locked into a battle for the village of Pervomaisk. In the course of several days, part of Rudaev's band escaped the encirclement. At the end of a year's fighting Russian forces were no closer to ending Chechen resistance.

Presidential Elections and the End Game

The Yeltsin government swung back and forth between repression and accommodation as the 1996 presidential elections approached. At the beginning of the electoral campaign, Boris Yeltsin's popularity had sunk to rock bottom. Some of his advisors favored postponing the presidential elections and outlawing the Communist Party, the chief opposition force led by Gennadiy Zyuganov. Those supporting the holding of elections mobilized their forces around the theme of preventing the restoration of communism and understood that the war in Chechnya was a chief source of discontent with the government. To win re-election Yeltsin needed both evidence of progress on the ground and an opportunity to begin negotiations with the Chechens. On April 21, 1996, Yeltsin got his evidence of progress when Russian intelligence was able to lock on to Dzhokar Dudaev's cell phone and provide strike coordinates for an Su-25 ground-attack aircraft to launch two laser-guided missiles that killed the Chechen president. With the death of Dudaev, the Yeltsin government proposed a cease-fire as a first step toward a negotiated settlement.

In the following months, the Yeltsin team used the cease-fire to defuse the war issue in the presidential elections, and finished first in the initial round of voting. They then ensured Yeltsin's re-election by forging an alliance with General Aleksandr Lebed, who had finished third in the voting behind Yeltsin and Zyuganov. Yeltsin treated Lebed as his anointed successor and appointed him secretary of the Security Council. Rumors of coups brought major shake-ups in the administration, including the removal of General Grachev and the appointment of General Igor Rodionov, a Lebed supporter, as minister of defense. Lebed had been an outspoken critic of the war in Chechnya.

In July, the Yeltsin administration began preparations for renewed fighting, but the Chechens preempted the Russian blow by striking at Grozny. Confronted by the Chechen reconquest of Grozny and serious divisions within the government over the further prosecution of the war, the Yeltsin government was forced to accept a cease-fire negotiated by General Lebed. The immediate axis of this dispute was between General Kulikov of the Ministry of Internal Affairs, who saw Russian control of Chechnya as vital to the territorial integrity of the Russian Federation and its survival, and General Lebed, who saw in Chechnya the collapse of the unreformed army. For Lebed, a cease-fire and settlement of Chechnya were the only way to save the armed forces from disintegration. The peacemakers won, the Russian Army withdrew, and Lebed and Maskhadov signed the Khasavyurt Accords on August 31, 1996. The cease-fire ended the fighting but left the ultimate status of Chechnya unresolved.

BETWEEN WARS, 1996–99

With Yeltsin now seriously ill, a struggle for leadership within the Kremlin became intense. Lebed, who was both popular and strong willed, seemed an immediate threat to the Yeltsin loyalists. They mounted a successful campaign, led by Minister of Internal Affairs Anatoliy Kulikov, to discredit him as a coup plotter and bring about his removal. Management of the Chechen question was left in the hands of the Security Council, with the oligarch Boris Berezovsky appointed deputy secretary for Chechnya. General Rodionov, a champion of military reform, found no support within the government and was removed in May 1997, replaced by General (and then Marshal) Igor Sergeev, the former commander of the Strategic Rocket Forces. Sergeev focused the reform efforts of the Ministry of Defense upon Russia's strategic nuclear forces. Preparation of Russian Army and Internal Forces for possible employment in response to further destabilization of Chechnya or the extension of unrest beyond its borders fell to the General Staff, the Ministry of Internal Affairs, and the North Caucasian Military District.

General Anatolii Kvashnin was appointed chief of the General Staff in June 1997. Former commander of the North Caucasian Military District during the First Chechen War, Kvashnin favored the reform of the Russian Armed Forces along lines that would enhance conventional military power and modernize the force to fight local wars.

Chechen military and political success strengthened the political hand of Colonel Aslan Maskhadov, who served as Dudaev's chief of staff and engineered the victory in Grozny. Maskhadov was elected president of Chechnya in early 1997, but his power base was quite limited. Personal and ideological/ religious conflicts projected an image that no one was in charge of a bandit republic. Law and order collapsed and kidnapping and extortion became widespread. Islam defined the splits among the Chechen leadership. Basaev, the most charismatic leader, was a throwback to Shamil's Sufism. Khattab, an Arab who had fought in Afghanistan and Tajikistan, brought foreign Mujahadeen, money, and Wahhabi fundamentalism to the struggle. Both leaders challenged Maskhadov's authority and promoted a renewed and expanded war.

For its part, the Russian government proved utterly incapable of developing a coherent political strategy to deal with Chechnya. Some Russians wanted revenge or had personal reasons to stoke the fires of ethnic hatred using a well-financed media campaign. Even Russian moderates came to view Chechnya as a criminal land and a source of chaos, where kidnapping had become a recognized business. By 1998, both sides were preparing for a confrontation.

THE SECOND CHECHEN WAR, 1999–

The five-year interlude provided by the Russian–Chechen agreement was supposed to provide sufficient time for a political resolution of the core issues: Chechen sovereignty and the territorial integrity of the Russian Federation. An interlude of peace ensued; however, it was marked by increasing violence, banditry, and kidnapping within Chechnya, and by growing Russian concern that the crisis in Chechnya would take a form requiring military action. In 1997–98 it appeared that Russian political and military leaders had agreed upon a limited response to such a crisis. Military command-post exercises, restructuring of command arrangements, and actions in theater all suggested a crisis response that would involve the military isolation of Chechnya from Russia, including an advance to the Terek River but no further.

Several events in the spring and summer of 1999 encouraged the resumption of hostilities. Many Russians viewed NATO's intervention in Kosovo as a precursor to intervention in support of Muslims in the Caucasus. Radical Islamic elements in Chechnya viewed the success of the Kosovo Liberation Army as a model for their armed struggle. The Russian leadership was aware of the possibility of renewed fighting and a raid into Dagestan but were divided over the response. Some saw the optimal response as a Russian attempt to support Maskhadov's authority in Chechnya. Others rejected this path as the surest way to legitimizing Chechen independence in 2001 at the end of the five years of the interim agreement between Lebed and Maskhadov. All sides recognized that Russia was not well prepared to deal with a renewed war. Stepashin's government accepted the military planners' recommendation for an advance to the Terek River in case of renewed hostilities.[26]

In August 1999, Khattab and Basaev led their military formations into Dagestan to ignite an Islamic insurgency. It is still unclear whether President Maskhadov endorsed or supported this move. Russian officials and press accounts stressed the chaos and disorder within Chechnya as a primary source of the external adventure. In his memoirs, General Gennadiy Troshev described Chechnya on the eve of the second war as "an international bandit enclave."[27] Foreign observers mentioned oil and geopolitics but also noted the risk of chaos spreading throughout the region.[28] Anatol Lieven, a leading expert on the First Chechen War, described the second as a struggle against the same extremism that threatened chaos for the entire Middle East.[29]

In response to the Chechen armed incursions into Dagestan, Moscow renewed hostilities and seemed initially to follow a limited course of action designed to drive the insurgents back into Chechnya and contain them. Tactically, Russian MVD commanders sought to inflict serious damage upon the enemy with indirect fire but to reduce the risks of close battle and Russian casualties. Chechnya was a security problem but not a crusade. This changed in September 1999 under a new prime minister as Yeltsin fired his latest, Sergei Stepashin, and replaced him with the head of the Security Council, Vladimir Putin. A series of bomb blasts in Russian apartment buildings brought the war home to the Russian people. Building upon media reports and speculations associated with the "Ryazan Incident," an event which the Federal Security Service (FSB) authorities described as an antiterrorism exercise but which critics have labeled a failed fourth bombing attempt, Boris Berezovsky, the oligarch with close ties to the "Family," has charged that the bombings at Moscow and Volgodansk were FSB provocations to justify the second war in Chechnya. The bombing in Moscow killed 215 people, and that in Volgodansk killed 18 and left 288 injured.[30] Berezovsky mounted an international multimedia campaign from exile. Colonel Aleksandr Litvineko, a former FSB officer and exile now living in England, provided additional details on the FSB conspiracy.[31] The Russian authorities denied the charges and responded by seeking to censor such reporting and limit the access of Russians to the charges. In late December 2003, the FSB seized 4,000 copies of Litvineko's book, *The FSB Blows Up Russia*, at the Latvian border as "anti-state propaganda."[32]

Unlike the First Chechen War, public opinion immediately rallied to the government's cause and has remained supportive. Putin took the war deep into Chechnya, sought to overthrow the Maskhadov government, and vowed to eliminate the bandits/terrorists wherever they were found. "Even if we find them in a toilet, we shall kill them in the outhouse."[33] Unlike the First Chechen War, Russian mass media has followed the government's line on the nature of the conflict and the threat. The advance to the Terek became the preparation for a general assault on Grozny.

Responsibility for the conduct of the campaign in Chechnya belonged to General-Lieutenant Gennadiy Troshev, commander of the North Caucasian Military District. This time the Russian government committed significant forces to the initial campaign. Coordination between army and MVD units had been greatly improved thanks to the efforts of Colonel-General Leontiy Shevtsov, who had served as Chief of the Operations Directorate of the General Staff during the planning of the first Chechen campaign. Shevtsov had gone on to be the Russian representative to NATO's SACEUR under IFOR/ SFOR and on his return had been selected by General Kulikov to command Russia's internal troops. When Stepashin became minister of Internal Affairs, Shevtsov took over the task of coordinating internal troop and army operational exercises.

After a deliberate advance to the Terek, MVD units, including Chechens loyal to Moscow, encircled the city of Grozny. A well-prepared Russian assault began on December 24, 1999, and after two months of fighting took Grozny, but only after flattening much of the city with air, artillery, and rocket strikes. The advancing Russian troops were ready for urban combat, using small-unit tactics to find and pin Chechen forces where they could be struck by indirect fire, including TOS-1 and *shmel* thermobaric weapons.[34] The Russian advance over the next two months was slow and methodical and cut the cities into isolated sectors. The Chechen resistance was broken and forced from the city. Russian units trapped the withdrawing Chechens in minefields and delivered devastating fire, inflicting heavy casualties. Shamil Basaev was seriously wounded in a Russian minefield.[35]

The war reverted to insurgency. Withdrawing into the mountains south of the Terek, the Chechen fighters returned to guerilla warfare and began to make greater use of territory outside of Russia for the resuscitation of their units. For example, Russian commanders complained of Chechen sanctuaries within Georgia. Colonel-General Valery Manilov, first deputy chief of the General Staff, charged in May 2000 that no fewer than 1,500 "mercenary gunmen" are based in Pankisi Gorge in eastern Georgia, poised to reenter Chechnya and mount renewed terrorist attacks.[36]

Putin staked his own rise to power on military success in Chechnya and achieved it with the capture and destruction of the Chechen capital, Grozny, in March 2000. The uneven struggle, however, continues, pitting regular Russian troops and paramilitary formations against Chechen fighters. Its roots are to be found in the history of the interactions between Russians and Chechens. Moscow has not found credible Chechen leaders to rule through and has not been able to suppress the armed insurrection. Atrocities mount, matched by terrorist incidents. In the spring of 2001, Putin announced the turnover of pacification to the FSB and reductions in troop levels in Chechnya. These have proven premature. After only 5,000 of the 80,000 troops in Chechnya were withdrawn, the government had to curtail the program in the face of mounting Chechen raids. Colonel-General Gennadiy Troshev, who had declared the war in Chechnya over in the fall of 2000, announced only six months later that Russian authorities should resort to the public execution of captured Chechen rebels.[37]

The longer and more bitter the war in Chechnya, the greater the risk of the territorial expansion of the conflict, and of external intervention. The war

proved a profound tragedy for Russian democracy and for Chechen nationalism, as violence has driven out any grounds for dialogue and compromise
and has made a compelling case for enhanced state power to fight the war
successfully. The second war has proven even more destructive than the first.
The assault on Grozny effectively leveled the city, leaving its population without basic services, and the counterinsurgency operations brought intense
physical destruction to outlying settlements, the concentration of refugees
into "filtration" camps, and increased brutality—a war without limits against
enemy combatants and civilians.[38]

Before the second war began, the Russian military claimed that its actions
would be selective, so as to keep damages and casualties among the peaceful
civilian population at a minimum. However, the first massive rocket attack
upon Grozny, during which hundreds of noncombatants died and Maternity
Hospital No. 1 was partially destroyed, serves as definitive proof to the contrary. The "antiterrorist" operations in the Chechen Republic have, in fact,
turned out to be large-scale warfare that inflicted serious casualties upon the
Chechen civilian population.[39] With neither side giving or asking for quarter,
the war became a protracted, low-intensity conflict. The actual number and
size of the armed formations opposing the Russian forces is relatively small,
estimated at 100 bands composed of between 1500–2000 fighters at any
given time, but the counterterror operations have not brought about a significant reduction in the opposing force.[40] As in the First Chechen War, Russian forces have had successes in strikes against leading enemy commanders,
including the capture of Rudaev and the killing of Khattab. Although the
Putin government was able to incorporate pro-Russian Chechen units into
the MVD forces that assaulted Grozny, it has been less successful in turning
the pro-Russian Chechen officials into a legitimate government that enjoys
the support of the Chechen population. Akhmed Kadyrov, a former mufti
who fought against Russia in the First Chechen War and became Moscow's
man in Grozny during the second, proved incapable of bringing stability and
legitimacy to the Russian civil administration. While dissatisfaction with the
Kadyrov administration mounted, no loyal alternative emerged to replace it.[41]
Kadyrov expressed his own displeasure with the efforts of the military and
special services to find the terrorist leadership, even as his own government
came under increasing terrorist attacks.[42] Even within the Russian government there was open conflict over the efficacy of "cleansing operations"
against villages that supposedly harbor terrorist elements. The dispute pitted
FSB operatives against military intelligence.[43]

In Chechnya, outsiders should be advised against picking sides and paint-
ing one as virtuous and the other evil. The level of chaos and disorder simply
overwhelms these categories. General Lebed, a veteran of Afghanistan, once
remarked: "I have had occasion to see a lot of combat, and I affirm this fact:
There are enough scoundrels in war on both sides—rape and sadism—all of

this is present on both sides."[44] Anna Politkovskaya, one Russian journalist who insisted on reporting what has transpired in Chechnya during the second war, described Russian military operations there as a "dirty war" and "military anarchy" and warned that such conduct fed the Chechen resistance and threatened to make Putin's campaign another bitter and protracted struggle like that fought under Nicholas I.[45] In part the problem is the nature of the Russian armed forces themselves, and in part the problem flows directly from the nature of the war itself, a protracted insurgency that has evolved into a vicious cycle of repression and retribution. Vengeance is an invitation to a perpetual blood feud. But the popular roots of revenge in an armed conflict lie in the pursuit to seek justice against those guilty of injustice. When visited upon a people, and not the culpably guilty, it becomes a source of injustice itself. Such has been the sad particular truth of Chechnya. By the summer of 2001 it appeared that no one involved in the Second Chechen War had found a way to end the bloodshed.[46]

PUTIN'S GAMBIT: THE ANTITERRORIST ALLIANCE AND ENDGAME IN CHECHNYA

The events of September 11 transformed the international security environment and gave President Putin an opportunity to transform the external contexts of the Chechen War. As we have noted earlier, Putin has taken full advantage of these circumstances, emphasizing the linkage between Islamic terrorists in Chechnya and those in Afghanistan, seeking to divide the Chechen nationalist insurgents from the Islamic extremists, and beginning a process of negotiations with the moderates via Victor Kazantsev, his envoy plenipotentiary to the federal district South. In the region, Putin has made clear the paramount importance of a Russian presence for stability. Russia's cause is just and its methods, in the face of this threat, are justified. Russia will negotiate with the Chechens, if they are willing to recognize the error of resisting Russian authority and break with the extremists. For this strategy to work, Putin required that the West stop its criticism of Russian tactics in Chechnya. In exchange, Putin shifted to a policy of finding Chechen partners for political negotiations. Boris Nemtsov, a leading Russian liberal and supporter of Putin, had been keen on such negotiations and declared that Putin's support for the United States and his policy of seeking a negotiated settlement in Chechnya made sense. The underlying premise for success in both ventures was to fight terrorism, but not to make war on the Chechen people.[47]

This emphasis on a political solution comes after two years of fighting in which the Russian armed forces proved effective in conventional war but unable to put down a dogged Chechen resistance. A bloody protracted conflict with its camps and atrocities brought condemnations of Russia's conduct. Western criticism of the Russian military's methods, calls for the creation of an international criminal tribunal to try Russian commanders and officials for war crimes in Chechnya, and unofficial contacts with the Chechen opposition brought sharp objections from Moscow. But this critique of Russian conduct was kept within discrete limits. As Secretary of State Madeleine Albright declared to the Senate Foreign Relations Committee, Chechnya was not Kosovo.[48] In January 2001, Putin placed the counterterrorist operations in Chechnya in the hands of the FSB. Putin stated that FSB leadership would bring "the use of different means and forces and with a different emphasis."[49] The different emphasis did not bring about an end to Chechen resistance, however. At the same time, Putin forcefully argued for linkages between Chechen rebels and international terrorist organizations, especially the Albanian resistance that took up arms in Macedonia in the spring of 2001. Both, he claimed, were terrorist organizations that posed a serious threat to European peace and stability.[50] Frustration with the inability to bring an end to armed resistance in Chechnya and the impact of conducting an antipartisan war brought calls for some sort of endgame for Chechnya—a negotiated settlement—but it was unclear through the spring and summer of 2001 with whom Moscow could conduct talks. Both sides still seemed to be looking for a military victory that neither could achieve.[51]

A gradual shift in U.S. policy toward Russia and the war in Chechnya became evident during the Ljubljana summit between Bush and Putin in June 2001. In addition to positive assessments of their trust in each other, the two had a frank exchange on Chechnya, each stating their positions. Bush mentioned freedom of the press and Chechnya, while Putin stressed Russia's security problems in the south. Bush then raised the problem of relations between Georgia and Russia. Russia claimed that Chechen forces enjoyed sanctuary in Georgia's Pankisi Gorge as part of an anti-Russian policy in the region. Russia and Georgia are divided over the solution to the Abkhazian question, where Russian peacekeepers effectively contribute to the continued inability of Georgian refugees to return to Abkhazia. Rebel forces in Abkhazia had driven out the Georgian population and Tbilisi saw the return of the refugees as a vital part of the solution to the conflict in Abkhazia. These exchanges took place in the context of intense discussions of national missile defense and the abandonment of the ABM Treaty.[52] After their second summit in the summer of 2001, Putin and Bush announced that they were seeking a new strategic framework that would address the issue of national missile defense. No solution had been found, but both parties accepted the idea of continuing dialogue.[53]

At the same time, the Bush administration was also reviewing its strategy on terrorism and preparing to mobilize a broader coalition for a determined fight. The focus of the struggle was to be Afghanistan and Pakistan. As Ahmed Rashid reported, one official defined the antiterrorism strategy as one of building a broad coalition. "We are building a global alliance to counter the terrorist threat from Afghanistan and force Pakistan to stop military supplies to the Taliban. . . . The alliance starts from Afghanistan's neighbors and extends to the G-8, NATO, the European Union (EU), East Asia, and the Middle East."[54] In short, before the events of September 11, Russia and the United States had acknowledged the linkage between the global terrorist threat to U.S. interests and the specific challenges in the North Caucasus and Central Asia. Thus, the Russian response to the events of September 11 should not be seen outside this larger context of changed priorities and perspectives.

After September 11, Putin moved Russian policy toward supporting the common struggle in Central Asia and seeking to resolve the conflict in Chechnya by negotiations and political means. In what could have been a major step toward a widened war in the Caucasus, Putin acted to defuse the results of the intervention of Chechen fighters in Abkhazia. The Russian press saw this intervention as part of Georgian policy to get the Chechen fighters out of Georgia at a time when their presence had become an embarrassment. Having denied the presence of such fighters on Georgian territory for over a year, President Shevardnadze had to act quickly or face serious complications that could threaten Georgia's stability,[55] as well as relations with Russia and the United States. As the fighting in Abkhazia escalated, Putin asserted Russia's preeminent role as a stabilizing power in the entire region and forced Shevardnadze to acknowledge their importance by threatening to remove Russian peacekeepers.[56] One Russian commentator, Alap Kasayev, spoke of the fighting in Georgia as "the Abkhazian front of the Afghan War," and suggested that Shevardnadze had sought to use Western support and military adventure to undermine Russian interests in the Caucasus.[57] But the outcome of the Abkhazian crisis strengthened Russia's position and Putin's authority as a regional leader.[58]

In Chechnya, Putin's seventy-two-hour deadline brought a positive response by President Maskhadov's government.[59] For six months the two sides sought a common agenda for talks.[60] Russian strategy here sought to divide the Chechen opposition between those seeking a political status less than independence and those set upon an Islamic revolution and state. Press reports took note of the close ties between Chechen Islamic extremists and the Wahhabis in promoting terrorist actions in Dagestan and Chechnya.[61] Russian special forces successfully eliminated Khattab, the charismatic Wahhabist leader, that spring. Western attitudes toward Russian policy also underwent a sharp change. In a radio interview in Moscow, Alvaro Gil-Robles, the human rights commissioner of the Council of Europe, declared that Chechnya was in transition to normality. He cited both the building of a civil society there and the desire of both Chechen and Russian peoples for peace.[62] While U.S. policy remains concerned about human rights violations in Chechnya and has begun broadcasts by Radio Liberty in Chechen, there is a recognition of the terrorist component to the Chechen conflict. In short, both the domestic and international ramifications of the war in Chechnya have been affected by the events of September 11. As one Russian commentator suggested, the geostrategic context of power and interests changed in September. The vital interests of the United States are to be found in the Middle East and Central Asia. Energy may still define the long-term picture, but the immediate threat is the terrorism of Islamic extremism, and in that regard, Putin's Russia and Bush's America shared a common if nebulous enemy, a chameleon that changes more than its color and manifests itself quite differently from state to state.[63]

In the course of the next two years, relations between Moscow and Washington deteriorated precisely over the definition of the common enemy. On the one hand, this involved the Bush administration's concerns over Russia's strong-arm tactics against Georgia. U.S. policy sought to uphold the territorial integrity and sovereignty of Georgia, viewing stability in the Trans-Caucasus as vital to regional stability and a precondition for the successful development of energy resources in the Caspian. From the beginning of the Second Chechen War, Putin, for his part, used his definition of the threat to justify a game of realpolitik over Georgia's role in providing de facto sanctuary to Chechen and Islamic extremists in Pankisi Gorge. For Georgia, Pankisi Gorge represented a classic spillover threat from an insurgency in a neighboring state: that is, the threat posed by transnational crime and violence, and the risk that the powerful neighboring state would threaten its territorial integrity and sovereignty. Given the complex role that Russia had played in Georgia's internal conflicts in South Ossetia and Abkhazia, Tbilisi had grounds for concern, especially with Russian troops deployed as peacekeepers and border guards within Georgia.

From the very beginning of the Second Chechen War, the Russian government, which considered the Chechen fighters to be bandits and terrorists, drew attention to Pankisi Gorge as a haven used by Chechen bands to reconstitute their forces during the winter pause in operations. Citing Georgian sources, the Russian media estimated the number of combatants in Pankisi Gorge at 450 fighters. The same article linked the concepts of a struggle against international Islamic terrorism and the haven in Pankisi Gorge.[64] In the summer of 2002, the Russian government mounted a sustained campaign of propaganda and intimidation against Tbilisi. The explicit linkage of the Pankisi Gorge to the War on Terrorism gave an international importance to the charges and counter-charges between Russia and Georgia and raises the question of Georgia's ability to protect its own sovereignty and territorial integrity, which was already under question in two secessionist regions, Abkhazia and South Ossetia, and by the continuing presence of Russian troops and bases in Georgia itself. On July 27, 2002, Russian military spokesmen reported a major incursion of 200 Chechen fighters from Georgia's Pankisi Gorge into the Itum-Kali District of Chechnya.[65] On July 28, Russian sources reported that border guard units had engaged the Chechen infiltrators near Kerigo Gorge and had killed nine of them.[66] What followed these announcements was a sharp rise in tensions between Georgia and Russia, with waves of charges and counter-charges. Radio, TV, and wire service reports provided hourly updates on the progress of the fighting. Citing intelligence gained in the course of the fighting, Defense Minister Sergei Ivanov spoke of the intense fighting in the area and then stated: "The problem of Georgia's Pankisi Gorge . . . can only be solved by force and with the participation of Russian subunits."[67]

The drumbeat for war out of Moscow grew as the weeks passed. On July 31, President Vladimir Putin rebuked the Georgian government for not preventing the incursion from the Pankisi Gorge.[68] The Russian Foreign Ministry signaled the internationalization of the crisis by raising the issue of raids from Georgian territory into Russian Chechnya as a matter under UN Security Council Resolution 1373 on the struggle against international terrorism.[69] At the same time, during the ASEAN Summit in Brunei, Foreign Minister Igor Ivanov spoke with Secretary of State Colin Powell about the cross-border raids and labeled them "an aggression" of international terrorism.[70] German media speculated that the United States had given tacit approval of Russian pressure on Georgia and speculated about U.S.–Russian military cooperation in cleaning out Pankisi Gorge. Given the Bush administration's interest in Russian cooperation in any action against Iraq, the author concluded: "At the same time the United States has no interest in spoiling things with Moscow."[71] In fact, the Bush administration warned Moscow about taking military actions that would escalate the Pankisi crisis.[72] The United States followed a policy of protecting Georgian sovereignty, even as it encouraged Georgia to take a more active role in addressing the situation in Pankisi Gorge. By the late fall of 2002 the Pankisi Gorge crisis had retreated from world headlines, but its aftermath left the Georgian government weak and increasingly unpopular at home. The end result was the "Rose Revolution" and the overthrow of the Shevardnadze government in the fall of 2003.

By the late fall of 2002 the central issue of global politics had become Iraq and the fate of its Baathist regime. Washington, acting upon its own calculation of the links among Saddam Hussein's regime, weapons of mass destruction, and Islamic terrorism, moved toward preemptive military action. When the Bush administration took its case to the United Nations, Russia allied with France and Germany in proposing more time for UN inspectors to continue the search for weapons of mass destruction and refused to back a U.S.-led military operation against Iraq. While Russia did not lead the forces of restraint on U.S. actions, it did call into question the notion of a common front against global terrorism. Washington had reason to regret the close ties between Moscow and Baghdad, stretching back to the Soviet era. With the war in Iraq, the U.S.–Russian alliance against terrorism was placed under considerable strain precisely over the definition of threat and the application of force to meet that threat.

CONCLUSION

In a series of steps, the Putin and Bush administrations had signaled their mutual interests in cooperation during the antiterrorism campaign against Afghanistan. Both have sought to place U.S.–Russian relations on a new foundation of cooperation. On October 17, 2001, at a meeting of the Security Council, Putin announced Russia's intention to close its intelligence facility at Lourdes, Cuba, and its naval base at Cam Ranh Bay, Vietnam.[73] While the rationale for the closing of the base was couched in monetary terms, the primary motive seems to have been to solidify the U.S.–Russian alliance against terrorism by a high-visibility step that marked a sharp break with Cold War logic.[74] The Bush–Putin sidebar conversations at the Asia-Pacific Economic Cooperation forum strengthened their mutual commitment to the war against terrorism.[75] National Security Advisor Condoleezza Rice reviewed the Bush–Putin interactions at Shanghai in positive terms and spoke of an emerging security arrangement that went beyond Cold War remnants to embrace new challenges arising from the war against terrorism, and speculated about the possibility of deeper cooperation. "I do not rule out the possibility, however, that as the war on international terrorism broadens, some new spheres may appear where our countries will find cooperation mutually beneficial."[76] Thomas Friedman, writing a month into the conflict, proclaimed that in the War on Terrorism, "We are all alone."[77] He was lamenting the fact that our allies in the fight against terrorism came with their own agendas and commitments. He made no mention of Russia as an ally. Only two days before, Gleb Pavlovsky had written that Moscow had to accept the idea that it would either join the antiterrorist coalition or face similar attacks on its own.[78] Putin has taken a significant domestic risk in supporting the antiterrorist coalition, leading to serious criticism from many former allies within the political elite. But he seems committed to the common struggle against terrorism.[79] Other former allies of the president have been quick to accuse him of selling out Russian interests to the United States. These critics portray the events of September 11 as serving America's efforts to gain global hegemony.[80] Putin had shown a willingness to embrace an American military presence in Georgia, if that military assistance will lead to the termination of a Chechen sanctuary in Pankisi Gorge. U.S. special forces began to train Georgian units to combat the terrorist threat in this area.

The Putin gambit of 2001 ran into problems precisely because a U.S.–

Russian alliance depended upon a shared perception of a common enemy. This was to be the very foundation for cooperation. Putin stressed that losses inflicted upon terrorists in Chechnya contributed to the global battle.[81] But the Putin administration's definition of the terrorist threat in Chechnya rested upon a larger concept of the revival of the power of the central Russian state. Putin might turn to the West as the source of relations to revive the national economy, but in the war in Chechnya he sought a free hand to deal with "bandits and terrorists" without external interference. He might seek negotiations as a tool to split the opposition, but he did not intend to limit the power of the Russian state or to compromise its sovereignty and territorial integrity. However much the Bush administration might recommend negotiations, it would not be allowed to call into question Russian power.

What mattered to Putin was that the United States recognize the war in Chechnya as one theater in the global War on Terrorism and grant Russia a free hand to resolve it. But Putin's solution through repression and state control looked less benign as the years passed. What might be excused as expedient for the prosecution of a counter-terrorist campaign came to look more and more like the creation of an authoritarian state order as the government increasingly took over the guidance of Russian society. For the United States, the assertion of such state power raised the issue of whether Putin was more committed to order than to democracy and freedom. U.S. Ambassador Alexander Vershbow stated: "If U.S.–Russian cooperation is to develop to its fullest, Russia must demonstrate a deepening commitment to democratic values and human rights."[82] Dmitri Trenin of the Carnegie Endowment Moscow addressed the connection between the Second Chechen War and the development of democratic values and human rights as a matter of finding an internal solution that would end the conflict, assure Russian security interests, and bring about internal political and economic development. External pressure will not bring about a settlement, but continuation of the conflict will continue to strain Russia's relations with the West.[83] Trenin referred to the conflict as "the forgotten war," but the continued violence, the ramifications of terrorist acts upon Russian society, and the state's efforts to impose order to fight the terror threat bring the war back to center stage nationally and internationally. The United States and the West are more likely to influence Russian conduct by raising the issues that call into question the legitimacy of the Russian course of action without calling into question the sovereignty or territorial integrity of the Russian Federation.

NOTES

1. Tom Heneghan, "Russian Memo Lists Bin Laden Camps in Afghanistan," *Reuters*, September 26, 2001.

2. "Putin Determines Russian Stance on Antiterror Cause," _RIA NOVOSTI,_ September 24, 2001.

3. "Putin Determines Russian Stance on Antiterror Cause."

4. "Putin Determines Russian Stance on Antiterror Cause."

5. "Putin Determines Russian Stance on Antiterror Cause."

6. Yegor Belous, "Black Widows on the Air Again," Pravda.ru, August 19, 2003, at english.pravda.ru/accidents/21/93/374/10735_kamikaze.html.

7. Abdul-Khakim Sultygov, _Chechenskyia respublika: Poisk ideologii politicheskogo uregulirovaniya_ (Moscow: Pomatur, 2001), 11.

8. "Vladimir Putin: Pozitivnye tendentsii est', no poka eto tol'ko tendentsii," _Moskovskiy komsomolets,_ December 26, 2001.

9. The Constitution of the Chechen Republic, at www.ln.mid.ru/brp_4.nsf/0/790652f54726fd7f43256d1800326fca?OpenDocument.

10. Sophie Lambroschini, "Chechnya: Elections Go According to Kremlin's Plan," RFE/RL, October 6, 2003, at www.rferl.org/nca/features/2003/10/06102003170118.asp.

11. "Russia: U.S. Criticizes Chechen Presidential Election," RFE/RL, October 6, 2003, at www.rferl.org/nca/features/2003/10/06102003184856.asp.

12. Anatol Lieven, _Chechnya: Tombstone of Russian Power_ (New Haven, Conn.: Yale University Press, 1998), 142–43.

13. Samuel P. Huntington, _The Clash of Civilizations and the Remaking of World Order_ (New York: Touchstone Books, 1998).

14. Much of this discussion is drawn from Jacob W. Kipp and Lester Grau, "Chechen Nationalism and the Struggle for Independence," _National Strategy Forum_ 10, no. 1 (Autumn 2000): 7–12.

15. ANS radio (Baku, in Azeri 1330 gmt 08 May 00) from _BBC Monitoring._

16. Kerim Fenari, "The _Jihad_ of Imam Shamyl," at www.amarelief.org/caucasus/news/Imam_Shamil.htm.

17. Robert F. Baumann, _Russian-Soviet Unconventional Wars in the Caucasus, Central Asia, and Afghanistan_ (Ft. Leavenworth, Kans.: Combat Studies Institute, U.S. Army Command and General Staff College, 1993).

18. Moshe Gammer, _Muslim Resistance to the Tsar: Shamil and the Conquest of Chechnya and Dagestan_ (London: Frank Cass, 1994).

19. N. I. Pokrovskiy, _Kavkazkie voyny i Imamat Shamilya_ (Moscow: ROSSPEN, 2000).

20. Steven Blank, "The Formation of the Soviet North Caucasus 1918–24," _Central Asian Survey_ 12 (1993): 13–32.

21. Carlotta Gall and Thomas de Waal, _Chechnya: Calamity of the Caucasus_ (New York: New York University Press, 1998), 56–75.

22. Lester Grau, "Changing Russian Urban Tactics: The Aftermath of the Battle of Grozny," Foreign Military Studies Office, at www.call.army.mil/fmso/fmsopubs/issues/grozny.htm.

23. Anatoliy Kulikov and Sergey Lembik, _Chechenskiy uzel: Khronika vooruzhennogo konflikta, 1994–1996 gg._ (Moscow: Dom Pedagogiki, 2000).

24. Lester Grau and William Jorgensen, "Viral Hepatitis and the Russian War in Chechnya," Foreign Military Studies Office, at www.call.army.mil/fmso/fmsopubs/issues/hepatiti/hepatiti.htm.

25. Raymond C. Finch, III, "A Face of Future Battle: Chechen Fighter Shamil Basayev," Foreign Military Studies Office, at www.call.army.mil/fmso/fmsopubs/issues/shamil/shamil.htm.

26. David Hoffman, "Miscalculations Paved Path to Chechen War," *Washington Post*, March 20 2000.

27. Gennadiy Troshev, *Moya voyna: Chechenskiy dnevnik okopnogo generala* (Moscow: Vagrius, 2001), 353.

28. Robyn Dixon, "In Dagestan, Rebel Leader Revives Russian Nightmare," *Los Angeles Times*, August 21, 1999, 1.

29. Anatol Lieven, "Let's Help Russia Against the Chechens," *Los Angeles Times*, September 21, 1999.

30. Patrick Henry, "Berezovsky Says Putin Knew About FSB Role," *Propaganda and Matrix*, March 6, 2002, at propagandamatrix.com/berezovsky_says_putin_knew_about_fsb_role.html.

31. "Russia: Former Agent Points Finger at FSB," *CDI Russia Weekly*, July 25, 2002, at www.cdi.org/russia/216-6.cfm.

32. "Russian Police Seize Book Implicating FSB," RFE/RL, December 29, 2003, at www.rferl.org/nca/features/2003/12/29122003191526.asp.

33. Moscow, *ITAR-TASS*, September 27, 1999.

34. Les Grau and Timothy Smith, "A 'Crushing' Victory: Fuel-Air Explosives and Grozny, 2000," Foreign Military Studies Office, at www.call.army.mil/fmso/fmsopubs/issues/fuelair/fuelair.htm.

35. Timothy L. Thomas, "Grozny 2000: Urban Combat Lessons Learned," Foreign Military Studies Office, at www.call.army.mil/fmso/fmsopubs/issues/grozny2000/grozny2000.htm.

36. "Russia and Georgia at Odds," *Monitor*, May 18, 2000.

37. David Filipov, "Putin Now Mired in Chechnya: Hopes Evaporate for Closure to War," *Boston Globe*, June 21, 2001; *Johnson's Russia List*, #5314, June 21, 2001.

38. Maura Reynolds, "War Has No Rules for Russian Forces Fighting in Chechnya," *Los Angeles Times*, September 17, 2000.

39. "Devastated by War, Chechnya's Civilian Population Faces Approaching Winter," *Dispatches from Chechnya*, no. 1 (September 18, 2000).

40. "100 Rebel Groups Numbering up to 2,000 Members Operating in Chechnya," *Agentstvo Voyennykh Novostey*, November 1, 2001.

41. Mikhail Ivanov, "Moscow's Muddled Thinking on Chechnya," IWPR's Caucasus Reporting, September 22, 2000.

42. Yevgenia Borisova, "Kadyorv's Nephew Fought for Rebels," *Moscow Times*, August 31, 2001, 3; and Marcus Warren, "Rebels Bomb Grozny Leaders," *London Daily Telegraph*, September 3, 2001.

43. Roustam Kaliyev, "Chechen Reality: GRU vs. FSB," *Perspective* II, no. 1 (September/October 2001).

44. *Ogenok*, no. 11 (March 1996): 11.

45. Anna Politkovskaya, *Vtoraya Chechenskaya*, 2nd ed. (Moscow: Igor Zakharov, 2002), 285, 290.

46. On the problem of ending conflicts see Charles W. Kegley, Jr., and Gregory A. Raymond, *How Nations Make Peace* (New York: St. Martin's/Worth, 1999), 235–36.

47. Yuriy Stroganov, "Boris Nemtsov on Putin's Economic Policies, Afghan Situation," *Trud*, October 16, 2001; *Johnson's Russia List*, #5498, October 19, 2001.

48. Miriam Lansky, "Caucasus: Chechnya, Echoes of Kosovo," *The NIS Observed: An Analytical Review*, Pt. *1*, 5, no. 7 (April 25, 2000).

49. Sarah Karush, "Putin Hands Chechnya War to FSB," *Moscow Times*, January 23, 2001, 1.

50. Sarah K. Miller, "US–Russian Relations: Cool Winds Are Blowing," *The NIS Observed: An Analytical Review*, Pt. *1*, 6, no. 6 (April 4, 2001).

51. Pavel Felgenhauer, "Chechnya Awaits Endgame," *Moscow Times*, June 28, 2001, 9.

52. "Transcript of June 16 White House Press Briefing by Secretary of State Powell and National Security Advisor [sic] Rice," and "Press Conference by President Bush and Russian Federation President Putin"; *Johnson's Russia List*, #4305, June 16, 2001.

53. David S. Broder, "Bush's Bet on Russia," *Washington Post*, August 1, 2001, 17.

54. Ahmed Rashid, "US Reviews Its Policy on the Taliban and International Terrorism," *World*, July 31, 2001.

55. Timofey Borisov, "'Fox' Blesses 'Wolf'; Before Attacking Abkhazia Gelayev Met with Shevardnadze" *Rossiyskaya gazeta*, October 21, 2001, 3. Some commentators in Moscow viewed the fighting at Kodori Gorge in Abkhazia as a "provocation" designed to set off a Georgian–Abkhazian war at an advantageous moment. The plan, according to these commentators, failed. See Dmitriy Nikolayev, "Failure of 'Kodori Action,' " *Nezavisimaya gazeta*, October 17, 2001, 1, 5.

56. "Putin Says Abkhazia Georgia's Internal Political Problem," Moscow, TV RTR, 1600 GMT, October 12, 2001.

57. Alap Kasayev, "Abkhazskiy Front Afganskoy voyny," *Nezavisimaya gazeta*, October 9, 2001.

58. Leonid Radzikhovsky, "Policing Asia," *Vremya MN*, October 16, 2001.

59. "Chechen Rebels Make Contact," Moscow: UPI, September 27, 2001.

60. Ron Popeski, "Chechens Seek Peace Talks, but Agenda Differs," Moscow: *Reuters*, October 24, 2001.

61. Robert Bruce Ware, "On the Roots of Extremism," *Moscow Times*, November 1, 2001.

62. "European Human Rights Commissioner Says Chechnya Is in Transition to Normality," *Echo Moskvy*, 0910 GMT, October 30, 2001.

63. Leonid Radzikhovsky, "Policing Asia," *Vremya MN*, October 16, 2001.

64. Viktor Yadukha and Mikhail Vignanskiy, "Terrorist International: Chechen Field Commanders Recruit Mercenaries and Prepare Winter Quarters," *Segodnya*, October 29, 1999, 3.

65. "Chechen Rebels Said to Have Entered Russia from Georgia, Clashes Reported," ITAR-TASS, 1121 GMT, July 27, 2002.

66. "Russia: Nine Chechen Rebels Killed in Clash near Georgian Border," ITAR-TASS, 1049 GMT, July 28, 2002.

67. "Russian DM Ivanov on Stopping Flow of 'Terrorists' from Georgia," ORT Television, 1100 GMT, July 29, 2002.

68. "Russian President Criticizes Georgia for Chechen Incursions," RFE/RL Newsline, August 31, 2002, at www.rferl.org/newsline/2002/08/2-TCA/tca-010802.asp; and Vitaliy Portnikov, "You Should Not Have Complained," Politi kum.ru WWW-Text, August 1, 2002.

69. "Moscow Holds Georgia Responsible for Crossing by Rebels," Interfax, July 31, 2002.

70. "Moscow Holds Georgia Responsible for Crossing by Rebels."

71. Barbara Oertel, "Hostile Partners: Russia Fighting 'Terrorists' in Georgia in the Same Spirit as US," *Tageszeitung*, Internet Version-WWW, August 1, 2002.

72. Scott Peterson, "US-Russia Ties Jolted by Crisis in Georgia," *Christian Science Monitor*, August 26, 2002.

73. "Putin Announces Russia to Withdraw from Radio-Electronic Center in Cuba," Moscow: *Interfax*, 12005 GMT, October 17, 2001; and Richard Balmforth, "Russia Ends Cold War Chapter by Quitting Cuban Spy Base," Moscow: *Reuters*, October 18, 2001.

74. Alexander Golts, "Putin Finds Way to Deal with Russia's Generals," *The Russian Journal* (October 26–November 1, 2001): 21.

75. Patrick Lannin, "Putin Backs Terror Fight, Says Russia Reforms Work," Shanghai: *Reuters*, October 19, 2001.

76. Yegenyy Bai, "The Threat of Terrorism Brings US Together," *Izvestiya*, October 15, 2001.

77. Thomas L. Friedman, "We Are All Alone," *New York Times*, October 26, 2001.

78. Gleb Pavlovsky: "Are We Prepared to Wait Until the Enemy Hits Us as It Hit America?" *strana.ru*, October 24, 2001, at www.strana.ru.

79. Otto Latsis, "No More Confrontation but Putin's U.S. Stance Faces Opposition," *The Russian Journal* (October 26–November 1 2001); *Johnson's Russia List*, #5511, October 28, 2001.

80. Aleksandr Dugin, "Terakty 11 sentryabrya (sic): Ekonomicheskiy smysl," at www.arctogaia.com/public/teract.html.

81. "Vladimir Putin Talks with American Journalists," *Kommersant*, no. 206, November 12, 2001; *Johnson's Russia List*, #5541.

82. Barry Schweid, "U.S. Ambassador Has Mixed Views of Putin," AP, January 9, 2004; *Johnson's Russia List*, #8008, January 10, 2004.

83. Dmitri Trenin, "The Forgotten War; Chechnya and Russia's Future," Carnegie Endowment for International Peace Policy Brief, No. 28 (November 2003).

Part Five

REGIONAL AND
FOREIGN POLICY

Chapter Twelve

Putin and the Regions

Nikolai Petrov and Darrell Slider

One of the first and most vital areas that Vladimir Putin identified for a major shift in policy was the relationship between Russia's regions and the federal (national) government. The Yeltsin period had seen a loosening of control by "the center" (the Moscow-based national political and administrative institutions) over Russia's eighty-nine regions. Struggles between Yeltsin and the Duma in the early 1990s ended with the shelling of the parliament building in October 1993, but the new parliament elected two months later was equally contentious. These difficulties forced Yeltsin to make concessions to regional leaders in order to gain their support at critical junctures, including during his campaign for a second presidential term in 1996. The administration was further weakened by the meltdown of the economy and the government's inability to raise taxes needed to finance its policies. This led regional leaders increasingly to take on responsibilities that would normally be carried out by federal agencies. Regional leaders used these opportunities to entrench themselves in power while often willfully flouting federal laws and presidential decrees.

Putin had witnessed the extent of the problem when he supervised Russia's regions for Yeltsin from March 1997 to July 1998. Putin was head of the department within Yeltsin's presidential administration (called the Main Oversight Department, or *glavnoe kontrol'noe upravleniie*) that gathered evidence on violations of federal laws and policies in the regions. Interestingly enough, Putin's predecessor as head of the department was Aleksei Kudrin, who was elevated to minister of finance and deputy prime minister, and his successor was Nikolai Patrushev, who became head of the FSB (the Federal Security Service, successor to the KGB). Both men are key figures in implementing elements of Putin's policy toward the regions. All three, not coincidentally, are from Russia's second city, St. Petersburg.

This chapter will examine the approach Putin has taken to deal with regional leaders through the creation of a new level of administration between the center and the regions in the form of seven federal administrative districts (*federal'nye okruga*) headed by specially appointed presidential representatives. Announced in May 2000, this initiative was one of Putin's first steps as president, and it has reshaped in a fundamental way the nature of the Russian political system.

One possible direction these changes could have taken would be to solidify Russia's federal system. Federalism requires a fairly explicit distribution of power between national and regional governments, and the new federal districts could have been used to implement and refine the Yeltsin constitution of 1993. Article seventy-one of the constitution defines the areas of federal jurisdiction, article seventy-two defines joint jurisdiction, and article seventy-three grants all other functions to the regions. The administrative changes adopted by Putin could have been used to reclaim federal powers that were grabbed by the regions and to flesh out the provisions of the constitution with the purpose of creating a functional federal system.

Instead, Putin is aggressively pursuing an anti-federal policy designed to take away or circumscribe most powers exercised by regional leaders. His goal appears to be to establish a unitary state under the guise of "restoring effective vertical power in the country," to use Putin's own description of his intentions. In keeping with Putin's background in the KGB, the main emphasis is on discipline and order. Overall, his approach represents a rejection of federalism—which is still very much a work in progress in Russia—and an attempt at recentralization. At the same time, it is by no means clear that the institutional and personnel choices that Putin has made will have the desired result; nor is it evident that recentralization will be an effective administrative strategy in post-Soviet Russia.

ORIGINS OF THE PROBLEM

Even after the fourteen other former Soviet republics became independent, Russia remained the world's largest country; thus, it is perhaps inevitable that there would be serious problems in administering its far-flung territories. This was true both before and after the Soviet state was established. The usual set of solutions involved efforts to tighten control from the center. Despite some outward trappings of federalism (the Russian republic, for example, was called the RSFSR—Russian Soviet Federative Socialist Republic), the Soviet Union was in essence a unitary state supplemented by a parallel hierarchy—the Communist Party of the Soviet Union (CPSU). Even under Stalin, however, "family circles" or cliques based on personal relations and patronage ties arose in the regions, insulating local politics from Moscow and allowing regional elites a free hand in many matters.[1]

In many of the former communist states of Eastern Europe—particularly those whose leaders set a reformist agenda—a comprehensive redrawing of subnational administrative boundaries took place. In Poland, the Czech Republic, the former German Democratic Republic, Hungary, and Croatia, communist-era regional entities were eliminated or replaced with new ones. In part this was done to meet European Union (EU) entry requirements, but often another important motivation was to break up political and economic power at the regional level that had emerged under communist rule.[2] No such redrawing of the political boundaries took place in Russia, with the consequence that political-economic elites of the communist era emerged largely intact at the regional level. Thus, Russia's current administrative structure closely mirrors that of the Russian republic under communism. Of the eighty-nine administrative entities, or "subjects of the federation," the most numerous are oblasts (forty-nine), followed by republics (twenty-one), six *krais* (which tend to be large territories or border regions), ten autonomous *okrugs* (located within the territory of other entities), one autonomous oblast (the Jewish AO in the Far East), and the cities of Moscow and St. Petersburg.

Russia's republics were, by and large, designated "autonomous republics" in the Soviet period. They received this special status because they were home to a non-Russian ethnic group (most often, though, Russians were the largest ethnic group even in republics; the eight exceptions were Dagestan, Chuvashia, Chechen-Ingushetia, Tuva, Kabardino-Balkaria, North Ossetia, Tatarstan, and Kalmykia). Unlike the "union republics" that became independent with the collapse of the USSR, autonomous republics were typically not in border regions.

Russian and Soviet history had never seen an attempt to apply a federal model as the basis for organizing the relationship between national and regional authorities. In this regard, Yeltsin's policies represented a revolutionary break from past methods of rule. However, because Yeltsin did not take the matter seriously, the result was an improvised series of steps that resulted in a redistribution of power between the center and the regions. As a consequence, Yeltsin's "federalism" was a product of a series of crises and struggles that characterized his nearly ten years in power.

First, there was the battle that took place in 1990–91 over the fate of the Soviet Union. Both Gorbachev and Yeltsin sought the support of regional elites, particularly those in the ethnically based autonomous republics within the fifteen union republics that became independent in late 1991. It was in the context of the struggle with Gorbachev for the loyalty of republic leaders that Yeltsin in 1990 encouraged them to "take as much sovereignty as you can swallow." In most of the republics, local leaders followed Yeltsin's example and created the popularly elected post of president, thus giving them a status and legitimacy lacked by heads of Russia's other regions at that time.

Almost immediately after the collapse of the Soviet Union, Yeltsin faced a new and lengthy conflict—this time with the Russian legislature. Their disputes covered a wide range of issues but centered on the relative powers of the parliament versus the president and on the strategy of economic reform that the country should pursue. In this struggle, Yeltsin sought the support of regional executives—the governors whom he had the right to appoint and dismiss—and the republic presidents. Ruslan Khasbulatov, the speaker of the Russian parliament who became Yeltsin's nemesis, appealed to the regional legislatures in an effort to build an alternative national power base. Since republic leaders had more independence than governors, Yeltsin tended to favor the republics with larger budget subsidies[3] and greater relative autonomy. These concessions were often codified in the form of bilateral agreements between the president and individual leaders. The most generous terms were granted to Tatarstan, Bashkortostan, and Yakutia, the republics with the most potential leverage because of their economic assets.

This battle culminated in the events of September–October 1993, when Yeltsin issued a decree dissolving the parliament. When Khasbulatov and Alexander Rutskoi, Yeltsin's own vice president, resisted and attempted to seize power by force, Yeltsin responded by having tanks shell the building. The new political context led to fundamental changes in regional politics.

First was the drafting of the Yeltsin constitution mentioned earlier, with its enshrined concepts of federalism, including the establishment of a new federal legislature, with an upper house—the Federation Council—comprising two representatives from each region. For the first time, this gave the regions a veto over laws passed by the lower house (the State Duma). Many governors successfully won election to this body and thus achieved additional independence and legitimacy. Yeltsin could not remove members of the Federation Council without its agreement, and council members also received immunity from criminal charges. Second was the dissolution of regional legislatures that had been elected in 1990 (though not in the republics) and the decision of a number of republics to adopt a presidential system to avoid ceding control to the center. Third, as was true at the national level, political power in the regions shifted dramatically toward the executive branch of government. Executive power in the regions was further strengthened in the mid-1990s when Yeltsin gave in to the demand by regional executives for popular elections. Yeltsin's last set of appointments to the post of governor took place in late 1995–early 1996, when he appointed thirteen.[4] After that, all governors were elected to office. This gave governors added legitimacy and made their removal by Yeltsin almost impossible.

In 1994–95, new regional legislatures were elected. The new assemblies were smaller in size than the soviets of 1990, and their powers were substantially reduced. With just a few exceptions, the new deputies tended to be made up of local officials, employees from sectors funded by the government (education and health care), or the regional economic elite—all groups that were dependent on the executive. Only a small proportion of deputies were full-time legislators, and in their legislative role they were both unwilling and unable to challenge the region's governor or president. Very few legislatures had more than token representation by national political parties.[5]

A year after the October 1993 attack on parliament, Yeltsin once again attempted to use force to solve a political problem—this time in Chechnya. Unlike republics such as Tatarstan and Bashkortostan, Chechnya refused to enter into a dialogue with the Kremlin and instead pressed for full independence. Under the leadership of General (and President) Dzhokhar Dudayev, Chechnya created its own military forces and expelled representatives of virtually all central Russian ministries, including the FSB and the Ministry of Finance. It should be said, however, that the Russian leadership did not make a serious attempt to achieve a negotiated solution to Chechnya's complaints, which contributed to the Chechens' resolve to secede. In December 1994, Yeltsin ended several years of neglect of the Chechen problem and ordered Russian Army and Interior Ministry troops into Chechnya in hopes of a quick military victory. The result was a disaster: the army was ill-prepared for a guerrilla war and suffered many casualties while directing much of its military might against the civilian population.

The war in Chechnya and ineffective policies in a number of other areas threatened defeat for Yeltsin in the 1996 presidential elections, and he again turned to regional leaders (as well as the country's business elite) for help. It was at this time that over twenty new bilateral treaties with oblasts and *krais* were signed. Yeltsin further strengthened the status of regional leaders by initiating a change in how the Federation Council was formed. Starting in 1996, sitting governors and chairmen of regional legislatures would automatically have seats in the Federation Council. With the help of regional "administrative resources" such as control over the local press, government workers, and simple vote fraud in some cases, Yeltsin came from behind to win re-election.

These serial political crises took place against a background of persistent economic emergencies that were stabilized in the mid-1990s only by resorting to "virtual" economics and financial trickery. These schemes eventually collapsed in the August 1998 devaluation and default. One common mechanism to formally balance tax receipts and expenses that was used both by central agencies and regional governments was sequestering funds—in other words, reducing expenditures by not paying salaries and not meeting obligations to suppliers of goods and services. In this way, the federal government effectively lost control of many of its agencies in the regions. Shortfalls in tax collection and nonpayment meant that regional leaders were almost forced to step in to provide funds or in-kind payments (office space, transportation, heat, hot water, electricity, and even food) in order to support the continued operation of federal institutions such as the criminal police, tax police, prosecutors, courts, and even Yeltsin's presidential representatives (created in 1991 to serve as his "eyes and ears" in the regions). Inevitably, federal entities in the regions shifted their loyalty from the center to the regions. Even the Russian military became increasingly dependent on regional leaders for logistical support. The result was "a sustained trend towards increasing compartmentalization and regionalization of military structures, driven primarily by the shortage of resources and underfinancing."[6] It should be emphasized that this was not a power play by regional leaders. In the face of the failure by the Kremlin to carry out its responsibilities, the regions were simply trying to cope.

Another feature of Yeltsin's policies toward the regions was the personalized and bilateral nature of many of the center-region relationships. This was in many ways a continuation of the informal operation of regional lobbying of the central institutions during the Soviet era; both Yeltsin and most regional leaders had practical experience dating back to the Brezhnev era. Some of this bilateralism was formally institutionalized in treaties negotiated between the Yeltsin administration and regional leaders. The first of these agreements was with republics, which provided a set of exceptions and exemptions that went far beyond what other regions were allowed under the 1992 Federation Treaty and the 1993 constitution. These agreements had the effect of making Russian federalism extremely asymmetrical, but in a way that was unsystematic and nontransparent.[7] Much of the enabling documentation at the ministerial level was kept secret. Later, most oblasts and *krais* also negotiated bilateral treaties with the center, though under less-favorable terms. The personalization of politics meant that Yeltsin often turned a blind eye to violations in a region (there were many in Kalmykia, for example) as long as its leader demonstrated loyalty to him in federal elections.

Overall, the institutional framework and dynamics of "federalism, Russian-style" had a number of dysfunctional elements and allowed regions control over other areas of federal responsibility that were atypical of a normal federal system.[8] The nature of federal relations also undermined efforts to democratize the political system as well as efforts to marketize the Russian economy. Governors and republic presidents obstructed the development of a national party system and used their powers to harass political opponents and independent news media. In an effort to protect local industries and markets, regional leaders created barriers to free trade between regions. They also preserved an economic climate that was hostile to outside investment and the rise of small business.[9]

PUTIN'S POLICY AND PERSONNEL CHOICES

Putin's initiatives toward the regions include the following:

1. the establishment of the seven federal districts ("super-regions") headed by presidential envoys, of whom five were generals;

2. increasing central control over federal agencies in the regions, including the courts, police, and television;
3. reforming the Federation Council by replacing sitting governors and chairmen of regional legislatures with full-time representatives who would be appointed by governors and legislatures (in the process regional executives and the heads of regional legislatures lost parliamentary immunity);
4. the adoption of laws that allow the president, under certain conditions, to remove governors and dismiss regional parliaments;
5. the creation of a new body for governors, the Presidential State Council, as a consolation for losing their seats in the Federation Council. The main advantage is that it allows governors to meet with the president four times a year. All regional leaders are members, but its working organ is a presidium (whose membership changes every six months) made up of one governor/president from each of the seven federal districts. The presidium is supplemented by working groups under the leadership of one regional leader (usually drawn from the most influential—such as Moscow mayor Luzhkov). The working groups prepare reports/proposals on important issues, but their role is strictly advisory. Putin directed that several of these reports serve as the basis for government drafts of new legislation, for example on policy toward exploiting Russia's timber resources. Other reports, especially ones that reflected the governors' perspectives on administrative reform and federalism, were ignored;
6. changes in interbudgetary relations through a new tax code, which increases the center's share and gives the federal government greater control over tax receipts and expenditures.

The first and most important of Putin's innovations, issued in the form of a presidential decree in May 2000, divided Russia into seven administrative districts. The ultimate goal of this new structure was not to replace existing regions, but rather to increase the effectiveness of the center by creating a new administrative structure to coordinate the operation of federal agencies in the regions. The top official in each of these new federal districts was called the "plenipotentiary presidential representative" (*pol'nomochnyi predstavitel' prezidenta* or *polpred* for short). As was mentioned above, this term had been used by Yeltsin to designate his representative in each region. Putin abolished this post in the regions; henceforth virtually every region would have a "chief federal inspector" who would be directly subordinate to (and appointed by) the presidential representative for the corresponding administrative district.

The decree creating presidential representatives provided for their direct accountability to the president. Yeltsin had initially given the same degree of access to his representatives, but later they were subordinated to a department within the administration.[10] In practice, though, while Putin appointed each of his representatives, they did not report solely to the president. The *polpreds* were still part of the presidential administration, which meant that they were supervised by Alexander Voloshin, then head of Putin's staff and a holdover from the Yeltsin era. This was a source of some consternation among the presidential representatives, since they wanted to be closer to the ultimate source of authority at the top of the administrative ladder. A symbolic indicator of the status of the seven representatives was Putin's decision to give each a seat on his Security Council, a body that has been important in establishing strategic priorities in government policy, both foreign and domestic.

The federal districts were not drawn anew based on any particular political or administrative purpose; they corresponded completely to the regional command structure of the Soviet/Russian Interior Ministry troops.[11] The "capital" or administrative center of each district in every case corresponded to the location of the headquarters of the corresponding Interior Ministry district. The following section describes the seven federal regions and Putin's appointees to the post of presidential representative:

1. The Central district is the largest in terms of the number of regions with eighteen. Naturally, Moscow is the center for the district; the capital and surrounding oblast dominate the district in both population and political importance. General Georgii Poltavchenko, named as Putin's representative in this district, was drawn from the upper ranks of the FSB. In the 1980s he served in the KGB in Leningrad oblast, where he first came in contact with Vladimir Putin, and for most of the 1990s he worked as head of the tax police in St. Petersburg. For a brief period before his appointment, Poltavchenko served as presidential representative in Leningrad oblast.

2. The Northwestern district is made up of eleven regions, the most important of which is Russia's "second capital," St. Petersburg. The large number of Petersburg natives in Putin's administration has added to the political significance of the region. One of the most controversial appointments was Putin's choice of General Viktor Cherkesov, first deputy director of the FSB, to serve as his representative in this district. Cherkesov had been a longtime KGB officer in Leningrad/St. Petersburg and was known for his role in the suppression of "anti-Soviet" dissent. His ties to Putin were the closest of any of the representatives, and they reportedly knew one another even before their KGB days. In March 2003, Cherkesov was given a new assignment, as head of a newly created "force ministry," the State Committee to Combat Drug Trafficking. Named in his place was a close Putin associate, Deputy Prime Minister Valentina Matvienko. It was clear at the time that the appointment was made in order to position her to win the upcoming elections to the governorship of St. Petersburg. She was duly elected in October

2003. Matvienko's replacement as polpred was Ilya Klebanov, also a former Deputy Prime Minister and then Minister of Science and Technology. Klebanov, also from St. Petersburg, had a background in the defense ministry. He is viewed as a much weaker figure than either Cherkesov or Matvienko.

3. The Southern district comprises the seven non-Russian republics of the unstable North Caucasus region, including Chechnya, as well as five frontline Russian regions. Particularly important regions from the economic standpoint are Krasnodar *krai* and Rostov oblast. The city of Rostov-on-the-Don is the administrative center. As his representative Putin chose General Viktor Kazantsev, at the time serving as commander of the military forces in the North Caucasus military district. As such he was a leading figure in planning the war in Chechnya.

4. The Volga district consists of seven republics, one autonomous *okrug*, and eight oblasts. Among the leaders of these regions are a disproportionate number of nationally known politicians: Presidents Mintimer Shaimiyev of Tatarstan and Murtaza Rakhimov of Bashkortostan, both among the most assertive of all the republics. Also in the district is the republic of Chuvashia, headed by President Nikolai Fedorov, one of the few regional leaders willing to speak out for the record against Putin's policies, and Samara governor Konstantin Titov. Nizhniy Novgorod, the third largest city in Russia after Moscow and St. Petersburg, is the administrative center. Perhaps because of the number of political "heavyweights" in the region, Putin chose a former prime minister, Sergei Kiriyenko, to be his representative there. Kiriyenko, prior to his brief stint as premier (he was dismissed in the wake of the August 1998 financial crisis), had been a Komsomol functionary in Nizhniy Novgorod, a banker, and briefly the federal energy minister. Kiriyenko is also the only presidential representative with a reputation as a liberal reformer; he was one of the founding members of the political movement Union of Right Forces (SPS). Kiriyenko became one of the most visible of the presidential representatives, in part because of effective self-promotion. For example, Kiriyenko launched a nationwide, internet-based search for staff for his office.

5. The Urals district has the fewest regions—only six. The dominant region is Sverdlovsk, along with its capital, Yekaterinburg. Putin named General Petr Latyshev as his representative to the district. Latyshev was at the time of appointment deputy minister of internal affairs and had spent virtually his entire career in the ranks of the MVD. In this capacity he had been active in investigating a number of cases of high-level corruption in regions including St. Petersburg, the most recent case.

6. The Siberian district is, like the Volga district, extremely diverse, made up of three republics, four autonomous *okrugs*, and nine oblasts/*krais*.

Novosibirsk, the traditional capital of Western Siberia, was designated as the administrative center of the district, though a number of other regions are of equal or greater importance, including Krasnoyarsk, Tomsk, Kemerovo, and Irkutsk. Despite the size and diversity of the region, it has perhaps the most developed sense of regional identity. Putin's appointee was Leonid Drachevsky. Once a professional athlete, Drachevsky worked for most of the 1990s in the Ministry of Foreign Affairs, where he served as ambassador to Poland and was deputy foreign minister under Yevgeny Primakov. In 1999 he was the Russian minister for the Commonwealth of Independent States (CIS). Drachevsky is considered the *polpred* with the weakest links to Putin's team.[12]

7. The Far Eastern district makes up the distant edge of the country, separated from Moscow by the Urals and Siberia. It comprises nine regions, including the largest single territorial entity—the republic of Sakha (Yakutia), five oblasts/*krais*, two autonomous *okrugs*, and the only autonomous oblast. Khabarovsk was chosen as the administrative center, though the most important regions are Yakutia and Primor'e (Vladivostok is the capital). The region as a whole is sparsely populated and has long felt isolated from events in Moscow. Konstantin Pulikovskii, a career general in the Russian army with experience in the first Chechen campaign, was named presidential representative for the district. His connection with Putin came when, after being dismissed from the military for his outspokenness, he served as Putin's campaign manager in Krasnodar *krai*.

Thus Putin's "magnificent seven," as they were referred to with some irony in the media,[13] were largely drawn from what are known as the "power ministries"—the FSB, military, and police. The contrast with the early Yeltsin period could not be more vivid. In 1991, Yeltsin created a new institution of "presidential representatives." The largest number of this first set of *polpreds* was drawn from the ranks of radical democrats who had worked with Yeltsin in the Soviet and Russian parliaments. In effect, the early Yeltsin appointees to this post were the type of people that several of the Putin appointees had worked to put in prison camps or psychiatric wards! (Later though, Yeltsin replaced his initial appointees with career bureaucrats, including several FSB officials. An even more major shift took place when Putin became acting president in January 2000. At that time about twenty new presidential representatives were appointed, most with FSB backgrounds.)

The first task awaiting the new plenipotentiaries was to set up their offices and assemble a staff. This process provided additional evidence on the institutional goals and capabilities of the new federal districts. Each was allowed to hire up to eight aides, who was given the title of deputy presidential representative. Each deputy in turn was assigned a specific functional area of responsibility, with two usually designated as the "first deputies." Evidence of the centralizing intent behind the districts is the fact that the vast majority of deputy representatives were not from the district in which they served. One of the first deputies typically came from the subdivision of the presidential administration's Main Oversight Department, which oversaw the region under the old system. Four of the presidential representatives (Kiriyenko, Drachevsky, Kazantsev, and Cherkesov) brought with them their own team of former advisors and close subordinates. Kiriyenko and Drachevsky brought the largest number of Muscovites (more even than Poltavchenko in the Moscow-based district). Kazantsev, since he simply moved from one office in Rostov to another, brought in mostly military aides. Cherkesov, though he had spent about a year in the central apparatus of the FSB in Moscow, continued to have a number of contacts from his Leningrad KGB days whom he tapped as top aides. (In January 2002, Putin named as Cherkesov's first deputy Admiral Mikhail Motsak, who recently had been dismissed in connection with the *Kursk* submarine disaster.) The other three presidential representatives were more dependent on appointees from the presidential administration. Poltavchenko assigned as his first deputy Anton Fedorov, the long-term coordinator of Yeltsin's system of presidential representatives. Pulikovskii brought some of his subordinates from Krasnodar, and was assigned one of Fedorov's deputies from the presidential administration. Latyshev's team was made up mostly of high-level administrators from other regions, including several from outside his district. All of the top aides to the presidential representative were based in the administrative center of the district.

In each of the component regions within the district, chief federal inspectors were appointed, though in a few cases one inspector was assigned two or more regions. Many of these inspectors, while appointed centrally, had roots in the regions to which they were assigned. In especially troublesome regions, however, outsiders—usually from Moscow—were named to the post. Unlike the practice that had emerged in the Yeltsin period, governors and republic leaders were not, as a rule, consulted. However, the ethnic factor was carefully taken into account in appointments to many of the more assertive ethnic republics (Tatarstan, Bashkiria, and Chechnya, for example). The backgrounds of chief federal inspectors are also revealing. There is a heavy predominance of inspectors who came from the "power ministries"; of those for whom biographical data are available, approximately three of every four came from the military, FSB, or MVD. The majority of federal inspectors are in their mid-forties, all are men, and virtually none of them had a background in any elective office.

FUNCTIONS OF THE
PRESIDENTIAL REPRESENTATIVES

Much of the work performed by presidential representatives is secret; as a result their actual role remains hidden. Putin meets regularly—once every three months—with his seven representatives in order to discuss future priorities. Since the system has been in existence, Putin has publicly emphasized three basic tasks:

1. To restore the preeminence of federal law. Much of the first year's work of the presidential representatives was spent overseeing the process of bringing regional legislation (including republic constitutions and regional charters) into conformity with federal law and the Russian constitution.

By the end of the first year's work, it was reported that thousands of regional laws had been "corrected." The effectiveness of this effort is questionable, however, since bringing regional laws into conformity with federal laws was approached as a technical exercise. Given the problems Russia has yet to address in establishing the rule of law, a massive effort to improve the content of laws appears to be premature. Russia, and this is even more true of the regions, is a country where the letter of the law often counts for little in the face of arbitrariness, incompetence, politicization, and corruption in the judicial system and in the bureaucracy.

2. To define the division of powers between the center, regions, and local government. Starting in the latter part of 2001, a major effort was undertaken to formalize relationships between center and regions. Part of this initiative has been to clarify the nature of bilateral treaties that were signed between over half the regions and Yeltsin's government. A commission headed by the deputy head of Putin's staff, Dmitry Kozak, took the lead in formulating the proper relationship between regions and the center, and worked with the presidential representatives in this area. The general perspective of the Putin team is that the bilateral agreements signed during the Yeltsin period have very limited legal standing; in effect, almost any other form of law or presidential decree takes precedence over them. The presidential representatives have created analogous commissions to inventory how powers are in fact distributed between particular regions and the center and to collect proposals on changes in federal laws defining the competencies of the respective levels.

Part of the division of powers consists of defining the role that would be played by subregional government. Under Yeltsin, the term "local self-management" meant that the regions enjoyed considerable autonomy. This was true both in the 1993 constitution and in the 1995 law on local government. However, resistance from governors turned these provisions into empty promises. Local budgets are completely inadequate to take on the obligations assigned to them, which puts local officials in the role of supplicants to regional leaders. In October 2003, Putin signed a new Law on Principles of Organizing Local Self-management which replaced the 1995 law. The law appears to increase the control of regional authorities over local officials, bringing mayors also into the "vertical of authority." The law establishes a new system of municipal entities that will encompass the entire country. Most of the law's provisions, however, do not go into force until 2007. Putin has pledged to guarantee local government the financial resources needed to carry out their functions, but he coupled this with a threat to remove elected officials who are not up to the task.

3. To coordinate and optimize federal agencies' activity in regions, including a role in appointing and monitoring personnel in federal agencies in the regions. This actually is an extension of actions taken in 1997–98, when collegia of federal agencies under the chairmanship of the presidential representative were created in most regions. These never worked well. Given the nature of the coordinating function, it is logical to expect appointments of FSB officers to play the coordinating role. No one else, after all, would have the authority to coordinate such powerful agencies as the FSB, FAPSI (the agency that controls communications security), the Ministry of Internal Affairs, the tax police, and federal prosecutors. As is shown in Table 12.1, during Putin's first term in office there were substantial personnel changes in the two key force ministries in the regions, the MVD and FSB. Over half the top regional officials at this level were replaced from 2000 to the end of 2003.

Perhaps more important than the stated functions of Putin's presidential representatives are the undeclared ones. It is here that the need for FSB functionaries becomes even clearer. These more or less covert assignments include:

1. Bringing military, police, and security organs out from under governors and back under the control of the center. This had been largely accomplished

Table 12.1. Replacement Rate of Regional Officials, 2000–2003

Year	Heads of Regions	MVD: Ministry of Internal Affairs	FSB: Federal Security Service	Chief Federal Inspectors
2000	13/89	3/88	10/87	13/75
2001	7/89	18/88	12/87	18/75
2002	6/89	10/88	14/87	9/75
2003	5/89	16/88	10/87	9/75
Total	31/89	47/88	46/87	38/75
As percent:	35%	53%	53%	51%

Note: Based on available data, which are incomplete. The total number of officials is less than the number of regions because some officials are in charge of several regions.

by 2002. Presidential representatives created security collegia in their districts, replacing informal structures of this type that had arisen outside the control of the center. Presidential representatives also helped the center establish control over the MVD (see following). In this they were aided by a change in the law in June 2001, which eliminated the governors' effective veto on appointments of regional MVD chiefs.

2. Overseeing and controlling the process of gathering compromising material (*kompromat*) on regional leaders. Officials from the Kremlin's Main Oversight Department have a substantial presence on the *polpred's* staff. Further capabilities that would allow the *polpred* to gather information on corruption or misdeeds in the regions are planned. Most importantly, the Audit Chamber is setting up offices in the districts and regions. This agency, formally under the control of the Russian parliament, in effect has become Putin's financial secret police, and it has been used actively against oligarchs, ministers, and others. The creation of Audit Chamber branches will form a new "financial vertical of power," in the words of its director, General Sergei Stepashin (Putin's predecessor in the posts of prime minister and FSB director). In 2003, for the first time serious criminal investigations were launched against several sitting governors, most typically those the Kremlin labeled as weak and ineffective.

3. Influencing political developments in the regions. Presidential representatives are clearly involved in efforts to remove from power those regional leaders who are considered obstacles by the Kremlin. In a number of regions—Kaluga, Kursk, Krasnodar, Primor'e, Yakutia, Ingushetia and St. Petersburg—political figures not to the liking of the Kremlin were removed from the political stage. Elections are a particularly propitious time for action, since it is when governors are at their most vulnerable (much like a crab that has molted and not yet grown a new shell). Under Putin, the Kremlin has tried to influence elections through the electoral process whereby Putin could use his popularity to help a favored candidate. In addition, secretive, behind-the-scenes maneuvering is common. Methods include exerting influence over the election commission or the local judiciary to remove a candidate from the ballot. In some cases it is clear that the *kompromat* gathered on regional leaders can be mobilized to pressure them not to seek another term in office (the use of blackmail, in other words). In other cases, various incentives are provided for leaders to step down, such as appointment to a new federal post or a seat in the Federation Council. Primor'e Governor Yevgenii Nazdratenko was named to head the agency that awards lucrative fishing quotas (he was later "promoted" from this post to a seat on Putin's National Security Council). Vladimir Yakovlev, a longtime political enemy of Putin who replaced Anatoly Sobchak as governor in 1996, was given the post of Deputy Prime Minister in charge of a massive reform of the country's infrastructure for the supply of heat and water. In other cases, such as Bashkiria and Kalmykia, pres-

sure was applied against incumbents, but they were allowed to remain in office after compromising with the Kremlin. Overall, as is shown in Table 12.1, approximately one-third of Russia's regional leaders were replaced during Putin's first term. The role that the president's representatives and their staff has played in these developments has not been publicized, but it is fairly obvious.

From the beginning, presidential envoys were denied many of the instruments of real power to control developments in the regions—the right to direct financial flows from the center, for example, or the power to appoint federal officials in the regions. They have, however, found other ways to attain leverage. It is apparent that *polpreds* have worked to expand their links with important regional actors, such as the business community. Behind-the-scenes alliances with prominent industrialists and other local oligarchs can provide presidential envoys the leverage they need to reduce the governors' room for maneuver. The fact that businesses often need to operate on a regional, national, and even international level gives Putin's representatives additional tools of persuasion. *Polpreds* also have power because they control access to the president. The presidential representatives prepare the agenda for meetings between the president and individual governors from their district, thus limiting direct communication with the president. As a result, governors are put in the position of having to work through the *polpred's* staff in order to get to the president. Finally, even though they lack direct appointment powers, *polpreds* can influence personnel decisions by federal agencies and the president in their district through their recommendations for promotions. In effect, over time they can create a kind of web of cadres in the district that could reduce governors' room for maneuver.

PARALLEL STRUCTURES IN THE FEDERAL DISTRICTS

The scheme that Putin established for improving the coordination of federal policy was replicated by many other agencies at the direction of the president. The strategy is to strengthen the vertical chain of command from the ministry in Moscow, to the federal district agencies, and from there to ministry officials in the region. The presence of these new district offices allows presidential representatives to play the coordinating role discussed earlier.

New territorial structures were established in the seven federal districts by the most important federal agencies and ministries—in all, about twenty federal agencies. To illustrate, within a year of Putin's reform there were nineteen federal agencies represented in the Volga district. These included the prosecutor's office, the Ministry of Justice, the Tax Police, the Federal Tax Service, FAPSI (the Federal Agency on Governmental Communication), the

Ministry of the Interior for Internal Troops, the Federal Criminal Police, the Federal Service on Financial Restructuring and Bankruptcy, the State Courier Service, the Committee on State Reserves, the Federal Securities Commission, the Property Ministry, the Federal Property Fund, the Ministry on Publishing and TV and Radio-Broadcasting, the Ministry of Natural Resources, the Pension Fund, the Ministry of Transportation, and Health Ministry, the State Committee on Statistics, and the Ministry of Anti-Monopoly Policy (the latter two had other regional branches within which they established federal district departments).[14] A new set of judicial organs—administrative courts—were set up in twenty-one districts, though they fit within the seven federal districts.

Some of the most important changes in administrative subordination took place in the Ministry of Internal Affairs. When Putin came to power, there was a symbiosis between police generals at the center and regional leaders that seemed to be unbreakable. Putin employed chesslike maneuvers to reassert dominance over this key lever of control. Instead of immediately appointing his own man as minister, he began by establishing a new intermediate level that separated the regional bottom from the central top. Seven MVD district directorates were created, headed by high-ranking police officials who are directly subordinate to the minister of internal affairs and appointed by decrees issued by Putin himself.[15] It took almost a year of personnel changes at the regional level to break up existing networks of relationships. Only then, in June 2001, did Putin replace then-minister Rushailo with his ally, Boris Gryzlov, and more far-reaching reforms of the MVD began in earnest. (At the end of 2003, Gryzlov, who was also leader of the pro-Putin party United Russia, resigned his police post to become the new speaker of the State Duma.) The MVD department that had responsibility for combating organized crime was completely reorganized to bring it under federal control. In this case, the *polpreds* provided a useful mechanism for restoring control by the central ministry over regional police chiefs. This was a source of some dissatisfaction later, when *polpreds* came into conflict with newly centralized police operations. The system of informal governors' control over prosecutors was broken as well, with seven prosecutors' general deputies appointed to head new district offices.

It should be emphasized, however, that none of the heads of the new district agencies is subordinate to the presidential representative in the district. While such a change would make sense from the standpoint of a clear and single vertical chain of command, it would represent a major assault on the prerogatives of the Moscow-based ministries. Ever since Khrushchev's attempt to undermine the ministries and transfer their powers to regional economic councils (the *sovnarkhozy*) the ministries have effectively fought reorganizations that would decentralize power to the district or regional level. The presidential representative cannot order the federal agencies in his district to do anything, though he can complain to Putin if there is resistance to his efforts.

One of the few federal ministries that did not create a new territorial structure based on the federal districts was the FSB. This suggests that the administrative district scheme was conceived by and is, in some respects, itself an extension of the FSB. Otherwise, the FSB would naturally seek to have a voice of its own at the federal district level.

RESTORING ST. PETERSBURG'S CAPITAL ROLE

Putin is the first of the country's Soviet and post-Soviet leaders who was born and raised in St. Petersburg, Russia's imperial capital, rather than coming from a far-flung province. (Interestingly, none has come from Moscow.) Moreover, unlike his predecessors, Putin did not spend a lengthy period of time in Moscow prior to becoming leader. This has had two major consequences. First, there has been a significant flow of elites from "Piter" (as St. Petersburg is known colloquially) to Moscow. The old eastern capital (Moscow) is now besieged by young, Westernizing newcomers. It is reported that on Monday mornings there is a traffic jam of limousines waiting outside the Leningrad railway station in Moscow to pick up officials returning from a weekend with their families in Piter. Second, some capital city functions have shifted from Moscow to Piter. President Putin himself visits the city often and the Constantine palace has been restored as an official presidential residence. There have been serious discussions about moving key institutions of the judiciary including the Supreme Court, Constitutional Court, and Higher Arbitration Court to St. Petersburg.

St. Petersburg's growing clout can be considered, at least partly, to be the consequence of Putin's reliance on his former colleagues from the Leningrad-St. Petersburg FSB.[16] However, the picture is more complicated than this, even in terms of personnel policy. There are at least three other sources of Petersburg elite recruitment in addition to the FSB: lawyers and former colleagues from Mayor Anatolii Sobchak's administration,[17] liberal economists,[18] and so-called "unallied individuals."[19] In addition to top presidential aides and government officials, the speakers of both the State Duma and Federation Council are from St. Petersburg.

One explanation for the dominance of the "Leningrad group" is Putin's need to fill key posts with people he trusts and who have demonstrated their loyalty to him. Another factor, though, is a desire to systematically dismantle the old Moscow-based bureaucratic machine. Officials from Piter, following long-standing practice, tend to bring with them their own subordinates, so that there has been an exponential explosion in the number of mid-level officials from Petersburg as well. While bureaucrats flow from Petersburg to

Moscow, the Kremlin is sending money the opposite direction—in particular, $1.5 billion in federal investment was allocated for the celebration of the city's three hundredth anniversary in 2003. There is increasing coverage of St. Petersburg life in the national media, and numerous projects have been proposed that would restore some capital city functions to St. Petersburg. Even if the construction of a new parliamentary center in Petersburg is unlikely in the short term, visiting foreign dignitaries are often taken to the "northern capital" as part of their official itinerary.

CONCLUSION

It is clear that the state of center-region affairs under Yeltsin was not sustainable—the regions had become too strong at the expense of the center. But it would appear Putin has swung the pendulum in the opposite direction. The policies he has undertaken threaten both federalism and democratic development in Russia.

There is a Soviet-era joke about a machinist from a defense plant who made Kalashnikovs (machine guns). When he retired from the factory, he decided to make toys for the children in his neighborhood. But whatever he made, whether it was a rocking horse, a doll, or a model ship, it always came out looking like a Kalashnikov! The Putin approach to the regions seems to suffer from a set of limitations that reflects his life experiences and background. Putin's choice of instruments and personnel make it evident that his policies for dealing with the regions will end up "looking like a Kalashnikov"—a recentralized, unitary system. This is in spite of the fact that the goal of his policies is often presented as one of "improving" or "correcting" Russia's federal system.

The methods used by Putin and his team are in large part derived from the standard operating procedures of the KGB and its successor organization, the FSB. These include gathering compromising materials against "targets," using this information to blackmail the target in order to gain its cooperation, planning and carrying out extralegal operations with a maximum degree of secrecy, and the use of diversions and feints to direct attention away from the real purpose of an operation. In the case of the shift of powers to the federal districts, a part of Putin's strategy seems to be to create new institutions that at first seem merely to duplicate functions of existing institutions, but that may later take their place. The emphasis on discipline, carrying out orders without question, and strict hierarchical relations also reflects the internal ethos of the KGB. Democracy and an effectively operating federal system, on the other hand, call for other modes of operation: politics as the sphere for resolving disputes; an emphasis on transparent, lawful action within existing political institutions; and the use of methods such as negotiation, persuasion and compromise.

If one sets aside the obvious exception of Chechnya, the Yeltsin presidency relied heavily on compromise and negotiation to achieve settlements with the regions. What prevented Yeltsin from building a more balanced system of federalism was the center's political and economic weakness. This weakness was exploited by republic presidents and governors to carve out substantial autonomy. Putin, with much higher levels of public support, an effective working majority in the Duma, and a much more favorable economic-budgetary situation, has a much stronger basis to exert leverage. The improvement of the Russian economy after the August 1998 crisis and as a result of higher oil prices cannot be overestimated in this regard. This led to enhanced tax collection and greater budgetary resources that could be used to pay off past debts and to finance federal institutions. The impression one gets from his regional policy is that Putin prefers to use his strength to force the changes he wants largely without bargaining and without employing constitutional mechanisms.

Will recentralization and the attempt to recreate a unitary system be effective in today's Russia? The first years of experience with the system of federal districts provides contradictory evidence. On the one hand, the new policies do seem to be removing gubernatorial control over the military, police, and federal agencies that rightfully belong under federal jurisdiction. On the other hand, there is little recognition among Putin's advisors that this strategy could go too far, or that excessive centralization was one of the weaknesses of the Soviet system. It is clear from Putin's statements on "restoring" vertical power that his main reference point is the USSR. To someone who is a product of the Soviet system, the elimination of checks and balances appears to increase the manageability and effectiveness of the political system. This may be true in the short run, but there is a huge risk entailed. A highly centralized system runs the risk of collapsing in the face of changing conditions or circumstances.

Putin's top aides and his presidential representatives have only a hazy notion of what constitutes federalism. To an extent this parallels Soviet-era misunderstandings about the nature of a market economy. The absence of a planned or command system for allocating resources was equated with chaos and anarchy. Similarly, the absence of a clear chain of command in the political-administrative sphere is viewed as disorder or a situation that is "out of control" (*bezobrazie*). The idea that certain important decisions would actually be made in Russian regions without a directive from the center is alien to this mindset. The same striving for clarity and order will likely encompass the subregional level—Russia's cities and towns—as well. Yeltsin's declared policy of creating autonomous institutions of local government was an important affirmation of federalist principles. Putin's plans are not likely to increase the effective powers exercised at the local level, and may result in the direct sub-ordination of mayors to governors.

Putin's policies not only threaten the development of a federal system, but democratization as well. The creation of new levels of administrative author-ity in the form of presidential representatives and new district offices of gov-ernment agencies does nothing to facilitate Russia's political maturation. Ultimately, the political center of gravity should be in the regions. In the 1990s, normal political institutions, the organizations that constitute civil society, and independent media have been victimized by the disproportionate power wielded by Russia's governors and republic presidents. If the center were to use its power to guarantee political freedoms and rights in the regions it would encourage participation and democratization. Instead, Putin's poli-cies are designed to create a new level of decisionmaking above the regions. This will have the effect of making policy less dependent on governors. But it also puts important policy decisions out of the reach of citizens and their nascent organizations. Needless to say, virtually none of the latter are orga-nized at the federal district level. The few regions that have shown some progress in democratization could very easily see these gains disappear as the locus of policy moves upward.

Illustrative of this point is Putin's policy toward political parties and elec-tions in the regions. Rather than encourage pluralism and allow the "bottom-up" development of grassroots parties, Putin pushed for the creation of a national superparty through the merger of three of seven parties represented in the Duma: Unity, Fatherland, and All Russia. This new party, "United Russia," is highly centralized under the control of Putin loyalists. As a result of the 2001 law on political parties, regionally based parties were not allowed to register and compete in national elections. At the same time, Putin's sup-porters in the Duma launched an effort to change the rules on electing regional legislatures to require a mixed single-member and proportional rep-resentation system (by party list). This appears designed to allow United Rus-sia to establish a foothold in regional legislatures and deprive governors of control over them. In addition, the presidential representatives were mobi-lized to assist in party formation in federal districts, obviously to benefit United Russia. Finally, plans were announced to establish an administrative vertical chain of command for election commissions, thus giving the center greater control over the conduct of regional and local elections. This is akin to a restoration of a Soviet-style system using a single party to provide a paral-lel integration of vertical authority that reaches from the top leadership to the lowest level of society. In 2003, United Russia changed its confrontational approach toward regional leaders, bringing subservient governors directly into the party's Higher Council and placing twenty-nine of them on the party list for the December Duma elections. Thus, the Kremlin mobilized the considerable "administrative resources" of governors and republic presidents to help elect an overwhelming pro-Putin majority in the new State Duma.

Thus, Putin's vision for Russia appears to be one of creating multiple instruments of strong vertical control: administrative (based on federal districts and presidential representatives), police (headed by one of Putin's closest allies), financial (headed by Sergei Stepashin), political party, electoral commission, and others. If implemented fully, the result will be a vertically integrated and horizontally fractured state.

When looking for parallels from Russian and Soviet history to understand Putin and his policies, the figure who most readily comes to mind is Yuri Andropov. As a long-term head of the KGB in the Brezhnev era, Andropov took part in a struggle between the KGB and party bureaucrats. When he became general secretary after Brezhnev's death, Andropov was considered a modernizer and Westernizer by some observers. He started by emphasizing discipline and order, but was prevented from doing much more due to ill health. Among his unrealized plans, by the way, was a reconfiguring (enlarging) of Russia's regions. Stalin, who like Putin, came to power through intricate bureaucratic maneuvers, also enlarged regions to be led by "loyal followers" and created a complicated system of power verticals that strengthened control over the regions. The leader considered the greatest reformer in Russian history, Peter the Great, introduced a new system of big *gubernias*, hated the city of Moscow and liked Germans, and then paved the road to Europe on the bones of his subjects. More and more frequently Putin is compared to Peter. Yet another historical figure might be a better fit, however— Paul I, Catherine the Great's unloved son. Paul liked Prussia and military parades; he disliked his mother and her reforms, and began his rule with the question of administrative-territorial restructuring. He could well have become the greatest counterreformer in Russian history if he hadn't been removed in a coup d'etat.

NOTES

1. See Graeme Gill, *The Origins of the Stalinist Political System* (Cambridge: Cambridge University Press, 1996) and Gerald Easter, *Reconstructing the State: Personal Networks and Elite Identity in Soviet Russia* (Cambridge: Cambridge University Press, 1996).

2. Peter Jordan, "Regional Identities and Regionalization in East-Central Europe," *Post-Soviet Geography and Economics* 42, no. 4 (2001): 235–65.

3. Daniel Triesman, "The Politics of Intergovernmental Transfers in Post-Soviet Russia," *British Journal of Political Science* 26 (July 1996): 299–335; and Daniel Triesman, "Fiscal Redistribution in a Fragile Federation: Moscow and the Regions in 1994," *British Journal of Political Science* 28 (January 1998).

4. Michael McFaul and Nikolai Petrov, *Politicheskii Al'manak Rossii 1997*, vol. 1 (Moscow: Carnegie Center, 1998), 149.

5. Darrell Slider, "Elections to Russia's Regional Assemblies," *Post-Soviet Affairs* 12, no. 3 (July/September 1996): 243–64.

6. Pavel K. Baev, "The Russian Armed Forces: Failed Reform Attempts and Creeping Regionalization," *The Journal of Communist Studies and Transition Politics* 17, no. 1 (March 2001): 34.

7. Steven Solnick, "Is the Center Too Weak or Too Strong in the Russian Federation," in *Building the Russian State*, ed. Valerie Sperling (Boulder, Colo.: Westview Press, 2000).

8. Alfred Stepan, "Russian Federalism in Comparative Perspective," *Post-Soviet Affairs* 16, no. 2 (2000): 133–76.

9. Darrell Slider, "Russia's Market-Distorting Federalism," *Post-Soviet Geography and Economics* 38, no. 8 (October 1997): 445–60.

10. Mathew Hyde, "Putin's Federal Reforms and Their Implications for Presidential Power in Russia," *Europe–Asia Studies* 53, no. 5 (2001): 719–43.

11. Nikolai Petrov, "Seven Faces of Putin's Russia: Failed Districts as the New Level of State Territorial Composition," *Security Dialogue* 33, no. 1 (March 2002): 219–37.

12. Ol'ga Blinova, "Polnomochnye predstaveiteli prezidenta Rossii: novaya vlastnaya vertikal" Tsentr politicheskoi informatsii (Moscow: 2000).

13. The reference is to the Western with this title, which was one of the first American films to be widely shown in the Soviet Union during the Cold War. The film was extremely popular in the 1960s when Vladimir Putin was growing up.

14. An additional eighteen federal agencies had regional offices in another location, while forty-three had no intermediate structures between their central headquarters and regional branches. "Federal Agencies on the Territory of Nizhniy Novgorod Oblast," 2001, scheme by the Volga federal district administration.

15. The number of staff (150) assigned to the federal district MVD offices was greater than that assigned to the staff of the presidential representatives.

16. Nikolai Patrushev (FSB Director), Sergei Ivanov (Defense Minister), Victor Ivanov (Deputy Head of Presidential Administration in charge of personnel), Victor Cherkesov (Chairman of the State Committee to Combat Drug Trafficking), Georgy Poltavchenko (Polpred), Viktor Zubkov (Chairman of Ministry of Finance Financial Monitoring Committee), Sergei Verevkin-Rokhal'skii (MVD Deputy Minister, head of Tax Police).

17. Igor Sechin (Deputy Head of Presidential Administration), Aleksei Miller (Chief of Gazprom), Dmitri Kozak (First Deputy Head of Presidential Administration), Vladimir Kozhin (Head of Presidential Administration Property Department), Ilya Yuzhanov (Minister of Anti-Monopoly Policy and Entrepreneurship).

18. Anatoly Chubais (Head of United Electrical Systems), German Gref (Minister for Economic Development and Trade), Aleksei Kudrin (Deputy Prime Minister and Finance Minister), Andrei Illarionov (Chief Economic Advisor to the President), Mikhail Dmitriyev (First Deputy Minister for Economic Development and Trade), Dmitri Vasilyev (Federal Securities Commission Chairman).

19. Boris Gryzlov (Speaker of the Duma, former Minister of Internal Affairs), Ilya Klebanov (Polpred), Leonid Reiman (Minister of Communications), Sergei Stepashin (Head of the Audit Chamber), Yuri Shevchenko (Health Minister), Sergei Mironov (Federation Council Speaker), Valerii Yashin (Director General of Svyaz-Invest, communications monopoly).

Chapter Thirteen

Putin and Russian Foreign Policy

Dale R. Herspring and Peter Rutland

In the foreign policy arena, Vladimir Putin marks a dramatic change from his predecessor. In the twilight of the Yeltsin era, it was increasingly common to hear Western commentators refer dismissively to Russia as a country of no consequence, a has-been with an economy the size of Portugal or Holland. While Yeltsin's primary concern was fending off domestic challenges to his authority, Putin has the opportunity and inclination to make the restoration of Russia as a great power a top priority. Putin realizes that the Soviet Union is no more, but he still sees the Russian state as an important player on the world scene.

If there is an "ism" that drives Putin, it is nationalism—nationalism built not on ethnic, cultural, or spiritual values, but on the centrality of state power, which in Putin's case embraces a deep-seated desire to restore Russia's former greatness. In his view, "Patriotism is a source of the courage, staunchness, and strength of our people. If we lose patriotism and national pride and dignity, which are connected with it, we will lose ourselves as a nation capable of great achievements."[1]

Putin is also an advocate of realpolitik. He understands better than most that Russia is playing with a very weak hand. The country's economy faces major problems, the political system is still unformed, and Russia as a whole is riven by social divisions and a profound crisis of identity. The military is in shambles despite Defense Minister Sergei Ivanov's reform efforts. Russia's neighbors view it with suspicion or hostility: its list of trusted allies does not extend much beyond the erstwhile Belarus.[2] Indeed, in the eyes of many, the only reason the country has been a significant actor in the foreign policy field was because it possessed nuclear weapons. But these have been deteriorating to the point that many have become both useless and dangerous to maintain.[3] In short, Putin faces a considerable challenge in trying to forge a coherent and effective foreign policy for Russia.

Putin has shown that he is prepared to tackle foreign policy problems head-on—to be an effective force for Russian interests in spite of the country's weaknesses. He has broken with the mind-set of the Soviet era and is seeking to defend and promote Russia's interests in the world as it is, and not as it used to be. Equally important, he expects other powers to base their policies on a realistic assessment of national interests. Putin is neither the kind of individual who gives something for nothing, nor does he expect such behavior from an adversary. In a sense, it was easier for the United States to deal with Russian and Soviet leaders like Mikhail Gorbachev and Boris Yeltsin, who saw the world in more ideological terms, than with Putin, who is a calculating pragmatist.

Before discussing the Putin administration's actions in some detail, let us turn to the Yeltsin regime, which is a critical backdrop for understanding the foreign policy world that Putin inherited.

THE PRE-PUTIN PERIOD

The Policy Framework

When he assumed control of a sovereign Russia at the end of 1991, Boris Yeltsin faced a foreign policy disaster. The USSR had collapsed, splintering into fifteen independent states. The Russian Federation took over as its legal successor and inherited what was left of the centralized institutions of the Soviet state, including its massive nuclear arsenal. Russia confronted an unprecedented task: to carve out a foreign policy for itself in the wake of a collapsed superpower.[4]

The effort to create a Commonwealth of Independent States (CIS) that could unify the newly independent states and project Russian power over the post-Soviet space was a failure virtually from the outset.[5] Too many of the former Soviet republics—and especially Ukraine—distrusted the Russians. Memories of the use of Soviet troops in the Baltics, Georgia, Azerbaijan, and other regions in an effort to hold the country together were fresh in their minds. Equally important, leaders such as Islam Karimov and Nursultan Nazarbaev enjoyed their new status as presidents of sovereign states and were understandably reluctant to give up the power that had serendipitously fallen upon them. Many feared that the Kremlin would again use the military to get its way if and when the former republics acted too independently. In the end, the CIS became little more than a fig leaf. Moscow could claim that it had good, close relations with the former Soviet republics, but the fact was that it was not a serious alliance. Russia was alone.

Yeltsin had to go back to the drawing board. He could hardly expect Russia to be the superpower the USSR had been, in spite of the country's nuclear weapons. Furthermore, confrontation with the West would do him little or no good. The country was in chaos. The political system was being reinvented and a new economy was being introduced as the state-owned system was rapidly privatized.

Yeltsin's primary concern was to create a benign external environment in order to free the Kremlin to deal with the critical tasks of domestic political and economic transition. Yeltsin had little alternative but to try to invent a new type of relationship with the West. Given that the United States was the world's only remaining superpower and, in Yeltsin's mind, the primary potential source of economic largesse, his strategy placed primary emphasis on U.S.–Russian relations.

It is important to keep in mind that the Cold War had left a residue of suspicion and even hatred on both sides. Overcoming this legacy would not be easy—and there was a significant part of the Russian populace that opposed Yeltsin's effort to improve relations with Washington; sometimes openly, at other times behind the scenes. Conservatives, and especially some military officers, were entrenched in Cold War habits. Taught for years to fear the West, including the United States, they now were being told that this "enemy" had become a friend.

Unfortunately, while there were certain elements of rationality in Yeltsin's policy, in time, it would become inconsistent, not only because of Russia's weakness and instability but also because Yeltsin himself was erratic, prone to headstrong and at times downright embarrassing behavior.

In addition to inconsistency, Yeltsin's reign was also marked by a lack of "geopolitical perspective or political planning, as well as general inertia," a point made by Oleg Levitin in his analysis of Yeltsin's Kosovo policy.[6] There was a tendency on Yeltsin's part to put off making hard decisions. So Moscow was prone to ignore problems like Yugoslavia, trying to postpone a decision on how to respond to Slobodan Milosevic and his barbaric actions in Kosovo.

These problems of erratic leadership were compounded by the administrative chaos in the foreign policy process. In the Soviet era, decisionmaking had been tightly centralized by the politburo, and its implementation overseen by the departments of the central committee. With the Communist Party's collapse, authority shifted from the politburo to the presidential administration, but the newly created security council failed to develop as an effective coordination institution. The huge bureaucracies of the ministries of foreign affairs and defense drifted out of control, often pursuing their own policy goals independent of other government agencies. New, influential players entered the foreign policy arena, such as oil companies, regional governors, and even regional military commanders, adding to the chaos of conflicting policy initiatives.

Yeltsin and the United States

The first official meeting between Boris Yeltsin and President Bill Clinton occurred in April 1993. Both sides declared their interest in and readiness to create a "dynamic and effective Russo–American partnership."[7] Clinton promised financial aid in the amount of $1.6 billion (half credits, half aid). Many believed it would be the beginning of a "special relationship" between Moscow and Washington.

While some may argue that critics such as Stephen Cohen exaggerate the impact the Clinton administration had on Yeltsin's Russia, there is no question that Clinton and his entourage believed that they could remake Russia in America's image. As Cohen put it, "In effect, the United States was to teach ex-Communist Russia how to become a capitalist and democratic country and oversee the process of conversion known as a 'transition.'"[8] Russia found itself swamped by Americans of all backgrounds and specialties, who were convinced that if only the Russians would listen to the West and especially the Americans, they would quickly rebound from the adversity of the transition process. In time, however, it became clear that the recovery process would be much more protracted and complex. Indeed, one could argue that in many ways, the Clinton administration's approach did Russia more harm than good.

In any case, despite growing doubts the Clinton administration continued to forge ties with the Kremlin. By September 1998 the two men had met fourteen times—an unprecedented event in U.S.–Soviet/Russian relations. The "Bill–Boris" relationship was in full bloom.

The problem for U.S.–Russian relations—and indeed for Russian internal politics—was that a combination of a U.S. failure to deliver the kind of aid that Russians believed was offered, together with an increasingly corrupt and inept Yeltsin regime, led to gradual disillusionment with the United States. Many Russians came to see the economic and social chaos of the early 1990s not as the product of a collapsed communist economic system, but as a result of the capitalist regime that was being forced on Russia at Western insistence. Many began to believe that U.S. aid was all part of a "plot" to both embarrass Russia and to enrich the United States at its expense. Not surprisingly, this did not go down well with nationalistic Russians. Accepting help and assistance from the outside world was bad enough; permitting the United States to take advantage of a prostrate country was unacceptable.

In the wake of the strong Communist showing in the December 1995 State Duma elections, Yeltsin appointed former spy chief Yevgeny Primakov as foreign minister. Under Primakov, Moscow adopted a more assertive foreign policy. The overt bias toward the West was replaced by a more even-handed approach, placing more emphasis on good relations with China and the Arab world. But rhetoric aside, Primakov effected only minor course corrections in the Moscow–Washington relationship. He even folded in the face of U.S. determination to enlarge NATO to include Poland, Hungary, and the Czech Republic.

The most serious test of the relationship was the Kosovo crisis in the spring of 1999. In the wake of the August 1998 financial crisis, Primakov was elevated to the post of prime minister, and he soon faced a deterioration in the security situation in the Yugoslav province of Kosovo. Moscow saw itself as having close historical ties with the Serbs (although in reality the relationship had been dormant since World War I). How could it now desert them in the face of American and NATO pressure—notwithstanding the atrocities committed by the Milosevic forces? In the beginning, Russian diplomats went along with actions such as sanctions against the Belgrade government and denying Yugoslavia the country's seat in the UN. But NATO, without consulting Moscow, commenced its bombing campaign on March 24, 1999, just as Primakov was en route to the United States for an official visit. Primakov's decision to turn his plane around above the mid-Atlantic was immediately seen as symbolic of a new chill in U.S.–Russian relations. Russia promptly withdrew from involvement in the permanent joint council that NATO had created in 1997 to give Moscow a voice inside the alliance.

During the crisis, Moscow's policy vacillated from one of limited support for the NATO pressure on Milosevic to vocal opposition. Russia came to realize that the allies were determined to press ahead with their military campaign, since NATO credibility was at stake, and when the opportunity arose to play the peacemaker in June 1999 Moscow seized the chance. Ex-prime minister Viktor Chernomyrdin was sent to Belgrade to deliver the bad news: Russian patience was exhausted; Milosevic could expect no more Russian support. Milosevic quickly decided that he had no alternative but to evacuate his troops from Kosovo, thus ensuring Russian participation in the military occupation of Kosovo and preserving Yugoslavia's formal sovereignty over the province.

As this sorry catalog illustrates, Putin inherited a foreign policy that was neither consistent nor effective. The world knew Russia was weak and not a serious player on the international scene. But recognizing the obvious did not prevent Russians from being deeply resentful of the position in which they found themselves, and of the role the Clinton administration was playing in Russia. Not only did the United States seem to be trying to turn Russians into Americans, in the eyes of many it was gloating over the country's weak position. U.S. involvement in Russia may have been intended to help overcome its problems—but in practice it merely served to draw attention to the unpleasant new reality and to implicate the United States in Russia's weakened condition.

As a result, the situation facing Putin when he took over as acting president at the beginning of 2000 was less than ideal. The country was in shambles, its relationship with the United States was troubled, the West seemed to be ignoring Russia, and even the Kremlin's few remaining allies (such as India) had lost faith. It was beginning to look like Moscow was irrelevant in the international arena. Yes, Moscow could be a spoiler by threatening to sell nuclear material or weapons to Iran, or by siding with Iraq in the interminable arguments in the UN Security Council over the sanctions regime, or by selling weapons to China. And it could exploit the presence of Russian "peacekeepers" in Kosovo, Moldova, Abkhazia, and Tajikistan to project Russian influence into those troubled countries. But such actions imposed costs on Russia itself that were equal to or greater than those inflicted on U.S. interests. And when the Russian Bear growled, who paid any attention? The answer was almost nobody.

PUTIN TAKES CONTROL OF FOREIGN POLICY

Putin's first priority was to attempt to rationalize foreign policy. He recognized better than Yeltsin not only how weak Russia was, but how important it would be for Moscow to project an activist, participatory image on the international stage. In redesigning Russian foreign policy, Putin had two objectives. First, he believed that Moscow had to be seen as an active global presence. Playing the isolationist game would get the Kremlin nowhere, and in fact would only reinforce the prevailing image of Russian weakness. Second, he decided that U.S.–Russian relations had to improve. Like it or not, the United States was the world's only superpower.

In carrying out these objectives, Putin's foreign policy has been characterized by a number of factors. First, he believes in a balance-of-power approach to foreign policy, as opposed to the Soviet-era concept of foreign policy as a clash between rival ideologies. As he stated in his millennium speech shortly after he took over from Yeltsin, "I am against the restoration of an official state ideology in Russia in any form."[9] For Putin, problem solving takes precedence over ideology, whether of the left or the right. U.S. preeminence obliges Russia to "bandwagon" with the U.S.-led coalition of leading powers. Putin understands that there will be times—most of the time, in fact—when he will hold a weak hand. Yet Putin is smart enough to know that the weak partner can deal from a position of strength on occasion.

To make this balance-of-power policy work, Putin adopted a calculated, practical approach to dealing with foreign (as well as internal) problems. Yeltsin himself described Putin as a "somewhat cold pragmatist."[10]

Putin made Russia's position very clear to Russians and the rest of the world shortly after assuming power. On June 28, 2000, he issued a new set of policy guidelines or "foreign policy concept." This replaced a 1993 document, and followed a new "national security concept" published in January and a "military doctrine" released in April. The concept stated that "Today our foreign policy resources are relatively limited. . . . And they will be concentrated in fields that are vital for Russia." Foreign Minister Igor Ivanov described the new approach as a pragmatic effort to help the country to solve its domestic problems.[11] The document itself offered a restrained but critical view of NATO and the West and highlighted the importance of Russia's ties to the Group of Eight (G8) and the European Union. At the same time it took a swipe at Washington by calling for a "multipolar world" in contrast to the "unipolar structures of the world with the economic and power domination of the United States," and reiterated Moscow's opposition to a limited national missile defense plan.[12] In tune with his more realist approach to foreign policy, Putin told an interviewer that Russia "must get rid of imperial ambitions on the one hand, and on the other clearly understand where our national interests are and fight for them."[13]

Putin has outstanding diplomatic skills. He appears to have produced a favorable impression on all of his interlocutors, from Tony Blair to Madeleine Albright to Jiang Zemin. At times he has gone overboard to make a good impression, displaying a Zelig-like enthusiasm for adapting to his current environment. In Japan he took part in a judo contest (allowing himself to be thrown by his fifteen-year-old adversary), in Canada he averred his enthusiasm for ice hockey, in Spain he praised the art of Velázquez, and in Rome he said he came because "we love Italy."

Relations with the United States in Putin's First Year

During Yeltsin's latter years in office, U.S.–Russian relations deteriorated to the point where one source noted that "Washington (was) all but estranged from Moscow for most of the past year over the U.S.-led air war in Yugoslavia and Russia's prosecution of the war in Chechnya. . . ."[14] These same observers argued that Washington hoped to return to a position of influence over the Kremlin, while the latter wanted U.S. assistance to restart its economy.

Putin immediately showed his interest in improved relations by persuading the State Duma to ratify START II, a feat that had eluded Yeltsin in the preceding five years. This treaty eliminated multiple warheads on land-based missiles and limited Russia and the United States to 3,000–3,500 strategic warheads each. Putin also announced that he wanted to see even deeper cuts—down to 1,500.

Arms control was very much at the fore when President Clinton paid his farewell visit to Moscow in June 2000. The United States again pushed for modifications in the 1972 Anti-Ballistic Missile Treaty so it could begin testing a national missile defense system (NMD). Moscow (and not only Moscow) found the U.S. determination to press ahead with NMD puzzling. Was it really based on the stated objective—fear of a possible nuclear strike on the

U.S. mainland (or against U.S. forces?) from a rogue state like Iraq or North Korea? Perhaps its real intention was to intimidate China. Or was it simply a boondoggle for U.S. defense contractors?

Whatever the true motivation behind Washington's enthusiasm, Moscow feared NMD for three reasons. First, no one could predict what kind of "spin-offs" in advanced weaponry the search for NMD might produce. Second, it would leave the United States in a position of unquestioned global strategic dominance with a potent combination of offensive and defensive forces. Third, in addition to lacking meaningful strategic defensive forces, the Kremlin knew that the number of nuclear weapons available to Russia's military leaders would steadily diminish due to lack of funds for maintenance and modernization. In future years Russia's offensive forces could conceivably shrink to the point at which they would be unable to guarantee second-strike retaliation against an overwhelming U.S. first strike.

Despite grave Russian objections, the U.S. Senate had approved in principle the development of theater missile defense in March 1999. In a bid to head off NMD, Putin persuaded the State Duma to ratify START II, signed in 1993, which they dutifully did on April 14, 2000. During President Clinton's June 2000 visit there was speculation that Putin was looking for a "grand bargain": Russian agreement to waive the ABM Treaty in return for deep mutual cuts in strategic missiles. However, Senate Republican Jesse Helms made it clear that he would block approval of any such treaty, distrustful of concessions made during the waning months of the Clinton administration. As a consequence, Clinton had to be satisfied with the dubious privilege of being the first U.S. president to address the Duma.

All in all, Clinton's visit to Moscow was anything but a success. "The Russians signaled their displeasure with the U.S. president by failing to broadcast his speech to the Russian legislature on TV. . . . There was an obvious chill in the air between Clinton and Putin at their final media conference—Clinton looked frustrated, exhausted and exasperated and there was no warmth from Putin. The days of the cheery Boris-and-Bill show are clearly over."[15] Strobe Talbott, at the time assistant secretary of state, has suggested that Putin erred in rejecting Clinton's proposal to loosen the ABM Treaty, since the following year he would be forced to swallow the "shredding" of the ABM Treaty by President Bush in the wake of September 11.[16] The result was that U.S.–Russian relations went into a "stall" for the duration of 2000, while the Russians waited to see who would replace Clinton. As far as they were concerned, there was no sense trying to do business with a lame-duck president. In the meantime, Putin busied himself establishing warm ties with European leaders.

During the American election campaign, Russians were hesitant to come out strongly in favor of one candidate or the other. Senior Russian officials were fully aware that in contrast to the days of the Soviet Union, Russia was not a major issue. There were some grounds for expecting Moscow to prefer a Democratic victory, given that Vice President Al Gore knew the ropes and had put considerable effort into building up the Gore–Chernomyrdin commission, which brokered bilateral relations in trade and technology issues. Others hinted that Moscow favored a Bush victory, since this would represent a clean break with the Yeltsin–Clinton era. Regardless of who won, Russian observers were well aware that Moscow was in a weak position and would have to deal with the United States when it came to regional problems, arms control, and especially economic issues.

Relations with the Bush Administration

U.S.–Russian relations got off to a poor start under the Bush administration. In fact, until the summit in Slovenia in June 2001, it appeared that Washington was simply not taking Moscow seriously as an international player. The new administration seemed to look upon Russia as an economic, political, and social basket case. For example, during his election campaign, Bush denounced Russia's actions in Chechnya and its pervasive corruption—in one presidential debate going so far as to charge former Prime Minister Viktor Chernomyrdin with pocketing Western loan money. Bush seemed to believe that since the Russians had gotten themselves into their present morass, it was up to them to straighten themselves out. Whether or not they had a democracy was a problem for them—not the United States. This was in sharp contrast to the Clinton approach, which was based on the theory of the "democratic peace"—the notion that democracies did not go to war with each other, thus giving the United States a strong stake in Russia's democratization.

Some actions by Putin seemed to confirm suspicions about Russian motives held by the conservatives in the Bush administration. In July 2000 on his way to the G8 summit in Okinawa, Putin stopped off in Pyongyang and tried to pull off a diplomatic coup by securing a pledge from North Korea to discontinue its missile program—a "pledge" it later denied. Then in December 2000 Putin made a trip to Cuba, the first by a Russian president since the collapse of the Soviet Union. Putin was well aware that this visit would irritate the United States, and particularly the conservative Bush. He presumably wanted Bush to understand that in contrast to his predecessor he would not kowtow to the United States. To quote an article in the *Guardian*:

> Since succeeding Boris Yeltsin last March, he has been busily challenging America's global hegemony, as seen from Moscow, at every opportunity. He has intervened directly in the US-led Middle East peace process, given succor to Iraq, and resumed arms sales to Iran and Libya. He visited North Korea, that most roguish of US-designated 'rogue states,' and cheekily claimed to have curbed its

menacing missiles. He went to India, bidding to revive Soviet-era ties in direct competition with Bill Clinton's efforts to woo Delhi last spring; and has increased military and political cooperation with China.[17]

It was also clear that problems remained between the two sides on issues such as Bush's favorite strategic initiative—a missile defense program. And it was clear from voices within the Russian leadership that Putin would face serious opposition if he tried to change Moscow's position. For example, in December 2000, Defense Minister Igor Sergeev stated that Russia would not agree to any compromise with the United States that modified the 1972 Anti-Ballistic Missile Treaty.

Despite the friction, the two sides shared at least some common interests. Both were concerned about international terrorism. Both worried about Afghanistan, Pakistan, and Islamic fundamentalism. Putin's pardoning of Edward Pope, a retired U.S. Navy captain and alleged spy, in December 2000 was an obvious effort to improve U.S.–Russian relations. And American policymakers had to realize that there were risks involved in ignoring the Kremlin. In spite of the horrible condition of its economy, society, and political system, Russia would remain vital to U.S. security for years to come. Indeed, after September 11, 2001, Washington would learn just how critical Moscow's role would be.

As the new Bush administration was sworn in, Putin was cagey as ever. When asked about the future of U.S.–Russian relations, he stated that "a lot would depend here on the policy of the new U.S. administration."[18] The Bush administration's policy was equally vague. When the issue of U.S.–Russian relations came up, Secretary of State Colin Powell argued that "Moscow was neither an enemy, nor a potential opponent of the United States." However, Powell pointed out that Washington could not consider Russia a strategic partner. According to commentator Valentin Kunin, this meant that if "the foreign policy of the Bush [administration] becomes the basis of Powell's guidelines, Russia–USA relations are unlikely to improve."[19] Condoleezza Rice, Bush's national security advisor, openly called for a decisive break with the "failed" policy of the Clinton administration. She reiterated what Bush had stated previously, that "Russia's economic future is now in the hands of the Russians." Leaving aside any pretense of diplomacy, she argued, "It would be foolish in the extreme to share defenses with Moscow as it either leaks or deliberately transfers weapons technologies to the very states against which America is defending."[20] As a result, the outlook for U.S.–Russian relations was anything but positive as Bush was sworn in.

In spite of this concern over the future of U.S. policy toward Russia, Moscow made it clear from the beginning that it was prepared to talk. On December 30, 2000, Foreign Minister Igor Ivanov said that Moscow wanted a "serious dialogue" with the Bush administration. He went on to note that he "did not believe that differences between the two countries on national missile defense are insuperable." If nothing else, his statement suggested that there were differences of opinion within the Putin regime on this highly sensitive topic.[21] Putin followed up immediately after Bush was sworn in by sending a letter in which he congratulated the new president on his position while at the same time calling for improved U.S.–Russian relations. Russia and the United States needed "to find joint answers to the serious challenges which confront us and the entire international community, in the 21st century."[22] Putin was clearly holding out an olive branch.

Lest anyone think that Putin was about to cave in to Bush, however, he made it clear in his dealings with the United States' West European allies that he was prepared to take the fight over NMD into America's own backyard. He went to Canada where he succeeded in persuading Prime Minister Jean Chrétien to say that "the stability which exists now" should not be "undermined by the plan put forth by the Americans" for missile defenses against rogue nations.[23]

Another key issue was the safeguarding of Russian nuclear materials. The country was clearly unable to spend the kind of money necessary to manage its stockpiles. As a result, the United States had poured $5 billion into an effort to safeguard this material, help destroy it, and pay Russian nuclear scientists enough to keep them from selling their expertise abroad. It was clear that more money would be needed to do the job, but the Bush administration, worried about waste and duplication in the thirty-plus programs being run as part of the weapons dismantling mission, launched an investigative study immediately after taking office. It also was concerned that Moscow was either encouraging or at a minimum permitting sensitive nuclear material to leak to Iran.

To make matters even worse, president-elect Bush gave an interview on January 14, 2001, in which he warned Moscow not to expect economic aid in the future except for nonproliferation projects unless Putin cleaned up the country's economic mess. "He has pledged to root out corruption. I think that's going to be a very important part, but it's his choice to make. That's the point I'm trying to make. It's hard for America to fashion Russia."[24]

The Russian response was mixed. Some, such as State Duma speaker and longtime Communist Party member Gennadii Seleznev, as well as Vladimir Lukin, the former Russian ambassador to Washington and a liberal, agreed with the U.S. president's comments. Others argued that Bush's statement "not only ends any hope of restructuring Russia's debt, but is likely to generate anti-reform reaction in Russia itself."[25]

Meanwhile, those who opposed any improvement in U.S.–Russian relations began repeating the oft-heard refrain that Washington was trying to force its will on others. As one Russian commentary put it, "Washington is trying to subordinate all independent countries to US dictate, to grab key industries and financial systems of the concerned countries and to control their policies. This amounts to Americanization and the assertion of US domination. However, the United States camouflages this process by the 'globalization' concept."[26]

In spite of the harsh polemics, Putin reiterated the Russian position on February 8, 2001, when he stated that he hoped to find common language with U.S. President Bush, especially with the ABM issue. Putin went on to note that he had recently spoken on the phone with Bush and observed that "I give a very positive evaluation to our conversation and its results. I feel that Bush and myself will find a common language."[27] Despite Putin's apparent optimism, Dr. Rice continued the Bush administration's hard line in an interview in *Le Figaro* on February 10, when she commented that "I believe Russia is a threat to the West in general and to our European allies in particular."[28] As if that were not enough, Secretary of Defense Donald Rumsfeld accused Russia of violating the nuclear nonproliferation regime.[29] That was followed by a huge scandal following the February 18 arrest of FBI agent Robert Hanssen, who had spied for the Russians for fifteen years. In response, the United States ejected fifty Russian diplomats: the largest number of expulsions since 1986. Not surprisingly, the Russians reacted by expelling an equal number of American officials. From all appearances, U.S.–Russian relations were headed even farther downhill.

Meanwhile, U.S. and Russian diplomats continued to meet. For example, Secretary of State Colin Powell held what was officially described as a "constructive dialogue" when he met Russian Foreign Minister Igor Ivanov in Cairo in February 2001 to discuss the apparent impasse in U.S.–Russian relations: diplomatic shorthand indicating that the two sides were at least still talking.[30] The two had another positive meeting in April. According to Powell, both countries wanted to put their past difficulties behind them and "move on."[31]

The two presidents met for the first time in Slovenia in June. The Ljubljana summit had a major, positive impact on U.S.–Russian relations, thanks largely to the personal chemistry between the two leaders.[32] Mr. Bush famously commented after his first meeting with Putin, "I was able to get a sense of his soul."[33] Despite substantive differences, it was clear that the atmosphere between the two countries had improved considerably. It helped that Putin, who had been intensively studying English since becoming president, was able to make some conversation with Bush in English. As Putin stated, "We found a good basis to start building on cooperation, counting on a pragmatic relationship between Russia and the United States." Bush, for his part, said, "I am convinced that he and I can build a relationship of mutual respect and candor."[34] Bush announced that he would support Russia's entry into the World Trade Organization (one of Putin's most important foreign policy goals), and Putin agreed to continue a discussion on a new strategic defense framework—a concession that seemed almost impossible only weeks previously. Both leaders agreed to exchange visits to their respective countries. Putin gave a newspaper interview in which he said he and Bush had forged a "very high level of trust," and referred to the American president as a "partner" and "a nice person to talk to."[35] Putin made no secret that there were significant differences on topics such as Chechnya, NMD, or the Kremlin's relations with Iran, but overall, he painted an upbeat picture. Bush reciprocated in mid-July by telling a *Novosti* correspondent that it was now important not only for the United States and Russia to agree on NMD, but that both countries needed to turn their attention to such threats as cyberterrorism, and—somewhat prophetically—Islamic fundamentalism.[36] In an interview, Bush spoke candidly of his relationship with Putin:[37] "I found a man who realizes his future lies with the West, not the East, that we share common security concerns, primarily Islamic fundamentalism, that he understands missiles could affect him just as much as us. On the other hand he doesn't want to be diminished by America."

The next meeting between Bush and Putin took place at the G8 meeting in Genoa in July 2001. It too went well, with Bush saying of Putin, "This is a man with whom I can have an honest dialogue."[38] The two sides issued a joint statement in which they agreed that the issues of antimissile defenses and strategic arms cuts were related and should be dealt with together. In practice it was assumed that this meant that any modifications in the ABM Treaty would be accompanied by large cuts in offensive nuclear warheads. The former was a long-term American goal, while the latter was being forced on the Russians by their increasingly outdated and inoperable nuclear arsenal.

It soon became clear that however much Putin might want to compromise on the ABM issue, he was not able to deliver the Moscow bureaucracy. The Russian military, one of the most conservative institutions in the country, was still locked into the mentality of the Cold War, deeply suspicious of anything that came from the United States and frozen by inertia into anti-U.S. policies—arms proliferation, nuclear deterrence, provocative military exercises.[39] Because of conflicting views and interests among senior commanders, Putin made virtually no progress with urgently needed military reform. In March 2001 Putin reshuffled his top security ministers. Defense Minister Igor Sergeev was replaced with Sergei Ivanov, a former KGB official and close Putin ally, who became the first civilian to head the Defense Ministry in Russian history. Ivanov was replaced as head of the Security Council by Vladimir Rushailo, formerly interior minister. In July Putin removed General Leonid Ivashov, an outspoken hawk, from his position as head of the Defense Ministry's international department.

Perhaps because of Russia's inability to move ahead with concrete concessions, Rice's visit to Russia shortly after the Genoa summit for consultations made little progress. She concluded by insisting that the United States would scuttle the ABM Treaty altogether rather than negotiate amendments to it. It was looking increasingly likely, therefore, that U.S.–Russian relations would founder on the rocks of the ABM Treaty. But then came September 11.

THE WORLD AFTER SEPTEMBER 11

The attack by terrorists on the World Trade Center towers and the Pentagon had a major impact on U.S.–Russian relations. Putin was the first leader to telephone Bush with condolences and an unequivocal condemnation of the terrorist act.[40] Despite Putin's reputation as a cautious and calculating leader, his swift response to September 11 seemed to be driven by instinct and emotion.[41] In a subsequent telegram to Bush, Putin decried the "barbarous terrorist acts aimed against wholly innocent people," and expressed Russia's "deepest sympathies to the relatives of the victims of this tragedy, and the entire suffering American people," calling for "solidarity" in the face of such actions.[42] Equally important was an offer of assistance by Defense Minister Sergei Ivanov to the U.S. Defense Department. Moscow took the unprecedented step of canceling a military exercise by the Russian air force at the request of the United States.

It was clear that September 11 had the potential to mark a sea change in international relations in general and in the U.S.–Russia relationship in particular. As Strobe Talbott noted, U.S. military action in Afghanistan would be targeting a former Russian enemy (Afghanistan) and current Russian threat (Islamic fundamentalism), in marked contrast to previous U.S. actions against Russian allies Yugoslavia and Iraq.[43]

The key question in Moscow, however, was, How big a role should Russia play in assisting the United States in retaliating for these actions—and what should it expect in return? The Russians made it clear that they were more than prepared to share intelligence, a gesture that was welcomed by the United States. But the real issue was access to bases in Central Asia, in countries that formerly were part of the USSR. Moscow was anxious to regain some of its former preeminence in the region and had reacted neuralgically to previous U.S. efforts to project its own influence—such as the U.S. military exercise in Uzbekistan in 1998 under the rubric of NATO's Partnership for Peace program. Russia was uncertain of the direction U.S. military action would take and had no desire to be associated with a policy that could involve large-scale conflict in Afghanistan and beyond. Russia was already engaged in what it considered to be a war against Muslim fundamentalists in Chechnya, where there was some evidence of fighters being supported by the same Osama bin Ladin who masterminded the attacks on New York and Washington. September 11 gave Russia a chance to legitimize its actions in Chechnya, the subject of intermittently harsh criticism by Europe and to a lesser extent the United States. More broadly, an alliance with the United States in the war on terrorism provided Putin with a golden opportunity to make Russia once again a major actor on the world stage.

Meanwhile, the initial response of those below Putin was far from unanimous. Foreign Minister Igor Ivanov said in Washington that the former Central Asian republics (i.e., Uzbekistan, Kazakhstan, Turkmenistan, Kyrgyzstan, and Tajikistan) would be free to make their own decisions when it came to aiding the United States. But Defense Minister Sergei Ivanov ruled out "even a hypothetical possibility" of a NATO military presence in these former Soviet territories. In addition, the chief of the general staff, General Anatolii Kvashnin, stated that "Russia has not considered and is not planning to consider participation in a military operation against Afghanistan." He also reminded the Central Asian republics of "their relevant bilateral and other obligations" to Russia.[44]

It took several weeks for Putin to enforce unanimity in the ranks of his top officials. By September 24 it was becoming clear that in spite of the opposition from some in the military, Putin had decided to actively aid Washington's campaign against the radical Taliban regime in Afghanistan. He agreed to step up support for opposition forces inside Afghanistan, and he gave "tacit approval for the United States to use former Soviet bases in Central Asia."[45] The same day, Defense Minister Ivanov, in a major reversal of his previous position, said that the United States could use military facilities in Tajikistan to launch strikes on neighboring Afghanistan "if the need arises."[46] Access to these facilities was especially important to Washington because of concern over the volatility of fundamentalist Muslim groups in Pakistan, its other major staging area. In addition, Putin agreed to take part in search-and-rescue operations and vowed to share intelligence about international terrorist groups. Presidents Nursultan Nazarbayev of Kazakhstan and Askar Akaev of Kyrgyzstan said that they were willing to provide the antiterrorist alliance with use of their airspace and military bases. By December 1, 500 U.S. troops were deployed at the Hanabad air base in Uzbekistan and the United States had signed agreements granting landing rights in Tajikistan and Kyrgyzstan.

There were limits to Russian cooperation, however. Moscow reportedly encouraged its longtime allies, the Northern Alliance, to move quickly into Kabul—before the United States had been able to patch together a coalition government with the southern Pashtuns. On November 26, several hundred paramilitary personnel from the Emergency Situations Ministry flew unannounced into Kabul to establish a Russian presence there, in a move reminiscent of the reckless "dash for Pristina" in June 1999, when Russian peacekeepers drove from Bosnia to seize the Kosovo airport before advancing British troops. However, the United States was able to forge a viable coalition government to their liking in the Bonn conference, without Russian interference. And on December 5, Foreign Minister Ivanov announced that Russia had no intention of sending peacekeepers to Afghanistan, signaling its unwillingness to engage more deeply in a country that had been a quagmire for its military in the 1980s.

The unprecedented introduction of U.S. military units into Uzbekistan, Kyrgyzstan, and Tajikistan, on what increasingly looks like a long-term basis, represented a projection of U.S. military power into Russia's "backyard" that would have been unthinkable prior to the September attack. As Dmitri Trenin has noted, Putin's foreign policy was ambiguously polygamous prior to September 11: he was seeking allies from Pyongyang to Ottawa and all points between.[47] After the World Trade Center attack, Putin was forced to prioritize, forced to choose. His decision to align with the United States caused a radical improvement in the tone of the U.S.–Russian relationship. In the summer of 2001, Putin had been getting increasingly bad press in the West because of Chechnya and the crackdown on the independent television station NTV, so as Yelena Tregubova observed, "the Russian president would hardly have made such a breakthrough on the world stage if not for the tragedy of September 11."[48]

Russian foreign policy elites seized upon September 11 as representing a fundamental shift in the international order. Academic Aleksandr Konovalov argued that the event "shattered the myth of absolute power and invulnerability, of the United States as a guarantor of stability," while leading liberal Duma deputy Aleksei Arbatov said it was "the end of the illusion of a unipolar world."[49] Sensing—incorrectly, as it turned out—that the United States was fundamentally weakened, the foreign policy establishment gleefully prepared wish lists of American concessions they expected Washington to proffer in return for Russia's cooperation. However, Putin's choice was a long-term strategic alignment, not a tactical maneuver. He expected—and received— little in the way of immediate payoffs.

Putin's visit to the presidential ranch in Crawford, Texas, in November 2001 symbolized the return of the feel-good factor in U.S.–Russian relations, but it failed to produce any specific rewards for Moscow. President Bush said "The more I get to know President Putin, the more I get to see his heart and soul, the more I know we can work together in a positive way."[50]

At an October meeting on the fringe of the Asia-Pacific Economic Council in Shanghai, Putin had asked Bush to exempt Russia from the 1974 Jackson-Vanik amendment, which forced Russia to vet its emigration policies if it was to maintain normal trade relations with the United States. The Crawford meeting produced a promise by Bush to ask Congress to lift the amendment—something that Bush was not able to deliver, given the skepticism about Russia in Congress.

Hopes that the Crawford summit would produce some kind of deal to bridge the gap between the two sides on national missile defense were dashed. There were some signs that Russia was open to a quid pro quo—an agreement to deep cuts in strategic forces in return for Russia acquiescing in a reinterpretation of the 1972 ABM Treaty to allow the American NMD program. However, the U.S. administration was reluctant to tie itself down in a major new arms control treaty. Bush suggested that the whole concept of formal treaties defining strategic arsenals was a redundant relic of the Cold War, and that a "handshake" deal was all that was needed.

On December 10, 2001, Secretary Powell traveled to Moscow to inform the Russians that the United States would be withdrawing from the ABM Treaty in six months' time. Russia's response was surprisingly muted. When the news was made public three days later, Putin made a brief televised announcement in which he assured viewers that Russian security was not threatened by the development. Some leading generals had threatened an aggressive response, such as withdrawal from the Start 2 treaty, which commits Russia to dismantle all its multiple-warhead missiles by 2007. But no such response was forthcoming.

However, by the time the two leaders met again, in Moscow in May 2002, the U.S. position had softened. President Bush agreed to sign off on a treaty under which each side pledged to cut its nuclear forces down to between 1,700–2,200 weapons by the year 2012.[51] However, the treaty, a mere three pages long, was vague on specifics. (In contrast, Start 2 ran to 700 pages.) It included no new agreement for verification procedures (still governed by the 1991 Start 1 treaty), and the United States insisted that the two sides be allowed to store and not destroy excess warheads. The treaty was regarded as a political sop to Putin, which did not substantively impact the military programs of either country. Secretary of State Colin Powell himself told reporters that "I'm more worried about chickens going back and forth than missiles going back and forth."[52] (He was referring to a recent trade dispute involving a Russian ban on chicken imports from the United States on health grounds, introduced in retaliation against new U.S. tariff barriers against Russian steel exports.) The ABM withdrawal came into effect on June 13, 2002; two days later, Washington broke ground in Alaska for its first installation of antimissile interceptors.

THE WAR IN IRAQ

During Putin's first years in office, Russia continued to observe the UN sanctions against Baghdad, while urging that they be lifted and protesting U.S. and British military actions enforcing the no-fly zones over Iraq. Russia had high hopes that once sanctions were raised, lucrative contracts for oil exploration with Russian oil companies would be honored. There was also the question of the $8 billion debt that Iraq owed to Russia. In November 2000,

Putin sent Foreign Minister Igor Ivanov to Baghdad to reassure Saddam Hussein that Russia wanted the status of Iraq to be normalized as soon as possible. At the same time, however, Russia recognized that Iraq would have to allow the return of UN weapons inspectors, expelled in 1998.

Things changed after September 11, 2001. In November 2001, Russia dropped its opposition to the U.S.-British plan to revise UN sanctions against Iraq. With Russian approval, the UN Security Council introduced "smart sanctions" allowing more oil sales but with specific bans on military-related purchases. The May 2002 summit in Moscow also cemented Russia's status as a partner in the war on terror—and thus by implication legitimized Russia's campaign in Chechnya. A "Joint Declaration on the New Strategic Relationship between the United States and Russia" pledged joint efforts to combat the "closely linked threats of international terrorism and the proliferation of weapons of mass destruction."

In the summer of 2002, as the United States began gearing up for war with Iraq, Putin had to decide whether or not to oppose President Bush's policy of preemptive intervention. Russia reluctantly acquiesced to increased pressure on Baghdad, approving UN Security Council Resolution 1441 in November 2002, which threatened Iraq with "serious consequences" should it block UN weapons inspectors.

French President Jacques Chirac and German Chancellor Gerhard Schroeder came out firmly against an invasion of Iraq. Most observers expected Putin to sit on the fence and avoid directly challenging the U.S. plan. They were taken by surprise on February 9, 2003, when Putin stood alongside President Chirac in Paris and condemned the U.S. invasion plan. Given that France and Russia were permanent members of the UN Security Council, with veto power, this meant that when U.S. forces invaded in March, it was without the imprimatur of the international community. On April 11, Putin, Chirac, and Schroeder held a summit in St. Petersburg at which they condemned the U.S. assault and called for an international conference under UN auspices to oversee the postwar reconstruction.

Putin objected to the war as a violation of international sovereignty and of the role of the United Nations. But his real reason for dissent seemed to be a gut feeling that the invasion would fail. Russian generals predicted a long and bloody struggle, and Putin himself warned of a "humanitarian catastrophe" and described the U.S.-led war as a "mistake with the most serious consequences." The war was also deeply unpopular within Russia. Before the fighting, 68 percent of Russians had a favorable view of the United States, but that fell to 29 percent after the U.S. invasion.

The stunningly swift U.S. military victory in Iraq made Putin's dire warnings appear foolish. But it also made it possible for the U.S.-Russian relationship to quickly recover, since attention soon shifted from the wisdom of war to the task of reconstruction. The White House decided to "punish France, ignore Germany, and forgive Russia," a phrase attributed to National Security Adviser Condoleezza Rice.[53]

President Bush agreed to attend the St. Petersburg summit at the end of May, which saw dozens of world leaders gather to mark the 300th anniversary of Putin's hometown. Immediately after the jubilee, Putin went to Evian, France, to attend the meeting of the Group of Eight leading industrial countries. For the first time, Russia was treated as a full member (formerly it had been excluded from the finance meetings).

Putin told a press conference in June that "the situation with Iraq really was a serious test for Russian-US relations, [but] we have managed to emerge from this situation with minimal losses."[54] And Bush invited Putin to a summit at Camp David in September 2003, at which the U.S. president reaffirmed that "Russia and the United States are allies in the war on terror." Bush went on to say, "I respect President Putin's vision for Russia: a country at peace within its borders, with its neighbors, and with the world, a country in which democracy and freedom and the rule of law thrive."

Meanwhile, critics were concerned by the rising power of the security services within Russia. In December 2002, Federal Security Service head Nikolai Patrushev shut down the U.S. Peace Corps in Russia and expelled its staff, claiming that the program was being used as cover for espionage. In October 2003, just one month after the Camp David summit, Yukos head Mikhail Khodorkovsky was arrested, triggering a torrent of American commentary criticizing the return of authoritarianism in Russia. The one-sided victory of United Russia in the December 2003 Duma elections gave more ammunition to the critics of Bush's pro-Putin rhetoric. Bush's loyalty to Putin seems to be driven more by the personal chemistry between the two men than by a cold calculation of Russia's utility to the United States in the war on terror.

Still, in December 2003, U.S. Ambassador to Moscow Alexander Vershbow told *Moscow News*: "We appreciate the fact that President Putin was among the first of world leaders who opposed the war in Iraq but then turned the page and looked for common ground with the United States. We appreciated Russia's help in securing the unanimous approval of UN Resolution 1511 in October [2003, lifting UN sanctions on Iraq]. Russia was key to bringing France and Germany from abstention to a positive vote for that resolution." Despite this reconciliation, Putin remained convinced that the invasion was a mistake. In his December 18, 2003, televised phone-in, he warned America that "feelings of invulnerability, of grandeur, of infallibility have always seriously impeded countries with aspirations to an empire."

The UN remained aloof from the U.S.-led political transition. Countries like Russia that opposed the war were barred from U.S. reconstruction contracts, and the question of Iraqi debt remained unresolved. In December 2003, Putin said Russia was ready to cancel two-thirds of Iraq's Soviet-era debts, but only if there was consideration given to Russian companies in the awarding of future oil contracts.

All in all, Putin's diplomacy survived the test of the war in Iraq rather well. He was able to make a statement of principle and show his loyalty to France and Germany without alienating the United States.

RUSSIA AND THE REST OF THE WORLD

Washington was far from Putin's only concern. In contrast to Yeltsin, Putin engaged actively with the rest of the world—to the point where one could call him the presidential tourist because he always appears to be traveling to one country or another. Between his election in March and the end of the year 2000 he made no fewer than twenty-four visits abroad and hosted dozens of foreign dignitaries in Moscow. These visits had a number of purposes. First, they were aimed at strengthening his hand vis-à-vis Washington by showing the Bush administration that he had alternatives, and that he could be a nuisance factor if he chose. No longer would Moscow's foreign policy be determined in Washington. The United States was far more powerful than Russia, but Putin would not permit his country to be taken for granted by Bush or anyone else. In addition, Putin believed that only by being active all over the world could the Kremlin restore Russia to its proper place. The latter goal is important not only for psychological reasons, but economic ones as well.

Moscow and Europe

Relations between Moscow and Europe initially developed smoothly under Putin—surprising given the continuing protests at Russian actions in Chechnya from West Europeans. With his fluency in German and familiarity with the European scene Putin was able to woo European leaders, who were more interested than their American counterparts in maintaining steady access to Russia's energy riches. The European Union is Russia's most important economic partner, accounting for 40 percent of Russia's foreign trade, in contrast to 5 percent to the United States.

In Soviet times, Moscow's overtures toward West Europe were aimed at trying to split the NATO alliance by playing on European doubts about American actions, as in the controversy over the deployment of new theater nuclear weapons in the early 1980s. While some commentators still see an anti-American undercurrent to Putin's courtship of Europe, one can equally argue that there is no contradiction in Putin simultaneously pursuing a pro-American and a pro-European policy. Russia is physically part of Europe,

Germany is its main trading partner, and it is only natural that a Western-oriented Russia will develop the closest ties with its European neighbors.

A steady stream of Western visitors trooped through the Kremlin corridors in the early months of 2000, sounding out the new Russian leader. Putin's relationship with Britain's Tony Blair ("my friend Tony") grew particularly close. Blair visited Russia in March 2000, in a visible endorsement of the acting president just two weeks before he faced election. Blair defended himself from human rights critics, saying "Chechnya isn't Kosovo. The Russians have been subjected to really severe terrorist attacks."[55] Putin repaid the favor by choosing London as the destination for his first foreign trip in April (although he stopped off in Minsk en route, a gesture to Aleksandr Lukashenko). By the time of Putin's official visit to London in December 2001, the two men had met on nine occasions over the preceding two years. Blair, like Putin, was trying to promote his country's international image beyond the level its actual influence would warrant. Putin continued his trips with an official visit to France in late October. Most noteworthy was the fact that the visit took place at all. Relations between the two countries had been strained by Paris's constant criticism of Russian actions in Chechnya and had led Putin to snub French President Jacques Chirac at the G8 meeting in June.

Of all of Moscow's relations with Western Europe, those with Germany have been the closest. Perhaps this was because of Putin's fluency in German and the number of years he lived in that country. In his June 2000 visit German Chancellor Gerhard Schroeder called for "a truly strategic partnership with Russia," and seconded Putin's concerns over the 1972 ABM Treaty.[56] The high point of German–Russian relations came with Putin's visit to Germany in September 2001. He was given the unusual honor of addressing the German Bundestag—which he did in German. In spite of all of this activity, German–Russian relations have been more rhetoric than substance to date. Germany, the largest holder of Russian scrip in the Paris Club of official lenders, has resisted Russian pleas to write down some of the Soviet Union's debts, which Russia took over in 1991. (By the end of 2001 Soviet-era debt stood at $66 billion, of which $36 billion was owed to the Paris Club.[57]) Since Bismarck's time, Germany had occasionally used Russia as a counterweight to rival Western powers. But with Germany finally a fully accepted member of the global community, it no longer needs to play such balance-of-power politics.[58]

By 2003, Putin's enthusiasm for closer ties with the European Union had started to fade. The EU had little time for Russia, being focused on its own concerns: absorbing its new eastern members and figuring out its political constitution. Putin was exasperated in dealing with the EU's clumsy bureaucracy over issues such as access to Kaliningrad and Russia's entry to the World Trade Organization (WTO).

In preparation for entry to the EU, the Baltic states and Poland had to end visa-free travel for Russians. This meant Russian residents of Kaliningrad crossing Lithuanian territory to and from the Russian "mainland" would also need a visa. Moscow vigorously protested the move, but the EU refused to budge. In November 2002, Moscow accepted a plan for "facilitated travel documents" for Kaliningrad residents that sounded suspiciously like visas.

Putin repeatedly stated that entry to the WTO was a top priority for Russia. China's entry into the WTO in 2001 left Russia as the only industrial power outside the 144-member club. But negotiations for Russian entry, which had begun back in 1993, bogged down. Although both the EU and United States formally recognized Russia as a market economy in 2002, it was clear that Russia's demands for protection from foreign competition in financial services, telecommunications, agriculture, aircraft, and cars were unacceptable to WTO negotiators. The United States protested the blatant piracy of software, music, and movies in the Russian market, while the EU complained that the gap between Russia's domestic energy tariffs and world market prices amounted to a subsidy for industrial exporters of $5–15 billion a year. During a state visit to Russia by Chancellor Schroeder in October 2003, Putin angrily refused to bargain about Russia's energy pricing policy with the EU. Russia's slow-motion negotiations with the WTO will continue, but actual entry will be postponed until 2006–07 at the earliest.

Another bone of contention with the EU was Russia's failure to ratify the 1997 Kyoto accord. By December 2003, 118 countries with 44 percent of the world's carbon emissions had ratified Kyoto, and Russia with its 17 percent of global emissions was needed to push the signatories above the 55 percent necessary for the treaty to come into effect. In 2001, President Bush withdrew the United States from the accord, and Russia felt some pressure to follow the U.S. example. In September 2002, Prime Minister Mikhail Kasyanov told the Johannesberg climate change summit that Russia was committed to Kyoto, but in 2003, Putin's idiosyncratic economics advisor, Andrei Illarionov, started denouncing the treaty, saying that it would crimp Russia's growth plans.

Putin had more trouble patching up Russia's relationship with some of its fellow Slavic countries. At the start of his first year, relations with Poland took a turn for the worse. In January 2000 Warsaw expelled nine Russian diplomats for spying, and on February 23 (Russia's Army Day) demonstrators protesting the war in Chechnya attacked the Russian consulate in Poznan. However, in July 2000 President Aleksander Kwasniewski made an official visit to Moscow and patched up the relationship. In January 2002 Putin reciprocated with a visit to Poland, the first by a Russian president since 1993. Good relations are important not least because NATO-member Poland borders the economically devastated and crime-infested Russian enclave of Kaliningrad, a potential flash point for future problems.

In Yugoslavia, Russia blundered by backing Slobodan Milosevic to the bitter end. At the G8 summit in July 2000, Putin had voiced some concerns over Milosevic's policies, but on August 28, 2000, Russia signed a free trade agreement with Yugoslavia, a propaganda coup for Milosevic in the run-up to the September 24 election. It took Moscow until October 6 to acknowledge that challenger Vojislav Kostunica had won the vote. Russia consistently defended Yugoslavia's interests in the NATO occupation of Kosovo, criticizing the UN administration for failing to disarm the Kosovo Liberation Army and protect the remaining Serbian population. Russia withdrew its remaining peacekeepers from Bosnia and Kosovo in August 2003.

NATO Expansion

The very existence of NATO is a problem for Russia, given that the alliance was set up to deter the Soviet military threat to central Europe. However, because it obstinately continues to exist, Russia is tempted to bow to the inevitable and regard it not as a barrier but as a bridge for future cooperation.

Russia broke off ties with NATO once the alliance began bombing Kosovo in the spring of 1999, an action that coincided with the entry of Poland, Hungary, and Czech Republic to NATO. But relations resumed shortly after Putin became acting president. In February 2000 NATO Secretary General Lord Robertson visited Moscow, and the next month the NATO–Russia Permanent Joint Council resumed its meetings after a break of nearly a year.

Putin surprised observers in a BBC interview on March 5, 2000, by floating the idea of Russia joining NATO, saying "it is hard for me to visualize NATO as an enemy." No one was quite sure how to interpret this strictly hypothetical suggestion, other than as a loose sign of goodwill. During his visit to Helsinki in August 2001, Putin for the first time implied that Russia would not violently object if the Baltic States were admitted to NATO. But Putin kept up the pressure on the Baltics to grant more civic and language rights to their Russian residents. Moscow protested the December 2001 decision of the Organization for Security and Cooperation in Europe to stop monitoring ethnic and language policies in Estonia and Latvia.

The question of Russia's testy relations with NATO acquired some urgency, given President Bush's proposal in Warsaw in June 2001 to enlarge the alliance by taking in new members from the Baltic and the Balkans. To calm Russian fears, in the wake of September 11, British Prime Minister Tony Blair proposed reviving Russian cooperation with NATO. The May 2002 Rome Summit saw the creation of a new Russia-NATO Council. Moscow pretended that this participation was something akin to associate membership in the alliance.

At NATO's November 2002 summit in Prague, Estonia, Latvia, Lithuania, Slovakia, Romania, Slovenia, and Bulgaria were invited to become full members in 2004. Putin reacted calmly to the development, although many Russian conservatives saw NATO expansion as part of a sinister plot to encircle Russia.

The Commonwealth of Independent States

The CIS that Putin inherited from Yeltsin was a hollow shell, and Putin had no serious initiatives to try to revitalize what was essentially a dead organization. On June 1, 2000, Putin officially launched the so-called Eurasian Economic Community, but actual trade ties between Russia and the member states remain anemic. In July 2001, the "Shanghai Five" (Russia, China, Kazakhstan, Kyrgyzstan, and Tajikistan) metamorphosed into the Shanghai Cooperation Organization with the addition of Uzbekistan. The grouping could have provided an important vehicle for joint Russian and Chinese supervision of the security situation in Central Asia, but its prospects were shattered by the September 11 attacks and the unexpected projection of U.S. military and economic power into the region. In May 2002, the Collective Security Treaty Organization (which includes Russia, Armenia, Belarus, Kazakhstan, Kyrgyzstan, and Tajikistan) agreed to form a rapid-reaction force, as part of which Russia deployed twenty-one aircraft at the Kant airbase near Bishkek, Kyrgyzstan, in December 2003. This is just a short distance away from the much larger U.S. airbase at Manas, which opened in December 2001.

Putin did find one new way to pressure uncooperative CIS members. In September 2000 Russia announced that it was withdrawing from the 1992 Bishkek agreement on visa-free travel for CIS countries, and would henceforth conclude agreements on a bilateral basis. The next month Azerbaijan's Foreign Minister Vilat Gulei traveled to Moscow and secured the continuation of visa-free travel for Azeri citizens: this was presumably a reward from Moscow in return for Azerbaijani concessions over the legal deadlock regarding the status of the Caspian Sea. Also, Baku leased the strategic Gabala radar station to Russia for another ten years. On December 5, 2000, Russia imposed a visa regime on Georgia, while exempting the separatist regions of South Ossetia and Abkhazia. This step threatened serious disruption for the estimated 650,000 Georgians living inside Russia, whose remittances were vital to the Georgian economy.

A most dramatic development in the wake of September 11 was the deployment of U.S. security personnel in Georgia. In February 2002, Georgia requested U.S. help in battling Chechen rebels holed up in the Pankisi Gorge in the north of the country. Russian forces had made occasional raids on Georgian territory in pursuit of Chechen guerrillas—most recently on the Khodori Gorge in the Abkhaz region of Georgia in October 2001. Washington agreed to provide $64 million worth of equipment (such as helicopters) and 150 Special Forces troops as trainers. Speaking on March 1, Putin raised no objection to the deployment, saying that it was "no tragedy," even though just a week before, Foreign Minister Ivanov had spoken out against the plan.[59]

At least, for the first time, Putin won public acknowledgement from Washington of the Russian argument that there were direct ties between the Chechen rebels and elements of al Qaeda. Tensions reached crisis point in August 2002, when Russian bombers hit the Chechen rebels in Pankisi. To forestall further Russian action, Georgian forces moved in and took possession of the valley.

In 2003, U.S.-Russian rivalry over Georgia expanded from the realm of security to that of economics. In May 2003, work started on the Georgian section of the Baku-Ceyhan oil export pipeline, a key element in U.S. strategy for the region. The same month, Russia's Gazprom took over a large segment of Georgia's gas system in compensation for unpaid bills, and in August, Russia's Unified Energy System took over the Georgian electricity holdings of the U.S. company AES. Things came to a head in November 2003, when blatantly rigged parliamentary elections led to public protests that toppled President Eduard Shevardnadze. Moscow saw the hand of Washington behind the "rose revolution" and reaffirmed its support for the leaders of Georgia's breakaway provinces of Abkhazia, Ajaria, and South Ossetia. But Russia reluctantly agreed to work with Georgia's new pro-Western leadership, in the form of U.S.-educated Mikheil Saakashvili, elected president by a landslide in January 2004.

At the Istanbul summit of the Organization for Security and Cooperation in Europe (OSCE) in 1999, Russia promised that it would negotiate the closure of its remaining bases in Georgia. But at the end of 2003, Russia was still occupying two of the installations and was saying it would need at least ten years to vacate them. Russia also provides the 1,500 troops of the nominal CIS peacekeeping force that guards the border between Georgia and the breakaway province of Abkhazia.

Likewise, in Moldova, Russia reneged on the promise it made at the Istanbul summit to withdraw its troops from the secessionist Trans-Dniestria region by December 2002. Russia proposed a plan to create a federal Moldova, which would have given effective veto power to Trans-Dniestria while locking in Russia's military presence. The plan collapsed in November 2003, due to popular protests in Moldova and a last-minute change of mind by the United States.

Developments in Ukraine seemed to signal a tilt back toward Moscow after several years of vocal enthusiasm for closer ties with NATO and the EU. In September 2000 President Leonid Kuchma fired the pro-NATO Foreign Minister Borys Tarasiuk and replaced him with Anatoly Zlenko, who had served in that post from 1990–94 and is regarded as pro-Russian. Meeting with Putin in Sochi in October 2000, Kuchma agreed to sell Russia an unspecified stake in Ukraine's natural gas transit system to offset the roughly $2 billion which Ukraine owed Moscow for gas deliveries. The huge scandal that erupted toward the end of the year, after the disappearance and murder of crusading journalist Heorhy Gongadze in September, seriously damaged Kuchma's credibility in the West, while Moscow remained loyally supportive.

Kuchma maneuvered to preserve his political power, preparing constitutional changes as he looked to the end of his second and final presidential term in 2004. As Western countries distanced themselves from Kuchma's authoritarianism, he drew closer to Russia. In January 2003, Kuchma was the first non-Russian to become head of the CIS Council of Heads of State. (However, Ukraine, unlike Russia, supported the U.S.-led war in Iraq, sending 1,600 peacekeepers.)

In September 2003, the presidents of Russia, Ukraine, Kazakhstan, and Belarus met in Yalta and signed an agreement creating a "single economic space," a Eurasian answer to the EU. Then just ten days later, a bizarre crisis erupted over the Ukrainian island of Tuzla, which lies in the Kerch Strait between the Black Sea and the Sea of Azov. Russia began building a causeway to connect Tuzla to the Russian shore. It looked as if Russia was about to seize the island and then dictate terms for the passage of ships into the Sea of Azov. Ukraine rushed troops to the island, and after a tense stand-off, the Russians halted the construction work.

By 2003, it was clear that Putin's foreign policy was putting a new emphasis on building closer economic and security ties with the CIS. In his state of the federation address in May 2003, Putin said: "The strengthening of relations with the CIS countries remains our indisputable priority in foreign policy." In part, this was in response to the U.S. post-9/11 military presence in Central Asia and the Caucasus, and in part a reaction to the cooling of ties with the EU.

But as the Tuzla crisis showed, suspicion of Russian motives remained high among its CIS partners. Even relations with the most fraternal of all the allies, Belarus, did not show any significant progress toward the creation of the common state that had been declared as a goal back in 1996. In September 2003, President Aleksandr Lukashenko declined Putin's suggestion to merge the two currencies forthwith, since Putin refused to give Lukashenko the right to print rubles in Minsk.

THE MIDDLE EAST

Russia continued to be active in Iran. In October 2000 it was revealed in Washington that Russia had agreed to terminate arms deliveries to Iran by 1999, in a confidential deal struck with Vice President Al Gore back in 1995. One month later, Moscow announced it was going to resume conventional arms sales, and in December 2000 Defense Minister Sergeev paid a visit to Tehran, the first of its kind since 1979, to explore the sale of missiles, patrol boats, diesel submarines, and spare parts. In return, President Muhammad Khatami traveled to Russia in March 2001 to talk directly with Putin about arms sales. Putin also reiterated Russia's intention to help Iran complete a long-stalled nuclear power plant in Bushehr—one that some American experts believe could advance Iran's nuclear weapons program.[60]

Putin tried to justify Russia's increased involvement with Tehran by claiming: "There are changes taking place in Iran. We must take into account our interests, we must help our companies work there."[61] In fact, the economic stakes in this budding relationship were significant. One source estimated that it could earn Moscow up to $7 billion during the next few years.[62]

In May 2003, news broke of Iran's secret uranium enrichment program. Although Russia refused to end its civilian nuclear cooperation program, it suspended nuclear fuel deliveries to the Iranian plant, pending inspection by the International Atomic Energy Authority, and supported pressure on Iran in September 2003 to sign an additional protocol allowing random IAEA inspections.

Russia was offended by not being invited to the Sharm-el-shaik Israeli–Palestinian peace talks in October 2000, despite the fact that it was a sponsor of the 1993 Oslo accords, and despite Foreign Minister Ivanov's feverish shuttle diplomacy in Syria, Lebanon, and Israel over the preceding weeks. Russia remained a powerless spectator as the situation in Israel deteriorated, with Palestinian suicide bombings triggering an Israeli crackdown in the West Bank and construction of a new security barrier. Unlike the United States and Israel, Russia continued to insist that Yasser Arafat was a legitimate interlocutor. Despite this, Putin developed good relations with Israel, visiting the country twice and hosting Prime Minister Ariel Sharon in Moscow in November 2003. In part, this was because of the presence in the Jewish state of more than one million emigrants from Russia.

CUBA

Putin made a highly publicized visit to Havana in December 2000. He clearly knew that this visit would irritate the United States, but he wanted to show the world that Russia was again a force to be reckoned with in the region. It was the first by a Russian leader since the collapse of the Soviet Union. The two sides signed agreements to "continue the long standing trading of Russian oil for Cuban sugar and to expand it to other products."[63] In addition, both sides denounced efforts by the United States to dominate the world. All in all, however, the talks were longer on rhetoric than substance. And Fidel Castro was stunned by the abrupt Russian decision announced in October

2001 to close down their 1,500-man electronic listening post in Lourdes, Cuba, complaining that the $200 million annual rent was too high.

Asia

Putin was determined from the outset that Russia would remain an Asian power. He is acutely aware of the economic and geopolitical precariousness of the Russian Far East, whose eight million residents are outnumbered one hundred to one by their Chinese neighbor to the south. Putin has sought to build trust with both China and India—the continent's two giants.

Apart from moral support, the one sphere where Russia could really be of help to China is in supplying military hardware. Russia's motives in these sales are strictly pecuniary: it does not want to strengthen China's military capacity, but it desperately needs China's cash to keep Russian defense plants afloat. Since 1994 China has bought four Kilo-class submarines, and two Sovremenny-class destroyers equipped with Sunburn antiship missiles. China has a license to produce the Zvezda H-31 antiradar missile, which can counter the American Patriot and Aegis systems. China is producing 300 SU-27 aircraft under license, and is buying sixty advanced SU-30 aircraft, four S-300 air defense systems, and the A-50 Shmel airborne early-warning radar aircraft. China needs such technology if it is to seriously threaten an invasion of Taiwan. But Russia is wary of strengthening its huge Eastern neighbor, and it is not clear how a confrontation over Taiwan would serve Moscow's interests.

In July 2001 Chinese President Jiang Zemin traveled to Moscow to sign a twenty-year Treaty on Good Neighborly Friendship and Cooperation, which reflected the two sides' joint opposition to U.S. supremacy, along with a desire to settle the border disputes that had been a source of friction for years. However, the treaty lacked substance. There was no reference to military cooperation and if anything, the document appeared aimed at regularizing the existing arms sales relationship.[64] The Russian press optimistically dubbed the meeting the "oil and gas" summit since the leaders revived the idea of an oil pipeline to China. However, September 11 would complicate Russo–Sino relations. Although Beijing welcomed the crackdown on Islamic terrorism, it was decidedly unenthusiastic about a U.S. military presence in Central Asia, which they saw as part of a plot to encircle China.

India is less than happy to see Russia adding to China's military arsenal. After two years of negotiations, and two months after Putin visited the country, Moscow finally signed a major arms agreement with India in December 2000 under which India agreed to purchase 310 Russian T-90 main battle tanks. India also signed a license to manufacture 140 Sukhoi-30MKI fighter aircraft over the next seventeen years—a deal worth around $3 billion.[65]

The frostiest relationship in Asia is that with Japan. The Soviet Union and

Japan failed to sign a peace treaty at the end of World War II, and Russia still occupies the southern Kuril Islands, which it seized in August 1945. Russia had agreed in the 1993 Tokyo Declaration that the territorial issue should be solved before a peace treaty could be signed, a step that Japan took as signaling the legitimacy of their claim. In 1997 Yeltsin and Premier Ryutaro Hashimoto set 2000 as a deadline for a peace treaty, a point reaffirmed in the 1998 Moscow Declaration. With the end-of-year deadline looming, Putin traveled to Tokyo in September 2000 and reportedly offered Prime Minister Yoshiro Mori two of the four disputed islands. Mori rejected the offer, and reaffirmed that Japan would not sign a peace treaty without the return of all the islands. The return of two islands was too little for Japanese conservatives, but too much for Russian conservatives, who vowed to block any such deal in the State Duma. A major scandal erupted in Tokyo in March 2002 when it was revealed that a leading Japanese parliamentarian had secured contracts for his constituency as part of the aid package that would have followed the return of two islands. This scandal sunk the prospects of a deal over the disputed territories in the foreseeable future.

Nevertheless, in January 2003, Prime Minister Junichiro Koizumi visited Moscow for a summit and proposed financing a pipeline to bring oil from Angarsk in Siberia to the port of Nakhodka on the Pacific coast, from where it could be shipped to Japan. The Russian oil company Yukos had already stated its intention to build a pipeline from Angarsk to Daqing in China. The Japanese pipeline would be twice as long and twice as expensive as the Chinese variant. But the Yukos plan was opposed by the state-owned Transneft, which controls most of Russia's oil export pipelines, and by Yukos's many enemies in the Kremlin. Routing the export pipeline to Japan would reduce Russian dependence on China, but the project may be prohibitively expensive.

Putin also spent some time and political capital visiting other Asian countries such as North and South Korea, and Vietnam. Putin's trip to Vietnam and South Korea in February 2001 was aimed at opening up business opportunities for Russian companies. But Russia's commercial presence in East Asia is marginal at present. For example, the United States conducts more than $55 billion in annual trade with Seoul, while Russia's trade reached $2.5 billion in 2000. Russia has almost no trade with its former close ally, Vietnam, while trade between the United States and Hanoi is close to $1 billion.[66] In October 2001 Putin announced that Russia would not renew its lease of the Cam Ranh naval base in Vietnam, due to expire in 2004. In the meantime, Russia agreed to permit North Korea to repair and modernize its Soviet-era tanks, fighter planes, and submarines.

As for North Korea, in August 2000, President Kim Jong-il made a bizarre state visit to Moscow—by train (the Dear Leader is afraid of flying). Things got more serious after President Bush identified North Korea as part of the "axis of evil" in January 2002. A scared Pyongyang announced in October

2002 that it had restarted its uranium enrichment program and hinted that it was already in possession of several nuclear weapons. Initially the Bush administration refused to negotiate, but at China's initiative, six-party talks opened in Beijing in August 2003. It was China that suggested the inclusion of Russia, in a bid to balance the bloc of South Korea, Japan, and the United States. Russia tried to persuade the United States to be more flexible and grant the security guarantees that Pyongyang requested. But Russia did not have any special influence over Pyongyang and was not a major player in the talks.

CONCLUSION

Despite its weakened position, Russia is a far more active and influential player on the international scene that it was when Putin took over as president. He is no longer Washington's vassal, as Yeltsin appeared to be during much of his presidency. Early signals by the incoming Bush administration that Russia would be relegated to the ranks of middle-range countries also seem to have reversed as relations between the two countries have improved significantly. The best example is the positive role Russia (and Putin) played during the American response to the attacks on the World Trade Center and the Pentagon. While it would be wrong to suggest that the United States could not have responded without Russian assistance, it is fair to say that Moscow's cooperation made the process much easier. Intelligence, access to air facilities, search and rescue assistance, etc., not to mention Putin's public support for the United States, all played important roles in helping the United States carry out its military and diplomatic operations.

Putin's assistance came with a price, of course. The West modified its position on Chechnya, linking the rebels to the terrorist Osama bin Laden and backing off the stringent criticism that had characterized Western policy in the past.

Putin also ensured that Russia would play a more important role in the world as a whole. Cuba, China, Iran: Putin was everywhere during his first two years in office. It could be argued that Russia was never a critical factor in key foreign policy decisions around the world, but what was important was that in contrast to the Yeltsin regime, other countries began to take Russia seriously, even in its weakened position. Putin's foreign policy success is all the more remarkable given the paucity of diplomatic experience in his previous career.

Most important, Putin paid a small price for Russia's higher visibility. In sharp contrast to Yeltsin, he avoided giving the impression that he was selling out Russia to the United States or anyone else. The main cost he incurred for this successful foreign policy was that his efforts and energies were to some degree diverted away from the domestic reform agenda. Although Putin was quite vigorous in pursuing political reform, his economic policy was sluggish and his willingness to grasp the nettle of military reform almost nonexistent. As a result, the gulf widened between Russia's Soviet-legacy military establishment and its twenty-first-century foreign policy rhetoric.

A further item of concern is that Putin's pro-Western stance, especially after September 11, moved him far ahead of the Russian security establishment. Even the most liberal foreign policy commentators were somewhat taken aback by the extent of Putin's cooperation with Washington. Polls indicate that the general public, while suspicious of U.S. motives, were prepared to trust their president to defend Russia's interests. So long as Putin's general approval rating remains strong, he will be able to continue defying the foreign policy establishment. However, should his domestic support falter (because of an economic crisis, for example), his pro-Western foreign policy could be a point of attack for his opponents.

For the future, we expect Putin will continue his efforts to make Russia an increasingly important player on the international stage. He knows that his success will be dependent to a large degree on the domestic scene—how successful Russia will be in getting its economy moving again, and in achieving and maintaining the kind of political stability the country needs for global influence. Regardless of what happens, however, there is no question that Putin has discovered the "bully pulpit," when it comes to foreign affairs—and he will continue to make as much use of it as possible.

NOTES

1. Vladimir Putin, "Russia at the Turn of the Millennium," *Parvitel'stvo Rossiyskoy Federatsii*, January 17, 2000, at www.government.gov.ru/english/stat VP_engl_1.html.

2. National Intelligence Council conference "Russia in the International System," February 2001, at www.odci.gov/nic/pubs/conference_reports/russia_conf.html (last accessed June 1, 2001).

3. See chapter 9.

4. Nikolai Kosolapov, "Stanovlenie sub'ekta rossiiskoi vneshnoi politiki" [Becoming a Subject of Russian Foreign Policy] *Pro et contra*, vol. 6 (Winter 2001) at www.ceip.org.

5. Martha Olcott and Anders Aslund, *Getting It Wrong* (Washington, D.C.: Carnegie Endowment, 2001).

6. Oleg Levitin, "Inside Moscow's Kosovo Muddle," *Survival*, vol. 42, no. 1 (Spring 2000): 130.

7. *Diplomaticheskii vestnik*, no. 7–8 (1998): 18, as cited in Stephen White, *Russia's New Politics* (London: Cambridge University Press, 2000), 224.

8. Stephen Cohen, *Failed Crusade* (New York: Norton, 2000), 7.

9. "Russia at the Turn of the Millennium," Government of the Russian Federation at www.pravitelstvo.gov.ru.

10. Cited in *Russian Journal*, November 2, 2001.

11. www.mid.ru/mi/eng/econcept.htm.

12. *Los Angeles Times*, July 11, 2000.

13. Jamestown Foundation *Monitor*, January 4, 2001.

14. Sharon LaFraniere and Steven Mufson, "Putin's Victory Could Bring Thaw in U.S–Russia Ties," *Washington Post*, March 28, 2000.

15. "Moscow's Chilly Rebuff Leaves Clinton in a Bind," *Time*, June 5, 2000.

16. Strobe Talbott, "Putin's Path: Russian Foreign Policy after September 11," lecture, Yale University, January 27, 2002.

17. "Mr. Putin Gets to Work. George Bush Will Find Him a Handful," *The Guardian* (London), December 15, 2000.

18. Valentin Kunin, "What Moscow Expects from the New US Administration," *RIA-Novosti*, December 19, 2000 in *Johnson's Russia List*, December 21, 2000.

19. Kunin, "What Moscow Expects."

20. Martin Walker, "Commentary: New Hard Line on Russia," *UPI*, January 5, 2001.

21. "Moscow Seeks 'Serious' Dialogue with the New US Bush Team," *RFE/RL Daily Report*, January 3, 2001.

22. "Putin Writes to Bush, Wants Better US-Russia Ties," *Reuters*, January 24, 2001.

23. "Putin Takes up Debt and Defenses with German Chief," *New York Times*, January 7, 2001.

24. "Excerpts from the Interview with President-Elect George W. Bush," *New York Times*, January 14, 2001.

25. "More Russian Reaction to Bush Interview," *RFE/RL Daily Report*, January 17, 2001.

26. "Russian-US Dialogue: Heeding Current Realities," *Krasnaya zvezda*, January 19, 2001.

27. "Russia's Putin Confident of Finding 'Common Language' with US President," *Interfax*, February 8, 2001.

28. "The President's Lookout," *Le Figaro*, February 10, 2001, in *Johnson's Russia List*, February 17, 2001.

29. "Rumsfeld's Accusations May Worsen Russia-US Relations," *ITAR-TASS*, February 15, 2001, in *WNC Military Affairs*, February 16, 2001.

30. "'Excellent' Talks Belie Chill in US-Russia Relationship," *Los Angeles Times*, February 25, 2001.

31. "Russia, US Appear to Mend Fences after Powell-Ivanov Meeting," *AFP*, April 12, 2001, in *CDI Russia Weekly*, April 12, 2001.

32. Sergei Oznobishchev, "Will the 'New Partnership' Succeed?" Jamestown Foundation *Prism* VII, no. 7 (July 2001); S. Oznobishchev and I. Runov, "Chto delat' s Amerikoi?" [What Is to Be Done with America?] *Dipkurier NG*, supplement to *Nezavisimaya gazeta*, May 24, 2001.

33. *Washington Post*, June 16, 2001.

34. *Los Angeles Times*, June 16, 2001.

35. "Not Quite Buddies, but Maybe Partners," *Washington Post/National Weekly Edition*, June 25–July 1, 2001.

36. "George Bush: USA and Russia Should Not View Each Other with Suspicion," *RIA/Novosti*, July 19, 2001, in *Johnson's Russia List*, July 19, 2001.

37. Peggy Noonan, "A Chat in the Oval Office," *Wall Street Journal*, June 25, 2001.

38. *New York Times*, July 23, 2001.

39. Alexander Golts, "Tough Challenge Ahead as Putin Looks West," *Russia Journal*, October 5, 2001.

40. Although he in fact talked to National Security Advisor Condoleezza Rice, and not President Bush himself. Dan Balz and Bob Woodward, "America's Chaotic Road to War," *Washington Post*, January 27, 2002.

41. Andrei Piontkowsky, "Putin Chooses US over Political Elite," *Russia Journal*, October 5, 2001.

42. "Russia Expresses Solidarity with US in Fight against Terrorism," Jamestown Foundation *Monitor*, September 12, 2001.

43. Strobe Talbott, "Putin's Path: Russian Foreign Policy after September 11," lecture, Yale University, January 27, 2002.

44. "Russia Joins Coalition," *Time.com*, September 23, 2001.

45. "Putin Vows to Aid Taliban Foes, Clarifies Position on Air Bases," *Washington Post*, September 25, 2001.

46. "Russia Says US May Use Facilities in Tajikistan," *Washington Post*, September 26, 2001.

47. Dmitrii Trenin, "Vladimir Putin's Autumn Marathon," Carnegie Endowment Briefing, November 2001 at www.ceip.org.

48. Yelena Tregubova, "The Results of 2001," *Kommersant-Vlast*, December 25, 2001.

49. Remarks at a conference organized by the Marshall Center for European Security and Ebert Foundation, Moscow, October 6, 2001.

50. *New York Times*, November 16, 2001.

51. Peter Slevin and Walter Pincus, "Treaty Means as Much Politically as Militarily," *Washington Post*, May 14, 2002.

52. Todd Purdum, "NATO Strikes Deal to Accept Russia in a Partnership," *New York Times*, May 15, 2002.

53. Carla Power, "Chirac's Great Game," *Newsweek International*, April 28, 2003.

54. Transcript at www.kremlin.ru, June 20, 2003.

55. *The Guardian* (London), March 11, 2000.

56. Jamestown Foundation *Monitor*, June 19, 2000.

57. Vladimir Kucherenko, "Russia's Book of Debt," *Rossiiskaya Gazeta*, January 9, 2001.

58. Point made by Hans Joachim Spanger at a conference organized by the Marshall Center for European Security and the Ebert Foundation, Moscow, October 6, 2001.

59. He was speaking at a meeting of CIS heads in Kazakhstan. Sebastian Alison, "Putin Says No 'Tragedy' in U.S. Troops in Georgia," *Reuters*, March 1, 2002.

60. "Putin to Sell Arms and Nuclear Help to Iran," *New York Times*, March 13, 2000.

61. "Putin Sees Positive US Ties but Defends Ties with 'Rogue' States," *AFP*, December 26, 2000.

62. "US Alarm at Russian Arms Sale to Iran," *The Times* (London), December 30, 2000.

63. "In Cuba, Putin Signals Russia's Return to Region," *Washington Post*, December 25, 2000.

64. It is worth noting that one of the authors was part of a high-level U.S. military delegation that traveled to Russia to visit the Far Eastern Military District. In private conversations with Russian military officers it became clear that many are suspicious of the Chinese and some are downright hostile, worrying aloud if these weapons would end up being used against Russia.

65. "India, Russia Sign Another Major Defense Deal," Jamestown Foundation *Monitor*, February 19, 2001.

66. "Putin, Ending Asia Trip, Appears Pleased with Renewed Stature," *New York Times*, March 3, 2001.

Chapter Fourteen

Conclusion
Dale R. Herspring

Based on the essays in this book, there are a number of reasons to believe that Russia under Putin is becoming more authoritarian than it was under Yeltsin. Nevertheless, there are some very tentative signs that *a limited form of democracy* may be possible in Russia in coming years.

First, as Colton and McFaul argue in their essay, improvement in the country's economy should help create a middle class in place of the one destroyed by Yeltsin's policies. If that happens, one could expect the middle class to demand more freedom and accountability on the part of the government. Furthermore, as they note, Putin supports a number of institutional and political projects that could at some point be critical in the development of democracy.

Second, it is worth noting that there are some aspects of a democratic polity still functioning in Russia. In contrast to Yeltsin, Putin has worked with the Duma and the Federation Council, even if he has a two-thirds majority in the Duma and a three-quarters majority in the Council. The structure exists and could be the source of a more democratic Russia if Putin or his successors decide to move in that direction. The same is true of political parties. They are a far cry from the kind of parties that exist in the West, and Putin has found a way to control them, too. Nevertheless, the potential for creating meaningful political parties exists.

Third, Russia's economy is doing very well under Putin. Under his presidency, the economy has expanded by about a third, which gives Russia the longest period of growth in a decade. He has "reduced the foreign debt by $17 billion, GDP increased 30% from 1999 to 2004 and the inflation rate went down three times."[1] Furthermore, Putin has begun to move Russia closer to the EU. Should this latter process continue, and should Russia's GDP continue to grow, and should that lead to the development of a viable middle class, another of the prerequisites for a democratic polity would appear.

Equally important, the picture for agriculture has improved since the days of Yeltsin. Wegren argues that the government's approach has been deradicalized. To use Wegren's term, Putin has been undertaking a "quiet revolution" in the agricultural sector. As a consequence, agriculture has produced positive growth rates for four consecutive years.

Fourth, Putin's effort to reform the legal system is a step in the right direction. Most important, a jury system was introduced. The idea of juries is a radical break with the past. The communist system outlawed them shortly after 1917. In their place, the communists introduced a three-member panel that served as judge, jury, and even on occasion the prosecution. However, in July 2003, Putin signed a law that gives defendants accused of the most serious crimes the right to demand a jury trial along with Western-style rights. It is difficult to know how well the new jury system will work in the long run.

Fifth, after years of neglect, Putin has begun to address the military's problems. While it may seem strange to some, military reform is critical to the future of democracy in an unstable country like Russia. The one thing that no one wants is a military that is demoralized, bitter, and prepared to work its will in the political arena. In spite of its involvement in the events of 1991 and 1993, and the decision of a number of Russian generals to go into politics, Russia thus far has been spared a politicized and politically active military. By attempting to resolve the military's problems, Putin is taking a very important step toward political stability.

Sixth, Putin's ability to use the events of September 11, 2001, to move Russia closer to the West could have a positive influence in the long run. Closer interaction between the West (including the United States and Western Europe) and Russia, in spite of the blowup over Iraq, in the economic sphere is bound to lead to some political spillover. Putin's most important diplomatic achievement came in the aftermath of Washington's invasion of Iraq. Putin was caught in the middle. He did not want to offend Washington, Paris, Berlin, or London. Yet he had to take a stand—was he for or against the invasion? Putin lined up on the side of the Germans and French against Washington. Rather than offend and irritate the Bush administration as the French and Germans did, he made it clear to Bush that he was opposed, but he avoided the kind of polemics that came out of Paris and Berlin. The latter undermined bilateral relations with Washington and led to a frosty relationship for a couple of years. Meanwhile, Putin's approach to Bush (i.e., we will agree to disagree on how to handle a major international crisis) left U.S.-Russian relations alive and well.

Unfortunately, there are also some negative signs on the road to democracy in Russia. First, there is the issue of media freedom. There is no doubt that Putin has restricted media freedom—or at least he sat by and did nothing while Russian bureaucrats restricted it for him. The only promising aspect for the future of democracy is that the media, especially the press, are still able to criticize the government.

It is also important to note that democratic institutions in Russia "have eroded" under Putin, as Colton and McFaul note. Putin is clearly more authoritarian than Yeltsin was. The amount of openness and democracy that was common to Yeltsin's rule is gone, although most analysts would agree that Russia is far from the repressive state that it was during the communist period.

Then there is the problem of the oligarchs. As far as he is concerned, Putin does not seem to consider them a problem—unless they openly challenge him, as Gusinsky, Berezovsky, and Khodorkovsky reportedly have. So far, Putin has treated the other oligarchs like the "robber barons" of the United States during the nineteenth century. For the most part, he seems to believe that what is done is done; it is now time to move on—but if they get out of line by trying to become major political forces, he is more than prepared to come after them.

The one chapter that is most depressing for the future of Russia is David Powell's discussion of demographic, health, and environmental conditions in the country. It seems almost impossible to believe, but Russia is losing population! It is already down to 143 million from 148 million in 1992, and as Powell demonstrates, it will almost certainly get worse. The health situation is abysmal, and if that were not enough, the mess the communists made of the environment has to be seen to be believed. Unfortunately, the Putin government has done little to attack any of these problems other than to talk about them. While the enormity of these problems is not Putin's fault, his tendency to ignore them certainly is. In the long run, it will make little or no difference what Putin does in other areas if he does not make serious progress in this one. What good will it do to have a viable economy if Russians find themselves "on the Endangered List," as Powell concludes?

The cultural world has also been impacted by Putin's policies. One of the most striking effects has been the greater role Putin has begun to play in this area. For example, he closed down the very popular, satirical TV program *Kukly*, and there has been an onslaught in the form of carpets, posters, and calendars with Putin's face on them. Putin seems to understand the political importance of theatrics, and as Lanin points out, he has not been bashful about using them to his advantage. While Moscow has not reentered the Cold War on the cultural front, it is clear that it has become more politicized—in Putin's favor.

There is no doubt that Putin has still not done much to fight corruption. He rails against it, and the police are sent out to arrest some here and some there—even though the police are considered by many Russians to be as corrupt as those they are arresting. The key question, however, is whether Putin understands the reasons for it, and if he does, is he prepared to make the fundamental changes that are needed in the Russian political system to get control of it. He is overseeing a reformation of the country's legal system, but that is only one aspect of it. To date, his record in this area is not encouraging.

Then there is the problem of Chechnya. It won't go away. Unfortunately, as long as Russian troops continue to butcher Chechens (and Chechens return the favor), it will be difficult to take advantage of the sprit of democracy that so many hope for in Russia. Tragically, the situation vis-à-vis Chechnya demonstrates to Russians all too clearly that, when confronted with a difficult problem, the best solution is to use force.

Finally, on the internal front, there is the issue of center-periphery relations, and here there is no question that Putin continues determined to limit local autonomy. For those who see local control as a key indicator of democracy, there is no doubt that Russia will move away from that kind of democracy for the immediate future. Putin clearly believes that Yeltsin gave away far too much authority to local and regional governments. He believes that if there is any chance for Russia to reform and reconstruct a stable political, economic, and social infrastructure, the Kremlin must get control of events in Russia. Otherwise, Russia will wallow in the depths of chaos and disorder for the indefinite future.

Now back to the man himself. As I see it, there are five factors that will continue to characterize Putin's approach to political and economic problems. The first, which should not come as a big surprise given his career in the KGB, is his devotion to the state. To Putin, the state is just a larger form of the bureaucracy he once served in. Indeed, this is key to his somewhat ambivalent attitude toward democracy. During his time in the KGB, Putin was part of an organization in which meritocracy, discipline, and order were paramount. If he was given an order, he was expected to carry it out, and for many years he did just that. He appears to be trying to impose that model on the country he is governing. While that approach appears authoritarian to many, to Putin is makes logical sense.

While Putin sees the whole Russian system as one big bureaucracy, he does not appear to be trying to reimpose a Soviet or Stalinist regime on Russia. That danger always exists, of course, but to date he has shown no interest in enforcing conformity throughout the system. Rather, as is normal in a bureaucracy, Putin believes the guy on top should be able to set the organization's parameters, and that those who work in it should operate within them. This helps explain his approach to the press. Putin's government has set certain parameters for what can be criticized and what is off limits to criticism, and it is up to the media to abide by it. Putin believes Russia must avoid the kind of political chaos that an unrestrained press would create.

Putin's bureaucratic mind-set also helps explain his approach to issues such as legal reform, the military, and even Chechnya. It is up to him to come up with a structural paradigm, and then he expects the rest of the system to fall in line. In his own mind, the answer to many questions he faces comes in the form of bureaucratic modifications. He seems to believe that once the bureaucracy is well ordered, the system will work better.

A second and equally important factor is political culture. While he does not use the political science term, Putin is very conscious of it and its implications for Russia. In short, he does *not* believe Russia should import a Western-style democratic system. Indeed, after "four years of Mr. Putin, it should finally be clear that he has no intention of grafting Western ideas and institutions onto the Russian body politic."[2] In Putin's mind, it goes against everything Russian. Transplanting those ideas and institutions would create chaos in Russia. To paraphrase Stalin with regard to the introduction of communism in Poland: Putin believes it would fit the Russian people "like a saddle fits a cow." Indeed, Putin openly expressed his doubts about the applicability of the Western experience in Russia in his Millennium Speech in January 2000.

> It will not happen soon, if it ever happens at all, that Russia will become the second edition of say, the US or Britain in which liberal values have deep historic traditions. Our state and its institutions have always played an exceptionally important role in the life of the country and its people. For Russians a strong state is not an anomaly that should be got rid of. Quite the contrary, they see it as a source and guarantor of order and the initiator and main driving force of any change.[3]

In essence, the above quote describes exactly what Putin has been doing since he took office—strengthening state authority while permitting freedom, but not if it gets in the way of the effective functioning of the country's bureaucratic structures. Besides, from his perspective, that is the way the average Russian wants it. And he appears to be right. Based on a public opinion poll conducted January 15–20, 2004, 78 percent of Russians said they would vote for Putin in the upcoming presidential election.[4] Very few politicians anywhere in the world could hope to have such a high approval rating.

This brings me to the third factor that seems to play a major role in Putin's decisionmaking approach—one that seems even stronger in Putin than his bureaucratic approach to solving problems. That is his anti-ideological attitude. As he put it in his Millennium Speech, "I am against the restoration of an official state ideology in Russia in any form."[5] What this means in practice is that, with the exception of his proclivity to look to the state to resolve problems, he is open and pragmatic when it comes to solving problems. The key question for Putin is "Does it work?" If the answer is yes, then let us do it that way. If the answer is no, then another approach is needed. This, too, should not come as a surprise, given his background. When it came to problem solving, the KGB was one of the least ideological organizations in the Soviet Union. The task was "to get the job done, to solve the problem at hand." Talking to KGB agents over the years, this writer has the impression that, while they believed they were the "shield and sword" of the state, they saw their primary task as solving the problems given to them by the "Center."

If Putin were convinced that the introduction of greater forms of what we in the West understand as democracy would help him deal with Russia's problems, even if it ran counter to his understanding of the Russian mind-set, he would probably move in that direction. If, on the other hand, he believed that further restrictions were required, he would have no hesitation about moving in that direction. While this pragmatic approach may be a bit unnerving to those who fear Russia could revert back to a more authoritarian state if the political and economic situation were to deteriorate, it also leaves open the option for a movement in the opposite direction.

The fourth characteristic of Putin's approach to political and economic problems is that Putin is not a long-range planner. His focus tends to be on the here and now, just as it was when he was in the KGB. This helps explain why he has yet to come up with a long-range plan for solving the country's economic problems. His focus has been on concerns such as the price of oil, or getting rid of obnoxious oligarchs, or forcing generals to go along with the American request to station troops in Central Asia. He has neither the time nor the temperament to look at problems from a long-term, conceptual standpoint.

Finally, as many writers have noted, Putin is cautious—a common characteristic among bureaucrats. His decisionmaking approach tends to be incremental. This is most evident in his dealings with the regions or in his attitude toward legal reform or his hesitation to adopt an economic reform plan. Rather than pursue the "hair-brained schemes" of a Khrushchev, Putin tries one approach after another, even if, as in the case of Chechnya, they do not seem to work very well. It is the approach of the tortoise rather than the hare.

This is not to suggest that Putin cannot move very quickly when the opportunity presents itself. This is clearly what he did in the aftermath of the attack on the United States on September 11, 2001. He used this tragic event not only to move Russia closer to the West, but to overcome opposition on the part of the military and other conservatives to his desire for closer ties with Washington. It is worth noting, however, that he is not out of the woods by any stretch of the imagination. A number of key individuals who opposed this move toward the United States remain bitter, and still in power. However, I would not be surprised if we reencounter this willingness to seize on events whenever Putin sees an opportunity to advance his political agenda.

In conclusion, what should we call Putin's form of governance? No title—especially one taken from another political system—would fit the Russian system exactly. No two cultures are exactly the same. However, Putin's preference for reliance on the state, his non-ideological approach, his pragmatic attitude, his belief in the importance of Russian political culture (a system of governance must fit the political beliefs and attitudes of the populace), as well as his cautious, incremental approach to problem solving suggest that the term "managed democracy" may fit best.

As Putin sees things, he was unexpectedly given the task of trying to bring Russia out of the mess it found itself in at the beginning of the year 2000. He accepted that responsibility and is trying to solve Russia's many problems as he "manages" the country. He fears that if he does not impose order through the power of the state, the Russian state will collapse. He is in charge of a country with almost no experience with democracy. He fears that if he does not take a strong hand in running the country, it could sink back into the anarchy of the Yeltsin period. As a result, he believes that the restrictions he has placed on the media are necessary while he guides Russia toward a more stable "democratic" political future. Besides, from Putin's point of view, this is the way the Russians want things. They long for a strong manager during their current "time of troubles."

How long will this period of "managed democracy" last? It is impossible to say. Since the first edition of this book was published, there is no doubt that he has tightened up the reigns of control, although the system is still a long way from the Soviet-type regime of the Brezhnev era. The one thing that is clear is that Putin has put the march toward democracy on hold for the present. What about the future? I suspect that if we asked Putin, he would not be able to answer that question. Nor would he be able to explain where he believes the country is heading. About the most I suspect he would say would be that it is clear to him that Russians prefer stability and a less democratic regime to the democracy and chaos of the Yeltsin years. "Russia is today a kind of plebiscite democracy, where one-man rule is preserved through democratic institutions," one Russian political columnist observed. "But as long as there is stability, people will be primed to trust this man, and only this man."[6] The fact is that Russians appear to have a more optimistic view of their future than they did four years ago. And to a large degree, Putin's presidency is the reason. "There is a totally different mood in this country from what we had four years ago," said Russian scholar Vyacheslav Nikonov. "Everyone was sunk in depression after all the disasters and humiliations of 1990s. Today there is optimism. The country is moving ahead, and we have things to be proud of again."[7]

It is worth noting, however, that Putin is betting on the economy and the high price of Russia's oil exports as the basis for a stable political system. If the economy should collapse, or another catastrophe should hit Russia, the progress that Nikonov spoke of could turn into stagnation, with all the political unknowns that such a situation could have for Moscow.

The French political scientist Bertrand de Jouvenel has argued that political questions are too complex to be "solved." As soon as one political problem is "solved," it gives rise to a new one. Political problems, he admonished us, can only be "settled," and even then, it is a temporary situation. I doubt that Putin has ever heard of Jouvenel, but I suspect he would agree with this comment concerning the temporary nature of political "solutions."[8]

NOTES

1. "Putin Believes That for Four Years of His Rule, Economic Situation in Russia Changed Drastically," *RIA-Novosti*, February 12, 2004, in Johnson's Russia List, February 12, 2004, 10–11; and Faulconbridge, "Putin Leading in Polls."

2. Peter Lavelle, "Popular Putin Holds Sway over Russians," *Washington Times*, December 21, 2003.

3. Vladimir Putin, "Russia at the Turn of the Millennium," *Pravitel'stvo rossiyskoy federatsii*, government.gov.ru/english/statVP_engl_1.html.

4. Faulconbridge, "Putin Leading in Polls."

5. Putin, "Russia at the Turn of the Millennium," 5.

6. Vitaly Tretyakov as quoted in "Why Russians Look to Putin," *Christian Science Monitor*, February 20, 2004.

7. Quoted in "Why Russians Look to Putin."

8. Bertrand de Jouvenel, *The Pure Theory of Politics* (New Haven, Conn.: Yale University Press, 1963), 207.

Suggested Reading

BOOKS

Arbatov, Alexei, et al., eds. *Eurasia in the 21st Century: The Total Security Environment*. Armonk, N.Y.: M. E. Sharpe, 1999.

Aron, Leon. *Yeltsin: A Revolutionary Life*. New York: St. Martin's Press, 2000.

Ashwin, Sarah, ed. *Gender, State, and Society in Soviet and Post-Soviet Russia*. Manchester, UK: Manchester University Press, 1999.

Barany, Zoltan, and Robert G. Moser. *Russia's Politics: Challenges of Democratization*. Cambridge: Cambridge University Press, 2001.

Breslauer, George W. *Gorbachev and Yeltsin as Leaders*. Cambridge: Cambridge University Press, 2002.

Brown, Archie, and Lilia Shevtsova, eds. *Gorbachev, Yeltsin and Putin: Political Leadership in Russia's Transition*. New York: Carnegie Endowment for International Peace, 2001.

Cohen, Stephen F. *Failed Crusade: America and the Tragedy of Post-Communist Russia*. Norton, 2000.

Colton, Timothy J. *Transitional Citizens: Voters and What Influences Them in the New Russia*. Cambridge, Mass.: Harvard University Press, 2000.

Cox, Michael, ed. *Rethinking the Soviet Collapse: Sovietology, the Death of Communism and the New Russia*. London: Pinter 1999.

Dunlop, John. *The Rise of Russia and the Fall of the Soviet Union*. Princeton, N.J.: Princeton University Press, 1995.

Ellman, Michael, and Vladimir Kontorovich, eds. *The Destruction of the Soviet Economic System*. Armonk, N.Y.: M. E. Sharpe, 1998.

Ellis, Frank. *From Glasnost to the Internet: Russia's New Infosphere*. New York: St. Martin's Press, 1999.

Field, Mark G., and Judyth Twigg, eds. *Russia's Torn Safety Nets: Health and Social Welfare During the Transition*. New York: Palgrave, 2000.

Fikke, Geir, ed. *The Uncertainties of Putin's Democracy*. Olso: Norwegian Institute of International Affairs, 2004.

Gall, Carlotta, and Thomas de Waal. *Chechnya: Calamity in the Caucasus*. New York: New York University Press, 2000.

Gustafson, Thane. *Capitalism, Russian-Style.* Cambridge: Cambridge University Press, 1999.

Handelman, Stephen. *Comrade Criminal: the Rise of the Russian Mafiya.* New Haven, Conn.: Yale University Press, 1997.

Hesli, Vicki, and William Reisinger, eds. *Elections, Parties and the Future of Russia: The 1999–2000 Elections.* Cambridge: Cambridge University Press, 2003.

Hill, Fiona, and Clifford Gaddy. *The Siberian Curse: How Communist Planners Left Russia Out in the Cold.* Washington, D.C.: Brookings Institute Press, 2003.

Huskey, Eugene. *Presidential Power in Russia.* Armonk, N.Y.: M. E. Sharpe, 1999.

Kivinen, Markku. *Progress and Chaos: Russia as a Challenge for Sociological Imagination.* Series B:19. Helsinki: Kikimora Publications, 2002.

Kivinen, Markku, and Katri Pynnöniemi, eds. *Beyond the Garden Ring: Dimensions of Russian Regionalism.* Series B:25. Helsinki: Kikimora Publications, 2002.

Klebnikov, Paul. *Godfather of the Kremlin: Boris Berezovsky and the Looting of Russia.* New York: Harcourt, 2000.

Kotz, David, and Fred Weir. *Revolution from Above: The Demise of the Soviet System.* New York: Routledge, 1997.

Ledeneva, Alena. *Russia's Economy of Favors. Blat, Networking and Informal Exchanges.* Cambridge: Cambridge University Press, 1999.

Lieven, Anatole. *Chechnya: Tombstone of Russian Power.* New Haven, Conn.: Yale University Press, 1999.

———. *Ukraine and Russia: A Fraternal Rivalry.* Washington, D.C.: United States Institute of Peace, 1999.

McFaul, Michael. *Russia's Unfinished Revolution: Political Change from Gorbachev to Putin.* Ithaca, N.Y.: Cornell University Press, 2001.

Marsch, Christopher. *Russia at the Polls: Voters, Elections, and Democratization.* Washington, D.C.: Congressional Quarterly Press, 2002.

Mickiewicz, Ellen. *Changing Channels: Television and the Struggle for Power in Russia.* Durham, N.C.: Duke University Press, 1999.

O'Brien, David J., and Stephen Wegren, eds. *Rural Reform in Post-Soviet Russia.* Washington, D.C.: Woodrow Wilson/Johns Hopkins University Press, 2002.

Odom, William. *The Collapse of the Soviet Military.* New Haven, Conn.: Yale University Press, 1999.

Putin, Vladimir. *First Person.* New York: Public Affairs, 2000.

Reddaway, Peter, and Dmitrii Glinsky. *The Tragedy of Russia's Reforms.* Washington, D.C.: United States Institute of Peace, 2001.

Reddaway, Peter, and Robert W. Ortung, eds. *The Dynamics of Russian Politics: Putin's Reform of Federal-Regional Relations.* Lanham: Rowman & Littlefield, 2004.

Remington, Thomas F. "Coalition Politics in the New Duma," in *1999–2000 Elections in Russia: Their Impact and Legacy,* ed. Vicki L. Hesli and William M. Reisinger 232–57. Cambridge: Cambridge University Press: 2003.

———. *Politics in Russia.* 2d ed. New York: Longman, 2001.

———. *The Russian Parliament: Institutional Evolution in a Transitional Regime.* New Haven, Conn.: Yale University Press, 2001.

Remington, Thomas F., and Steven Smith. *The Politics of Institutional Choice: Forma-*

tion of the Russian and State Duma. Princeton, N.J.: Princeton University Press, 2001.

Sachs, Jeffrey D. and Katharina Pistor, eds. *The Rule of Law and Economic Reform in Russia*. Boulder, Colo.: Westview Press, 1997.

Simes, Dmitri K. *After the Collapse. Russia Seeks Its Place As a Great Power*. New York: Simon & Schuster, 1999.

Shevtsova, Lilia. *Yeltsin's Russia: Myths and Reality*. Washington, D.C.: Carnegie Endowment for International Peace, 1999.

Smith, Gordon B., ed. *State-Building in Russia: The Yeltsin Legacy and the Challenge of the Future*. Armonk, N.Y.: M. E. Sharpe, 1999.

Sperling, Valerie, ed. *Building the Russian State: Institutional Crisis and the Quest for Democratic Governance*. Boulder, Colo.: Westview Press, 2000.

Stoner-Weiss, Kathryn. *Local Heroes: The Political Economy of Russian Regional Governance*. Princeton, N.J.: Princeton University Press, 1997.

Varese, Federico. *The Russian Mafia*. Oxford: Oxford University Press, 2001.

Wedel, Janine.*Collision and Collusion: The Strange Case of Western Aid to East Europe*. New York: St. Martin's Press, 1998.

Wegren, Stephen K. *Agriculture and the State in Soviet and Post-Soviet Russia*. Pittsburgh: University of Pittsburgh Press, 1998.

Weigle, Marcia. *Russia's Liberal Project: State-Society Relations in the Transition from Communism*. Philadelphia: Pennsylvania State University Press, 2000.

Woodruff, David. *Money Unmade: Barter and the Fate of Russian Capitalism*. Ithaca, N.Y.: Cornell University Press, 1999.

Yeltsin, Boris N. *Midnight Diaries*. New York: Public Affairs, 1999.

———. *The Struggle for Russia*. New York: Times Books, 1994.

ARTICLES

Aslund, Anders. "Russia and the International Financial Institutions." February 2000. At www.ceip.org/files/Publications/IFIAC.asp?pr=2&from=pubdate

Gel'man, Vladimir. "Regime Transition, Uncertainty and Prospects for Democratisation: The Politics of Russia's Regions in a Comparative Perspective." *Europe-Asia Studies* 51, no. 6 (September 1999).

Hellman, Joel. "Winners Take All: The Politics of Partial Reform." *World Politics* 50, no. 2 (January 1998).

Herspring, Dale, and Jacob Kipp. "Searching for the Elusive Mr. Putin." *Problems of Post Communism* (September/October 2001).

Hyde, Mathew. "Putin's Federal Reforms and their Implications for Presidential Power in Russia." *Europe-Asia Studies* 53, no. 5 (2001).

Luong, P. J., and E. Weinthal. "Contra Coercion: Russian Tax Reform, Exogenous Shocks, and Negotiated Institutional Change." *American Political Science Review* 98, no. 1: 139–52.

Lynch, Allen. "The Realism of Russia's Foreign Policy." *Europe-Asia Studies* 53, no. 1 (January 2001).

Menon, Rajan, and Graham Fuller. "Russia's Ruinous Chechen War." *Foreign Affairs*, March 2000.

O'Brien, David J., Stephen Wegren, and Valeri V. Patsiorkovski. "Contemporary Rural Responses to Reform from Above." *Russian Review* 63, no. 2 (April 2004): 256–76.

Remington, Thomas F. "Majorities without Mandates: The Federation Council since 2000." *Europe-Asia Studies*, 55, no. 5 (2003): 667–91.

———. "Putin and the Duma." *Post-Soviet Affairs* 17, no. 4, (November/December 2001).

———. "Russia and the 'Strong State' Ideal." *East European Constitutional Review* 9, no. 2 (Winter/Spring 2000).

"Russia: Ten Years After." Carnegie Endowment Conference, June 2001. At www .ceip.org/files/programs/russia/tenyears/panel8.htm.

Rutland, Peter. "Putin's Path to Power." *Post-Soviet Affairs* 16, no. 4 (December 2000).

Stepan, Alfred. "Russian Federalism in Comparative Perspective." *Post-Soviet Affairs* 16, no. 2 (April/June 2000).

Treisman, Daniel. "Fighting Inflation in a Transitional Regime." *World Politics* 50, no. 2 (January 1998).

Wegren, Stephen. "The Rise, Fall, and Transformation of the Rural Social Contract." *Communist and Post-Communist Studies* 36, no. 1 (March 2003): 1–27.

———. "Why Rural Russians Participate in the Land Market: Socio-Economic Factors." *Post-Communist Economies* 15, no. 4 (December 2003): 483–501.

Wegren, Stephen, K., David J. O'Brien, and Valeri V. Patsiorkovski. "Russia's Rural Unemployed." *Europe-Asia Studies* 55, no. 6 (2003): 847–67.

———. "Why Russia's Rural Poor Are Poor." *Post-Soviet Affairs* 19, no. 3 (July-September 2003): 264–87.

———. "Winners and Losers in Russian Agrarian Reform." *Journal of Peasant Studies* 30, no. 1 (October 2002): 1–29.

Index

Abkhazia, 224, 225–27
Abramovich, Roman, 168, 169, 172, 175, 176
Adamov, Yefgeny, 166
Aeroflot, 165
AFL-CIO Solidarity Center, 23
Aganbegyan, Abel, 127
Agrarian Party of Russia, 148
agriculture, 141–60; agrarian revolution, 141; agricultural land sales, 33; Agroindustrial Union, 150; financial credit system, 154–55; food import policy, 150–54; Ministry of Agriculture, 151–52
agricultural unions: grain union, 152, 153; meat union, 152–153; poultry union, 152–153; sugar union, 152
Akaev, Askar, 273
Aksenenko, Nikolay, 166, 173
Albright, Madeline, 224, 265
Alekseeva, Ludmila, 25
Alfa group, 60, 163
All Russia (OVR), 38, 40, 41, 44; Fatherland–Unified Russia, 39
Andropov, Yuri, 257
Anishchenko, Mikhail, 76
Anti-Ballistic Missile Treaty (ABM), 265, 266, 268, 270–72, 275
Arbatov, Alexsey, 274
Astrakhanova, Natalia, 170

AvtoVAZ, 168
Ayatskov, Dmitri, 77

Babeva, Svetlana, 171
Babitsky, Andrei, 62
Balabanov, Aleksei, 85
Basaev, Shamil, 206, 216, 218, 220
Belianinov, Andrei, 171
Berezovsky, Boris, 19, 23, 25, 48, 57, 60, 66, 80, 81, 163, 166, 176; calls Putin a dictator and a criminal, 65; continues to finance NTV from abroad, 65; clashes with Putin, 169, 172, 173, 295; gives up his Duma seat, 169; investigated, 165; leaves Russia for fear of arrest, 63; ousted as kingmaker, 132; sets up opposition to Putin, 169
Beria, Lavrenti, 212
Bezborodov, Nikolay, 188
Billington, James, 128
bin Laden, Osama, 205, 272
Biryukov, Nikolay, 13
Bishkek Agreement (1992), 282
Blair, Tony, 265, 279
Boone, Peter, 175
Borodin, Pavel, 2, 166
Bortsov, Yuri, 4
Boucher, Richard, 65, 207
Bova, Russell, 14

Brezhnev, Leonid, 75, 79, 83, 124, 125, 127, 130, 136–37, 257
Bush administration, 26, 65, 294
Bush, George W., 197, 269, 270, 271, 272, 274, 277
Butov, Vlaldimir, 174

Castro, Fidel, 285
Catherine II, 210
Center for Strategic Planning (St. Petersburg), 46–47
Center for the Study of Public Opinion (Moscow), 13
Chazov, Evgeny, 97
Chechnya, xviii, 4, 6, 8, 14, 20, 22–23, 25, 55, 85–86, 205–33; assault on Grozny, 215–16, 222; Chechen Rebels compared to al Qaeda, 283; crime and terrorism in, 184; First Chechen War, 1994–1996, 213–19; geography, 209; Gorbachev and, 213; history, 209–12; human rights, 63–64; independence, push for, 241; media, coverage of, 59, 61–62, 216–17; Second Chechen War, 1999–, 165, 219–23; seizure of Moscow Theater, 67, 84, 176; September 11, impact on U.S. policy toward, 272–75; Stalin, Joseph, 212
Chekists, 167, 170, 171
Chemezov, Sergei, 171
Chemical Weapons Convention, 102
Cherkesov, Viktor, 167, 244, 247
Chernomurdin, Viktor, 162, 263, 267
Chiburaev, Vladimir, 98
Chirac, Jacques, 276, 279
Chubais, Anatoly, 2, 20, 60–61, 67, 134, 162, 167, 168, 169, 171, 173, 177–78
Chudakova, M. O., 78
Civic Forum, 25
civil code, 34
Clinton, William, 265–67; addresses Duma (June 2000), 266; visit to Russia (January 1994), 262; visit to Russia (June 2000), 266
Cohen, Stephen, 14, 262

Collective Security Treaty Organization, 282
Collins, James, 5
Colton, Timothy, 7, 293, 295
Commonwealth of Independent States (CIS), 246, 260, 282–84; CIS Council of Heads of State, 284
Communist Party of the Russian Federation (CPRF), 6, 15, 19–20, 21, 35–36, 39, 40, 67
Communist Party of the Soviet Union (CPSU), 124, 125, 128, 163, 165, 178; abolished by Yeltsin, 129; opposes Yelstin's agrarian reforms, 148–49; rural vote for, 145–48, 156
Connor, Walter D., 106
Constitution (1993), 14, 16–18, 25
Council of Factions, 49
Coulloudon, Virginie, xviii
Cretien, Jean, 269
crony capitalism, 164
Cuban Missile Crisis, 125
customs code, 34

Dagestan, 22, 24
Daniel, Yuli, 79
Danilov-Danilan, Viktor, 95, 99
Davos World Economic Forum, 170
demographic problems, 89–94
Denisov, Valentin, 149
Deripaska, Oleg, 166, 169–70, 173, 176
Diachenko, Tatiana, 165, 170
Diskin, Joseph, 177
Dmitrieva, Tatiana, 95, 98
Donath, Klaus-Helge, 76
Dorenko, Sergei, 23
Drachevsky, Leonid, 246
Dubov, Vladimir, 176
Dudaev, Dzhokar, 213–14, 215, 217, 241
Duma, xvii, 15, 31–44; "Coalition of the Four," 36–44; Coordinating Council, 41; factions, 36–44; shelling of, 237

economy, Russian, 121–40, 293; agriculture, 141–60; European Union,

impact on Russian economy, 137;
growth of, 122; market reforms, 57;
reform, criteria for success, 130–31
Ekho Moskvy, 58, 64, 68, 80
elections, Russian: presidential election,
1996, 60; presidential election, 2000,
61, 148; parliamentary election,
December 1993, 145; parliamentary
election, December 1995, 145; parliamentary election, December 1999,
61; parliamentary election, December
2003, 69, 176
Ernst, Konstantin, 69
Eurasian Economic Community, 282
European Union (EU), 130, 137–38,
225, 239, 278, 279, 280

Fadeev, Gennady, 173
"Family," 19, 166, 171
Fatherland–All Russia (OVR), 16, 19,
25, 35, 40, 61, 165, 256
Federal Counter-Intelligence Service
(FSK), 215
Federal Districts, creation of, 18, 238,
243–47; Presidential Representatives,
role of, 248–51
Federal Security Service (FSB), xii, 2, 18,
22, 23, 165, 167, 173, 220, 224, 253
Federation Council, xvii, 16–17,
240–42; reform of, 33, 35, 44–46,
49, 55, 175, 243
Federation of Independent Trade Unions
of Russia (FITUR), 47
Fedorov, Nikolay, 245
Feshbach, Murray, 95, 100, 102
financial crash, August 1998, 59, 150,
165, 263
Friedman, Thomas, 228
Friendly, Alfred, 95

Gaidar, Yegor, 122, 128
Gazprom, 23, 59, 63–64, 68, 70, 132,
163, 168, 171, 174, 177, 283
Gazprom-Media, 59, 168
Gelman, Marat, 83
Georgia, U.S. troops deployed in,
282–83

Gerashenenko, Viktor, 171, 172
Gil-Robles, Alvaro, 225
Glazev, Sergei, 20
Goldovsky, Yakov, 174
Gongadze, Heorhy, 284
Gorbachev, Mikhail, 35, 49, 56–57, 70
79, 123, 260; compared with Khrush-
chev, 126–27; compared with Yeltsin,
128–29; economic reforms, 125–28;
foreign policy, 260; influence of
Khrushchev on, 125, 126; new think-
ing, 127; place in history, 127; policy
of *glasnost*, 56–57, 125, 161; policy
of *perestroika*, 126–28; regions, 239;
tolerance of independent media, 70
Gordeev, Aleksey, 143, 144, 149, 151,
155
Gore, Al, 267, 284
Gosplan, 137
Grachev, Pavel, 214, 217
Graham, Thomas, 162
Gref, German, 15, 46, 47, 134, 167, 172
Gref Plan, 134–35
Grishin, Yuri, 187
Gryzlov, Boris, 170, 252
Gulei, Vilat, 282
Gusinsky, Vladimir, 23, 25, 48, 57, 58,
60, 63–66, 69, 79, 80, 132, 163,
167–68; arrest of, 168; clashes with
Putin, 169, 172, 295; criminal
charges brought against, 62–63; emi-
gration to Spain, 168; gives up media
assets, 73, 132; Media-MOST offices
raided, 168; released from jail, 169;
sale of media assets, 63–64
Gutseriev, Mikhail, 176

Helms, Jesse, 266
Hewett, Ed, 126
HIV/AIDS in Russia, 110–12
Human Rights Watch, 22
Humes, Graham, 3
Huntington, Samuel, 208

Igrunov, Viacheslav, 20
Illarionov, Andrei, 15, 134, 167

income tax, flat, 16
India, relations with, 286
Inkombank, 163
International Monetary Fund (IMF), 137
International Research and Exchanges (IREX), 55–56
Ishayev, Viktor, 134; Ishayev Plan, 135
Itogi, 23
Ivanov, Igor, 136, 265, 268, 270, 274, 285
Ivanov, Sergei, 22, 167, 170, 185, 190, 193–94, 196, 227, 259, 271, 272, 273, 285
Ivashov, Leonid, 271
Izmerov, Nikolai, 92

Jackson-Vanik, 274
Jiang Zemin, 265, 286
Jordan, Boris, 23, 63, 67
Jouvenel, Bertrand de, 300
judicial reform, 34

Kadyrov, Akhmed, 207, 222; assassination, 207
Kaliuzhnyi, Viktor, 166
Karimov, Islam, 260
Kasayev, Alap, 225
Kasyanov, Mikhail, 15, 134, 168, 173, 176, 196, 280
Kaverin, Veniamin, 84
Kazantsev, Victor, 223, 245, 247
Khasaavyurt Accords, 22, 218
Khasbulatov, Ruslan, 49, 240
Khloponin, Aleksandr, 175
Khorodrkovsky, Mikhail, 20, 48, 67, 132, 176, 177, 277, 295
Khrushchev, Nikita, 76, 79, 81, 130, 136–37, 252, 298; catching up and surpassing the West, 125; compared with Gorbachev, 126, 127; compared with Putin, 136; importation of grain, 124; reform efforts, 124; removal from power, 125
Kim Jong-il, 287
Kim, Yuly, 84
King, Larry, 81

Kipp, Jake, 8
Kirpichnikov, Valery, 166
Kiryenko, Sergey, 20, 245
Kiselev, Evgeny, 23, 58, 63, 66, 68, 79, 80, 172
Kisilev, Aleksei, 100–101
Klebanov, Ilya, 167, 245
Kogan, Vladimir, 172
Koizumi, Junichiro, 287
Kokh, Alfred, 168
Komoyedov, Vladimir, 187
Konovalov, Aleksandr, 274
Korzhakov, Aleksandr, 162
Kosygin, Alexei, 125
Kosygin Reforms, 124
Kovalev, Sergei, 20
Kozak, Dmitri, 34, 47, 167, 248
Kristenko, Viktor, 167
Kuchma, Leonid, 26, 283–84
Kudrin, Aleksei, 15, 167, 171, 237
Kulikov, Anatoly, 218, 221
Kunin, Valentin, 268
Kursanov, Pavel, 78
Kursk, sinking of, 21, 62
Kutovoi, Grigory, 171
Kvashnin, Anatoly, 193, 198, 218
Kwasniewski, Aleksander, 280
Kyoto Accords, 280

land reform (code), 33, 34, 40, 133–34
Lanin, Boris, xiv, 295
Lapshin, Mikhail, 149, 150
Latyshev, Petr, 245
Lavigne, Marie, 138
Law on Principles of Organizing Local Self-management, 249
Lebed, Aleksandr, 217, 218, 219, 221
Lebedev, Platon, 132, 177
Lesin, Mikhail, 63, 168
Levitin, Oleg, 261
Liberal Democratic Party of Russia (LDPR), 15, 37, 44
Lipman, Masha, 7
Lisin, Vladimir, 67
List, Friederich, 135
Litvineko, Aleksandr, 220
Logovaz, 163, 165

Lukashenko, Aleksandr, 284
Lukin, Vladimir, 269
LUKoil, 65, 168, 172–73, 177
Luzhkov, Yuri, 3, 38, 40, 67, 80, 165
Lysenko, Vladimir, 17
Lyubimov, Aleksandr, 81

Malashenko, Igor, 60
Malenkov, Georgie, 123
Mamut, Aleksandr, 167
"managed democracy," 14, 26, 55, 299
Manilov, Valery, 221
Markov, Georgy, 79
Maskhadov, Aslan, 207, 209, 215, 218–19, 225
Matvienko, Valentina, 244
McFaul, Michael, 7, 293, 295
Media Freedom, Russia, 55–74, 294
Media-MOST, 21, 58, 59, 62, 63–64, 68, 69, 70, 79, 163, 168
Media-Socium, 66
Menatep, 163
Mikhalkov, Nikita, 84
military, Russian: arms control, attitude toward, 271; Chechnya, 188; Conscription, 194–95; contract service in, 191–92; crime in, 188; desertion from, 187; hazing (Dedovshchina), 187; Non-Commissioned Officer (NCO), 187, 188, 195–96, 199; professional military, 191; Pskov Experiment, 191–93, 199; reform of, 22, 189–96; training, 187; women in the military, 195
Millar, James, 8
Miller, Aleksei, 132, 171
Milosevic, Slobodan, 26, 261, 263, 280–81
Mironov, Sergei, 36, 46
Mordashov, Aleksey, 175
Mori, Yoshiro, 287
Morozov, Oleg, 40, 83
Motsak, Mikhail, 247
Moving Together, 75–76, 83

National Missile Defense System (NMD), 265, 266, 269, 271, 275

NATO: expansion of, 281–82; Partnership for Peace, 272–73; Russian relations with, 263, 265, 278–83
Nazarbayev, Nursultan, 260, 273
Nazarov, Vadim, 78
Nazdratenko, Evgeny, 18, 175, 250
Nemtsov, Aleksandr, 107
Nemtsov, Boris, 20, 104, 191, 196, 223
Nikonov, Vyacheslav, 299
Nosov, Sergei, 78
NTV (First Private Russian TV Organization), 23, 24, 25, 57–58, 59, 60, 80, 168, 172; arbitration court considers case, 74–75; coverage of Putin, 61–63; goes off the air, 67; lack of public support for, 66; takeover of, 63–64; Yeltsin offers support for, 65

Oligarchs, 48, 161–182; conflict over ownership of regional companies, 171, 174–75; financial crisis of 1998, impact on, 165; Putin, crackdown on, 167–70; Yeltsin, 1996 election, 163, 164
Onishchenko, Gennady, 110, 111
Organization for Security and Cooperation in Europe (OSCE), 22, 23, 283
ORT (Russian Public Television), 23, 57, 60, 69, 80, 165
Orttung, Robert, 175
Oster, Grigory, 78
Our Home Is Russia (NDR), 19, 49

Paris Club, 279
parties, law on, 48
Patrushev, Nikolai, 22, 167, 237, 277
Paul I, 257
Pavlovsky, Gleb, 178, 228
Peace Corps (U.S.), 23, 277
Pekhtin, Vladimir, 40
People's Deputy faction, 15, 37, 38, 39, 40, 41, 44
People's Party, 39
Pereyaslov, Nikolai, 83
Peter the Great, 5, 257
Petlyura, Nikolai, 77
Petrov, Nikolai, 8

Pokrovsky, Vadim, 110
political parties, 33–34, 35–44, 293
Politkovskaya, Anna, 62, 223
Poltavchenko, Georgy, 244
Pope, Edward, 268
Potanin, Vladimir, 80, 86, 163, 168, 172
Powell, Colin, 227, 268, 270
Powell, David, xiv, 295
presidential decree (*ukaz*), 31, 32
Presidential State Council, 243
presidential veto, 32
Primakov, Yevgeny, 3, 19, 23, 38, 61,
    66, 178; anti-corruption campaign,
    165; foreign minister, 246, 262;
    NATO expansion, 263; prime minis-
    ter, 263
Pristina, dash for, 273
Pristavkin, Anatoly, 78
Privatization, 162
procuracy, 48
Prokhanov, Aleksandr, 178
Proskurin, Petr, 79
public health problems, 91–112; birth
    rate, 91–92
Pugachev, Sergei, 172
Pulikovsky, Konstantin, 246, 247
Putin, Vladimir, xi–xv, xvii; agriculture,
    141, 144–56; approach to politics,
    3–5, 13–14, 296–300; becomes pres-
    ident, 1, 3; biographical details, 1–3;
    Bundestag, speech before, 280; Bush,
    George W., relations with, 197,
    267–78; Chechnya, xiv, 61, 62, 81,
    205–7, 208–29, 296; corruption,
    fight against, 296; culture, 75–87;
    democracy, 14–26; demography,
    89–94; Director, Federal Security
    Service, xii; Duma, 15–16, 31–35;
    economy, 129–136; "Family," 19,
    166, 171; federal-regional relations,
    237–58, 296; Federation Council,
    17, 33, 36, 44–46, 55; foreign policy,
    259–60, 264–92; foreign policy con-
    cept, 264–65; governing style, 31–
    35, 48–50, 55–56, 293; Iraq, war in,
    275–78; Kursk, sinking of, 62; legal

reforms, 25, 294; "managed democ-
    racy," 14, 26, 55, 299; market
    reforms, xiv, 132–36; media, 55–74;
    meeting with businessmen (May 31,
    2001), 171; military reform, 185–
    203, 294; Oligarchs, 167–79; person-
    ality, xi–xiii, 185–86; personal
    popularity, 55; political parties, 33;
    preemptive intervention, policy of,
    276; "Putinomania," 75–78; replaces
    Yeltsin, ix; rural vote, 147, 156; Sep-
    tember 11, 2001, response to, xii,
    186, 288, 294; United States, rela-
    tions with, 229, 265–75
Putin, compared with other leaders:
    Brezhnev, 136; Gorbachev, 136;
    Khrushchev, 299; Yeltsin, 5–6, 31,
    61, 136, 178, 251
Putin and negotiations: Crawford sum-
    mit, 274–75; Genoa summit, 271;
    Ljubljana summit, 224, 270;

Radio Liberty, 62
Raikov, Gennadii, 39
Rakhimov, Murtaza, 245
Rashid, Ahmed, 224
Rasputin, Valentin, 79
Regions of Russia, 15
Reiman, Leonid, 172
Rekshan, Valdimir, 78
Reporters Without Borders, 56
Rice, Condoleezza, 228, 268, 270, 271–
    72, 277
Rimashevskaya, Natalia, 107
Rodionov, Denis, 175
Rodionov, Igor, 217, 218
Rodionov, Sergey, 81
Rogozhkin, Aleksey, 85
Romanov, A., 216
Rosprom, 163
Rossel'khozbank, 154, 155
Rossiisky Kredit, 163
Rosugol, 163
RTR (TV Channel 2), 57–58, 62, 80
Rudaev, Salman, 217
rule of law, 6
Rumsfeld, Donald, 270

Rushailo, Vladimir, 167, 170, 252, 271
Russia, relations with: China, 286; Cuba, 267, 285–86; Iran, 285; Israel, 285; Japan, 286–87; North Korea, 287–88; Poland, 280–81; United States, 262–64, 265–75
Russian Agrarian Movement, 149
Russian Union of Industrialists and Entrepreneurs (RUIE), 47, 169, 174
Russia's Choice, 19
Russia's regions, 15, 19, 37, 38, 40, 41, 44
Rutland, Peter, 8
Rutskoi, Aleksandr, 21, 240

Saakashavili, Mikheil, 283
Sabitov, Gabit, 78
SBS-Agro, 163
Schroeder, Gerhard, 276, 279, 280
Sechin, Igor, 167
Security Council, 18, 48, 189, 190, 215, 250
Sekatsky, Aleksandr, 78
Seleznev, Gennadii, 15, 20, 269
September 11, 2001, Russian response to, 197, 223, 272–73, 288
Sergeev, Igor, 167, 179, 268, 271, 285
Shaimiev, Mintimer, 165, 245
Shamil Iman, 211
Shanghai Five, 282
Sharon, Ariel, 285
Shedler, Andreas, 21
Shenderovich, Viktor, 68, 79
Shevardnadze, Eduard, 225, 283
Shevtsov, Leontiy, 220–21
Shevtsova, Lilia, 5, 185
Shiryanov, Bayan, 83
Shmelev, Nikolay, 137
Shoigu, Sergey, 40
Shpak, Georgy, 187, 199
Shtyrov, Viacheslav, 175
Shvydkoi, Mikhail, 86
Sibal, 166
Sibneft, 166, 168, 176, 177
Sinyavsky, Andrei, 79
Slavneft, 176
Slider, Darrell, 8

Sobchak, Anatoly, xi, 2, 3, 15, 178, 253
Sokurov, Aleksandr, 85
Solovev, Nikola, 109
Sorokin, Vladimir, 76, 82, 83
Soros, George, 60, 172
Soskovets, Oleg, 162
S. S. Shatalin Plan, 126–27, 128–29
Stalin, Josef, 76, 79, 123–24, 127, 257
START (Strategic Arms Reduction Treaty), 31
START II (Strategic Arms Reduction Treaty, II), 265
state bureaucracy, reform of, 34
State Council, 17
Stephashin, Sergey, 173, 219, 220–21, 250, 257
Stevensen, Irene, 23
Stogov, Il'ya, 78
Stroev, Egor, 44
Strugatsky, Boris, 82
Sukhanov, Yuri, 176
Svyazinvest, 60, 61, 172

Talbott, Strobe, 266, 272
Tarasiuk, Borys, 283
Tennenbaum, Johnathan, 135
Titov, Konstantin, 245
Transneft, 287
Tregubova, Yelena, 274
Trenin, Dmitri, 229, 274
Troshev, Gennady, 219, 220, 221
Tsereteli, Zurab, 77
Turner, Ted, 59, 172
TV-6, 23, 25, 63, 65–66, 70, 172–173
Tyumen Oil Company, 168, 176

Unified Energy Systems (EES), 163, 168, 171
Union of Rightist Forces (SPS), 15, 40, 67, 188, 190, 193, 245
United Nations, 205, 277
United Russia, 19, 21, 67, 69, 256
Unity, 15, 16, 19–22, 36, 37, 38, 39, 40, 41, 44, 61, 165, 256
Unity bloc, 15, 16
Ustinov, Vladimir, 166, 167, 174

Venediktov, Aleksei, 80
Vershbow, Alexander, 229, 277
Viakhirev, Rem, 171
Vietnam, relations with, 287
Virgin Lands Project, 124
Voloshin, Aleksandr, 166, 244
Vol'skii, Arkady, 47, 66, 169
Vorob'ev, Kirill, 82
Vrob'ev, Edvard, 214
Vyakhirev, Rem, 132

Wegren, Stephen, xiv, 293–94
Witte, Sergei, 135
World Bank, 137
World Health Organization (WHO), 94
World Jewish Congress, 168
World Trade Organization (WTO), 152, 153, 279, 280

Yabloko, 15, 20, 35, 37, 40, 61
Yablokov, Aleksei, 96
Yakovlev, Vladimir, 250
Yanshin, Aleksandr, 95
Yashin, Valery, 171
Yavlinskii, Grigorii, 20, 23
Yeltsin, Boris, ix, 13, 19, 24, 123, 260; abolishes Communist Party, 129; agriculture, 141–45, 150–51; Chech-nya, 59, 208, 213–18; Communist Party, 129; economy, 122, 128–29, 131; Federation Council, 17; foreign policy, 259, 260–64; Gorbachev, relations with, 129, 162; governing style, contrast with Putin, 5–6, 24–25, 31–35, 49, 174, 185; media, relations with, 57, 58, 59, 60, 61, 65, 70; military, 189, 192; and Putin, 2–3, 4, 14; regional relationships, 237, 248, 255; retirement of, xi; United States, relations with, 262–64; Y2K, xi; Yugoslavia, relations with, 262–63
Yukos, x, 132–36, 175, 176, 287
Yumashev, Vlaentin, 167, 170
Yurakov, Viktor, 77
Yushanov, Ilya, 167

Zhirinovsky, Vladimir, 38
Zhitnik, Aleksandr, 154, 155
Zivenko, Sergei, 171
Zlenko, Anatoly, 283
Zolotatrev, Boris, 175
Zolotov, Viktor, 167
Zyagintsev, Andrey, 84
Zyazikov, Murat, 77
Zyuganov, Gennady, 15, 60, 147, 165 166, 217

About the Contributors

James F. Collins is a retired Foreign Service officer with the Department of State. Mr. Collins served as U.S. ambassador to Russia from 1997 to 2001.

Timothy J. Colton is Morris and Anna Feldberg Professor of Government and director of the Davis Center for Russian and Eurasian Studies at Harvard University. He is the author of a number of books on Russian politics, most recently *Transitional Citizens: Voters and What Influences Them in the New Russia* (2000).

Dale R. Herspring is professor of political science at Kansas State University, a member of the Council on Foreign Relations, and a retired Foreign Service officer with the Department of State. He is the author and editor of ten books and more than seventy articles dealing with civil-military relations in the former East Germany, Poland, Russia, the USSR, and the United States. His most recent book is *Admirals, Generals and Presidential Leadership: Civil Military Relations in the United States from Franklin Roosevelt to George W. Bush* (University Press of Kansas, forthcoming).

Jacob W. Kipp is senior analyst with the Foreign Military Studies Office of the U.S. Army Training and Doctrine Command at Fort Leavenworth, Kansas. He is the past editor of *European Security* and the author of numerous articles on Russian military matters, including Soviet and Russian concepts of space as a theater of military actions.

Boris Lanin is head of Literary Studies at the Russian Academy of Education, and a professor at the Tax Academy of Russia. A native of Baku, he received a Ph.D. in 1994 from Moscow Pedagogical University with a dissertation entitled *Anti-Utopia in Russian Literature*; he has published or edited half a dozen books on literary themes. He has been a visiting fellow at the Slavic

Research Center in Hokkaido, Japan, and the Kennan Institute, Woodrow Wilson Center, in Washington, D.C.

Masha Lipman regularly writes op-ed articles about Russian politics for the *Washington Post*, and she is a research scholar at the Moscow Carnegie Center.

Michael McFaul is associate professor of political science and the Peter and Helen Bing Senior Fellow at the Hoover Institution. He is also a senior associate at the Carnegie Endowment for Peace. His latest books are, with Timothy Colton, *Popular Choice and Managed Democracy: The Russian Elections of 1999 and 2000*, and with James Goldgeier, *Power and Purpose: US Policy Toward Russia After the Cold War*.

James R. Millar is professor of economics and international affairs at George Washington University, where he previously served as director of the Institute for European, Russian, and Eurasian Studies. He is the author and editor of six books and more than forty articles, the editor of the journal *Problems of Post-Communism*, and editor in chief of the four-volume *Encyclopedia of Russian History* (2004). Millar served as president of the American Association for the Advancement of Slavic Studies as well as treasurer of the American Council of Learned Societies. He is currently vice president of the International Council for Central and Eastern European Studies and a member of the board of governors of the International Research and Exchanges Board. Millar has been a Guggenheim fellow and Woodrow Wilson Center fellow.

Nikolai Petrov is scholar-in-resident at the Carnegie Moscow Center, head of the Center for Political Geographic Research, and a research associate with the Institute of Geography at the Russian Academy of Sciences. Dr. Petrov earned his Ph.D. in Geography from Moscow State University in 1982. From 1990 to 1995, he served as an advisor to the Russian parliament, government, and president. Petrov was the chief organizer of the Analysis and Forecast Division in the Supreme Soviet and head of a governmental working group on regional problems. He also served as an analyst in the Analytical Center of the President. He leads the regional project center at the Carnegie Endowment for International Peace in Moscow, where he published numerous works, including *Political Almanac of Russia* (1997).

David E. Powell is the Shelby Cullom Davis Professor of Russian Studies at Wheaton College (Norton, Mass.), as well as an associate of the Davis Center for Russian and Eurasian Studies (Harvard University) and a lecturer in health policy and management at the Harvard School of Public Health. He has written widely on social problems in the USSR and Post-Soviet Russia.

Thomas F. Remington is professor of political science and chair of the Political Science Department at Emory University. Among his publications are two books on the Russian parliament: *The Russian Parliament: Institutional Evolution in a Transitional Regime, 1989–1999* (2001) and, with Steven S. Smith, *The Politics of Institutional Choice: Formation of the Russian State Duma* (2001). Other books include *Politics in Russia* (1998; second edition, 2001; third edition, 2003), *Parliaments in Transition* (1994), and *The Truth of Authority: Ideology and Communication in the Soviet Union* (1988). His research focuses on the development of representative institutions in post-communist Russia, particularly the legislative branch, and legislative-executive relations.

Peter Rutland is professor of government at Wesleyan University. From 1995 to 1997 he was assistant director for research at the Open Media Research Institute in Prague, and in 2000 he was a Fulbright visiting professor at the European University in St. Petersburg. His most recent book is the edited collection *Business and the State in Contemporary Russia* (2001).

Darrell Slider is professor of government and international affairs at the University of South Florida. He has been the recipient of numerous awards and is the author of more than thirty-five articles dealing primarily with regional and local politics in the former USSR and Russia.

Stephen K. Wegren is associate professor of political science at Southern Methodist University. His books and monographs include: *Land Reform in the Former Soviet Union and Eastern Europe* (1998), which won the Hewett award for the best book in political economy from the American Association for the Advancement of Slavic Studies; *Rural Reform in Post-Soviet Russia* (2002); *Russian Policy Challenges: Security, Stability, and Development* (2003); and *Building Market Institutions in Post-Communist Agriculture: Land, Credit, and Assistance* (2004).